NEW GEORGIA

TWENTIETH-CENTURY BATTLES

Edited by Spencer C. Tucker

NEW GEORGIA

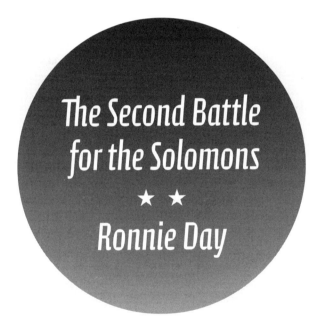

The Second Battle
for the Solomons

★ ★

Ronnie Day

INDIANA UNIVERSITY PRESS

Bloomington & Indianapolis

This book is a publication of

INDIANA UNIVERSITY PRESS
Office of Scholarly Publishing
Herman B Wells Library 350
1320 East 10th Street
Bloomington, Indiana 47405 USA

iupress.indiana.edu

The paper used in this publication
meets the minimum requirements of
the American National Standard for
Information Sciences – Permanence of
Paper for Printed Library Materials,
ANSI Z39.48–1992.

Manufactured in the
United States of America

Library of Congress
Cataloging-in-Publication Data

Names: Day, Ronnie.
Title: New Georgia : the second battle
    for the Solomons / Ronnie Day.
Description: Bloomington : Indiana
    University Press, 2016. | Series:
    Twentieth-century battles | Includes
    bibliographical references and index.
Identifiers: LCCN 2015025411| ISBN
    9780253018779 (cloth : alk. paper) |
    ISBN 9780253018854 (ebook)
Subjects: LCSH: World War, 1939–1945 –
    Campaigns – Solomon Islands – Munda.
    | Munda (Solomon Islands) – History,
    Military – 20th century.
Classification: LCC D767.98 .D39 2016 |
    DDC 940.54/265931 – dc23 LC record
    available at http://lccn.
    loc.gov/2015025411

1 2 3 4 5   21 20 19 18 17 16

Contents

A Note from the Publisher

RONNIE DAY DID NOT LIVE TO SEE THIS BOOK INTO PRINT. FOR all intents and purposes, however, the manuscript was complete at the time of his death. Day delivered the finished manuscript to IU Press in June 2014, lacking only the maps and photographs, and he continued to work on his manuscript while those were being prepared. Revisions to the manuscript were found on the author's computer by his son, John, and that version of the manuscript was proofread by Edward Speer, who had worked with the author on corrections to the draft. Spencer Tucker, the editor of the series Twentieth-Century Battles, read the Press's draft and offered a number of helpful suggestions. The two versions of the manuscript were compared, collated, and corrected at IU Press, and some additional text from an earlier, longer draft was restored to the manuscript for the sake of clarity and improved narrative flow. Peter Woodbury made corrections to the final draft and maps, supplied scans of the U.S. National Archives photographs, and compiled the index section. The maps were drawn by Bill Nelson.

Preface

IN JANUARY 1989 I FLEW UP TO MUNDA FROM GUADALCANAL, spent a few hours, and then caught the plane back to Henderson Field. The picture-postcard beauty of the view from Munda left an indelible impression on me, and so in 1992 I went back, this time with a veteran of the battle there, and got a much better look at the islands. Evidence of the war can be found everywhere, ranging from the Munda elementary school bell, which is stamped USN, to the marine light tank sitting where it was knocked out in September 1943. But the most impressive legacy is the airfields, and I like to think that it was walking the 8,000-foot strip at Munda that aroused my curiosity about what had happened there and that eventually led to this book.

Not much has been written about the battle for New Georgia. The official historians of the belligerent powers gave it coverage in volumes devoted to the larger campaign of which it was a part. While these histories are the indispensable starting point for any study of the Pacific War, most were written a few years after the end of the war, the Japanese account being the exception, and are dated. To my knowledge, only two monographs dealing exclusively with New Georgia have since been published. Both focus mainly on the ground battle for Munda Field, which is only part of the story. But as the bibliography will show, there are a number of works that touch on New Georgia in one way or another – histories of the South Pacific theaters, biographies and personal accounts, unit histories, and specialists' studies of aircraft and naval architecture. Some of these are extremely good; others less so. (Recently, too late for use here, several books have been published on the overall campaign of which New Georgia was a part.)

Unlike many Pacific War battles, however, New Georgia has never been erased completely from the public memory. This is due mainly to the continued interest in two men who fought there. One was John F. Kennedy, whose PT boat was sliced in two by a Japanese destroyer and whose elevation to the presidency resulted in the incident becoming a lasting icon of the Pacific War; the other was Gregory "Pappy" Boyington, whose Black Sheep Squadron passed into the realm of mythology via a popular television series that unfortunately for history got it all wrong. To date, a half dozen books, one movie, and one National Geographic documentary have been devoted to PT-109 and another half dozen to Boyington's Marine Fighting Squadron 214.

My version of New Georgia was written to satisfy my curiosity, but nonetheless with the hope that it might add to our understanding of the war in the Solomons. It attempts to portray both sides – Allied and Japanese – locked in a three-dimensional struggle – ground, air, and sea – for possession of the airfield sites. For the Allied side, I have used the official histories and other published works, and I have done considerable research in the major archives. For the Japanese side, my lack of language skills has imposed severe limitations. The account, therefore, rests primarily on the relevant volumes in the War History Series (*Senshi sosho*), a few Japanese memoirs and secondary works, the large collection of captured (and translated) documents in American archives, and some very selective research in the National Institute of Defense Studies Archives in Tokyo. It goes without saying that the Japanese language sources were translated for me, and the people who labored so hard are listed in the acknowledgments.

For the Allied Command, New Georgia served up some very valuable lessons, which had to be learned the hard way; for this writer, trying to put the story together has also proven to be a lesson learned the hard way.

Acknowledgments

A GREAT MANY PEOPLE HELPED ME OVER THE YEARS THAT I worked on this New Georgia campaign project, and without doubt I will inadvertently leave out others that have helped me – for which I apologize.

First and foremost, I am in lasting debt to Naoko Suesada. Without her generous and reliable translation of Japanese records and diaries, a balanced two-sided historical account of the New Georgia campaign would not have been possible. Hitomi Deneen did additional Japanese translations for which I am grateful.

In North America, I express my appreciation to the following institutions and persons for their contributions: U.S. National Archives and Still Picture Reference section at Suitland, Maryland; U.S. Library of Congress; Charles Haberlein at the Naval Historical Center, Washington Navy Yard; U.S. Army Center of Military History; Archie DiFante at the Air Force Historical Research Agency at Maxwell Air Force Base; U.S. Navy Seabee Museum at Port Hueneme, California; Helen Morriss Wildasin for her husband Mack Morriss's diary; Associate Professor Daryl Carter at ETSU; Ed Speer, my former student and researcher; Matt Poole of Wheaton, Maryland; Tom McLeod of Texarkana; the late Colonels Jefferson J. DeBlanc and Berton H. "Tex" Burns.

During my trip to Japan, I received assistance from the Military Archival Library, National Institute for Defense Studies in Ebisu, Tokyo; Nobuhiro Moriya; and my daughter-in-law's parents, Kenichi and Katsuko Tsunoda.

In the South Pacific area, I extend my thanks to my long-term Australian friend and Solomons research collaborator, Peter Woodbury of Sydney. Also from Australia, I am indebted to the late coastwatcher Martin Clemens; Peter Flahavin of Melbourne, for his local knowledge and record sharing on Guadalcanal; Dr. Peter Stanley of the Australian War Memorial; and the Australian National Archives in Canberra. In New Zealand, Ewan Stevenson of Auckland shared valuable information on the Western Solomons, and David Duxbury of Christchurch was a reliable source on the RNZAF and its aircraft. In the Solomon Islands itself, my thanks to the Solomons Islands National Museum at Honiara, Agnes Lodge, and Alfred A. Bisili of Munda and Danny Kennedy of Gizo.

Lastly, I want to thank my family who have supported me throughout this labor of love – John and Rima, Anna, Joe, and Stephanie.

Ronnie Day
Johnson City, Tennessee

Maps

American and Japanese Aircraft

B-17 "Flying Fortress" Four-engine heavy bomber, built by Boeing.

B-24 "Liberator" Four-engine heavy bomber, built by Consolidated.

B-25 "Mitchell" Twin-engine medium bomber, built by North American Aviation.

F4U-1 "Corsair" Single-engine fighter aircraft, built by Chance Vought.

F4F "Wildcat" Single-engine carrier-based fighter aircraft, built by Grumman.

F5A Photo-reconnaissance version of the P-38 fighter.

F6F "Hellcat" Single-engine fighter aircraft, built by Grumman as replacement for F4F Wildcat.

Hudson MK III-A Light bomber and coastal reconnaissance aircraft, built by Lockheed.

P-38 "Lightning" Twin-fuselage, twin-engine fighter, built by Lockheed.

P-39 "Airacobra" Single, mid-engine fighter with tricycle landing gear, built by Bell Aircraft.

P-40 "Warhawk" Single-engine fighter, built by Curtiss-Wright Corporation.

PBY "Catalina" Twin-engine flying boat, built by Consolidated.

PBY-5A "Black Cats" Version of PBY adapted for nighttime reconnaissance.

PB4Y-1 "Liberator" Navy four-engine patrol bomber designation for
  B-24.

PB4Y-2 "Privateer" Navy four-engine patrol bomber derived from
  the B-24.

PV-1 "Ventura" Twin-engine patrol and reconnaissance aircraft, built
  by Vega Aircraft Company, a division of Lockheed.

SB-24 "Snooper" Version of the B-24, radar equipped with extra
  crew member as radar operator, used for night strikes and path-
  finder operations.

SBD "Dauntless" Single-engine dive bomber and scout plane both
  land and carrier based, used by USN and USMC, built by Douglas.

TBF "Avenger" Single-engine torpedo/glide bomber, built by
  Grumman.

JAPANESE AIRCRAFT (ALLIED CODE
DESIGNATION IN QUOTES)

A6M2 "Zero," "Zeke" Navy single-engine, carrier-based fighter,
  built by Mitsubishi. During the first years of WWII the Zero was
  considered the finest fighter in the world.

A6M2-N "Rufe" Seaplane based on the Zero, built by Nakajima.

A6M3 "Hap" (later "Hamp") Redesign of the Zero with a larger engine, stronger armament, and clipped wings, built by Mitsubishi.

B5N2 "Kate" Navy carrier-based, single-engine torpedo bomber,
  built by Nakajima.

D3A2 "Val" Navy carrier-borne, single-engine dive bomber, built by
  Aichi.

D4Y1 Suisei (*Comet*) Carrier-borne, single-engine dive bomber,
  notably faster than the D3A, built by Yokosuka.

E13A1 "Jake" Navy single-engine, long-range reconnaissance
  seaplane, built by Aichi.

F1M2 "Pete" Bi-wing, single-engine reconnaissance seaplane, built by
  Mitsubishi.

G3M2 "Nell" Long-range, land-based, twin-engine attack bomber,
  built by Mitsubishi.

G4M1 "Betty" Long-range, land-based, twin-engine attack bomber, built by Mitsubishi. Lighter and faster than the G3M, it was also susceptible to catching fire when hit.

H6K4 "Mavis" Four-engine flying boat used for patrol, built by Kawanishi.

H8K2 "Emily" Four-engine, heavily-armed flying boat, longer and with greater range than the H6K, built by Kawanishi.

J1N1 Gekkō (*Moonlight*) "Irving" Navy twin-engine night fighter and reconnaissance aircraft, built by Nakajima.

Ki21 "Sally" Twin-engine heavy bomber, built by Mitsubishi.

Ki43 "Oscar" Air force single-engine, land-based fighter, built by Nakajima.

Ki46 "Dinah" Twin-engine reconnaissance aircraft, built by Mitsubishi.

Ki48 "Lilly" Twin-engine light bomber, built by Kawasaki.

Ki61 "Tony" Single-engine fighter, built by Kawasaki.

Japanese Air Force Organizations

Kōkū kantai Air Fleet (carrier- or land-based).

Kōkū sentai Carrier Division (or Air Flotilla for land-based units).

Kōkū bokan Carrier-based Air Group.

Kōkūtai Naval land-based Air Group.

Hikotai Flight Echelon of Kōkū bokan or Kōkūtai.

Hikō buntai Usually the administrative equivalent of a Chutai.

IMPERIAL JAPANESE NAVY AIR FORCE

OPERATIONAL ORGANIZATION

Hikokitai Carrier-based aircraft Echelon or Wing, or the Flight Echelon of a Kōkūtai. Air group (such as attached to a ship).

Daitai Squadron of 18 to 27 aircraft (Sentai for IJAAF).

Chutai A unit of six to nine aircraft.

Shōtai A unit of two to four planes (usually three).

Buntai Two-plane element, adopted late in the war as part of a four-plane Shōtai.

Chutai Three to four Shōtai.

Daitai Three to six Chutai.

Hikotai/Kōkūtai Two to three Daitai.

Seikūtai Air Superiority Unit.

Kōgekitai A split division of a Seikūtai.

IMPERIAL JAPANESE ARMY AIR SERVICE ORGANIZATION

Kōkū gun   Air Army of two Air Divisions (Hikō Shidan), plus some independent units.

Hikō Shidan   Air Division made up of two or more Air Combat Groups, plus base and support units. Previously designated Hikō Shodan = Air Corps.

Hikōdan   Air division of two or more air combat groups.

Kōkūtai   Air combat group

Hikō Sentai   Air combat group of three squadrons.

Hikō Chutai   Squadron of three flights.

Hikō Shōtai   Flight of three aircraft.

Acronyms, Abbreviations, and Code Names

COMMAND ACRONYMS

AAF	Army Air Forces (Arnold)
BSIPDF	British Solomon Islands Protectorate Defence Force
COMAIRSOLS	Commander Aircraft Solomons (Mulcahy; Mason)
COMINCH	Commander in Chief, United States Navy (King)
COMSOPAC	Commander South Pacific Area (Halsey)
COMAIRSOPAC	Commander Aircraft South Pacific (Fitch)
CINCPAC	Commander in Chief, Pacific (Nimitz)
IMAC	First Marine Amphibious Corps
IGHQ	[Japanese] Imperial General Headquarters
SOPACSOUTH	South Pacific Area

MILITARY ACRONYMS AND ABBREVIATIONS

APA	Attack Transport
AKA	Attack (Cargo) Transport
APC	Small Coastal Transport
APD	High-speed Transport
CB	Naval Mobile Construction Battalion (commonly called Seabees as a play on the initials CBs)
FA	Field Artillery

LCI	Landing Craft Infantry
LCT	Landing Craft Tank
LST	Landing Ship Tank
MAW	Marine Aircraft Wing
NGAF	New Georgia Air Force
NGOF	New Georgia Occupation Force
RCT	Regimental Combat Team
RNZN	Royal New Zealand Navy
SCAT	South Pacific Combat Air Transport
SNLF	Special Naval Landing Force (Japan)
SWPA	South West Pacific Area Command (MacArthur)
TF	Task Force
TG	Task Group
VB	Navy Bomber Squadron
VF	Navy Fighter Squadron
VMF	Marine Fighting Squadron
VMSB	Marine Scout Bomber Squadron
VMTB	Marine Scout Torpedo Squadron

CODE WORDS

CACTUS Guadalcanal; later code name changed to MAINYARD

CARTWHEEL Operational name for overall strategy to retake New Guinea and the Solomon Islands (United States)

CLEANSLATE Operational name for occupation of Russell Islands

TOENAILS Designation for the New Georgia operation (United States)

ULTRA Deciphered information from encrypted enemy communications (United States)

I-gō aerial offensive launched against Guadalcanal (Japan)

Ka-gō Operation to withdraw from Guadalcanal (Japan)

Ke-gō Operation to reinforce the Solomons (Japan)

Se-gō Operation to evacuate Kolombangara (Japan)

To-gō Operation to establish new defense line on New Guinea (Japan)

NEW GEORGIA

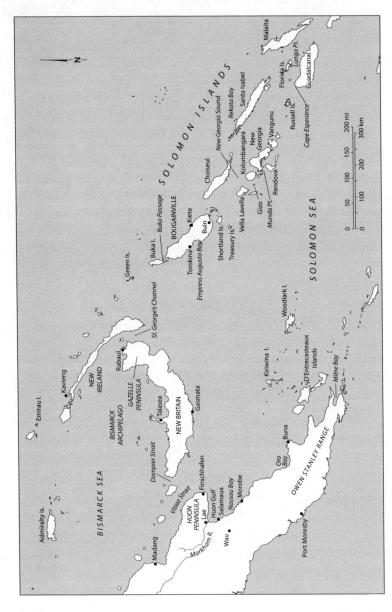

Map 1.1. Battle Area, 1943.

ONE

The Japanese Occupation

WHEN EUROPEANS WERE EVACUATED FROM THE SOLOMON Islands following the fall of Rabaul on the island of New Britain in January 1942, the Reverend John Metcalfe stayed at the Kokenggolo Methodist Mission at Munda Point. He was certain that New Georgia had nothing of value to the Japanese. But on the stormy night of 13 November 1942, the Reverend Metcalfe was forced to set out on his escape route up the trail to Bairoko Harbor when the destroyer *Hakaze* began landing an airfield surveying party and a detachment from the Sasebo 6th Special Naval Landing Force (SNLF) to secure the area.[1]

Even on the run, Metcalfe was still puzzled about the Japanese motives until he learned on 17 December that they had built an airfield in the plantation. On the one hand he was surprised; on the other he immediately saw the implications. "I've wondered why the Yanks gave so much attention to Munda, now I know," he wrote in his diary. "The prospect is not pleasant though, since it may mean the Y's [Yanks] using it after the J's [Japanese] which will mean a prolonged battle ground and make this a rather dangerous spot."[2]

The Japanese move into New Georgia was driven by events on Guadalcanal and mirrors the Japanese situation there, which was going from bad to disastrous. At Imperial General Headquarters (IGHQ) in Tokyo, New Georgia was first planned as a forward air base for a new attack on Guadalcanal, then as an intermediate base to help supply the starving troops there, and finally, as the forward base in the defense against a renewed Allied drive up the Solomons.

THE JAPANESE AT MUNDA

The Japanese surveying party completed its work and returned to Rabaul on 17 November. During the three days it had worked among the palms, the situation in Southeast Area had altered drastically in favor of Allied forces. In Papua, New Guinea, General Douglas MacArthur had initiated his attack on the Japanese bases at Buna-Gona, while off Guadalcanal the Imperial Navy had lost a series of surface and air engagements – the Naval Battle of Guadalcanal – in an attempt to force through a large convoy. Ten of the eleven transports were lost and with them desperately needed rations and ammunition for Lieutenant General Hyakutake Harukichi's beleaguered Seventeenth Army. Both sides realized that this was a turning point in the four-month struggle, and historians have since agreed. "It was the decisive battle for the campaign," historian Richard B. Frank has written, "and in retrospect, it became clear that it was decisive for the Pacific War as a whole."[3]

Too late, the Japanese finally recognized that they were locked in a two-front war in Southeast Area, one in which the Allied forces on each front possessed superior forces. Nonetheless, IGHQ went ahead with plans to hold eastern New Guinea and to make another attempt to retake Guadalcanal. The Imperial Army dramatically increased its commitment. Until mid-November, the Japanese had three commands in Southeast Area – the army's Seventeenth Army (Hyakutake), 11th Air Fleet (Vice Admiral Kusaka Jinichi), and 8th Fleet (Vice Admiral Mikawa Gunichi). Now, with the army committed to bringing in additional infantry divisions as well as an air division, Lieutenant General Imamura Hitoshi activated Eighth Area Army at Rabaul. The Seventeenth Army on Guadalcanal would come under this command, as would the new Eighteenth Army, which had been created to defend New Guinea. Since the Japanese practice in joint operations was to maintain parallel headquarters, in late December Southeast Area Fleet was formed with 11th Air Fleet and 8th Fleet, which came under the command of Kusaka. Kusaka, however, retained direct command of the 11th Air Fleet (Base Air Force).

As the Japanese realized, any hope of success hinged on gaining air superiority over their convoy routes in order to get reinforcements and

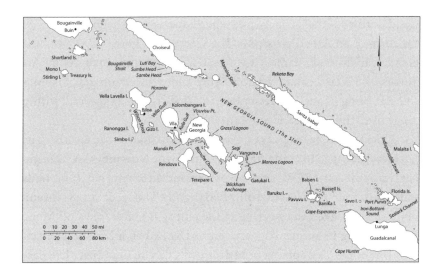

Map 1.2. Central Solomons.

supplies to Guadalcanal. To this end, the Army Air Service was to reinforce the 11th Air Fleet, and both services were to cooperate in building
the necessary airfields. Four fields were to be built immediately: Rapopo,
near Rabaul, for the army; Munda for the navy; Vila, on Kolombangara,
for joint use; and Ballale Island, off the Shortland Islands, for the navy.
Munda, which a Japanese army/navy reconnaissance team had selected
over Rekata Bay on Santa Isabel, was 120 miles from the Japanese airfield
at Kahili and 180 miles from the American airfields at Lunga. This would
be an ideal base, therefore, from which to provide convoy protection.[4]

The Japanese faced three obstacles in their move into Munda. The
first was logistical. The barrier reef enclosing Roviana Lagoon guarded
Munda Point, and the only direct access from the sea was by way of
the Munda Bar – and this only for small vessels with experienced pilots
who were familiar with local landmarks. Consequently, men, materiel,
and equipment had to be off-loaded into barges for the three-mile trip
through the lagoon reefs. The second obstacle was American intelligence.
Coast-watcher stations had been in operation on both Choiseul and Vella
Lavella since October, and the chances of approaching the Munda Bar
undetected were not good. The third obstacle was sure to arrive from

Guadalcanal – if the Japanese were spotted and if weather permitted – in the form of an Allied air strike. The Cactus Air Force – CACTUS was Guadalcanal's code name – was made up of marine, navy, Army Air Forces, and New Zealand aircraft flying under the command of 1st Marine Air Wing (from late December, 2nd MAW). Munda was well within range of all the assorted Cactus aircraft.[5]

Nonetheless, taking advantage of darkness and/or bad weather, the Japanese managed to evade air strikes during the November and December transport runs. While some ships were forced to return only partially unloaded, none were lost and only two slightly damaged. On 28 November, B-17s damaged the steering of the empty *Chihaya Maru* off Mono Island during its return trip, and on 16 December, a Marine Douglas SBD Dauntless dive bomber pilot dropped a flare to illuminate Japanese destroyers off the Munda Bar and then damaged *Kagerō*'s stern with a near miss.[6] Submarines, however, drew blood. On 10 December, *Wahoo* torpedoed *Kamoi Maru* off Buka Island, and, a week later, *Grouper* sank *Bandoeng Maru* in the same area. Both were small army freighters, but both were carrying munitions, and the loss was keenly felt at Rabaul.[7]

The November transports brought in the occupation force and the construction units. On the night of the 20th–21st, *Kamo Maru* landed Major Satō Giichi's 2nd Battalion, 229th Infantry, 38th Division, and two batteries of 75mm guns of the 41st Antiaircraft Battalion. Within the week the navy's 22nd Construction Unit and part of the 4th and the army's 10th Construction Unit followed. Captain Iwabuchi Sanji, who had lost the battleship *Kirishima* in the Naval Battle of Guadalcanal, took command of the base. Altogether, the construction units numbered 2,500 men, equipped with hand tools, a few trucks, and eleven rollers. "Japan had bulldozers and other earthwork machines, but had not thought about using them for airfield construction," the Army Air Service historians wrote. This was a serious weakness, especially in the tropical forest of the Southeast Area. But the Kokenggolo Mission plantation offered an excellent site with level terrain and a solid coral base, and while the Japanese had no tanks to push over the palms, which was their usual practice when tanks were available, the palms could be blasted out. To avoid detection for as long as possible, they left the palms standing and worked around them, hurrying the construction because of fear of an

American preemptive landing like that at Guadalcanal. But there was no hiding the work from the scouts of the coast watchers, and on 5 December, a Marine PB4Y photographic plane confirmed that an airfield was taking shape beneath the palms. Five days later, eighteen B-17s unloaded on the plantation, damaging eight of the rollers. Thereafter, the Japanese worked under continual air attacks; so many bombs hit Kokenggolo Hill that the Japanese named it Bomb (Bakudan) Hill.[8]

By 15 December, a rough 3,300 by 130–foot field with thirty revetments was operational, and the next night the December transports began bringing in antiaircraft units of Colonel Shiroto Shunichi's 15th Field Antiaircraft Regiment, aviation gasoline, and base personnel. On 23 December, twenty Zeros of the 252nd Kōkūtai (air combat group) under the command of Lieutenant Suhō Motonari flew in, immediately touching off an air battle; in fact, the 252nd lost one Zero to Cactus fighters before sunset. On Christmas Eve morning, the SBDs arrived early and caught a dozen Zeros on the eastern end of the field, and as the Marine Scout Bomber Squadron VMSB-142 War Diary recorded, "bomber pilots dove immediately on this spectacular target." Suhō recalled that five planes were lost on the ground and others damaged, while in the air two pilots were killed and three wounded. The 252nd never recovered from the Christmas Eve battles. By 28 December, only three of the original twenty Zeros, plus four or five replacements, were flyable, and Base Air Force sent three Mitsubishi G3M "Nell" medium bombers to take out the pilots. A barge-hunting P-39 fighter shot down one of these. The other two G3Ms, with the surviving pilots, and the three flyable Zeros returned to Rabaul. Ground personnel were left behind.[9]

Sending in well-trained pilots and good aircraft to fight from such an inadequate base was meaningless, Suhō noted after the war. Apparently, Base Air Force drew the same conclusion, for it never again tried to use the airfield on a permanent basis. The Army Air Service's 12th Hikōdan (air division) used the airfield on and off during the Guadalcanal evacuation, and it served as an emergency landing field right up until marine 155mm guns, emplaced on Rendova, brought it under fire. But judged by its objective, building the airfield at Munda had been a futile effort – the first of a number of setbacks in New Georgia as the Japanese expanded into Vila, Kolombangara, and Wickham Anchorage.

THE MOVE INTO KOLOMBANGARA

Kolombangara is a volcanic island some fifteen miles northwest of Munda. The tallest of its four peaks has an elevation of just over 5,800 feet, and the island would be perfectly round were it not for Vila Point, which juts out into Blackett Strait like the tab on a can lid. The Vila River empties into Blackett Strait at the point, and the largest expanse of level terrain on the island runs north and south on each side of the river. Here, Lever Brothers operated three plantations,[10] Stanmore on the north side and Vila and Lady Lever on the south, and here the Japanese planned to build an airfield and a shipping base. The airfield was to be built in Vila Plantation, while the base facilities and supply dumps would be located in Stanmore and on north to Jack Harbor. Blackett Strait narrows to 1,200 yards at Vila before connecting to Kula Gulf, but the channel is deep, and transports and destroyers could unload into barges 300 to 400 yards from shore. Ringgi and Vavohe Coves provided excellent bases for the barges on which Japanese interisland logistics depended. Since the Japanese were lacking in heavy construction equipment, Vila provided the only solution available to the logistical problem posed by the Munda Bar. (Later, after Munda changed hands, the Navy Seabees solved the problem by first blowing a channel through the bar for LSTs and then dredging it for use by small tankers.)[11]

The Japanese scheduled the last December transport for the 2nd Roadstead, as they called Vila. *Nankai Maru*, carrying construction materials, was to depart Rabaul on Christmas Day, followed two days later by *Kagu Maru*, carrying the 17th Naval Construction Unit. All that could go wrong did. *Nankai Maru* and *Uzuki* sailed at 1500, and at 1930 *Seadragon* torpedoed *Nankai Maru*, flooding the two forward holds. Twenty-five minutes later, the wildly maneuvering *Uzuki* collided with the transport. While *Nankai Maru* was able to make it back to Simpson Harbor under its own power, *Ariake*, scheduled to escort *Kagu Maru*, had to be sent to tow *Uzuki*. Early the next morning, three of MacArthur's Fifth Air Force B-24s flying from Port Moresby scored a near miss on *Ariake*, damaging the hull and killing twenty-six men and wounding forty. If that was not enough, in the early hours of 27 December, Fifth Air Force sank a transport and inflicted serious damage on *Kagu*

Maru, which had suffered some slight damage from the bombing early on Christmas morning. The Japanese canceled the shipments, while in Truk a disgusted Vice Admiral Ugaki Matome, Chief of Staff, Combined Fleet, wrote in his diary: "That should be called a case of going into the forest to cut wood and coming back shorn."[12] The construction at Vila was delayed for two weeks.

THE MOVE INTO WICKHAM ANCHORAGE

The occupation of Wickham Anchorage on the southeast tip of Vangunu Island was part of a plan to supply Guadalcanal using small cargo ships of 500 tons or so, which the Japanese called sea trucks. This was a joint army/navy operation that originated at the very top of the Southeast Area command in Rabaul, and the army units involved reported directly to Imamura. The plan called for the sea trucks to move by stages at night, while hiding out by day along "the secret course" from Rabaul to Kamimbo Bay on the western tip of Guadalcanal. The hideout bases were planned for the Shortland Islands, Wickham Anchorage, and the Russell Islands.[13]

Perhaps reflecting the desperate situation on Guadalcanal, the army sea trucks *Iwami Maru* and *Takashima Maru* (one was towing a large barge) set out on the secret course before the main occupation force went to Wickham Anchorage. They were loaded with compressed, dehydrated rations and sealed drums of rice. A machine-gun section and a signal unit were also on board, most likely intended for Wickham Anchorage. In any case, the two units ended up at Wickham. Unknown to the Japanese, Wickham Anchorage was in the backyard of the coast watcher at Segi, Major Donald Kennedy, BSIPDF (British Solomon Islands Protectorate Defence Force). A radio message to Guadalcanal was all that it took. As the sea trucks neared the entrance to the anchorage on 26 December, Cactus dive-bombers literally split them open. For days thereafter, Kennedy's scouts raced the Japanese in recovering the rations and drums of rice that floated ashore; the scouts brought back an estimated five tons of rice and an equal amount of rations, while the Japanese recovered about 900 cases. The starving troops on Guadalcanal would have greeted this food as a gift from the gods.[14]

Despite this setback, the Japanese persisted, and the next night, six destroyers of the 8th Fleet Reinforcement Force (what the Americans called the "Tokyo Express") boarded the 1st Battalion, 229th Regiment, at Buin and landed it without incident at Wickham.[15] The following night, 28 December, two sea trucks, *Azusa Maru* and *Kiku Maru*, arrived with a SNLF detachment, one army battery of heavy antiaircraft guns, along with ammunition and supplies. But they were spotted, and again, Kennedy radioed Guadalcanal. The next morning, Cactus dive-bombers sent both to the bottom and with them two of the four heavy guns, all of the observation instruments, most of the ammunition, and all of the supplies. On 30 December, the Marine SBD Dauntless dive-bombers returned to sink four large barges sent down from Vila and damaged another, leaving the Wickham Occupation Force with only five that could be used.[16]

Rabaul canceled the secret course plan. The anchorage played no further role in the Guadalcanal campaign, except that the garrison would rescue a number of airmen who ditched in the vicinity during the air battles that attended the Japanese withdrawal from Guadalcanal.[17]

IGHQ – THE JANUARY DECISION

In the last weeks of December, IGHQ came to the difficult decision to withdraw from Guadalcanal, and on 28 December, Admiral Nagano Osami, Chief of the Navy General Staff, and General Sugiyama Hajime, chief of the Army General Staff, informed the emperor of their intention. But Hirohito wanted not only the plans for the evacuation but their plans for halting the American advance. Consequently, on New Year's Eve, the first Imperial Conference with IGHQ since the start of the Pacific War was held.

While the evacuation of Guadalcanal was the major concern, the fate of New Georgia was also decided. Prior to the Imperial Conference, the navy and the army had reached agreement on all major points except the Solomon Islands defense line. The army, fearing a new Guadalcanal in the making, wanted to withdraw all the way back to Bougainville, but the navy was adamant on holding New Georgia and Rekata Bay, a seaplane base on northeast Santa Isabel. What Nagano and Sugiyama laid before the emperor was an army/navy compromise worked out on 29 December: the army would be responsible for Bougainville and the navy for New Georgia and Rekata Bay. But the navy exacted from the army an agreement to keep at least two battalions in New Georgia and troops at Rekata Bay. This was the first step toward committing the army to the defense of New Georgia.[18]

Waiting in the adjoining room with other staff members, Commander Sanagi Sadamu, at the time serving in the War Planning Section of the Navy General Staff, overheard Hirohito ask Nagano what they planned to do to halt the American advance up the Solomons. Nagano assured the emperor that once the New Georgia bases had been completed "[they] could inflict great damage on the Allied forces at Guadalcanal."[19] Hirohito would not forget Nagano's promise.

IGHQ made the Army/Navy Central Agreement official on 4 January 1943. The details were already in the hands of the responsible commanders, Admiral Yamamoto Isoroku, commander, Combined Fleet at Truk, and Imamura and Kusaka at Rabaul. As usual, IGHQ stressed cooperation between the services in what was clearly a switch to the defensive in the Southeast Area. There were three main provisions. First, the withdrawal from Guadalcanal (Ke-gō) was to be completed "using every imaginable means," while the army was to strengthen positions in the Northern Solomons and the navy those in the Central Solomons (Ka-gō). Second, in eastern New Guinea a strong defensive position would be established along the line of Salamaua–Lae–Mandang–Wewak, and the units at Buna (now all but destroyed) were to withdraw to Salamaua (Operation To-gō). Third, in regard to air operations, the army, which by the November agreement had committed Lieutenant General Itabana Giichi's 6th Air Division, was to have responsibility for New Guinea. Kusaka's Base Air Force had responsibility for the Solomons, as well as areas in New Guinea not covered by the 6th Air Division.

Based on the IGHQ directive, Yamamoto issued his specific instructions to Kusaka for the defense of the Central Solomons. First, during January all bases in Santa Isabel and New Georgia were to be reinforced and the supply lines secured, so long as nothing interfered with Ke-gō, scheduled to begin at the end of the month. Second, Rekata Bay was to be the hub for the Santa Isabel defense line, and Munda the hub for

New Georgia, with the forward post at Wickham Anchorage. Third, the airfields in New Georgia were to be completed as quickly as possible and underground storage facilities built at Munda for aircraft. Fourth, after the completion of the Guadalcanal evacuation, and in line with what Nagano had told the emperor, the air and naval forces were to cooperate in the defense of the bases, the air force and submarines were to cut off all supplies to Guadalcanal, and the air force was to renew nighttime attacks.[20]

Yamamoto's instructions revealed a serious lack of understanding of the real situation in the Central Solomons: to underscore this – although of course it was simply a coincidence of timing – on the same night that Kusaka received his instructions, Admiral William F. Halsey Jr., commander, South Pacific Forces (COMSOPAC), added a new dimension to Munda's travails – naval gunfire. Rear Admiral Walden L. Ainsworth, with light cruisers *Nashville*, *St. Louis*, and *Helena*, and two destroyers, broke off from the covering force of a large troop convoy that was unloading at Guadalcanal and headed northwest to Munda. The course was set to skirt Rendova to the south and come onto the firing track west of the island. The night was dark with an overcast sky and passing showers, and the darkened ships navigated using surface search (SG) radar. The submarine *Grayback* served as a navigational aid, and two PBY-5A "Black Cats" were out ahead to search the night and then to serve as spotters. All went according to Ainsworth's well-laid plans – the first that would coordinate surface, submarine, and aircraft units in a night bombardment. At 0102, *Nashville* came on to the firing track and opened fire, each ship following in turn; forty-eight minutes later, having put over 4,000 rounds on the target, the task group turned and headed back southeast. Yet, the damage was not that great. The Japanese recorded thirty-two men killed and ten buildings destroyed, while the construction crews had the runway repaired in two hours. But this marked the beginning of a series of bombardments that continued until Munda fell.[21]

THE JAPANESE DEFENSE EFFORT – JANUARY 1943

The official Japanese Navy historians write that the January buildup of the defense forces in the Central Solomons fell short of expectations.

They blame this on the preparations for Ke-gō, but give no specifics as to where the navy came up short. What is known, however, is that the Japanese dispatched twenty transports, some to Rekata Bay, but most to Vila, and all but the final one made port (see below). To build the field at Vila, the Japanese sent in the navy's 17th and 19th Construction Units and a detachment of the army's 5th Engineer Regiment, as well as the 3rd Battalion, 66th Infantry, 51st Division, to build roads and base facilities. The 51st had been brought in to reinforce Hyakutake's 17th Army on Guadalcanal, but with the decision to withdraw, the division had been reassigned to Lieutenant General Adachi Hatazō's Eighteenth Army in New Guinea. At Rekata Bay, the Japanese sent in a miscellaneous force of SNLF troops, the Masuda Battalion, formed out of replacements that had been intended for Guadalcanal, and an antiaircraft unit.[22]

The relative tranquility at Vila – compared to Munda, at least, where bombing continued unabated – came to an abrupt end on the night of 23–24 January. The coast watcher's scouts had again spotted the activity, and Ainsworth with *Nashville, Helena,* and four destroyers again headed northwest – this time up the Slot,[23] marking the first time that American warships traveled these waters. With one destroyer going ahead to sweep deep into Kula Gulf and with Black Cats overhead to spot, the bombardment went off as planned. On the delivering end, the destroyer *DeHaven*'s commander reported seeing six salvos from *Nashville* in the air at the same time; on the receiving end, a POW from the 17th Construction Unit recalled that he saw shells make big craters everywhere, the fuel depot hit and burn all night, the ration dump hit, and many men hit, "as he saw bodies flying through the air after an explosion."[24] Actually, only five men were killed. Come sunrise, the entire *Saratoga* air group, based at Guadalcanal the day before, struck the still-smoking Vila area. But despite the construction delays, the bombardment, and the bombing, on 26 January, the airfield was deemed ready enough for use, and a sentai (roughly the equivalent of a USAAF group) of the 12th Hikōdan was scheduled to land there on its return from a mission to Guadalcanal. This apparently did not occur, and Army Air Service units used Munda instead during Ke-gō.[25]

Near the end of the month, Kusaka began moving the navy's main defense force – Rear Admiral Ōta Minoru's 8th Combined SNLF – to

New Georgia. Ōta was an experienced SNLF commander, but the 8th Combined was a new unit activated on 20 November 1942, comprising the Kure 6th and the Yokosuka 7th. Both units had been configured as heavy artillery units for the mission of supporting the major attack on Guadalcanal, planned for January, by shelling the airfields and American positions. The guns and their crews had been drawn largely from battle-ships undergoing a major refit – *Fusō*, *Ise*, and *Hyūga* – and the heavy 14cm, 12cm, and 8cm guns with fixed mounts were not maneuverable, giving them a limited field of fire.[26] Antiaircraft and support units, two rifle companies, and a heavy weapons company made up the rest of the Special Naval Landing Forces. The troops comprising the rifle compa-nies were mostly raw recruits, and when the unit arrived at Rabaul in December 1942, they were given more training at the big army base at Raluana Point, between Rabaul Town and Kokopo. To call these troops Japanese marines, however, is to invite an erroneous comparison to the amphibious-assault-trained U. S. Marines; as the navy advised the army, a Special Naval Landing Force was primarily a defensive unit, and if the rifle companies were to be used in "moving battle," this characteristic needs to be taken into account.[27]

The Cactus Air Force exacted a toll on the late January transports. On the 27th, SBDS and TBF Avenger torpedo bombers with the usual fighter escort caught *No. 20 Mikage Maru* as it was about to enter Vella Gulf carrying cargo and Kure 6th troops. While the ship made port at Vila, ten men were killed and thirty wounded in the attack.[28] Worse was to follow. On 29 January, Ōta and his headquarters, along with the Kure 6th Headquarters, departed Rabaul for New Georgia in the 7,000-ton *No. 2 Tōa Maru*. After a stopover at Buin, the *No. 2 Tōa Maru*, with the large torpedo boat *Hiyodori* and a subchaser as escort, sailed for Vila on 31 January. Three FIMS "Pete" bi-wing floatplanes provided air cover. A Royal New Zealand Air Force (RNZAF) Hudson first spotted the little convoy, confirmed by the coast watchers on Choiseul and Vella Lavella. On board *No. 2 Tōa Maru*, Lieutenant Commander Imai Akijiro, chief of staff, 8th Combined, was concerned when he saw the Hudson turn away to the south. "Commander," one of his fellow officers said to him, "the sunset is coming soon, so we won't have to worry about an enemy attack." "Yes," he replied, "it seems we are going well." But he continued to watch the eastern sky, and then he "saw something like a grain of millet on the horizon." The grain of millet gradually grew bigger; it was a number of enemy planes.[29]

Thirty-one altogether – SBDS, TBFS, F4F Wildcats, and P-39s – caught the convoy in Vella Gulf. As *No. 2 Tōa Maru* began a slow turn to starboard, the dive bombers peeled off to port and pushed over, making their attack stern to bow. They scored no hits, but near misses killed a number of men on board the transport, and four of the F4Fs strafed the ship with good effect. As the SBDs leveled out and the TBFs made their run, Lieutenant Jefferson DeBlanc saw what he expected. Two FIMs were racing in to attack the SBDs, what he called "the usual old 'Munda Airfield' set-up."[30] With his wingman covering him, he immediately was on the tails of the FIMs and sent both flaming into the sea. In the meantime, a torpedo from one of the marine VMSB-131 TBFs struck home on the port bow of *No. 2 Tōa Maru* (which could be visually confirmed), while another may have hit forward on the starboard bow. As the bombers with the P-39s headed home, a chūtai (squadron) of Ki-43 fighter planes from the 11th Sentai in route to Munda intervened, and DeBlanc and his wingman climbed into the battle. Both were shot down (and rescued), but not before the F4Fs downed four of the Ki-43s, with three credited to DeBlanc.[31]

Down below, *No. 2 Tōa Maru* was smoking from fires that had been caused by the strafing, and the two forward holds were flooding rapidly from the torpedo hit. (No. 1 hold was loaded with bags of concrete mixture.) *Hiyodori* took off the seriously wounded and headed for Vila; as the sun set, all available barges came out from Vila, and they along with the subchaser removed the rest of the personnel and what cargo they could. Unable to stop the flooding, and with the ship down by the bows, the captain managed to run the ship aground on the reef at Gizo. But it soon slipped off into deep water, and with it went seventy-five barge loads of valuable cargo, including trucks, an automobile, two tractors, and two Type 97 light tanks that belonged to the Kure 6th Headquarters Company. It was a significant loss for the Japanese.[32]

Ōta assumed command at Munda 5 February, relieving Iwabuchi, who soon after disappears from New Georgia records.[33] For his headquarters, Ōta selected one of the crests of a hill north of the airfield, a hill that the Japanese named Kongō Yama (Golden Mountain) and that the Americans later called Twin Hills (and that I shall call Kongō Hill). With the army firmly in control of the Munda defenses, Ōta deployed the 8th Combined SNLF to defend the northern approach to Munda by way of Kula Gulf and the all-important shipping base at Vila. Consequently, he placed the headquarters of the Kure 6th (Commander Takeuchi Shizushichi until May, then Commander Okumura Saburō) at Bairoko Harbor, with its heavy 14cm gun battery at Enogai Inlet. Commander Takeda Koshin would defend Vila with the Yokosuka 7th, minus its 14cm battery, which was emplaced on Poporang Island. The army units at Munda, Shinoro's 15th Field Antiaircraft Regiment, Satō's 2nd Battalion, 229th, and 1st Battalion, 229th, at Wickham and Viru Harbor, also came under Ōta's command. But all army units reported through Colonel Shinoro, the ranking officer, except those engaged in construction on Kolombangara, which were under 8th Area Army.[34]

Ōta organized logistics with Vila as the hub. Both services had barges of various types, the most common being the 50-foot, bow-ramped Daihatsu, which could carry around one hundred men or 15 tons of cargo. Ōta consolidated all these and other small craft under one command, the New Georgia Area Boat Unit. With its main base at Ringgi and Vavohe Coves and a second base at Bairoko Harbor, the unit had responsibility for all transport in New Georgia. Barges transported men, guns, and supplies to the outposts at Wickham Anchorage and Viru Harbor, and later to those on Rendova Island and Vella Lavella. But the heaviest traffic was in the triangle formed by Vila, Bairoko Harbor, and Munda. Barges went directly to Munda through Hawthorne Sound and the Diamond Narrows to the Kokenggolo Mission pier at the western end of the airfield. The other well-traveled route, and one used for troop movements to Munda, was between Vila and Bairoko Harbor. From Bairoko Harbor, the troops marched down the trail to Zieta, where the Kure 6th cultivated a large farm, and thence to Munda. Sea trucks later unloaded rations at Bairoko Harbor, where a 2,000-ton dump was located.[35]

This was the extent of the Japanese defense preparations in New Georgia and Rekata Bay at the completion of Ke-gō on 8 February 1943. The army had an antiaircraft regiment with units at Munda and Vila, and three infantry battalions scattered from Vila to Wickham Anchorage.

The navy had part of the Kure 6th and the 8th Combined Headquarters in place, but the Yokosuka 7th, with the exception of an antiaircraft unit at Vila, was still to come in.[36] The Japanese did not anticipate an easy time. As the 10 February transport order for the Yokosuka 7th warned, "Furthermore, enemy torpedo and bombing attacks, like those suffered by the *No. 20 Mikage Maru* and *No. 2 Tōa Maru*, are to be expected in the future, with considerable losses by damage and sinking." This is a story we will take up in chapter 3.[37]

COMSOPAC – THE JANUARY DECISION

Even though Japanese intentions regarding Guadalcanal were not clear in mid-January, Halsey's staff in Nouméa, New Caledonia, and the staff of Admiral Chester W. Nimitz, commander in chief, Pacific Fleet (CINCPAC) at Pearl Harbor, were studying the situation in the Solomons. They were working under the Joint Chiefs of Staff 2 July 1942 Directive, which stipulated three tasks for the capture of Rabaul. Task 1 was the seizure of Tulagi-Guadalcanal; Task 2 was the seizure of the remainder of the Solomon Islands and the Huon Peninsula of northeast New Guinea; and Task 3 was the seizure of Rabaul. While Task 1 was not yet completed, the American planners were certain of the outcome and focused their attention on Task 2, the occupation of the rest of the Solomons. General Douglas MacArthur, commander in chief, Southwest Pacific Area (SWPA), would have responsibility for New Guinea and would exercise overall command over the Task 2 operations in the Solomons, since the Central and Northern Solomons lay in his theater.[38]

The Japanese base at Buin was the primary objective in the Solomons; located 300 miles from Guadalcanal, the base lay outside the range of fighters, making the construction or capture of an intermediate airfield necessary. Like the Japanese before them, the Nouméa and Pearl Harbor planners considered both Rekata Bay and New Georgia, but they came to different conclusions. Nimitz's staff, while admitting that it was a "close call," opted for Rekata Bay, primarily because of the hydrographical difficulties at Munda. Halsey, on the other hand, was set on New Georgia. The expected arrival of the new large landing craft, LCTs, LCIs, and LSTs, would enable him, he thought, to overcome the hydro-

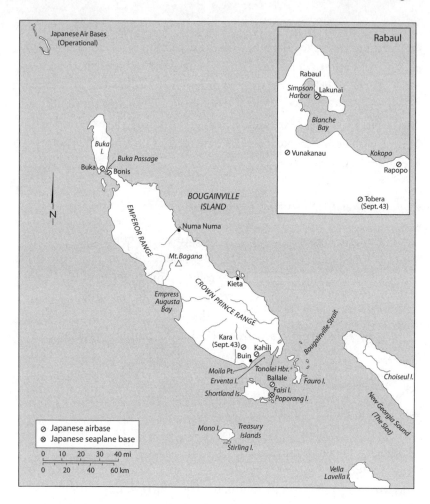

Map 1.3. Bougainville/Rabaul.

graphical problems; the airfields were already in existence; and aircraft based in New Georgia would be in the best possible position to cover the convoys to Bougainville, which would be routed south of Gizo and Vella Lavella. "After the Yellow Bellies have got the field in good condition for us," Halsey wrote Nimitz, "we will go up and take it away from them."[39]

Nimitz tended to side with his field commanders, so the nod went to New Georgia. But MacArthur would time the operation. After the bruising he received in the Papua campaign, he was in no hurry, which he indicated in a five-part message to Nimitz on 13 January. He reasoned that conditions had changed considerably since the Joint Chiefs 2 July Directive, and time was needed to rebuild and strengthen his forces before moving against formidable Japanese positions. Consequently, an immediate offensive in s w pa was not possible. On 9 February, the day Guadalcanal was declared secure, Nimitz and Halsey learned through Admiral Ernest J. King, commander in chief, United States Fleet (COMINCH), and a member of the Joint Chiefs, that MacArthur contemplated no continued offensive in the Solomons at the present time.[40]

Nor, as it turned out, for the immediate future – in fact, the New Georgia invasion forces would not depart Guadalcanal until 29 June.

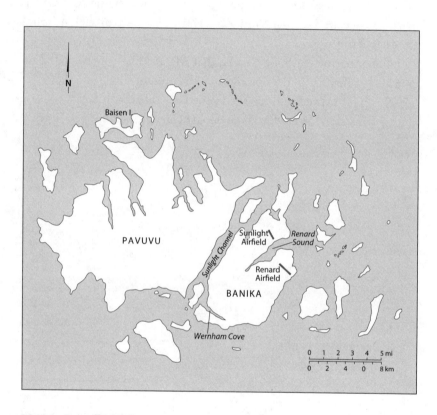

Map 2.1. Russell Islands.

TWO

SOPAC

BASES AND LOGISTICS

DURING A TRIP TO PEARL HARBOR, BRIGADIER GENERAL DEWITT Peck, USMC, Halsey's war plans officer, stayed with Nimitz, and the next morning he was told to go down and visit the CINCPAC staff. Peck did. "They were laying for me," he recalled. "They had one question: 'What have you learned as a result of the Guadalcanal Operation?' I had no hesitancy in replying, 'the importance of logistics.' Guadalcanal was operated on a shoestring – of necessity then – but I found out then, and we all did, that without adequate logistics, you are in a mess; and the 4 Section is one of the most important sections that you have, as important as the 3 [operations]."[1]

Thus CINCPAC's Estimate of the Situation, Solomon Islands, dated 15 January 1943, began with a list of what had to be done to turn Guadalcanal into a satisfactory base: completion of storage ashore, particularly for aviation gasoline; completion of airfields now underway and projected; provision of as many aircraft as the airfields could handle; construction of unloading facilities at beaches and roads for the distribution of supplies; and development of Port Purvis as a large anchorage.[2]

These projects were all underway or in the planning stage. The one major item missing from CINCPAC's checklist was the occupation of the Russell Islands, an objective that would be added by the end of the month.

THE RUSSELL ISLANDS – COMPLETING THE BASE COMPLEX

The Russell Islands lie 30 miles off the northwest tip of Guadalcanal, about 60 miles from the naval bases in the Florida Islands and the airfields at Lunga on Guadalcanal. Two small islands, Banika and Pavuvu, and a number of islets make up the group. Pavuvu, the larger of the two main islands, was no more than 10 miles across and hilly. But Banika, separated from Pavuvu by the narrow Sunlight Channel, was relatively level and extensively planted in coconut trees, while Renard Sound on the east coast afforded a small but good harbor (which was later found to be capable of handling Liberty ships).

Occupying the islands was the idea of Halsey's amphibious commander, Rear Admiral Richmond Kelly Turner, and General Peck. Halsey was not very enthusiastic about such a short step up the Solomons but gave Peck the go-ahead to raise the issue with Nimitz at a conference in Nouméa on 23 January. As Peck explained it, a marine raider battalion and part of a marine defense battalion would be used to occupy the islands, then establish a staging base for landing craft, a PT boat base, and possibly a fighter field as a first step in the advance on Munda. The record shows no discussion, but thereafter things moved quickly. Nimitz approved the move on 28 January, and Halsey issued his warning order on 7 February.[3]

Turner had his plan for operation CLEANSLATE ready by 15 February. Contrary to what Peck had told Nimitz, the plan called for an occupation in force using two regimental combat teams (RCT) of Major General John H. Hester's 43rd Infantry Division (earmarked for New Georgia), which would constitute the occupation force, with the 3rd Marine Raider Battalion temporarily attached to deal with any Japanese in the Baisen area. The Japanese had established a temporary barge base there during Ke-gō that was not used, and the personnel had left on the last destroyer run. A Solomon Islands patrol inserted the night of 12–13 February confirmed that the Japanese were gone, but both Turner and Hester persisted in their belief that up to a battalion remained. The support units included a PT boat squadron, an antiaircraft detachment of the 11th Marine Defense Battalion,[4] a radar unit, a fighter director group, the 33rd Naval Construction Battalion (Seabees), and a boat pool. Movement was to be shore-to-shore from Koli Point, Guadalcanal, and Gavutu Harbor, Florida, using destroyers and a variety of landing craft including the newly arrived LCTs, which could carry 150 to 180 tons of cargo.[5]

The two regimental combat teams of the 43rd Infantry Division – the 103rd and the 169th – had to be brought in from New Caledonia, and this gave Kusaka, who had moved a half dozen G4M "Betty" attack bombers from the 705th Kōkutai to Ballale to conduct searches, an opportunity to implement Yamamoto's instructions to cut communications to Guadalcanal. This was an impossible task, and failed miserably. The G4Ms missed the first convoy led by Turner in his flagship, the navy (amphibious) attack transport (APA) *McCawley*, carrying the 103rd, but they spotted the second carrying the 169th southeast of San Cristobal shortly after midnight on 17 February. The Bettys continued to shadow the convoy, and in the afternoon, eleven G3M "Nells" of the 701st Kōkutai, the only unit of Base Air Force still equipped with the old bomber, took off from Vunakanau at Rabaul. Soon after darkness had settled in, the torpedo-armed Nells caught the convoy off northeast San Cristobal and made their attack in the usual manner, with the contact plane dropping flares to illuminate the convoy. But the attack was badly coordinated, the American ship handling superb, and the antiaircraft fire thrown up by the escorts and transports devastating. Not a ship was hit, while the 701st lost four aircraft, including that of the group leader.[6]

CLEANSLATE began the night of 20–21 February, with the landings scheduled for dawn. As the scouts had reported, no Japanese were there to oppose the landing. The Marine Raiders who landed at Baisen found abandoned equipment, rotting fish and rice, and one Japanese – the skeleton of a pilot sitting in the cockpit of his downed Zero.[7] By D+2 Turner had put 7,000 men ashore, and 15,500 by 15 March. Beginning on the morning of the landing, Guadalcanal-based fighters maintained a dawn to dusk patrol over the Russells, but no Japanese aircraft showed up. For two weeks the Japanese were oblivious to the American construction of a new base.[8]

Airfields were given a high priority because they would cut 120 miles from the roundtrip of the fighters covering the New Georgia operation. Two naval construction battalions were quickly at work, and by 15 April, a fighter field was operational on the south side of Renard Sound, while a second field on the north side would be operational by June. The construction of shipping facilities, aviation fuel tank farms, roads, and housing went along apace.[9]

When Nimitz asked for an explanation of the large forces used, Halsey replied that the Russells were a "stepping stone" to New Georgia, his forces had been moved in the right direction, and valuable experience in using landing craft had been gained in the operation. (In his autobiography, he dated the beginning of the battle for the Central Solomons from the seizure of the Russells.)[10]

FLORIDA AND GUADALCANAL

The naval bases were in the Florida Islands, which lie 26 miles north of Lunga across Iron Bottom Sound, so named for all of the American and Japanese ships resting on the bottom. During the height of the battle for Guadalcanal, the 6th Seabees worked on the PT boat base at Calvertville and the seaplane base at Halavo Bay. With the arrival of additional battalions, the Seabees began to complete and expand Halavo, to build landing craft and large boat bases, and to repair facilities at Turner City and Carter City. The most pressing project was to convert Port Purvis into a forward base for light cruisers and destroyers, which would advance them 565 miles from the main forward base at Espíritu Santo in what was then the New Hebrides. Halsey had ordered the harbor surveyed in January, and work started soon thereafter. But progress was slow. Part of the problem was oil storage, for the tank farms had to be carved out of the hillside on the south shore. Hulks were towed in to serve as temporary storage, and a light cruiser task force returning from a bombardment mission in Kula Gulf refueled there in early March. The hundreds of thousands of gallons of fresh water needed were piped down from sources far up the hill on the north side. But not until 11 August did *Argonne*, a repair ship, arrive to take up station.[11]

Guadalcanal – the code name changed from CACTUS to MAINYARD – was the hub of the base complex, with the airfields, installations such as hospitals, and supply depots situated on the narrow Lunga plain that ran from the Nalimbu River in the east to Point Cruz in the west. Over 100

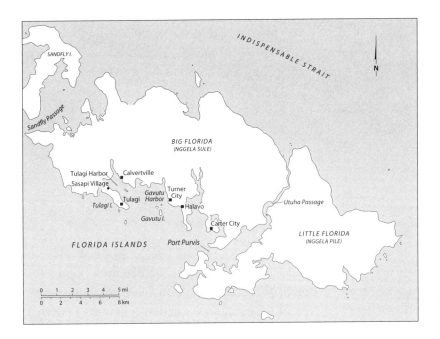

Map 2.2. Florida Islands.

miles of roads had to be built to tie it all together, and with four sizable rivers dividing the plain, numerous bridges strong enough to withstand the constant flooding had to be built and maintained.[12]

In January, Halsey's able air commander, Vice Admiral Aubrey W. Fitch, commander, Air, South Pacific Force (COMAIRSOPAC), introduced systematic planning for the construction and administration of all airfields under his command. Guadalcanal was first in priority. Of the three existing fields, Henderson Field, the strip taken from the Japanese, was the largest and was often called Bomber No. 1. The Dauntlesses, Avengers, and Black Cats based there, as did the B-17s and B-24s coming in from the main fields at Espíritu Santo. Fighter No. 1 field had been built just southeast of Henderson and Fighter No. 2 some distance west at Kukum. Major work in drainage, construction of taxiways, Marston matting, and housing for air crews had to be completed. In new construction, the most pressing concern was the completion of a heavy bomber

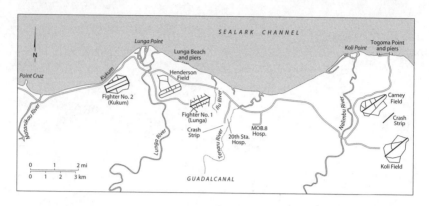

Map 2.3. Guadalcanal.

field at Koli Point. The 14th Naval Construction Battalion and the 2nd Marine Aviation Engineer Battalion were both on the job, but unstable soil and heavy rains made the going slow. On the night of 23–24 March, 705th G4Ms exacted a price for the delay when they hit the heavy bombers packed on one end of Henderson, destroying four and damaging sixteen more, some beyond repair. After that, even the air personnel pitched in to help with building quarters, and on 1 April the 307th Bomb Group (H) and the Navy's VB-101 and VB-102 Squadrons (flying B-24s, navy designation PB4Ys) moved to the new field, which was named Carney.[13] The 5th Bomb Group (H) remained at Henderson until Koli Field, adjacent to Carney, was completed in early October.[14]

The Japanese raid also highlighted another problem – careless airfield management. Little effort had been made at aircraft dispersal. On Fitch's recommendation, in April Halsey established an Air Center Command on each of the islands with an airfield or seaplane base. The command would be responsible for all of the details of operation, from housing and communications to procurement and emergency firefighting and rescue facilities. Each airfield or seaplane base was allocated to one of the services, with a commander subordinate to the Air Center commander. At the Solomons Air Center, for example, the center commander was navy; Henderson Field, Fighter No. 1, and the Russell Islands fields went to the marines; Carney and Fighter No. 2 to the Army

Air Forces; and Halavo to the navy. This was a step in the right direction, but as late as June, Fitch was still calling for better dispersal.[15]

OPERATION DRYGOODS

To ensure logistical support for the upcoming move up the Solomons, Turner recommended to Halsey on 14 January that 50,000 tons of supplies and 80,000 barrels of gasoline be stockpiled on Guadalcanal and the Russells. Halsey approved, and thus began operation DRYGOODS.[16]

Even though the Japanese were unable to interfere effectively, the operation was no small task. Transports and cargo ships had to anchor in the Lunga Roads, and troops and cargo moved ashore in landing craft and barges tied up at finger piers. From there trucks carried the supplies to their destination. "The small craft plying from ship to shore reminded one of streams of industrious ants," one observer noted.[17] Stevedore battalions (Seabee "special" battalions) were scarce, and any available man was pressed into service when the ships were in the Lunga Roads. But as primitive as port conditions were, unloading proceeded at a surprisingly fast rate in the heat and humidity. On 19 April, for example, the veteran navy APA, *President Hayes*, arrived off Kukum, bringing in the 1st Battalion, 1st Fiji Infantry Regiment (for the defense of Florida) and the 1st Commando Fiji Guerrillas (slated for the New Georgia operation). The Fijians broke the previous record for unloading a transport, 104 tons per hour, by unloading at the rate of 131.5 tons per hour. In just over five hours, the Fijians unloaded 657 tons. They received a message of congratulations from the captain, Commander F. W. Benson.[18]

At the beginning of the operation, two terminals were operating, one at Lunga and the other just west at Kukum (also the location of a huge aviation fuel tank farm). During the operation, a third was established at Koli Point, the site of more and more installations. Work was underway on a tank farm with a 36,000-barrel capacity and an underwater pipeline for unloading the tankers. A temporary branch of a naval hospital was there, and the army's 48th Station Hospital was slated to be located there. When Fitch visited Guadalcanal in March, he recommended to the Commander Service Squadron, Rear Admiral C. H.

Cobb, that Koli Point be designated a terminal and the necessary port battalion be brought in. (The battalion arrived in May.)[19]

By June, Turner had met his goal and then some, and in the meanwhile, at SOPAC Headquarters at Nouméa, Halsey worked to improve the logistical system. Nouméa was the principal port of entry for the theater, and while it possessed one of the finest harbors in the Pacific, port and shore facilities had to be built from scratch. Ships rode at anchor, sometimes for weeks, until they could unload. But by mid-May, Halsey could write Nimitz that he had the shipping problem "pretty well licked in Nouméa." A few days later, on 20 May, he created the Joint Logistic Board, composed of the supply chiefs of the various services under his command, to impose order on procurement and supply. One of the board's important duties was to provide interservice emergency logistical support in the theater.[20]

REORGANIZATION OF AIR COMMAND

During the battle for Guadalcanal, the aircraft based there – the CACTUS Air Force – had flown under 1st Marine Air Wing (MAW), Major General Roy S. Geiger, until November, then Brigadier General Louis Woods, both designated Senior Naval Aviator, Guadalcanal. At some point, Fighter Command under a squadron leader and Strike and Search Command under Marine Air Group MAG-14 came into use, but the chain of command with the squadrons was informal. When a new squadron arrived, the commander was advised to have a pilot at the air headquarters dugout at all times to serve as liaison. In late December 1942, Brigadier General Francis Mulcahy, 2nd MAW, arrived with his entire staff. According to Colonel W. O. Brice, MAG-14, "that was the first *real* staff set-up at the highest echelons."[21]

Shortly after the Japanese evacuation, Fitch began to organize Guadalcanal-based aircraft into an offensive air force for the drive up the Solomons. The first step was to send in Rear Admiral Charles P. Mason to activate Solomon Islands Air Command (COMAIRSOLS) on 15 February. Because he brought in only five staff members, these fused with Mulcahy's staff, with Mulcahy becoming Mason's chief of staff.

Colonel John. D. Munn, USMC, an air intelligence officer with months of experience on Guadalcanal, recalled this setup as being "the first real heterogeneous staff (insofar as it included Navy, Marine, and Army personnel)."[22] But the operational organization of both a Fighter Command and a Strike and Search Command remained the same. Fitch retained the Army Air Forces heavy bombers under his control.

Fitch's employment of the heavy bombers became a point of contention over the next few weeks. This had been brewing for some time, both in the theater and in Washington, between Admiral King and Lieutenant General H. H. Arnold, commander, Army Air Forces (both members of the Joint Chiefs). The AAF's major complaints were logistical failures, tardiness in providing suitable airfields, and above all, the navy's use of the heavy bombers for long-range reconnaissance, which reduced the number of aircraft necessary for an attack on moving ships. The last was a particularly touchy subject, since the navy loudly criticized the performance of the heavy bombers against shipping. The arrival of the Navy's PB4Y squadrons in the early months of 1943, however, went far in resolving the search issue, since they took on these missions.[23]

What officially brought the matter to a head, was COMAIRSOPAC bypassing the newly activated 13th Air Force under Major General Nathan F. Twining[24] and dealing with its units directly. But still the crux of the problem was the employment of the heavy bombers (the heavy losses incurred in February may have had something to do with it). Twining's superior, Lieutenant General Millard F. Harmon, who commanded all army forces in the South Pacific, went to Halsey to handle the matter in the theater. The two men had a good working relationship, and Halsey acknowledged on more than one occasion how fortunate he was to have Harmon. Halsey's solution was for Harmon and Fitch to work out the problems and reach an agreement that Halsey would accept. Accordingly, the veteran airmen, Harmon and Fitch, met for two days in the first week of March. At the conclusion, they reached agreement along the lines of the position paper Harmon had prepared, "Principles and Policies Governing Employment of Air Force Units," which can be summarized in three points. First, AAF officers would have the closest participation in planning the details of missions, especially in regard to "proper formations, bomb loadings, escort and combat techniques." Second, any disruption of normal command channels would be held to a minimum (in other words, 13th Air Force Headquarters would not be bypassed in dealing with the various units). And third, "Army bombardment aircraft should be used primarily on bombardment missions, and their employment for purposes of search and patrol be limited."[25]

For all intents and purposes, the Harmon-Fitch agreement integrated 13th Air Force into COMAIRSOPAC on an equal footing with the other services. Twining moved his headquarters near Fitch's at Espíritu Santo. In April, an advanced bomber headquarters detachment moved to Guadalcanal and set up at Carney Field, and a detachment from fighter command moved to Fighter No. 2. Most importantly, COMAIRSOLS created a bomber command under a 13th Air Force officer who would have operational control over all heavy bombers, AAF and navy, as well as the medium bombers.[26]

To further interservice harmony, command of COMAIRSOLS was rotated. Rear Admiral Marc A. Mitscher relieved Mason in early April after Mason was evacuated with cerebral malaria. Twining was to relieve Mitscher on 25 July and in turn was to be relieved by Major General Ralph L. Mitchell, USMC, on 20 November. Chiefs of staff were in each case drawn from another service from that of the commander: Mitscher had Brigadier General Field Harris, USMC; Twining would have Captain Charles Coe, USN; and Mitchell would have Captain L. A. Moebus, USN. In the subordinate commands throughout the period, Fighter Command was rotated between the marines and the army, but Strike Command was always under a marine commander, and Bomber Command was always under the commander of the 13th Air Force Bomber Command.

COMAIRSOLS was undoubtedly one of the more distinctive combat forces in World War II. Late in the New Georgia campaign, a formation bound for Kahili could be made up of army and navy B-24s, with marine F4US, navy F6FS, army P-38s, P40s, and P-39s, and New Zealand P-40s flying escort. As a long-serving staff officer put it in his history of COMAIRSOLS, "Our private war in the Solomons was a two-bit penny arcade compared to the big show going on in Europe. However, for sheer color, fighting spirit, and a unique little show, there was probably nothing like it on earth while it lasted."[27]

THE COASTWATCHER NETWORK

The coastwatcher organization was top secret during the war, but much has since been written about it, especially regarding the important role the network played in the struggle for Guadalcanal. The coast watchers played a no less significant but somewhat different role in the New Georgia campaign.

The headquarters for the coastwatching network in the Solomons, call sign KEN, was located in the shattered plantation near the northwest end of Henderson Field. A direct telephone line ran to COMAIRSOLS headquarters, located not far away on the ridges overlooking the Lunga River. Lieutenant Commander Hugh A. Mackenzie, RAN, was in charge until early spring 1943, when a series of misfortunes struck. First, his assistant, Lieutenant C. H. C. Train, was lost over Ballale on 5 March, when the B-24 in which he was flying as a spotter was shot down (Brigadier General Mulcahy also flew the mission in an aircraft that returned safely). Then in late March, Mackenzie's superior, Commander Eric A. Feldt, RAN, suffered a major heart attack while on an inspection trip to KEN, and he was out of the war for some time, recovering in the naval hospital at Tulagi. Australian Naval Intelligence ordered Mackenzie to leave for Brisbane and take over Feldt's job, and Lieutenant Commander I. Pryce-Jones, RANVR, replaced him at Guadalcanal. By the time Pryce-Jones took over, the coastwatcher stations for the New Georgia campaign were in place.[28]

One of the most significant changes in the organization as it had existed during the battle for Guadalcanal was the Japanese elimination of the Bougainville stations at Buin (11 November) and Teop (7 April). They were able to so because the Bougainville natives in the coastal villages, enough of them at least, were not loyal to the Australian administration and helped the Japanese. As Mackenzie put it, "the experienced coast watcher can continue operating just so long, and only so long, as the local natives do not cooperate with the enemy against him."[29] Both coast watchers escaped, but the radios on Bougainville went silent.[30]

The Choiseul and Vella Lavella coastwatcher teams, which had been landed by the submarine *Grampus* back in October, were now closest to the Japanese southern Bougainville bases. On Choiseul, Sub-lieutenant

A. N. C. Waddell, RANVR, and Lieutenant C. W. Seton, AIF, located two stations on the northwestern side of the island, which afforded them a good view of shipping entering or departing the Shortland-Bougainville Straits area. Waddell estimated that 99 percent of the Choiseul people were loyal Waddell, but the other 1 percent posed a danger, especially after the Japanese decision to hold Rekata Bay led to the establishment of a barge route with way stations along the western coast. Despite orders to the contrary, Waddell and Seton waged their own little war with the Japanese, killing ninety-seven, while losing one of their scouts.[31]

On Vella Lavella, Lieutenant R. E. Josselyn, RANVR, and Sub-lieutenant John R. Keenan, RANVR, operated their station between Mundi Mundi plantation and Iringila on the northwest coast. Unlike Waddell and Seton just across the Slot, they operated in relative security. The population was loyal, and the village headmen supplied the necessary scouts, while the Japanese paid little attention to the island other than to establish barge relay bases during the battle for New Georgia. The Reverend A. W. E. Silvester, who had rescued the American pilots shot down during the sinking of *No. 2 Tōa Maru*, kept his medical station running at Biloa for the duration.[32]

At the airfields at Munda and Vila, coast watchers also moved in with the Japanese. The problem at both places, given the terrain, was finding a site from which the airfields were visible. Sub-lieutenant D. C. Horton, RANVR, went in first, on 23 December 1942, by PBY to Kennedy's station at Segi to keep watch over Munda. With scouts provided by Kennedy and accompanied by Sergeant Harry Wickham, BSIPDF, who lived in Roviana Lagoon and knew the area well, Horton made his way to Munda overland and by canoe. After a week inspecting the Japanese perimeter, however, his scouts reported that no satisfactory site could be found. Horton then decided to locate across the lagoon on the steep slopes of Rendova Mountain, ultimately building several alternative camps, one as high as 3,000 feet up the mountain. Observation posts had to be built high in the trees in order to get a view of Munda Field some 6 miles distant. As usual, the headmen provided a number of scouts. Horton kept with him at least fourteen scouts, since it took that many men to carry the radio, while the others he placed under Wickham to operate farther west in Vonavona Lagoon.

For a time, Horton operated freely, since the Japanese had no posts on Rendova; later, mixed detachments of the 229th and the Kure 6th SNLF occupied Ugeli Village (now Egholo) on the northeast coast in January and Rendova Harbor in March. Wherever they located on Rendova, one of Horton's scouts kept watch on their camp, so at all times he knew what they were doing. The supply route from Segi would be rerouted accordingly.[33]

In March, KEN sent in Lieutenant A. R. Evans, RANVR, to keep watch on Vila. By this time, Japanese barges could be encountered anywhere in New Georgia waters, so Evans and his party went by canoe from Segi up the north coast of New Georgia, crossed the narrow neck of land on foot, and then went by canoe up Roviana Lagoon to Honiavasa Passage. The moon was full and the night bright, so they crossed to Vonavona Island by way of the weather side of the Munda Bar. By 21 March, he was at his camp, which Wickham's scouts had already built some 9 miles northwest from Vila and 3 miles from the coast. Observation posts were built nearer Vila, some in trees as Horton had done, and a village sentry system was established along the coast of Blackett Strait. But Evans was never able to get a clear view of Vila due to the terrain and instead had to depend on the information the scouts brought back.[34]

At Segi Point, Donald Kennedy had operated his station since early July 1942, and his reports on passing Japanese air formations had been invaluable to the Americans on Guadalcanal. He lived in considerable comfort with his Rennell Island mistress and their child at Harold Markham's plantation. Markham, who had intended to retire there before the Americans bulldozed his plantation for an airfield, had built a spacious European-style bungalow on a hill overlooking the narrow Njai Passage that separates New Georgia from Vangunu Island. As district officer for the Western Solomons, Kennedy requisitioned food from the villages on a rotational schedule, set the prices at their prewar level, and paid with a signed receipt for later payment. Americans passing through on various reconnaissance missions were surprised at the table his servants set for them.[35]

As district officer, Kennedy was the law in New Georgia, and to ensure that his instructions were carried out, he appointed as his administrative assistant Willy Paia, a Kokenggolo Mission School graduate. Paia worked with the headmen to ensure that the local populace at Munda, most of whom had fled to the eastern part of Roviana Lagoon, had no contact with the Japanese. He also saw to it that the levied food supply reached Segi in the long canoes that plied the routes in relays. Occasionally, a violator of Kennedy's regulations was in one of the canoes. The guilty party could expect a whipping while tied over a barrel. From the oral accounts of the New Georgia people recorded after the war, they apparently were more afraid of Kennedy than of the Japanese. Feldt described Kennedy as "a spider at the center of a huge web" that stretched southeast to Gatukai and northwest to Munda.[36]

As we have seen, during the final days at Guadalcanal, Kennedy played a major role in foiling the Japanese sea truck route operation, but after the evacuation, his position grew more exposed as the Japanese rearranged their defenses in southeast New Georgia. In late February, the 1st Battalion, less 4th Company, was withdrawn to the Munda area. One platoon of the 4th remained at Wickham Anchorage, joined by a rifle company of the Kure 6th. The rest of 1st Lieutenant Takagi Masao's 4th Company was transferred to Viru Harbor, where both the Yokosuka 7th and Kure 6th had antiaircraft units. A COMAIRSOLS strike on 4 March killed twelve men and badly wounded four but did not hit the guns.[37]

Kennedy was now in the middle of two substantial Japanese outposts, and what ensued was a small-scale guerilla war. As a major in the British Solomon Islands Protectorate Defence Force (BSIPDF), he had recruited about three dozen well-armed scouts and another three dozen armed with traditional weapons. In addition, he had appropriated a cutter that belonged to the deserted Seventh Day Adventist mission, and he had a captured Japanese barge, both well-armed. While his final report is brief and short on detail, there is no doubt that any Japanese who nosed too close to Segi never returned to tell about it. Kennedy justified the operations on the grounds that Segi's value as a coast-watching base and a safe point of entry for the PBYs outweighed other considerations, and by June he had killed fifty-four Japanese and captured two.[38] Years later, Kennedy's second-in-command, Billy Bennett, the son of a New Zealand man and a New Georgia woman, was even more explicit. After an encounter with a whale boat in which eight Japanese had been captured, Bennett told an interviewer, "We took everybody ashore, marched them into the bush and killed them secretly. And we burned and sank the ship."[39]

The impunity with which the New Georgia coast watchers operated was of course due to the loyalty of the New Georgia people. The population of just fewer than 8,000 lived entirely on the coasts, with almost half concentrated in Marovo and Roviana Lagoons. This was significant for three reasons. First, there was none of the usual class antagonism between "the people of the sea" and "the people of the bush," as those living in the interior of the larger islands were called, which the Japanese on Bougainville had turned to their advantage. Second, Kennedy's task of maintaining colonial government was made easier since the natives were readily accessible. Third, the cooperation of the natives made the work of the missionaries equally as easy, with the result that New Georgia was heavily Christianized. Almost the entire population, if the claims of the missions are to be believed, had some connection with either the Methodists or the Seventh Day Adventists. The Adventists had their headquarters at Batuna on northeast Vangunu, while the Methodists had their headquarters at Kokenggolo. Of the two, the Methodists had by far the most elaborate establishment and the most influence. At Kokenggolo, they had a number of schools, including what was regarded as the finest higher school in the Solomons, as well as hospitals staffed with a resident medical doctor and trained nurses, a medical station on Vella Lavella, and a school on Choiseul. The churches of both denominations dotted the islands, and many of the outstanding scouts for both the coast watchers and the Americans were mission educated.[40]

Given this situation, KEN was extremely sensitive to reports of COMAIRSOLS pilots mistakenly bombing villages or strafing canoes. Mackenzie reported that he had constantly to be in touch with the air intelligence officers on this matter, and COMAIRSOLS duly issued orders not to attack a village unless specifically ordered, and under no circumstances, even if Japanese were present, to strafe a canoe. A briefing paper for New Zealand Hudson pilots put it best: "Never use natives in their canoes for front gun practice" because they might help downed pilots. "There are lots of long range Zero tanks floating in the sea, or someday you may happen to see honorable Jap sitting in his rubber dinghy armed with a revolver praying to Tojo to help him. This is war. Try him."[41]

Historian John Prados has called the coast watchers one of the Pacific war's "three pillars of Intelligence," the other two being ULTRA (the interception of Japanese communications) and the air searches that fanned out each morning in all directions from Guadalcanal.[42] Of equal importance, the coast watchers served as the point of entry and provided the scouts for American reconnaissance teams surveying the terrain or looking for airfield sites, and they worked in tandem with COMAIRSOLS to destroy a large number of barges and fishing boats. Finally, the coast watchers rescued Allied airmen – one count for the Solomons campaign put it at 118 – while capturing and sometimes executing Japanese airmen. At this point in the Solomons war, therefore, the image of "Lonely Vigil" – the title of the most popular book on the subject – does not quite fit. The coast watchers moved freely and had their own well-armed forces and the support of the populace. Only once did the Japanese locate a station: fleeing from American troops on Rendova, the Japanese stumbled on Horton's camp. Horton's replacement managed to escape with the codebooks.[43]

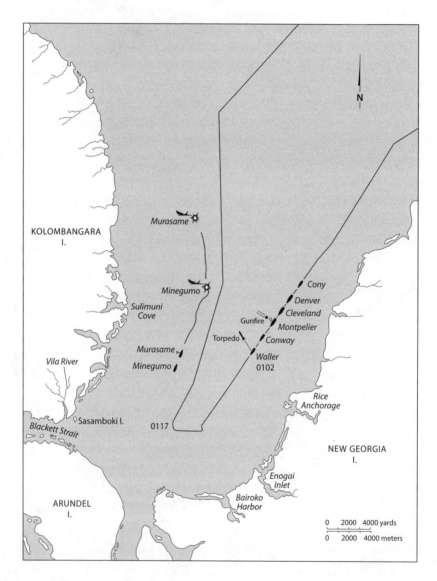

Map 3.1. Kula Gulf Naval Action, 5 March 1943.

THREE

SOPAC's Air and Naval Offensive

ON THE MAP BOARDS OF THE SOUTH PACIFIC IN WASHINGTON and Tokyo, no flag marked New Georgia as either a critical objective to be taken or an important position to defend. On the American side, the Joint Staffs' March 1943 directive for an advance on Rabaul does not even mention New Georgia (although it was assumed that Halsey would take it for the airfields needed to provide air cover for the Bougainville operation).[1] On the Japanese side, the IGHQ directives, also issued in March 1943, put the emphasis on the army's need to hold eastern New Guinea while relegating the Solomons to a secondary area and New Georgia to a navy outpost.[2] As it turned out, however, the battle for possession of New Georgia took all summer, and not long into the fighting, comparisons were being made to Guadalcanal and Buna.

"It does not seem possible, in view of the daily increasing power of our forces, that the enemy will be able now to hold this primary defensive line [New Georgia] for very long," Major Frank S. Owen, intelligence officer of the 5th Bomb Group (H), had written in his February 1943 report. "But in the Buin area the Japanese have a 'Gibraltar' capable of defending itself for an indefinite time against tremendous odds."[3]

In the months leading up to the invasion of New Georgia, SOPAC's air and naval forces took the offensive, with the aim of isolating the battlefield. COMAIRSOLS, under the command of Vice Admiral Aubrey Fitch, had three tasks as stipulated by Fitch's 11 March Air Operation Plan: (1) the destruction of enemy shipping; (2) the destruction of shore installations; and (3) the protection of friendly surface forces operating up the Slot. Weather permitting, therefore, the air war went on around the clock, day in and day out. SOPAC's naval forces (3rd Fleet from 15 March) joined in the effort by conducting bombardments of Munda and Vila, making runs up the Slot to intercept Japanese shipping, and mining Blackett Strait and Kula Gulf.

SOPAC, as we shall see, enjoyed some spectacular successes, but overall failed to stop the Japanese buildup in New Georgia and Rekata Bay. The close proximity of the Buin base complex, which COMAIRSOLS judged to be beyond its means to hit with heavy daylight formations, was a major problem.

MUNDA, VILA, REKATA BAY – THE BASES

COMAIRSOLS kept up the relentless bombing of the Japanese bases in the Central Solomons. Vila and Rekata Bay both got attention, but the primary target was Munda. From 8 February to the end of the month, for example, the Japanese recorded sixteen attacks. With each passing month, the number of aircraft increased, as did the weight of the ordnance. When half-ton and one-ton "daisy cutters" became readily available, the SBD Dauntlesses carried the 1,000-pounders and the TBF Avengers, the 2,000-pounders. On 20 June, on a typical mission, eighteen SBDs and twelve TBFs put nearly 21 tons of bombs on Munda. Two 1,000-pounders and one 2,000-pounder fell in the sea due to release hang-ups, and two SBDs and one TBF were hit by 25mm fire but suffered no casualties. As was the usual case, damage was hard to assess. The VT-11 TBF pilots who went in at 3,000 feet, as the SBDs pulled out of their dives, reported a large explosion in Lambete Plantation, while a hit in the south loop area "was seen to throw into the air an object which could have been either a gun barrel or a log." Overhead, the thirty-two F4Fs covering the bombers encountered no opposition.[4]

Kusaka, in command of the Japanese Southeast Area Fleet (11th Air Fleet and 8th Naval Fleet), did not have the capability to defend Munda. With the departure of the units brought in for Ke-gō, Base Air Force was left with two understrength flotillas. Rear Admiral Ichimaru Toshinosuke's 21st Air Flotilla (1st Air Attack Force), based at Kavieng had responsibility for New Guinea, and Rear Admiral Kosaka Kanae's 26th Air Flotilla (6th Air Attack Force), based at Lakunai in east Rabaul, with units at Kahili and Ballale, had responsibility for the Solomons. From February until the invasion of New Georgia, Kosaka tried to keep around thirty Zeros at Kahili, drawn either from the 204th Kōkūtai (Zeros) or from the composite 582nd Kōkūtai (Zeros and D3A "Val" dive bombers). But there was much shifting of air units back and forth to Rabaul, especially for big operations such as cover for a convoy to New Guinea or an attack on Guadalcanal, and the number of fighters at Buin fluctuated. All the Japanese could do was to send out Zeros once or twice a month to patrol over New Georgia for a few hours. This was a hit-or-miss affair in terms of making an interception, and to the good fortune of COMAIRSOLS, these were almost always a miss. For the American airmen, the Munda missions were routine enough to take along a *Life* photographer in a Navy SBD for a mission in March. Early the next month, Americans at home were treated to a three-page spread of the place called Munda that had been cropping up in the news.[5]

Without air support, the Japanese relied on pick and shovel. Massive tunnels for men, munitions, and supplies honeycombed Kokenggolo and Bibilo Hills, and the heavy antiaircraft guns defending the airfield and 8cm coastal guns covering the Munda Bar were well dug in northwest of the airfield. Fortifications were constructed from coral and logs and covered with vines and other foliage. Combined with the heavy forest and plantation palms, this camouflage largely defeated photographic intelligence's efforts to identify targets. The antiaircraft guns were so well hidden that often the SBD leader would make a feint dive to draw fire, and when the Japanese responded, the rest of the squadron would attack. The airfields, of course, could not be camouflaged, so they were almost always on the target list. Vila, which had a drainage problem, was largely a wasted effort, first for the Japanese who built it, then for the Americans who bombed it. Munda, on the other hand, rested on solid coral and was quickly repairable; as we have noted, the Japanese kept it operational as an emergency strip for shot-up aircraft right up through the first days of the invasion.[6]

VILA, REKATA BAY – SHIPPING

In mid-February, the Japanese resumed the transports to Vila. Priorities were defense units, beginning with the rest of the 8th Combined, and sufficient supplies of food, ammunition, and fuel to last several months. Kusaka thought the situation urgent enough to ignore Combined Fleet's directive to use sea trucks and instead opted for his large transports. But with the loss of *No. 2 Tōa Maru* still fresh on their minds, the Japanese were careful now to schedule departures from Shortland in the morning, so transports would arrive at Vila at night, unload, and depart before sunup. In addition, each transport had an escort of destroyers or auxiliary ships, and during daylight hours Zeros and seaplanes provided cover. This worked well at first, and three separate transports made the trip safely. Then, on 27 February, the Choiseul coast watchers spotted *Kirikawa Maru* (4,000 tons) carrying two 14cm guns, four 8cm dual-purpose guns, 600 tons of ammunition and supplies, and SNLF personnel as the ship and its two escorts cleared the Shortlands. A search plane and the coast watchers reported their course, and the COMAIRSOLS strike force of fourteen SBDs, with an escort of twenty-four fighters, caught them three miles off the northeast tip of Vella Lavella. The escort took on the thirteen Zeros and two F1Ms flying cover, and in the fight that followed each side lost two aircraft. But Marine Scout Bombing Squadron VMSB-144 SBDs went about their business with deadly effect; a surviving Japanese medical officer later wrote that the bombs were exploding in the ship like a fireworks exhibition at Ryōgoku Bridge in Tokyo. Watching from across the New Georgia Sound, Waddell radioed KEN that "we had the satisfaction of seeing the cargo vessel burning from stem to stern – this was the first occasion we had seen the results of our reporting."[7]

For the Japanese at Rabaul, the loss of *Kirikawa Maru* was a shock. As a result, they decided that the use of cargo ships was unfeasible and fell back on the destroyers of the Reinforcement Force to carry out the transports. Captain Tachibana Masao, with *Murasame* (Lieutenant Commander Tanegashima Youji) and *Minegumo* (Lieutenant Commander Uesugi Yoshitake), would make the first run. Accordingly, Tachibana sailed from Rabaul on 4 March with the intention of laying over at Buin and making the run into Vila the next night. On the way out of the harbor, his two destroyers passed *Uranami* and *Hatsuyuki* coming in with survivors of the worst naval disaster the Japanese had suffered since Guadalcanal. MacArthur's air forces had sent all eight transports, which carried the Eighteenth Army, to the bottom, along with four of the eight destroyers in what was named the Battle of the Bismarck Sea.[8]

For Tachibana, the crowded decks of the *Uranami* and *Hatsuyuki* were to prove an ill omen. At noon on 4 March, Rear Admiral Aaron S. Merrill with TF 68 – Cruiser Division 12, *Montpelier* (F), *Cleveland,* and *Denver,* and seven destroyers – left Espíritu Santo, also bound for Kula Gulf. At Nouméa, SOPAC had been viewing the Japanese activities with some alarm, and intelligence had concluded, erroneously, that they were preparing to base aircraft at both airfields and had established a torpedo boat base. On 27 February, therefore, Halsey had ordered the bombardment of both Munda and Vila on the night of 5 March.[9]

With the exception of the submarines *Grampus*[10] and *Grayback,* which were being directed to Vella Gulf to block any shipping trying to escape Vila, Merrill's plan differed little from Ainsworth's back in January. Four destroyers would break off just past the Russells and conduct the Munda bombardment from west of Rendova; Merrill with the main force would go up the Slot and into Kula Gulf; and both groups would open fire simultaneously at 0017. Three Black Cats would search ahead, with Merrill's own officers aboard to spot for the bombardment, while COMAIRSOLS would provide air cover at dawn for the retiring ships. The destroyers would refuel at Port Purvis.

Night fell, clear and moonless over New Georgia. A mild sea was running. Relying on his SG radar for navigation, Merrill hugged the coast of New Georgia in the hope that the breakers might obscure the wakes of his ships. At 2115, TF 68 intercepted the COMAIRSOLS relay of the Choiseul coast watchers' report of two ships, either destroyers or cruisers, leaving the Shortlands at high speed two hours earlier. Shortly afterward, a Black Cat reported two cruisers on a course for Blackett Strait. Thinking he had been spotted, Merrill had to consider the possibility that he might soon be facing two heavy cruisers lurking in Blackett Strait to intercept him. At the least, he knew that Japanese warships were present. Accordingly, he increased speed slightly in order to round Visuvisu

Point at 0010 instead of 0017, to ensure that the Munda group did not open fire first and so give the enemy warning. Gunnery officers got the armor-piercing (A P) shells ready.

Off Visuvisu Point, Merrill slowed speed slightly and entered the gulf, with the destroyer *Waller* 6,000 yards ahead. At the same time, the two Japanese destroyers had unloaded and were underway through Blackett Strait to Kula Gulf, with *Murasame* leading. Passing to the east of Sasamboki Island, even as American radars were searching for Sasamboki as a navigational marker, the destroyers were picked up. Aiming by radar, *Waller* launched a spread of five torpedoes at 0102, and a minute later *Montpelier* opened fire, followed immediately by the other cruisers – all of them concentrating on the largest of the two destroyers, *Minegumo*. As Merrill reported, "Perhaps because it developed a better pip on the radar screen, early concentration was on the second ship in the column." Two minutes later the *Minegumo* was on fire, and an explosion sent flames shooting several hundred feet into the air. Possibly one of *Waller's* torpedoes had hit home; certainly Commander Arleigh Burke, who had ordered them fired, thought so.[11] At 0108, all guns shifted to the trapped *Murasame*, still making its way up the gulf. The *Montpelier's* sixth salvo hit home, and within minutes *Murasame* was a blazing wreck. At 0114, the cruisers ceased fire; Merrill turned onto the firing course, star shells lit up the sky over Vila, and at 0125, the guns opened up. Spotting was excellent; a Yokosuka 7th 12cm gun attempting to return fire was knocked out, and the Japanese reported much damage to aviation equipment on the shore. At the same time, the Munda bombardment group was putting 1,585 5-inch shells on the airfield area; the major damage was a hit on an ammunition dump that destroyed 1,000 8cm shells.[12]

Bombardment ceased at around 0134, and Merrill wasted no time in clearing Kula Gulf and heading back down the Slot at thirty knots. But when the expected Japanese air strike finally materialized, it missed T F 68 completely. With his destroyers refueled at Purvis, Merrill was headed east in Sealark Channel when Guadalcanal went to Condition Red around 1330. T F 68 went to battle stations. But as the puzzled air controllers watched, the Japanese strike force of eight D3As and thirty-five Zeros came in from southeast of Guadalcanal and headed straight for the Russells. (Rabaul had just learned of American activity there the day before.) But Kosaka's strike force was in no semblance of a formation, and the bombers, separated from the Zeros, came in low, skimming the water to attack Pavuvu. For the P-39 pilots on patrol at 9,000 feet, this was a dream come true, and they promptly shot down three of the bombers before finally being chased off by Zeros. The Japanese pilots reported the airfield under construction – confirmed the next day by a Ki-46 photographic reconnaissance plane – but were oblivious to the presence of TF 68. Merrill steamed on east, confident that he had sunk two cruisers. When this proved not to be the case, he was still satisfied that the fight at Kula Gulf had been the first night torpedo/gun action fought entirely by radar.[13]

Back in the gulf, the survivors struggled ashore. For once, the Japanese had been caught completely by surprise. In *Murasame*, the gunnery officer, Lieutenant Kayama Homare, had just discovered to his disgust that mice had beaten him to the rice ball he was about to eat, when he saw flashes like lightning. The picture he paints is one of complete confusion. Astern, *Minegumo* was on fire almost immediately. Tachibana thought they were under air attack – a notion he still clung to after the battle – and ordered antiaircraft action. Then the hail of shells hit *Murasame* and electrical power was lost. Water quickly flooded the destroyer.

With orders to abandon ship, Kayama made his way to his dark cabin, retrieved his sword and a book, and came back on deck, which was littered with dead and badly wounded men. He stopped to try to help them get off the ship, but they said that they would die with the ship, so Kayama stepped off into the oil-covered sea. He swam toward Kolombangara and made shore after sunrise, where he ran into some seamen making their way south. Some were not so fortunate. At an isolated patch of beach, scouts working for Wickham watched three Japanese seamen stagger ashore and promptly shot them out of hand. A total of 174 men survived, among them Tachibana and Tanegashima.[14] We will hear more of Tanegashima later.

The loss of *Murasame* and *Minegumo*, hard on the heels of the four destroyers that went down in Bismarck Sea, was a severe one for the Imperial Navy. Once again, Kusaka and Mikawa reshuffled the deck. To avoid Kula Gulf, they began using a new route that skirted Vella Lavella to the south and entered Blackett Strait by Ferguson Passage. To guard against surprise, they put E13As over Kula Gulf, to the west of Rendova, and near Guadalcanal.

After two successful runs to Rekata Bay, the Reinforcement Force resumed the transport to Vila on 13 March. Using the new route, three destroyers took in the Yokosuka 7th Headquarters and as much supplies as they could carry. All went well. When an American task group of four destroyers bombarded Vila again on the night of 15–16 March, it found the gulf empty, with no blips of enemy aircraft on the radar screen, and the shore batteries remained silent. For 1,799 rounds fired, the Japanese called the damage minimal, with one man killed.[15] The Japanese now pressed sea trucks and large barges into the Vila run. The route was in two stages, using Horaniu on the northeast coast of Vella Lavella as the intermediate layover base. *Kyosei Maru* made the first run, on 16–18 March, directly to the Kure 6th at Bairoko Harbor, thereby saving a lot of labor in transshipment by barge from Vila. Thereafter, throughout the rest of March, April, and early May, the Japanese suffered only one loss, the 543-ton sea truck *Gishō Maru* on 2–3 April. Josselyn's scouts spotted the ship hidden at Horaniu, Vella Lavella, on its way back to Buin, and the fighters sent out by COMAIRSOLS improvised their attack. The P-38s of 339th Fighter Squadron went in first at masthead height and "bombed" with their belly tanks, and the F4Us followed strafing. *Gishō Maru* burned all night and sank next day.[16]

From Evans on Kolombangara, COMSOPAC was well aware of the Japanese traffic in Blackett Strait. Halsey had intended to mine the strait in early April, but Yamamoto's air offensive (see chapter 4) caused a delay. But on the night of 6–7 May, with Ainsworth's cruisers blocking Vella Gulf, the destroyer *Radford* led the minelayers *Preble*, *Gamble*, and *Breeze* through the poorly charted Ferguson Passage. The weather was squally and visibility low, and *Radford* relied entirely on the SG radar and sound plots. In seventeen minutes, the minelayers laid three rows of mines across Blackett Strait to within 1,000 yards of the Kolombangara shore. The minelaying group exited through Vella Gulf, linked up with Ainsworth, and retired down the Slot without incident. Neither Evans's scouts nor the Japanese spotted the minelayers.[17]

The next night, 7–8 May, Captain Mutaguchi Kakuro's Destroyer Division 15, *Oyashio, Kuroshio,* and *Kagerō,* left Buin for the fifth consecu-

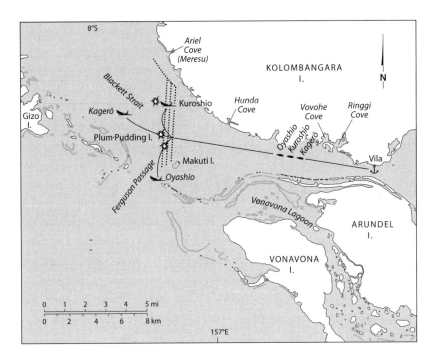

Map 3.2. Blackett Strait.

tive run of the early May transport. Mutaguchi was bringing in 3rd Battalion, 13th Infantry, and he was to take back 3rd Battalion, 66th Infantry. The weather was worse than the night before, when the minelayers were doing their work, with a strong southwest wind and heavy rain squalls. The Japanese lookouts could not pick out the islands on either side that marked the entrance to Ferguson Passage; *Oyashio* turned on its searchlight, and the destroyers slowed to a crawl to navigate the passage. Evans's scouts saw the light and awakened him to have a look. He recognized the light for what it was, radioed KEN, and went back to sleep. Meanwhile, the Japanese destroyers made it to Vila, but so much time had been lost that the barges waiting to unload them had gone back to base and had to be called out again. The destroyers were unloaded, the last troops of the 66th taken on, and they were heading home through Blackett Strait when *Oyashio,* in the lead, hit the first mine. The other two destroyers immediately began searching for the submarine they believed responsible; both hit mines. At first light, Evans could make out the three destroyers, one of which was burning, and radioed KEN.[18]

The weather over Blackett Strait had again closed in, with rain squalls and the ceiling low at around 900 feet, when the COMAIRSOLS strike force of three TBFs, nineteen SBDs, eight P-40s and thirty-two F4Us arrived. The F4Us and the TBFs turned in to attack Munda instead, but the VB-11 SBDs and the New Zealand No. 15 Squadron P-40s (the two had trained together in Fiji) went in, the SBDs pushing over at 4,500 feet into a glide bombing attack and the P-40s going in with them to strafe. The *Kuroshio*, the hardest hit, had already sunk, and the dive bombers concentrated on the remaining two, breaking through the overcast to be met by intense antiaircraft fire. Nonetheless, the SBDs scored a number of near misses and one direct hit around No. 3 gun mount on the *Oyashio*. Both the *Oyashio* and *Kagerō* eventually sank. The Japanese barge crews braved the attacks of the New Zealanders to rescue 770 men, but 192 Navy and approximately 140 Army personnel were killed. One VB-11 SBD was lost to navigational error, but the San Cristobal coast watcher rescued the crew.[19]

As a result of the loss of Destroyer Division 15, the Japanese cancelled the final scheduled destroyer run, with the intention of resuming regular runs during the next "dark of the moon" period, the nights of late May and early June.[20] These would have to use Kula Gulf until minesweepers from Buin could clear Blackett Strait; in anticipation Halsey ordered a minefield laid off eastern Kolombangara's coast. This was done on the night of 12–13 May under cover of a bombardment of Vila and Munda, the heaviest yet in volume of fire, with Ainsworth using four light cruisers and seven destroyers. The three rows of mines began 1,000 yards off the shore and extended nearly 8,500 yards east, but there is no record of a Japanese ship hitting one. On the other hand, an explosion in the *Nashville*'s No. 3 turret killed eighteen men, injured seventeen more, and sent the ship home to the States for repair.[21]

The late May-early June transports used Kula Gulf and suffered no losses. But the American invasion 30 June interrupted the late June-early July schedule, and the reinforcement runs then touched off the July naval battles off Kula Gulf. But by the day of the invasion, the Japanese had brought in the bulk of the navy and army troops assigned to defend New

Georgia, along with approximately three months' supply of ammunition and food. In addition, the Kure 6th had a large farm, described by one veteran as the size of the Tokyo baseball stadium, under cultivation at Zieta on the site of an abandoned banana plantation. The Japanese had learned a lesson from their experience at Guadalcanal, where their troops had been reduced to starvation. But given the growing scarcity of shipping, the cost had been high – one cargo ship, one sea truck, and five destroyers.[22]

THE BUIN COMPLEX

Buin was the key to the Japanese defense of the Central and Northern Solomons. As we have seen, the 26th Air Flotilla based units there. The fighters used Kahili while land-based bombers used Ballale, when they shifted from Rabaul to the Solomons for an operation. The anchorages were the principal relay points for the reinforcement of New Georgia and Rekata Bay. Rear Admiral Itagaki Akira's 1st Special Base Force controlled the subchasers, minesweepers, and patrol craft, the 1st Transport Group (barges and fishing boats), and as many as 6,000 naval base personnel. After 15 April, when the 11th Seaplane Tender Division was dissolved,[23] the 938th Kōkūtai, equipped with F1M "Pete" and E13A "Jake" reconnaissance planes under Commander Terai Kunizou, was regimented into 1st Special Base Force.[24] For its part, the Imperial Army kept Hyakutake's 17th Army Headquarters at Erventa Island. Of the divisions that had fought on Guadalcanal, Eighth Area Army retained 38th Division at Rabaul, and 2nd Division was sent out of the Southeast Area for rehabilitation. Hyakutake's command thus consisted of Lieutenant General Kanda Masatane's newly arrived 6th Division (Kumamoto), minus its 13th Infantry, which was retained at Rabaul until moved to New Georgia, as well as support, antiaircraft, and shipping units.[25]

In the first months of 1943, SOPAC did not have the strength in heavy bombers and long-range fighters to mount a sustained, large-formation, daylight bombing campaign against Buin. Anything less invited unacceptable losses, as Fitch learned in February. On the first day of the month, in the midst of the air battles attending Ke-gō, nine B-17s of the 72nd Squadron, 5th Bomb Group (H), with eight P-40s and P-38s,

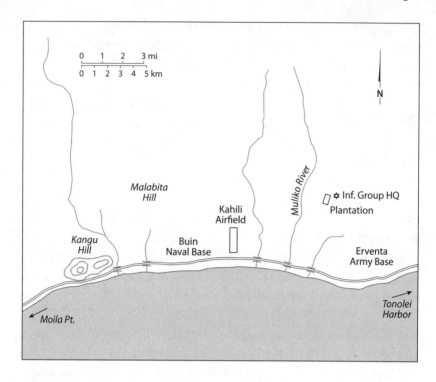

Map 3.3. Buin.

hit shipping at Buin, damaged the seaplane tender *Kamikawa Maru* off Shortland Island, but lost three B-17s to Zeros, while a fourth was badly damaged. Shortly thereafter, the 72nd Squadron, which flew at Guadalcanal and since September had been attached to 11th Bomb Group (H), was withdrawn. Its remaining aircraft were turned over to the 23rd and 31st Squadrons of the 5th Bomb Group (H), which had no planes, and its personnel rested while they awaited reequipping with B-24Ds. The 11th Bomb Group (H), which had been in combat for the duration of the Guadalcanal campaign, was also being withdrawn before being sent out of the theater for reorganization.[26]

In mid-February, with the arrival of new squadrons, Fitch again attacked Buin. On 11 and 12 February, VMF-124, equipped with the new F4U-1 Corsairs, arrived at Guadalcanal along with about twenty B-24Ds, half belonging to the Navy's VP-51 (shortly designated VB-101) and half belonging to the 370th and 424th Squadrons, 307th Bomb Group (H).

The debut of the F4Us and B-24s in the Solomons was scheduled for the next day, 13 February. This was unfortunate timing, especially given the inexperience of the pilots and crews. While the Zeros from *Zuikaku* and *Junyō* had just returned to Truk following Ke-gō, Kusaka had retained part of the reequipped 252nd, apparently to provide cover for the March convoy that met its demise in the Bismarck Sea, and a chūtai was based at Ballale. In mid-February, 6th Air Attack Force at Buin could put more than thirty fighters in the air.[27]

Air Command at Guadalcanal planned two missions for 13 February. At 0930, nine VB-101 PB4Y bombers with eleven F4Us and four P-38s took off for Buin; they met no opposition, and all aircraft returned. An hour later, six B-24s of the 424th Squadron followed, with twelve P-40s and P-38s. By the time the six bombers reached the target, a large cargo ship, the escort was down to six fighters after some planes had been forced to turn back. Thirty-three Zeros and eighteen seaplanes intercepted. Two B-24s fell victim to the intense antiaircraft fire over the target, and Zeros shot down a third, which had lost an engine (part of this crew was rescued). Three of the American fighters were shot down and their pilots lost, while the Japanese lost two Zeros, with their pilots killed, and three Zeros badly damaged.[28] Despite the heavy losses, Guadalcanal air command tried again the following day, Sunday, 14 February, St. Valentine's Day. Nine VB-101 PB4Ys, twelve F4Us, and ten P-38s took off for Buin. The target was the 6,500-ton cargo ship *Hitachi Maru*. The PB4Ys sank it with four high altitude hits, but as they turned away, thirty-one Zeros and eleven seaplanes attacked. For the cost of one Zero, the Japanese shot down two PB4Ys, four P-38s, and two F4Us. This was enough for Fitch, who suspended daylight missions against Buin and switched to night harassment missions. But the first mission flown on the night of 15 February cost the 307th two more B-24s due to bad weather (survivors from both crews were rescued). The mid-February missions cost a third of the Guadalcanal B-24s, and on the night of 6 March, VB 101 lost two more over Buin to antiaircraft fire.[29]

In late February, Halsey decided to mine the Buin anchorages using TBF Avengers that SOPAC air commanders believed had the range. Twelve Avengers of VMSB-143, carrying full bomb loads (4 × 500 lbs.), with nine VB-101 PB4Y bombers to drop flares and bomb the shore, flew what was probably a test mission on the night of 28 February. One TBF was lost to the concussion from its own bombs,[30] but the rest returned, most with a safe margin in gasoline reserves. Halsey, therefore, sent in the squadrons of Carrier Division 22 – *Sangamon* (CVE 26), *Suwanee* (CVE 27), and *Chenango* (CVE 28)[31] – to base at Guadalcanal, adding to the number of available TBFs. The Mark XII magnetic mine had to be laid in water of 20 fathoms or less, so two lines were planned parallel to the coast and both well within the 20-fathom line. The forty-two TBFs assigned to the mission would sow the line closest to shore on the first night, returning the second night to sow the outer line. To keep the Japanese antiaircraft crews occupied, eighteen heavy bombers loaded with fragmentation clusters would hit the gun positions as the TBFs went in at 1,500 feet to drop the 1,500-pound mines that were attached to parachutes. A Black Cat on one night and a Hudson on the other would be on station just north of Vella Lavella to drop flares as a navigational aid for the returning TBFs. The missions went off as planned on the nights of 20 and 21 March with the loss off the Russells of one B-17 to engine failure (the crew was rescued) and one TBF shot down by antiaircraft fire on the second night.[32]

The minelaying operation – the first of its kind in the Solomons war – resulted in only one ship being damaged, *Kazagumo*, which hit a mine off Kahili on 3 April during the reinforcement runs to Vila. Nonetheless, the ship was able to return to home waters under its own power. But avoiding the minefield hampered ship movements and the reinforcement runs to New Georgia. All the Japanese could do defensively was to put up two or three seaplanes each night to provide warning. (Coincidently, this policy was implemented just days before a F5A pinpointed the seaplane anchorage at Poporang; at dawn on 29 March, moments after the watch planes landed, six COMAIRSOLS fighters came skimming in just over the trees, destroyed six seaplanes and damaged five more in a single pass, and on the way out shot up a subchaser, killing a number of the crew.) Ironically, the Japanese were installing the first radar set on Poporang, which was in operation around 30 March.[33]

In May, Halsey ordered a second minelaying operation. With the heavy bombers flying diversion, the TBFs went to work again. On the nights of 19, 20, and 23 May, VMSB-143 and VT-11 sowed fields off both

Buin and Shortland Island. Losses were heavier than in March, with four TBFS going down, all on the first mission. For all the effort, there seems to have been no immediate damage to Japanese shipping, even though by July the minesweepers had cleared only thirty mines. Later, the light cruiser *Yūbari* was damaged by a mine 5 July 1943, and the submarine RO-100 was sunk the following November by another.[34]

From February onward, TBFS flew regular night missions to Buin. On 5 June, VT-11 flew a daylight strike against shipping as part of a formation that for the first time included SBDS. To give the VB-21 SBDS the required flying time, mechanics installed a F4F-4 wing tank on each plane and loading was limited to one 500-pound bomb.[35] Around thirty AAF and RNZAF fighters led the way to make a sweep of Kahili; the bombers with an escort of F4US followed. The attack went in at noon and did not go smoothly. Eleven of the thirty-two F4US turned back, causing spotty coverage for the bombers, and the fighter sweep was sent in high, which prevented these fighters from filling in the gaps. Two SBDS and one TBF went down and another TBF crash-landed in the Russells with a crew member dead. Among the fighters, one American P-40 pilot and two Japanese pilots were killed. With the early June transports to Vila in progress, there was considerable shipping in the area, including four destroyers, but the only loss the Japanese suffered was the 780-ton *Shintoku Maru* and the large barge it was towing. On the positive side, the improvised drop tanks worked, bringing Kahili within range of the SBDS.[36]

There were no further daylight missions to Buin in June. With the New Georgia invasion date looming, Strike Command intensified the effort against Munda-Vila. With its strength steadily growing, Bomber Command increased the night attacks on Buin, on the night of 26 June, for example, sending over three squadrons of B-24s and one of B-25s from the 42nd Group (M), which was now operating from Guadalcanal.[37] One can only speculate as to what the effect would have been if only a significant fraction of the ordnance put on Munda had instead been placed on Buin in a few heavy daylight raids.

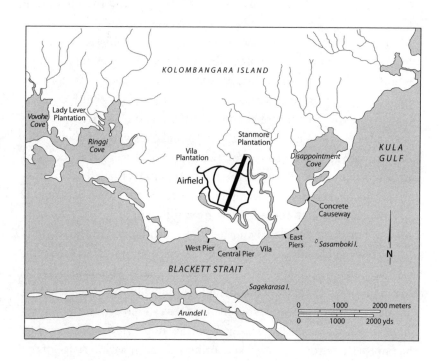

Map 4.1. Vila.

The Japanese Air Counteroffensives

ON 3 APRIL, YAMAMOTO AND UGAKI FLEW TO RABAUL TO command the air offensive against Guadalcanal and Papua. That afternoon, Ugaki met with Kusaka, Mikawa, and Vice Admiral Ozawa Jisaburō, commander, Third Fleet, who had flown in the day before with Vice-Admiral Kakuta Kakuji, commander, Carrier Division 2. That evening, Imamura joined the admirals for dinner at Kusaka's headquarters at the New Guinea Club. Yamamoto and Ugaki were billeted in Mikawa's quarters on a hill in east Rabaul, and there, with thunder rumbling over the hill and the area engulfed in a rain squall, Ugaki entered a passage in his diary that was very revealing of the mood in Combined Fleet. "When we decided to come down south to take command of operations, we of Combined Fleet made an important resolution," he wrote. "If and when this attempt fails to achieve satisfactory results, there will be no hope of future success in this area." But after what he had seen and heard in Rabaul, he "wondered if this has been fully brought home to those concerned with operations."[1]

THE APRIL AIR OFFENSIVE

According to Commander Wanatabe Yasuji, Yamamoto's plans officer, discussions on how to thwart the Allied buildup at Guadalcanal and Papua began in late February. Pressure from the emperor may have played a part. Commander Sanagi, who was in a position to know, said that, after the Guadalcanal evacuation, the emperor had sharply questioned the Navy General Staff as to why, since the bases at Munda and

Kolombangara had been completed, nothing had been accomplished as had been promised at the Imperial Conference. While Sanagi did not think the emperor's displeasure was officially communicated to Yamamoto, the staff officers at Tokyo and Truk were gossiping about it, and Sanagi suggested that this may have served as a psychological trigger for I-gō. If the emperor's rebuke to the Navy General Staff was the origin, then the events of early March served as the catalyst. Wanatabe was definite that the crushing defeat in the Battle of the Bismarck Sea caused the date for the operations to be moved up and serious planning to begin. The army, as could be expected, was furious with the navy for yet another failure to get one of its major convoys through, and at IGHQ the army was pushing for a new agreement on Southeast Area operations that would commit the navy to making eastern New Guinea its first priority (see chapter 5).

On 13 March, Wanatabe notified Eighth Area Army of Yamamoto's intentions to carry out major air operations, and five days later officers of Combined Fleet, 3rd Fleet, and 11th Air Fleet held a strategy meeting. What resulted from this meeting is not known. But there were major differences within Combined Fleet that had to be resolved. The first was Ozawa's reluctance to use his 3rd Fleet carrier groups in a land-based operation, since it was thought that at least three months would be required to replace the anticipated losses. These objections were overruled on the grounds that American carrier strength had been depleted as a result of the Battle of the Santa Cruz Islands back in October (as had the Japanese), and no carrier operations were expected in the near future. In Combined Fleet's assessment, the greatest threat came from Allied land-based airpower. The second issue was one of command. Kusaka was senior to Ozawa, who objected to entrusting his carrier groups to a land-based air commander. On this point, Yamamoto agreed, and settled the issue by assuming command.[2]

The original Combined Fleet order for I-gō, which was issued on 26 March, has been lost. But the official Japanese navy historians, using other sources, especially Ugaki's report requested by the Navy Ministry and dictated from his bed in *Musashi*'s sickbay, have reconstructed what they consider to be a reasonable outline. The objective of I-gō was nothing less than the smashing of the Allied bases and airfields in Guadalcanal and Papua, using every available aircraft of the 3rd Fleet and Base Air Force. The operation was divided into two phases, with the main effort directed at Papua (another indication of the army's influence). Phase 1 (Operation X), scheduled for 5–10 April, would be against Guadalcanal, while Phase 2 (Operations Y, Y-1, and Y-2), scheduled for 11–20 April, was aimed at Papua. The available forces totaled 339 aircraft, of which 184 came from Ozawa's 3rd Fleet – Carrier Division 1, *Zuikaku* and *Zuihō,* and Carrier Division 2, *Junyō* and *Hiyō* – and 155 from Base Air Force – Ichimaru's 1st Air Attack Force and Kosaka's 6th Air Attack Force.[3]

At Rabaul in late March, as destroyers brought in personnel and supplies for 3rd Fleet, Kusaka realigned Base Air Force. Ichimaru transferred his headquarters from Kavieng to Rabaul, and Kosaka moved his from Lakunai to Buin. For reasons that are not clear, Kusaka sent a fighter sweep of fifty-eight Zeros over the Russells on 1 April. Forty-two F4FS, F4US, and P-38s intercepted. In the battle that followed, the Japanese lost nine planes and seven pilots killed, and COMAIRSOLS lost nine planes with three pilots killed. While the battle was in progress, a transport plane landed at Henderson Field carrying Rear Admiral Mitscher, who was coming in to relieve the seriously ill Mason as commander of COMAIRSOLS.[4]

Operation X, which had been scheduled for 5 April, was delayed twice because of weather. But on 7 April, the skies cleared and the aircraft advanced to the forward bases in Bougainville, where they refueled. Only carrier bombers and fighters made the strike on Guadalcanal. The 253rd (Lieutenant [JG] Saitō Saburō) and the 204th (Lieutenant Miyano Zenjirō), with a total of forty-eight Zeros, moved to Buka and made up the Air Superiority Unit (seikūtai). The carrier groups joined the 582nd at Kahili and Ballale, arriving in time for the cameras of a COMAIRSOLS F5A to photograph them jammed on the two airfields. Since only *Zuihō's* fighters came in, its shōtai were divided among the four attack forces (kōgekitai); otherwise unit integrity was maintained. The plan called for an attack in two waves. The first wave consisted of the Buka fighters and *Zuikaku* and 582nd attack forces, which took off around noon; the second wave made up of *Hiyō* and *Junyō* attack forces followed an hour later – altogether 157 Zeros and 67 D3As. Their passing did not go unnoticed. Jack Reed at Teop reported the Buka fighters just minutes after they took off, and farther down the chain the other coast watchers called in as the planes flew over. At Munda, Horton reported that the antiaircraft crews, accustomed as they were to seeing only American planes, opened a vigorous fire on their own planes as they passed.

As Japanese air reconnaissance had shown, shipping was abundant in the Guadalcanal area. At Lunga, four transports that had brought in the 145th Infantry, 37th Division, were loading the 132nd Infantry, Americal Division, which was being withdrawn to Fiji. Three ships were loaded and waiting for the other, *Hunter Liggett*, to finish taking on the last personnel. Five cargo ships were at various points at Guadalcanal, and the fleet tanker *Tappahannock* was pumping fuel into the underwater pipeline at Koli Point. Across the sound, Tulagi Harbor was crowded with smaller shipping and the fleet tanker *Kanawha*. Rear Admiral Ainsworth's TF 18 – the light cruisers *Helena*, *Honolulu*, and *St. Louis*, and six destroyers – which had been making nightly sorties up the Slot in the hope of making another Kula Gulf interception, was at Port Purvis making preparations for a night bombardment of Munda and Vila. In the Russells area, a group of LCTs and a destroyer transport were on a supply run, with the destroyer *Aaron Ward* as escort to guard against submarine attack. Just two nights before, the destroyer *O'Bannon*, returning with TF 18 from a run up the Slot, had sunk the RO-34, sent to provide weather reports for the air attack and to perform lifeguard duty.[5]

COMAIRSOLS staff was at lunch when Reed's report from Teop came in. It bought Mitscher precious time. From ULTRA he knew that a major air attack was imminent, but only earlier that morning did he get a date from Halsey – 8 April, the next day. In the same message, Halsey suggested that Mitscher move up the scheduled strike on Kahili by one day, and down on Henderson Field, five B-17s and twenty-four TBFs were being readied to take off for Kahili at 1330.[6] The troop transports quickly got underway and made for Sealark Channel and the open water to the east. The cargo ships, with the destroyer *Sterett* as escort, headed through Lengo Channel followed by *Tappahannock*, which rapidly overtook the slower cargo ships. At Tulagi, the smaller vessels dispersed as well they could in the harbor, but the failure to order *Kanawha* to get underway immediately was to prove fatal. TF 18, which by that time was just northwest of Savo Island, was ordered to round the Florida Islands to the north and then stand down Indispensable Strait, where it could take cover under the heavy black clouds and rain squalls that engulfed the area from eastern Florida to Malaita. Thus, the Japanese were deprived of what they considered to be a prime target.[7]

As the Japanese formations filled the radar screens and Guadalcanal went to Condition Red, Mitscher sent off the bombers to circle over eastern Guadalcanal. A few minutes after 1300, he began sending up seventy-six marine, navy, and army fighters. Fifty-six of these fighters – about half F4FS, the rest P-38s, P-39s, P-40s, and F4US – made contact. On the ground, RNZAF Radar Unit No. 52, with its advanced British-made ground control of interception (GCI) radar, provided Fighter Control with a radar that could both plot altitude and track more accurately than the SCR 270-B.[8]

The air battle developed over a wide area stretching from the Russells to the eastern end of Lengo Channel. As the fighters engaged, the D3AS made for Tulagi, no doubt hoping to catch TF 18. At least two bombs sank the New Zealand corvette *Moa* in four minutes, and *Kanawha*, caught in the entrance to the harbor after finally being ordered to get underway, was badly hit by two more. Although the fleet tug *Rail* and other nearby ships were able to get the tanker beached on a reef, it slipped off into deep water before daylight the next morning and was lost.[9] Lieutenant James E. Swett, leading a division of VMF-221, made the D3AS pay the price, shooting down seven before he himself was shot down by the rear gunner of the eighth plane he attacked. Swett very likely accounted for loss of the commander of the 582nd, Lieutenant Takahata Tasuo, whose plane did not return. The *Hiyō* and *Junyō* D3AS of the second wave accounted for the destroyer *Aaron Ward*, which had been ordered to leave the ships returning from the Russells and cover LST-449, which was nearing Koli Point fully loaded. The two ships were retiring east toward Lengo Channel when the destroyer took one direct hit and two damaging near misses, sinking while being towed to Tulagi. Some of the Japanese pilots sighted the cargo ships farther ahead and attacked the rear of the convoy, but with the exception of a number of casualties and some damage from near misses, all ships escaped to the east.[10]

The last Japanese planes headed for home around 1530 (a total of thirteen landed at Munda and spent the night). Based on the wildly exaggerated reports of the pilots – ten transports, one cruiser, one destroyer, and forty-one aircraft destroyed – the Navy General Staff named it the Battle of Florida Island. COMAIRSOLS and the ships also made equally excessive claims of fifty aircraft shot down. Actual losses were twelve Zeros and nine D3As for the Japanese, and seven fighters, with six of the pilots rescued, for COMAIRSOLS. That night, Mitscher evened aircraft losses somewhat by his ill-considered decision to send off the strike against Kahili in the face of extremely bad weather up the Slot. The mission was a failure, with seven TBFS going down in the weather. Only three crew members from two different aircraft were rescued.[11]

Expecting another attack, Mitscher on 9 April sent some of his bomber squadrons to Espíritu Santo in order to bring in additional fighters. But, as planned, the Japanese turned their attention to Papua and eastern New Guinea and the Y Operations. On 11, 12, and 13 April, they raided Oro Bay, Port Moresby, and Milne Bay, in that order, but inflicted minimal damage. An attack on the Huon Gulf area – where 3rd Australian Division was pressing 51st Division – planned for 16 April, was called off when air reconnaissance found no shipping. Yamamoto then ordered I-gō ended. The overall effort had cost twenty-five Zeros, twenty-one D3A Vals, and fifteen G4M Bettys (the latter in the New Guinea operations). On 17 April, Ugaki held a conference of the top commanders to assess the situation. He warned that another effort by Combined Fleet could not be expected, and he was critical of Base Air Force, citing three major weaknesses: reconnaissance, inability to deal with the American heavy bombers, and poor training. Kusaka took this as an insult, and some heated words were exchanged afterward.[12]

The final act of I-gō was played out in the skies over southern Bougainville. Yamamoto had resolved to visit Buin on 18 April, and his detailed itinerary was intercepted by ULTRA on 14 April (Oahu date). Nimitz decided to attempt to intercept Yamamoto and sent the order to COMSOPAC, who forwarded the message to Fitch and thence to

Mitscher. Major John W. Mitchell, commander of the 339th Fighter Squadron, planned a mission that would take a 412-mile route south of New Georgia entirely over water, with the P-38s skimming the waves at fifty feet to avoid detection. At a point west of the Treasury Islands, the formation would dogleg to make the interception just northwest of Kahili. The best pilots were picked from the 70th and 339th Squadrons. The flight was divided into three sections: a killer section of six, a covering section of ten, and a spare section of two, which was to fill in anywhere a pilot had to abort.

On Easter Sunday, the Japanese and American flights took off; the timing of each was exact. When contact was made, the killer section was down to two, Captain Thomas Lanphier and Lieutenant Rex Barber. From that point on, what happened is controversial, but the most plausible reconstruction of the action is that of author Carroll V. Glines.[13] As the two P-38s climbed to attack the two G4Ms, one carrying Yamamoto and the other Ugaki, the six 204th Zeros flying escort spotted them and began their dive to attack. Lanphier met three of them head-on and broke up their attack, while Barber closed in behind the lead bomber, and with the other three Zeros trying desperately to shoot him off its tail, shot the bomber down. As it turned out, this was Yamamoto's plane. Ugaki's plane had veered over the water, where Lieutenant Besby F. Holmes closed in on it and set one of its engines afire. Barber finished it off at such close range that pieces of the G4M were imbedded in his P-38, which also sported 104 bullet holes from the Zeros. Ugaki survived, though badly injured.

The P-38s, missing one of their number that was never accounted for, turned for home and a controversy that has lasted until the present day. As Donald A. Davis writes, "Admiral Isoroku Yamamoto, who had been larger than life, was to prove larger than death as well. As the killer flight dashed away, it was almost as if the C-in-C reached up from the jungle with his samurai sword and struck each of the four pilots."[14] The first controversy originated before all of the P-38s touched the ground, when Lanphier shouted over his radio that he had got Yamamoto. He was duly given the credit – then. The second blowup began on 11 May, when J. Norman Lodge, veteran Associated Press correspondent in the South Pacific, filed a story that contained the mission details, including the fact that American intelligence had known Yamamoto's every move in advance. A lot of people on Guadalcanal knew at least something about the mission. Even Sergeant Mack Morriss of *Yank,* who was about as low on the pecking order of correspondents as one could get, knew about the mission and named Barber as the shooter in his diary.[15] But, Halsey, in a fit of anger that did not reflect well on him, blamed Mitchell, Lanphier, and Barber for the leak and tore up Mitscher's recommendation that the three receive the Medal of Honor. One episode never seems to make its way into the literature on the aftermath of the Yamamoto incident: it very nearly put a black mark on the record of Major General Alexander M. Patch, commander, XIV Corps, on Guadalcanal at the time (and later, lieutenant general, commander, Seventh Army in Europe), and probably would have done if Admiral Earnest King, the supreme navy commander of the Pacific, had gotten his way.[16] Since the war, the mission has been the subject of several books, court actions, controversy with the air force and the like. As it stands today, Lanphier and Barber have each been awarded half credit for killing Yamamoto.

Judged by its objective, I-gō had been a failure. Air reconnaissance gave the lie to official Japanese claims of success, and Kusaka concluded that more I-gō–type operations would be necessary. But Ugaki had made it clear that Combined Fleet would not intervene again, and Yamamoto's successor, Admiral Koga Mineichi, sent Carrier Division 1 home on 3 May, since Navy General Staff was planning on using 3rd Fleet in the Aleutians, a plan that Koga opposed and that was soon discarded. Koga, in *Musashi,* followed the carriers home a few days later, with Yamamoto's ashes in a coffin and the badly injured Ugaki in sick bay. He was just as pessimistic as had been Yamamoto, telling a staff meeting on 8 May that he put the chances of success in the present war as three in ten.[17]

KUSAKA'S AIR OFFENSIVE, JUNE 1943

During late April and early May, there was a lull in the Guadalcanal air war. After I-gō, Base Air Force was busy with aircraft repair and maintenance, which was completed by the end of April.[18] In early May, as Koga instructed before he left for Japan, Kusaka concentrated on New Guinea, using mainly using Ichimaru's 1st Air Attack Force. Finally, Base

Air Force was undergoing reorganization, which merits discussion. Kusaka had planned for the 25th Air Flotilla under the command of Rear Admiral Ueno Keizō, which was in Japan undergoing rehabilitation after suffering heavy losses in the Guadalcanal campaign, to relieve the 21st Air Flotilla, which would return to Japan. It also appears that Kusaka intended to bring the 24th Air Flotilla down from Saipan to relieve the 26th Air Flotilla. But growing Japanese concern with the American offensive in the Aleutians forced major changes in this plan. Navy General Staff activated the 12th Air Fleet, with responsibility for the area 24° N 160° E, and shifted the 24th Air Flotilla to the 12th to join 27th Air Flotilla. Kosaka's 26th would not be relieved and, in fact, fought on for the duration of the campaign against Rabaul. In place of the 24th, Ichimaru's 21st would move to Saipan for rehabilitation. Ueno's 25th would return to Rabaul but without its 801st Kōkūtai, which went to the Marshalls, leaving the 25th with the 251st (sixty Zeros and ten J1N1 reconnaissance planes) and the 702nd (fifty G4Ms). The 25th was late coming in and did not complete its redeployment until 17 May, the day that the last of 21st Air Flotilla left for Saipan. With the activation of 12th Air Fleet (2nd Base Air Force), 11th Air Fleet became 1st Base Air Force.[19]

The hiatus in air combat over Guadalcanal ended in the middle of May. Ainsworth's heavy bombardment on the night of 12–13 May, which coincided with the American landing on Attu, set off alarm bells in Rabaul. Fearing that the American move against New Georgia was imminent, Kusaka launched two operations on 13 May. The first was a fighter sweep over the Russells by fifty-four Zeros from the 582nd, 204th, and 253rd. Fighter Command put up 102 fighters, a record number to date, but the interception was marred by miscues, and only a third made contact. Fighter Command lost five aircraft with three pilots, while the Japanese lost four planes shot down and five damaged. Kusaka gained nothing in the tradeoff. Fighter Command learned a valuable lesson in managing a large number of aircraft of many types from all services – marine F4Us, navy F4Fs, Army Air Forces P-39s, P-40s, and P-38s as well as New Zealand P-40s.[20]

The second Japanese operation, scheduled from 13 to 24 May, was carried out by the G4Ms of the 702nd and 705th, aimed by day at the destruction of shipping southeast of San Cristobal, and by night the airfields in the Russells and on Guadalcanal. The antishipping formations, made up of six to twelve Bettys, with a patrol plane scouting ahead, flew a route north of the Solomons and then doglegged down to the shipping route. Four attacks were made on American shipping, but their only success came on 23 May, when six 702nd G4MS bombed the PT boat tender *Niagara* in route from Tulagi to Milne Bay with six PT boats. Damage was heavy, and the ship's commander had it sunk. CINCPAC was not pleased and called the decision precipitate.[21] Against the airfields on Guadalcanal and the Russells, the G4MS made six night attacks, with forces ranging from three to seventeen planes. In the heaviest of these, on the clear, moonlit night of 19–20 May, fourteen men were killed and twenty wounded, but damage to installations was slight. Major Louis Kittel, flying a P-38, shot down two of the G4MS. In addition, the 705th, which based at Ballale for the operation, had so many planes damaged by night bombing that a contingent of maintenance men had to be flown down from Rabaul to make the repairs.[22]

The meager results of the May operations convinced Kusaka that nothing less than an I-gō–type effort would be necessary "to buy time to increase the defensive force in the Central Solomons."[23] In late May, he proposed a plan to Koga for a Combined Fleet/1st Base Air Force air offensive, but Koga rejected it. He intended to concentrate Combined Fleet at Truk in July to have it ready by August for a decisive battle if necessary with the U. S. Fleet. Consequently, after a conference with Navy General Staff, he ordered the carriers, now including *Shōkaku*, which had been badly damaged in the Battle of the Santa Cruz Islands, back to Truk. On the other hand, Koga approved of Kusaka going it alone with 1st Base Air Force.[24]

Kusaka decided to go ahead with his offensive, and planning began. The use of the 702nd and 705th G4MS in the operation was ruled out; they would repeat operations against American shipping east of San Cristobal and night missions over Guadalcanal. This decision left Kusaka with 105 Zeros and 25 D3AS. Operations were set for 5–16 June with two objectives: first, the fighters would attempt to gain control of the air with fighter sweeps and bombing of airfields by Zeros carrying some type of gasoline bomb (this was a 204th innovation); second, having dealt with the COMAIRSOLS fighters, the D3AS, with an escort of all available fighters, would attack shipping in the Guadalcanal-Tulagi area. The first phase was called So Operation and the second phase Se Operation. Kosaka was in command and Lieutenant Commander Shindō Saburō, 582nd, would lead the first attack.[25]

The Rabaul-based Zeros advanced to Buka, Kahili, and Ballale on 6 June, and the next morning, Shindō led eighty-one Zeros, eight carrying gasoline bombs, toward the Russells. Over Gatukai, the Japanese ran into eight VF-11 F4Fs, which had not turned back when a strike on Vila had been aborted; the Japanese shot down three, but all three pilots were rescued by Kennedy's scouts.[26] Fighter Command put up ninety-six fighters, in addition to the eight on regular patrol over the Russells, but kept fifty-two over Savo Island to protect shipping. In the battle that followed over the Russells and Cape Esperance, the Japanese claimed forty-one and lost nine; COMAIRSOLS claimed twenty-six, with four lost in combat, two lost to operational causes, and one pilot killed.[27]

The next day, a conference was held in Rabaul to evaluate the operation. Given the claims made, the results seemed positive, but the second So Operation was postponed to the 12th, so that the pilots of the 582nd and the 251st could train in the four-plane sections that the 204th was using, and maintenance work could be completed on the aircraft. Lieutenant Miyano Zenjirō, 204th, led the seventy-four Zeros on the second So Operation strike. The usual assortment of fighters from Fighter Command met them in a battle that was fought over the Russell Islands. This time the Japanese claimed twenty-four planes, while recording the loss of seven (one pilot was rescued), with seven more damaged. American losses were six planes, with four pilots rescued. Despite a photo reconnaissance over the area after the battle that showed a total of 250 Allied aircraft on the fields, Kusaka decided to go ahead with the Se Operation against shipping.[28]

For the 16 June operation, twenty-four D3As would make the attack, with most of the seventy available fighters arrayed on both sides and in the rear, and with one group slightly ahead. Shindō, once more the flight commander, planned to swing south of the Russells, turn in at Beaufort Bay, and make his approach from the south. His progress southeast was duly called in by the coast watchers, and radar picked up the formation at 1309. One minute later, Fighter Command began putting up 104 fighters, of which, to its considerable satisfaction, 74 made contact. Fighter Control scrambled the first group to fly cover over shipping at Lunga and Koli – four cargo ships, some destroyers, and LSTs and LCTs – and then sent off a dozen 339th P-38s, followed by VF-11's F4F Wildcats, to intercept the incoming attack from the south. The P-38s met the Japanese over Beaufort Bay, and as the air battle between the opposing fighters rolled north over the mountainous spine of Guadalcanal, a dozen F4Fs fought their way in to attack the D3As, causing considerable disruption in the formation before they could reach the coast and push over against the shipping. As the coastline neared, the battles of the 339th and VF-11 merged into the main battle, fought from 20,000 feet to just above the water, from Cape Esperance to east of Koli Point.

Each pilot carried away a snapshot of the wild battle. Here are just a few. A P-40 pilot of the 44th Fighter Squadron reported that he "saw a large dog fight going on 5 miles SE of Savo. I came down in a dive and saw a Grumman and a P-40 collide close to the water. They were making opposite passes on a Zero." A VF-11 pilot saw two of his colleagues collide and both F4Fs fall together into the water. (In fact, all three VF-11 losses were due to collisions.) A P-39 pilot – the P-39s were the last to scramble – was impressed by the many weird combinations he saw, which included some strange bedfellows. "One P-38 and an F4F were scissoring together like they had been training for it all of their life," he reported. "I saw two F4Us and a P-40 working together as a perfect combat team. I saw many other weird combinations. Weird but they work." A F4U pilot from VMF-121 – which had just flown in to base in the Russells, the first squadron to do so – reported that as he climbed to join up, "one flaming Zero almost fell on his plane."[29]

American intelligence officers, trying to piece together the battle later, were unimpressed with the performance of the Zero pilots but showed some admiration for the 582nd's D3As. "The Jap dive bombers again showed their doggedness in pressing home their bombing runs." Nonetheless, only two ships were badly hit – the cargo ship *Celeno* and LST-340 – and both were saved.[30]

For 1st Base Air Force, the raid had been a disaster. As usual, surviving pilots gave greatly exaggerated reports of sinking at least four midsized cargo ships, one large transport, and one destroyer, hits on four large transports, and twenty-eight aircraft shot down. (IGHQ inflated these scores even more and named it the "Air Battle of Lunga.") But only two ships were hit, and casualties from the ships and strafing at Lunga were twenty-five men killed, twenty-nine wounded, and twenty-two missing. For this, 1st Base Air Force paid an exorbitant price: fifteen Zeros and thirteen D3As failed to return, two D3As and three Zeros made emergency landings at Vila, and four D3As and two Zeros returned damaged. Among the first-rate pilots who failed to return was the 204th's Lieutenant Miyano. Kusaka could not believe the extent of his losses and was convinced that a number of aircraft had made emergency landings. The next day, reconnaissance planes and Zeros searched Santa Isabel, Choiseul, and the south coast of New Georgia but found nothing. An evaluation meeting on Se Operation came to the obvious conclusion that Allied fighter performance had become more sophisticated (nothing was said about the declining Japanese fighter performance), and until the more advanced carrier bombers arrived, a daylight attack on the Guadalcanal base complex by D3As was impossible. Had they known the true losses on the Allied side, the Japanese commanders would have been even more pessimistic. COMAIRSOLS lost six aircraft and five pilots (four of these from collisions), and two P-40s crash-landed with damage.[31]

Compounding the Japanese failure over the Russells and Guadalcanal was that of the G4Ms east of San Cristobal. During the Se Operation fighter battles, Captain Paul Theiss had brought his large convoy to Guadalcanal and unloaded a number of Seabee battalions, including some scheduled for New Georgia, and the 1st Marine Raiders. He then embarked the 172nd RCT and a section of the 24th Seabees, which were to make the Rendova landing for Efaté, arriving there 16 June for rehearsals. The Japanese patrol planes spotted this convoy inbound on 10 June, and three G4Ms were sent off to attack. Fighter Command sent eight F4Us and four P-38s to intercept in extremely bad weather, and off northeast Malaita these shot down one of the bombers and damaged the other two. Other G4Ms lurked around the convoy as it went back out but did not attack. The Japanese missed the outbound convoy altogether.[32]

In the aftermath of the June air battles, Kusaka urgently requested reinforcements. He received the promise of the 201st and the 501st Kōkūtai for the 25th Flotilla, with the 201st arriving around mid-July. The

501st, however, was newly formed and still training, and so its arrival date was indefinite (in fact it did not arrive until the end of the New Georgia campaign). In addition, Combined Fleet promised the bombers of the small carrier *Ryūhō* to the 26th Flotilla to replace the 582nd's losses, with the arrival set for around 1 July (they arrived on 2 July, three days into the New Georgia invasion).[33]

On the ridge at the Lunga River, COMAIRSOLS intelligence officers got the Japanese losses somewhat higher than they actually were. But their conclusion that COMAIRSOLS could "look forward to continued superiority in planes" was correct. Japanese formations would never again appear over Guadalcanal in daylight.[34]

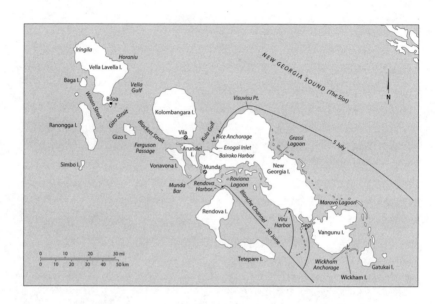

Map 5.1. Operation TOENAILS Landings.

FIVE

Plans and Preparations

TO UNDERSTAND THE PLANNING, PREPARATIONS, AND CONDUCT of operations in the battle for New Georgia, a brief discussion of the command structure is necessary. As a result of the division of the South Pacific between the army and the navy, the Allies had two theaters, South Pacific, SOPAC (navy), and South West Pacific, SWPA (army), but a unified command – or a semblance thereof. The Japanese, on the other hand, had one theater, Southeast Area, but no unified command. At IGHQ, the army and navy general staffs worked out an agreement for the direction of operations; the local commanders, in turn, worked out an agreement to carry out the operations. While there was plenty of room for friction on both the Allied and Japanese sides, each conducted joint operations with relative harmony. This was due in large measure to the personal relationships of the top commanders.

As we have noted, MacArthur would have overall command of the final operations against Rabaul, while Halsey would be in tactical command in the Solomons. "Although this arrangement was sensible and satisfactory, it had the curious effect of giving me two 'hats' in the same echelon," Halsey wrote after the war. "My original hat was under Nimitz, who controlled my troops, ships, and supplies; now I had another hat under MacArthur, who controlled my strategy." Given the less than cordial relationship between MacArthur and the navy, the command setup could have become awkward, but that was prevented by the lasting friendship that developed between Halsey and MacArthur. "We had arguments, but they always ended pleasantly," Halsey wrote. "Not once did he, my superior officer, ever force his decisions on me. On the few occasions when I disagreed with him, I told him so, and we discussed the issue until one of us changed his mind."[1] In this regard, it was not always Halsey who changed his mind.

In Rabaul, a similar relationship had developed between Kusaka, who answered to Combined Fleet, and Imamura, who answered to the Army General Staff. Both men had arrived at Rabaul at roughly the same time – Kusaka from the presidency of the Naval College at Etajima in early October to take command of the 11th Air Fleet, and Imamura, described as "a sober, reflective, somewhat bookish officer,"[2] from command of Twenty-Third Army to activate Eighth Area Army. Since then, the two men had developed a close relationship; they and their staffs had lunch together once or twice a week, where Southeast Area affairs were discussed informally and the respective staffs got to know one another personally. The latter was important since the staff officers were frequently the source of discord between the top commanders on both sides. In his war memoir, Kusaka credited the good relations between the navy and the army to Imamura, whom he called "a very great person."[3] Their friendship was of key importance in a military establishment that gave wide latitude to commanders in the field.

MACARTHUR AND HALSEY

Planning for the coming offensive got underway on 10 March, when delegations from SWPA (MacArthur), SOPAC (Halsey), and CINCPAC (Nimitz, Commander in Chief, Pacific) were summoned to Washington to confer with the Joint Chiefs. The problem was MacArthur's request for an astounding 1,800 additional aircraft (mainly heavy bombers), five new divisions, and naval reinforcements (this grew even more when Halsey's requests were added). The magnitude of the requests put the Joint Chiefs in a quandary. Europe took precedence over the Pacific for the still limited resources, and in January 1943, at the Anglo-American conference in Casablanca, the United States and Great Britain had agreed to invade Sicily and launch the Combined Bomber Offensive against Germany. The continuation of the offensive against Rabaul had been approved, but only with the forces already allocated.

In the Washington discussions, three options soon became apparent: (1) provide MacArthur with what he requested (which General H. H. Arnold, the Army Air Forces commander, vehemently opposed); (2) get MacArthur to scale back his requests (which he refused to do); or (3) cancel the decision to take Rabaul in 1943 and limit the effort to roughly that of Task Two of the Joint Chiefs 2 July 1942 Directive. The Pacific delegation opted for the third option, with one additional operation added: the occupation of Kiriwina and Woodlark Islands in order to have airfields in medium bomber range of Bougainville (the islands were unoccupied, and the airfields were Halsey's idea). Queries to both Halsey and MacArthur brought agreement on the issue of a limited offensive.

With the major issue resolved, the Joint Chiefs issued a new directive on 28 March 1943. Now the objective was to maintain the initiative by operations designed to lead to the capture of the Bismarck Archipelago. Again, the operation was divided into three tasks: Task One was the establishment of airfields on Kiriwina and Woodlark Islands; Task Two was the capture of the New Guinea's Huon Peninsula (Salamaua, Lae, Finschhafen, and Madang) and western New Britain; and Task Three was the occupation of the Solomon Islands up to and including southern Bougainville.[4]

Soon after the conference in Washington, Halsey made an appointment to see MacArthur, flying to Brisbane on 15 April, just as the wheels were being set in motion to intercept Yamamoto. This was the first meeting between the two men, and it marked the beginning of their friendship. For two days, Halsey and MacArthur went over the plans at the latter's lavish headquarters in the AMP Building on Queen Street. Some of the discussion was taken up with Task One, the occupation of Kiriwina and Woodlark Islands, for which Halsey was to supply part of the forces (this operation proved a dead end).[5] But the real problem from Halsey's (and King's) point of view was the timing in the plan – Halsey was not to move until MacArthur had secured Salamaua and Lae, and since this was not scheduled until around September, most of the Pacific naval forces then available would remain idle for months. Halsey wanted to move simultaneously with MacArthur's occupation of Woodlark and Kiriwina and, with the one qualification that he would not bring on a major battle requiring SWPA's assistance, he secured MacArthur's approval.

In support of MacArthur's main effort, Halsey's operations were divided into three phases: (1) infiltration of New Georgia; (2) seizure of the Buin area and/or Rekata Bay; and (3) seizure of Kieta and neutralization of Buka.[6] The tentative date set for Phase 1 was 15 May, but MacArthur soon pushed it back to 15 June and finally to 30 June. On 26 April, MacArthur issued the revised plans for the operation, code-named CARTWHEEL, which incorporated Halsey's changes and used language so general in regard to New Georgia as to give Halsey a relatively free hand.

Halsey issued his operational plan, code-named TOENAILS, on 3 June. The Munda Bar ruled out a direct attack on Munda, and after a thorough reconnaissance of Kolombangara, the idea of bypassing Munda by attacking Vila was discarded.[7] Instead, in an operation Halsey described to Nimitz as "infiltration and staging," four simultaneous landings would be made on 30 June: (1) Wickham Anchorage for a landing craft layover base; (2) Segi Point for its airfield site;[8] (3) Viru Harbor for a small craft base; and (4) Rendova Harbor as the base from which to stage the troops to New Georgia for the attack on Munda. (In late June, a fifth landing at Rice Anchorage on Kula Gulf on 4 July was added to serve as a base from which to attack Enogai Inlet and Bairoko Harbor.) Four task forces would carry out the operation: TF 31 under Turner, amphibious operations; TF 33 under Fitch, air support; TF 36 under Halsey, naval support; and TF 72 under Captain James Fife, submarine operations.[9]

Forces allocated to the New Georgia Occupation Force (NGOF) were as follows: from the army, the 43rd Division and the 136th FA Battalion (155mm howitzers) from the 37th Division (toward the end of the month two additional battalions from the 37th were allocated for the Rice Anchorage landing); from the navy, eight destroyers, twenty-four PT boats, Acorn 7 (built around the 47th Naval Construction Battalion),[10] the 24th and one section of the 20th Naval Construction Battalions, and the communications and naval base units; from the Marine Corps, the 1st Marine Raider Regiment less 2nd and 3rd Battalions, and the 9th Defense Battalion, which had a 155mm gun unit and a light tank platoon; and from the Fiji Military Forces, the 1st Commando Fiji Guerillas.[11]

The one-division limitation produced the most serious dissension among the planners. American intelligence estimates of Japanese strength in New Georgia were fairly accurate. Turner put it as 3,000 at

Munda and from 5,000 to 7,000 at Vila, while Hester put it at 4,000 to 5,000 at Munda and 8,000 to 10,000 at Vila. The last complete count of the official Japanese historians was dated 31 May, at which time they had 11,701 men, including 1,291 construction personnel. But at least one more infantry battalion arrived before the late June to early July transports were disrupted by the Allied landing. This was a considerable force to be reckoned with, and Major General C. Barney Vogel, commander, I Marine Amphibious Corps (IMAC), held out for two divisions as the minimum required. Vogel's position was probably behind Turner's request of 12 June for two more divisions, additional Marine Raider and defense battalions, and other support troops.[12] Halsey rejected the request (and he later cited Vogel's obstructionist behavior in the New Georgia planning in securing his relief).[13]

Since, in fact, two divisions were needed to capture Munda and a third to compete the occupation of New Georgia, Halsey has been criticized for his refusal to commit a larger force at the start. He had the divisions. XIV Corps, now under the command of Major General Oscar W. Griswold, had the 37th (less a regiment) and the 25th Divisions at Guadalcanal and the American at Fiji. On the other hand, both the 25th and the American had fought on Guadalcanal; the former was badly understrength, and the latter was undergoing extensive reorganization. Perhaps Halsey was looking ahead to Bougainville, where the major battle was expected. He knew that he would have the 3rd Marine Division for this operation, but otherwise he would fight with what he had. As Halsey well knew, his superiors considered the drive on Rabaul unfinished business; the new business – and from King's point of view, the most important – was the impending drive through the Central Pacific. A letter from Nimitz in mid-May is revealing in this regard. "I wish you all success with the coming operations, and you may rest assured that my Staff and I will continue to look out for your interests, although it may appear to some of you occasionally that your Force has been forgotten," Nimitz wrote. "We have a good over-all view of what is happening in the Pacific, and will see that you are not left without tools when the time comes."[14]

Halsey's plan specified only the objectives and the forces allocated; the detailed planning was left to the individual commanders. To carry out the multiple landings, Turner divided his forces into two groups: the Western Force, under his command, would make the Rendova landing; and the Eastern Force, under Rear Admiral George H. Fort, commander, Landing Craft Flotillas, would make the landings at Wickham Anchorage, Segi Point, and Viru Harbor landings. For the Rendova Harbor landing, Turner planned to use four APAS and two AKAS on 30 June to take in the 172nd RCT and the 24th Seabees; thereafter, his large landing craft, LSTS, LCTS, and LCIS, would complete the initial movement of the NGOF over the next the next few days. For his three scattered landings at Wickham Anchorage, Segi Point, and Viru Harbor, Fort would use destroyer-transports, landing craft, and coastal transports (APcs).[15]

To provide air support, Fitch (COMAIRSOPAC/Task Force 33) estimated that he would have a total of 1,182 aircraft, of which 626 would go to Mitscher (COMAIRSOLS/Task Group 33.1). Seventeen specific missions were assigned – from having PBYs available for aircrew rescue to having aircraft available on six hours' notice for supply drops on New Georgia – but they all boiled down to establishing air supremacy over New Georgia and providing support for the ground troops in any way possible. To control air operations, Fitch created the New Georgia Air Force (NGAF), or Air Command New Georgia, which consisted of Brigadier General Mulcahy, his 2nd MAW staff, and Argus 11 (one advanced base fighter direction unit with one New Zealand and two U.S. radar units). On takeoff, COMAIRSOLS aircraft assigned to New Georgia missions came under Mulcahy's control; all requests originating with the New Georgia commanders for air support went to him, and if approved, went on to COMAIRSOLS. Fitch specifically directed that COMAIRSOLS maintain a minimum of eighteen SBDs on ground alert in the Russells for missions requested by Mulcahy.[16]

In Halsey's plan for the deployment of TF 36 (3rd Fleet), the New Georgia veterans, Cruiser Division 9 (Ainsworth/TG 36.1), and Cruiser Division 12 (Merrill/TG 36.2), along with three destroyer squadrons, would provide close support. Merrill would open the D-Day operations with a bombardment of the Shortland Island area, and under this cover, the minelayers would lay fields across the southern entrance to Bougainville, while detached destroyers would shell Vila as a diversion. Ainsworth would be at sea in striking distance of Rendova. One battleship division would move forward to Havannah Harbor, Efaté, while his two carriers and a battleship division would operate out of Nouméa. Fife's submarines would establish a picket line to the north to watch for any movement south of Combined Fleet units, as well as operate in the Solomons.[17]

The New Georgia Occupation Force plan to capture Munda quickly was simple in concept. Hester's 172nd and the 169th infantry would move to Zanana through Honiavasa Passage, and from there overland to the departure line on the Barike River. On 7 July, under the tactical command of Brigadier General Leonard F. Wing, assistant divisional commander, the two regiments would advance astride the east–west track known as the Munda Trail, the 169th on the right and the 172nd on the left. A destroyer bombardment, followed by heavy air attacks, would precede the jump-off, and three battalions of artillery (two 105mm, the other 155mm) emplaced on either side of Honiavasa Passage would support the attack – in addition to the 155s at Rendova. Two days later, on 9 July, with the 172nd and the 169th closing in on the airfield from the east, 3rd Battalion, 103rd, supported by the 9th Defense Battalion's tank platoon would hook around Munda Point and seize the airfield from the west. All the while, the Northern Landing Force would hold the Enogai-Bairoko Harbor area, prevent reinforcements from reaching Munda, block the Bairoko Harbor–Munda Trail, and link up with the 169th on its right flank.[18]

KUSAKA AND IMAMURA

In March, at roughly the same time the Joint Chiefs were scaling back operations against Rabaul, IGHQ was revising the 4 January 1943 Army/Navy Central Agreement for operations in the Southeast Area. The Army General Staff had never been satisfied with the navy's determination to defend the Central Solomons, and Eighth Area Army wanted some clarification of its obligation in that regard. But the catalyst was the Bismarck Sea disaster, where once again the army had thousands of its troops drowned or strafed in the water before they could reach the battlefield. In the immediate aftermath, army and navy staff officers met at IGHQ on 6 March. There was much finger pointing. The army accused the navy of being focused on the Solomons rather than on New Guinea (the official navy historians admitted this) and requested an additional 200 naval aircraft to protect the supply lines. The navy in turn criticized the Army Air Forces for inability to carry out missions over water.

Under these circumstances, IGHQ set up a Joint Army/Navy Investigation Board to study the matter. At the conclusion, the army declared that it viewed New Guinea as vital for the national defense and proposed that if a retreat was necessary – the implication being because of the lack of naval support – then it would set the defense line from northwest New Guinea to Timor. The navy's representatives argued that the Huon Peninsula must be held or its loss would swing open the western gate to Rabaul and force the Combined Fleet to withdraw from Truk. But the navy recognized the army's proposal for what it was – an ultimatum – and quickly agreed that army/navy operations should focus on eastern New Guinea. The army wanted this in writing, and the result was the Army/Navy Memorandum on Southeast Area Operations, signed off on around 20 March.

On the basis of this memorandum, the two services completed the Southeast Area Army/Navy Agreement on 22 March, which canceled the 4 January agreement. The preamble stated that the army and the navy "would literally operate as one unit" and that the "primary operation of the two forces will be directed against New Guinea," while operations in the Solomons and Bismarcks were to be strictly defensive. As in the earlier agreement, however, the army would defend the Northern Solomons and the navy the Central Solomons, but – and this is the key wording in regard to New Georgia – *some* army units would be placed under navy command according to agreements between the local commanders in Rabaul. Thus, the army was still committed to the defense of New Georgia.

To ensure that the front commanders, Yamamoto, Kusaka, and Imamura, fully understood the primary objective and that they were to work as one to achieve it, their chiefs of staff – Vice Admiral Ugaki, Rear Admiral Nakahara Yoshimasa, and Lieutenant General Katō Rimpei – were summoned to Tokyo, where the new agreement as well as the operational instructions were presented. The latter spelled out in detail the army/navy cooperation expected in both the primary and secondary areas; for example, the navy had the responsibility for supplying army units in the Central Solomons, but the army was to cooperate. In the all-important matter of gaining some parity in the air, the two air forces were to operate in both areas, with the Army Air Forces mainly in New Guinea and Base Air Force mainly in the Bismarcks and Solomons, but "depending on the status of the operations, the Army and Navy units will cooperate to execute the operations, regardless of the roles stated in the previous paragraphs." For the period May to September, and including units scheduled to arrive in that time period, IGHQ estimated that Lieutenant General Teramoto Noriichi's 4th Air Army (activated in early August) would have a total of 241 aircraft of all types, and Kusaka's Base Air Force would have 315 of all types.[19] It goes without saying that in the air the Japanese were facing hopeless odds – they were outnumbered by either of the two air forces arrayed against them.

In arranging the defense of the Central Solomons, Imamura and Kusaka adhered to both the letter and the spirit of the 22 March agreement. Vice Admiral Baron Samejima Tomoshige, who had arrived on 6 April from command of 4th Fleet to relieve Mikawa as commander of 8th Fleet, had the overall responsibility. Imamura substantially increased the army's commitment in May and June. The 229th Infantry, which had been scattered from Buna to Guadalcanal, was reconstituted, and Colonel Hirata Genjiro, with his headquarters, was sent in to take command. The same transports took in Major Kojima Bunzō's rebuilt 3rd Battalion, and Major Hara Masao to take command of the 1st Battalion (although it does not seem that this battalion was brought up to full strength). In May, Imamura began the movement of Colonel Tomonari Satoshi's 13th Regiment, 6th Division, to Kolombangara, and by June, Tomonari and his headquarters, Major Takabayashi Uichi's 3rd Battalion, and elements of Major Kinoshita Seishu's 1st Battalion and Major Obashi Takeo's 2nd Battalion had arrived. (The remainder arrived in early July.) To command the army forces, Imamura appointed Major General Sasaki Noboru, a cavalry officer with service in China, who came to Rabaul from the Armored Warfare Department of the Ministry of War. Sasaki activated Headquarters, Southeast Detachment, under 17th Army at

Erventa on 26 May, and then immediately passed to Samejima's command. With Lieutenant Colonel Kamiya Hoshiharu as his chief of staff, Sasaki located his headquarters on Kongō Hill near Ōta's on 2 June.[20]

On directions from Samejima, Sasaki's first order of business was to arrange command responsibilities with Ōta. The result was the Navy/Army Agreement on Defense in the New Georgia Area, which set up the joint command for what was called the New Georgia Defense Unit. Ōta was in charge of the northern sector, the Enogai and Bairoko area, and Sasaki the Munda area. In all areas, however, the senior officer would be in command, regardless of the troops involved. To this was added the important provision that if the situation demanded, command would be unified under the senior officer in New Georgia – and by date of commission this was Sasaki. Ōta had responsibility for coastal artillery defense, radio communications with the rear, and the all-important barge operations that would transport troops and supplies from Kolombangara and evacuate the sick and wounded. The army had responsibility for all land operations, while antiaircraft defense was a shared responsibility. "It was a ground breaking development," the official Japanese army historians wrote, "for the Imperial Army to be placed under the Navy from the early stages of operations preparation and to assign roles that maximized the strength of both the Army and the Navy."[21]

Unlike the Rabaul commanders, who steadfastly maintained that the Americans would attack in late July or early August, Sasaki quickly reached the conclusion that it would probably come in late June. But even with the gift of a month's time afforded him by MacArthur's delays, he was far from ready by that date. He had a shortage of labor due to illness, especially malaria,[22] and the materiel and equipment he needed did not arrive. Terrain was an obstacle everywhere, whether in digging deep enough in the coral on the south side of the airfield or in establishing communication lines with the defense line he ordered built east of Lambete Plantation. In the northern sector, he found that while the four Kure 6th 14cm guns had been emplaced at Enogai Point, little had been done at Bairoko. An adequate field of fire had not been cleared, and the trenches were too shallow because of the difficulty in digging deep. He solved the latter problem by using blocks of coral to construct the emplacements, as was being done on the beach at the airfield. East of the airfield, practically nothing had been done to prepare the defenses. Sasaki established the main line running inland from Ilangana and made excellent use of the low ridges that ran in all directions. Two-tier log and coral pillboxes were constructed that could withstand anything except a direct hit by a heavy shell, and a tunnel was dug into what the Americans later called Horseshoe Ridge to house Hirata's headquarters. Officers dug alongside the enlisted men. It was "very unusual for the Japanese Army," a POW told his interrogators, to see officers with picks and shovels in their hands.[23]

Communications was a major problem. Other than a motor vehicle road that ran along the beach to Lambete and 1,000 meters of completed road between Southeast Detachment HQ and 229th Infantry HQ, no roads as such existed – only trails, which, as Sasaki wrote, the rains turned into "slush ponds." To maintain contact with his thinly spread troops, he requested underground cable, but there is no record that he received it. Likewise, it is doubtful that the underwater cable he requested for communications with Vila ever came. Naval signaling centers for contact with the rear, however, were all underground and withstood continual bombing and shelling. Considerable ammunition had to be stored close to the gun emplacements and dugouts, while food and ammunition were in dumps near the bomb shelters of the bivouac area in Lambete Plantation.[24]

In the short time that he had been in command, Sasaki had accomplished a great deal. But there was still much to be done. Sasaki did not rule out a frontal attack across the Munda Bar, for the Japanese had come to have an almost exaggerated respect for American landing craft. This accounts for extremely strong bunkers being built near the beach at the northwestern end of the airfield, defenses along the shore of Roviana Lagoon from Munda Point past Lambete Plantation, and the emplacement of a Yokosuka 7th SNLF 12cm gun section on the tip of Baanga Island. As we have seen, Sasaki also considered an attack from the east by forces staging through Roviana Lagoon, and he had constructed the defensive line from Ilangana north. But he seems to have considered Roviana Island, west of Honiavasa Passage, as the likely staging point. This last assumption was not too far-fetched, since large ships could unload on the southern shore, and the Americans, after the Seabees had built a road across the island, did use it as the main supply route to Munda until the Munda Bar was made navigable. But an enemy landing at Rendova Harbor was also considered a possibility after the Japanese noted the increase in COMAIRSOLS aerial reconnaissance from mid-June on. Finally, the Kula Gulf–Vila area had to be considered another possibility, especially after air attacks on Vila increased dramatically in June. Then, on the 15th, a heavy raid hit Bairoko Harbor for the first time. The Japanese took notice. "The enemy objective seems to be Kolombangara Island rather than Munda," a mid-June intelligence report concluded. "It is thought that this may be part of the enemy's plan to cut off our rear."[25]

With his forces stretched thin, the question remains as to why Sasaki kept company-size units in exposed locations at Wickham Anchorage, Viru Harbor, and Rendova Harbor. Together, these added up to roughly one battalion, with the troops drawn from the two rifle companies of the Kure 6th and the 1st and 2nd Battalions of the 229th. From hindsight it seems that the former would have served him better in the Dragons Peninsula (Enogai and Bairoko) and the latter in the Ilangana line.

THE OPPOSING FORCES – 30 JUNE

The time has come to look at the forces arrayed against each other as the battle opened in all three dimensions. Of the infantry units, with the exception of the 1st Marine Raider Battalion, none had fought in the Solomons. For the most part, however, the Japanese units did have some prior combat experience in other theaters, while the Allied units had none. The air and naval units, on the other hand, were made up of mostly long-serving veterans.

Ground Forces

The 43rd Division, expected to take Munda Field in a few days, was a New England National Guard Division brought up to strength by draftees. The division had shipped to the South Pacific in October 1942, the 103rd and the 169th Infantry Regiments to New Zealand, then to New Caledonia, and then to the Russells. The 172nd went directly to Espíritu Santo, but as the transport, *President Coolidge*, entered the harbor, it hit a friendly mine and sank. The regiment had to be completely reequipped before moving on to Guadalcanal in the spring of 1943.

The inexperienced 43rd Division had several months to prepare. According to the division's history, Hester had pillboxes constructed, modeled after those of the Japanese on Guadalcanal, for training exercises, but how effective this was is debatable. Neither the Guadalcanal terrain nor that in the Russell Islands bore any resemblance to that encountered in New Georgia. The two regiments seem to have spent much time on occupational duties. In April, XIV Corps arranged for the 147th RCT, veteran of the fighting on Guadalcanal during the Japanese retreat west, to conduct several one-day orientation courses for 43rd officers and selected NCOs, but again the terrain bore little resemblance to that on New Georgia.[26] In mid-June, the 103rd Infantry and the 169th Infantry conducted exercises on Guadalcanal using landing craft (one of the LSTs was hit during Kusaka's big air raid), while Turner sent the 172nd and part of the 24th Naval Construction Battalion – the units scheduled for Rendova – to Efaté for landing exercises from his transports. The 9th Marine Defense Battalion reported that it only conducted simulated exercises. At the same time, Strike Command and XIV Corps conducted four days of what was described as "extensive air-ground exercises" to test munitions, target marking, and radio communications in preparation for close air–ground support. No troops, however, were involved.[27]

The Eastern and Northern Landing Forces came from the 43rd's 103rd RCT, the 1st Marine Raider Regiment, and the 37th Infantry Division. The 4th Raider Battalion, formed at Camp Linda Vista near San Diego in late 1942, arrived at Espíritu Santo in late February 1943. A few veterans from the 1st Raiders joined the battalion, but as a unit it had no combat experience. The one veteran unit, the 1st Marine Raider Battalion, which had earned legendary fame on Guadalcanal, was in the Northern Landing Force. But as its historian, Joseph H. Alexander, wrote, it was "distinctly different from the original version – fewer superstars, mainly a tried and tested core of veteran junior officers and NCOs leading an enthusiastic group of newcomers."[28] Two battalions from the 37th Division, an Ohio National Guard Division with no combat experience and a history similar to that of the 43rd, comprised the rest of the force.

On the Japanese side, ground defense was the responsibility of the Imperial Army. The troops came from two regular army divisions, the 38th (Nagoya) and the 6th (Kumamoto). The 38th had taken part in the capture of Hong Kong and the Dutch East Indies, and later the division, less the 229th Regiment, had been sent to Guadalcanal. In November 1942, the 229th was split up. Regimental headquarters and part of 1st Battalion made it to Guadalcanal and were evacuated to Rabaul, so that on New Georgia the battalion apparently consisted of only the 3rd and 4th Companies and the 1st Machine-Gun Company.[29] The 2nd Battalion, as we have seen, was sent to Munda as the occupation force and retained its organic organization. The 3rd Battalion had been sent to Buna, where it was virtually destroyed. On New Georgia, the reconstituted 3rd Battalion was composed almost entirely of replacements for the 38th Division, with a sprinkling of sick or wounded veterans evacuated from Buna. The replacement troops were almost certainly called-up reservists. While they were older than fresh recruits, they had gone through the rigorous and harsh training that was standard in the Imperial Army.[30]

The 6th Division, which contributed the 13th Regiment (and later the bulk of the reinforcements) had seen heavy fighting, with the attendant heavy casualties, in the first years of the Sino-Japanese War, including the sack of Nanjing, but then settled in as part of the occupation forces in Hunan Province. The 6th Division was assigned to Imamura's Eighth Area Army in November 1942, for the planned renewal of the attack on Guadalcanal, and its depleted ranks were brought up to full strength by newly trained conscripts. The division began its movement to Southeast Area in late December, arriving in Truk in January. Since by that time the decision had been made to evacuate Guadalcanal, the 13th Regiment, the cavalry regiment, and a battalion of the field artillery regiment were directed to Rabaul and the rest of the division to Bougainville. The Rabaul convoy arrived safely, but submarine *Silversides* sank three transports in one of the Bougainville convoys with considerable losses, especially to the medical and engineering units. At Rabaul, the 13th was taught American tactics, based on the experience at Guadalcanal, and trained in night-fighting before beginning the movement to New Georgia.[31]

Thus, both the 229th and the 13th contained sizable numbers of men with no combat experience. But even the veterans had never faced the volume of artillery fire to be expected from the Americans. Just before leaving China, an IGHQ staff officer briefed the 6th Division battalion commanders on American artillery fire, which he described as "tremendously fierce and concentrated."[32]

Air Forces

As COMAIRSOLS predicted, after following Kusaka's June air offensive, it could look forward to continued numerical superiority in aircraft. Out of 533 aircraft assigned (roughly 100 less than Fitch's initial projections), Mitscher had 455 combat planes available. Of these, Fighter Command (Colonel E. L. Pugh, USMC) had 213 aircraft, 82 of which were second-generation fighters, F4US (65) and P-38s (17), while the rest were the older F4FS (72), P-40s (47), and P-39s (12). Strike Command (Colonel C. F. Schilt, USMC) had 170 light and medium bombers. Seventy-seven SBDs and 72 TBFs, roughly divided between marine and navy squadrons, made up most of the force, but the 21 AAF B-25s were listed under this command. Bomber Command (Brigadier General G. C. Jamison, AAF) had 72 heavy bombers. Nine were B-17s of the 5th Group, while the rest were B-24s, split almost equally between the AAF and the navy. In addition, COMAIRSOLS had 48 noncombat aircraft – search, utility, and photographic reconnaissance – available.[33]

The Japanese, on the other hand, could muster fewer than 200 planes. Kusaka's 1st Base Air Force, 25th and 26th Air Flotillas, had approximately 120 combat planes along with 4 reconnaissance types. Of these, 71 were Zeros, 38 were G4Ms, and 11 were D3As. All of the land-based bombers and two-thirds of the fighters were at Rabaul, while the D3As were at Kavieng undergoing rehabilitation and reorganization after the 16 June battle.[34] Itabana's 6th Air Division had roughly 50 operational aircraft. The 14th Hikōdan was in the midst of relieving the 12th, and the 11th Sentai of the latter, which had suffered heavy losses in New Guinea, had already departed the theater. The 1st Sentai was scheduled to follow, but at the time of the Rendova landing was temporarily merged into the 14th Hikōdan. The 14th Hikōdan, the only newcomer to the Solomons among the air units, was comprised of the 14th Sentai, equipped with Ki-21 heavy bombers (what the AAF would designate a medium bomber), and the 68th and 78th Sentai, equipped with the new Ki-61 fighters, which boasted Daimler-Benz liquid-cooled engines. But the 68th had lost 10 of its aircraft to navigational/operational problems en route to Rabaul, while the 78th was in transit at the opening of the Rendova landing (and was not included in the estimated strength given above).[35]

Naval Forces

At sea, the Japanese were also badly outnumbered. On 30 June, Same-jima's 8th Fleet consisted of his flagship, *Chōkai*, the only heavy cruiser in the South Pacific, the old light cruiser *Yūbari*, used as a training ship, and one destroyer squadron. As we have seen, Halsey allocated two destroyer divisions to Turner, with two light cruiser divisions and three destroyer squadrons in close support. Neither Halsey nor Koga had any intention of using their battleships or heavy carriers, but both committed the air groups of their light carriers to the battle. In submarines, both sides were roughly equal. Halsey had his eleven deployed north of the Bismarcks on the shipping lanes Truk–Rabaul and Palau–Rabaul. Kusaka, with the eight boats of Rear Admiral Harada Kaku's 7th Squadron, had two submarines operating in New Georgia waters on 30 June.[36] American intelligence had a fairly accurate picture of Combined Fleet's strength, and Halsey was certainly aware of the eight to ten heavy cruisers at Truk that could be deployed to Rabaul – as in fact they were – and make things interesting for his light cruisers.[37]

Numbers of ships, of course, are not the whole story. On land, inex-perienced troops would have to attack Japanese defenders, many of them veterans, in prepared positions, with the terrain overwhelmingly favor-ing the defenders. And the Japanese were tenacious defensive fighters. MacArthur had learned this the hard way at Buna; Halsey, despite the experience at Guadalcanal, still had to be taught. In the air, the Japanese could choose the time of attack, and consequently, COMAIRSOLS had the formidable operational task of keeping, from sunup to sundown, from bases 120 to 180 miles distant, a strong air patrol over the battle sites and convoys. Likewise, the navy, even with the intelligence provided by ULTRA, aerial reconnaissance, and the coast watchers, faced the same problem of interdicting the Japanese Reinforcement Force from bases 180 miles away.

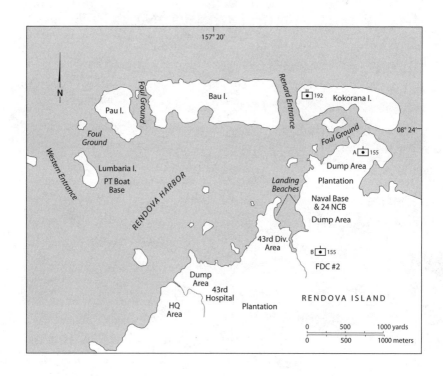

Map 6.1. Rendova.

SIX

The Landings

HALSEY'S PLANNED "INFILTRATION" OF NEW GEORGIA, AS WE have seen, called for five separate landings scattered throughout the islands. With the exception of Rice Anchorage, the initial landings were to be made simultaneously, but events at Segi would lead to a preemptive landing on 21–22 June. To further complicate matters for the historian, Rear Admiral Turner failed to file an action report. One can speculate that the report was a victim of the shift in the center of gravity of the navy's war to the Central Pacific. King wanted Turner back at Pearl Harbor to set up the amphibious command for operations in the Central Pacific. Consequently, Nimitz wrote Halsey on 26 June, "I desire that you release Turner not later than the completion of your move into Rendova."[1]

In the absence of an after-action report, reconstruction of the operations has been pieced together from Turner's loading orders and from various other records.

SEGI AND THE PREEMPTIVE LANDING

Trained reconnaissance teams arrived at Segi by PBY on 14 June. The 47th Seabee team stayed at Segi to work on the landing sites for their heavy equipment, while the other teams, with scouts Kennedy provided, headed out by canoe for their various assignments. One went to Viru Harbor; another to Oloana Bay on Vangunu two miles west of Wickham Anchorage; another to Rendova Harbor; and another to Rice Anchorage. At Rendova and Oloana Bay, members of the teams stayed behind to man beacon lights on 30 June to guide in the landing craft, while a coast watcher, Flight Officer J. A. Corrigan, with a party of native laborers, would be waiting at Rice Anchorage. The reconnaissance teams then returned to Segi for the trip back to Guadalcanal, only to discover that during their absence the situation had changed. The 4th Raiders and the 103rd Infantry were dug in around Markham's plantation. Obviously, something had happened.[2]

The situation at Segi began to develop two days after the reconnaissance teams arrived, on 16 June, when Kennedy with just a dozen scouts attacked the bivouac of a Japanese platoon on patrol from 4th Company, 229th Regiment, at Viru Harbor. The site was near Nazareth Village in Nono Lagoon, about a mile west of Segi. All of the Japanese escaped, leaving behind their equipment and documents, and reported being attacked by fifty native guerillas led by a Caucasian. Sasaki responded by sending Major Hara, the new commander of 1st Battalion, with his 3rd Company and a machine-gun platoon to Viru Harbor the following night with orders "to settle things."[3] Hara seemed in no great hurry, and he had no exact knowledge of Kennedy's whereabouts, but Japanese activity in Nono Lagoon increased. As a result, Kennedy believed he would soon be under attack from two directions, since two Kure 6th barges were working around the north coast of Vangunu toward Segi, searching for an overdue surveying party that Kennedy and his scouts had killed a month before. He informed KEN that he might have to vacate Segi, but no action was taken. But on 20 June, when Kennedy radioed that the Japanese had landed troops in Nono Lagoon (which turned out to be in error, as they soon departed), Turner acted.[4] Late that night, he loaded two companies of the 4th Raiders under the battalion commander, Lieutenant Colonel Michael S. Currin, on destroyer transports and sent them to Segi. Two companies of the 103rd followed the next night, along with Fitch's engineer, Commander Wilfred L. Painter, and his party to survey the airfield site.[5]

The threat to the airfield site outweighed alerting the Japanese that something was afoot – for Rabaul did take notice. When lookouts at Wickham reported the passage of what was correctly reported as fast transports, Kusaka put Southeast Fleet on alert, ordered Harada to direct submarines to the area, and with a headquarters detachment flew down to Buin. But when reconnaissance planes reported no unusual activity between Gatukai and Rendova, he canceled the alert on 27 June. Kusaka remained convinced that the invasion would not come until late July or early August.[6]

Just three days later the Japanese would be taken by tactical surprise. Less than thirty Zeros would be on the field at Kahili, while the D3AS were at Kavieng; 8th Fleet's destroyers would be scattered from Rabaul to Buka and Buin; and no prior warnings would be sent to the outposts at Wickham Anchorage, Viru Harbor, or Rendova.

THE MOVEMENT INTO NEW GEORGIA

SOPAC's final plans called for Turner to use the attack transports (APAS) *McCawley* (F), *President Jackson, President Hayes,* and *President Adams* and the attack cargo ships (AKAS) *Libra* and *Algorab* to land the 172nd RCT, the 24th Seabees, support units, and supplies at Rendova Harbor on 30 June. Two groups of infantry dubbed the "Barracudas" would go ahead of Turner in fast transports, one to seize the Rendova Harbor beaches, the other the Honiavasa Passage, through which the 43rd would stage to New Georgia Island. Thereafter, landing craft in echelons timed to arrive daily would take in the remainder of the Western Force. Embarking mainly from the Russell Islands, Fort would simultaneously land the 103rd RCT, minus its 3rd Battalion, the rest of the 4th Raider Battalion, and the 47th Seabee Battalion at three points: Oloana Bay on Vangunu, Segi Point, and Viru Harbor (the latter to be taken from the land side by the 4th Raiders). Subsequent echelons would complete the movement of the Eastern Force.[7]

Naval and air forces would strike the Japanese from New Georgia to Bougainville. On the night of 29–30 June, Rear Admiral Merrill with his cruisers would take the minelayers up to the Shortland Islands, mine the southern entrance to Buin, and bombard Ballale, Faisi, and Poporang Islands. On the way up, two of his destroyers would give Vila a brief shelling. In the early daylight hours of the 30th, Bomber Command planned to put twenty-seven B-24s and B-17s over Kahili. Beginning at daybreak, Fighter Command would keep thirty-two fighters over Rendova, and Strike Command would hit both Munda and Vila.

Across the Solomon Sea, where MacArthur's forces were poised to occupy Woodlark and Kiriwina Islands as originally planned, a new operation had been added. During the night of 29–30 June a heavily reinforced battalion from 41st Division would land at Nassau Bay just south of Salamaua. The objectives were: (1) a base for seaborne supply to the Australian 3rd Division, which was pressing the Japanese 51st Division back toward Salamaua, and (2) a staging base for landing craft for the September attack on Lae. But it would also divert Eighth Area Army's attention away from New Georgia. In addition, to support his and Halsey's landings, MacArthur's 5th Air Force would hit Rabaul with a heavy raid on the night of 29–30 June.[8]

THE WESTERN FORCE – RENDOVA

The night of 29–30 June was dark and stormy. Both COMAIRSOLS and 5th Air Force canceled their scheduled missions, and Merrill's task group ran into a solid front that even the Black Cats could not penetrate. The bombardment and minelaying was carried out in driving rain with visibility sometimes dropping to zero.[9] Kolombangara and Buin immediately reported the bombardments, but Kusaka attached no importance to them; he thought them no different than past bombardments. A report that would have gotten his attention, however, was either not received or else mishandled upon receipt: at around 2200 submarine RO-103, fresh from sinking 14,000 tons of American shipping south of San Cristobal, had reported Turner's convoy south of Wickham Anchorage. Instead, the first message to set off alarm bells in Rabaul came in around 0500, reporting the landing at Nassau Bay. At 0650, a message from 8th Combined reported Turner's destroyer screen off Rendova, and as a radio intelligence analyst (ULTRA) at Pearl Harbor noted, "This set the ball rolling." The volume of traffic increased to the point that radio intelligence could not tabulate it, but as the analyst commented, "impression is given that frantic counter-measures are being taken by Jap forces in New Georgia against Allied units."[10] Both Imamura and Kusaka were surprised. Eighth Army senior staff officer, Lieutenant Colonel Imoto Kumao, concluded his log entry by writing, "On this day, battle situations were quite unknown, and everything was in chaos."[11]

Turner's trip up had been uneventful. The Barracuda groups, on the other hand, both ran into difficulties. The Honiavasa Passage group, made up of two companies from the 169th Infantry, landed on Honiavasa Island, on the east side of the passage, and Dume Island, on the west side. No opposition was encountered, but the fast minesweeper *Zane* ran hard aground, and Turner had to send for *Rail* to pull *Zane* off. Their crews would later witness the biggest air battle of the day.[12] The Rendova group, made up of two companies from the 172nd, missed the flashing light marking the narrow Renard Entrance to the harbor. By the time the group found its way back, Turner was unloading. In what army historian John Miller called a "somewhat disorderly" landing, it seems that the regimental commander, Colonel David N. M. Ross, Headquarters Company, 1st Battalion, and the Barracudas went in at roughly the same time.[13]

The fight in Levers Plantation was brief. The Japanese defense force of 140 men – half from the Kure 6th SNLF 1st Rifle Company, half from 2nd Battalion, 229th Infantry – was taken by surprise as the men ate breakfast. Radio communications with Munda had been lost due to low batteries, but at any rate the warning came too late. A week of steady rain had left water standing on the ground, and depressions and drainages ditches filled, so that the troops were sometimes fighting knee-deep in water. Ross with his headquarters company was in the thick of the fight. He took a bullet in the arm, but kept on fighting; his orderly was killed. But the overwhelming American forces quickly pushed the Japanese back into the plantation, and the survivors scattered. The Americans estimated they had killed seventy to seventy-five, while suffering four killed and five wounded. As for the remaining Japanese, American patrols searched out and killed or captured the groups scattered on Rendova, while a few tried to make it to the mainland on makeshift rafts and were picked up by American vessels.[14]

Japanese interference with unloading was ineffective. A few minutes after the first troops landed, visibility cleared somewhat, and the Yokosuka 7th SNLF 12cm guns at Baanga opened fire on the westward destroyers, with one shell hitting the *Gwin*, killing four men and wounding seven. The destroyers returned fire, and while Japanese guns fired intermittently throughout the day, they caused no further damage. Likewise, submarine RO-101, which was west of Rendova, found it impossible to penetrate the screen to attack the transports.[15] At 0900, a false air alert cost Turner an hour as he maneuvered his ships, and two hours later the first air attack did come in, twenty-seven 582nd Zeros from Kahili, with fourteen carrying bombs. Fighter Command's Rendova Patrol, sixteen VMF-121 F4US and sixteen VF-21 F4FS, intercepted southwest of Rendova. The crews of a strike force of marine and navy SBDS and TBFS that was headed for Vila, but that had swung south to avoid a storm over the Slot, witnessed the battle and counted four Zeros going down in flames – the same number the Japanese reported losing, with two pilots killed. The Rendova Patrol lost none.[16]

Despite the delays, the unloading went at a satisfactory pace. The problem was the landing site, complicated by Turner's loading scheme. The weeklong rain had turned the area behind the east landing zone into what the 24th Seabees described as a marsh, with no firm substrata to support roads. After a few trips, equipment and trucks were mired in two to three feet of mud. Turner's loading added to the difficulty. Tons of bulky B Rations, hundreds of barrels of petroleum products, and thousands of barracks bags belonging to personnel were piled on the beaches. Missing from the cargo were the Seabee's heavy bulldozers, the army engineers, adequate medical personnel, and military police to prevent rampant pilfering. The situation only got worse. The rain continued on and off, and the daily convoys dumped even more tonnage into this morass. (Even as Turner completed unloading, the second echelon of LSTs was under way with the heavy 155mm howitzers of the 192nd FA Battalion and the 155mm guns of the 9th Defense Battalion.) Why Turner loaded for an unopposed occupation rather than an offensive action is not clear. But both marine observers were critical. Lieutenant Colonel W. J. McNenny reported that "equipment and stores carried in the New Georgia operation were excessive. It appears the forward base must be considered as an assembly area for launching the assault." Colonel George W. McHenry wrote in his notes, "Believe too much gear for initial landing. Stress what [is] necessary to fight and eat. Bring other up after secure." Griswold agreed, and he included these criticisms in his "Lessons Learned from Joint Operations." But the battle with the mud would continue day after day in Rendova Plantation.[17]

A few minutes before 1500, with all but about 50 tons unloaded, Turner decided it was time to go. Peck, who was on the *McCawley*'s bridge as an observer, recalled Turner as saying, "The Japanese will attack – their planes will come in around three o'clock."[18] He was off by about forty-five minutes. Just after 1545, as his convoy stood down Blanche Channel in two columns and the destroyers in a circular screen, the 5th Air Attack Force's strike from Rabaul came in. Lieutenant Commander Nakamura Genzō led the twenty-six 702nd and 705th G4Ms, and Lieutenant Mukai Ichirō led the escort of twenty-four 251st Zeros.

Nakamura brought his torpedo-armed G4Ms in over New Georgia in a perfect V of Vs formation, circled over Roviana Island, and, dropping as low as 50 feet over the water, bore in on the convoy from the port side. A shift change was in progress for the Rendova Patrol, and about forty-eight marine and navy fighters were on hand to intercept. Major Gregory J. Weissenburger's VMF-213 went after the Zeros and shot down ten, including Group Leader Mukai, who was one of eight 251st pilots killed that day. VMF-221's F4Us and VF-21's F4Fs went after Nakamura's bombers. "Go get 'em, boys," came over the radio from Vega (Rendova Fighter Control) and, as VMF-221 reported, "Twenty seven [sic] Bettys in a Vee of Vees began to catch hell."[19] Nakamura's bombers, with the swarm of American fighters attacking them, flashed by *Zane* and *Rail*, and the crews marveled at the bravery of the fighter pilots who continued to press home their attacks through the heavy antiaircraft fire thrown up by the ships. Nineteen G4Ms went down; most but not all were victims of the fighters. A 702nd tail gunner told his captors that, as his G4M was making its run on a ship at an altitude of 60 feet, he was exchanging fire with an attacking Corsair. About 3,000 yards from the ship, a direct hit from antiaircraft fire sent his plane plowing into the sea. He credited his survival to the impact throwing him clear.[20]

For this expenditure in aircraft, the Japanese scored one hit. A torpedo struck the *McCawley* amidships on the port side, as it began an emergency 90° turn to the right, and blasted a truck-size hole in the engine room. Fifteen seamen were killed. With the *McCawley* dead in the water, Turner and his party transferred to a destroyer. Rear Admiral Theodore Wilkinson, slated to take command of the amphibious force when Turner returned to Pearl Harbor, stayed behind to take charge of the salvage operation.[21] At 1720, shortly after Turner left to rejoin the convoy, the final Japanese air attack came in. Made up of twenty-one Zeros and nine D3AS in one group and thirteen F1MS in another, the attack was as confused as it was improvised.[22] The Zeros turned away from the intercepting F4US and P-40S, and the D3AS scored no hits but lost one plane. On the other hand, the American fighters shredded the seaplanes, shooting down seven out of the thirteen.[23]

At the end of the day, COMAIRSOLS had destroyed one-quarter of 1st Base Air Force's strength and struck the 938th a serious blow. The price paid was fourteen fighters downed in combat, with ten of the pilots rescued, and three more lost to operational causes, with one pilot killed.[24] *McCawley,* under tow by *Libra,* was settling aft fast and was beyond saving, but Wilkinson kept at it. At 2022, in a case of mistaken identity, the Rendova PT boats sent *McCawley* to the bottom with two torpedoes and settled the issue. The fleet tug *Pawnee,* which was taking the tow from *Libra,* escaped being hit by a hair's breadth.[25]

In the aftermath of the 30 June battles, Kusaka ordered his 21st Air Flotilla at Saipan to send down detachments from the 253rd and 751st, appealed to Combined Fleet for reinforcements in addition to *Ryūhō's* bombers due to arrive on 2 July, and persuaded Imamura to commit the 6th Air Division. But for the following day, 1 July, he could mount only one feeble strike of six D3AS with thirty-four Zeros from Kahili. These attempted to hit LCIS unloading the 3rd Battalion, 103rd Infantry, at Poko Plantation on the west coast of Rendova. But twenty P-40S and F4FS broke up the attack in a battle that saw three D3AS, five Zeros, and five P-40S go down. No bombs hit the landing area. COMAIRSOLS, on the other hand, was able to put twenty-seven B-24S and B-17S, with an escort of seventy-two fighters, over Kahili, as well as keep the Rendova Patrol in the air.[26]

On 2 July, however, the combined army/navy strike was ready, and at Rabaul, Major Endō Misao led off his eighteen 14th Sentai Ki-21 bombers with an escort of twenty-three Ki-43 "Oscars" and Ki-61 "Tonys"; twenty-nine Zeros joined up over Kahili. At 1330, Endō's bombers came in from the east under low cloud cover. There was no opposition in the air and no warning on the ground. Mitscher had recalled the Rendova Patrol due to bad weather, and the portable radar was down (the long range SCR-270-D sat on the beach, still crated). Endō's bombers hit the congested area at the head of the harbor, killing or wounding around 200 men, with casualties especially heavy in the 2nd Battalion, 172nd, the 24th Seabees, the 9th Defense Battalion, and staff officers of the various headquarters. A VMF-213 pilot, who had been picked up after his F4U suffered engine failure, was talking with a marine 40mm gun crew when he looked up, saw the bombs dropping, and dove into a mud hole. When it was over, he found the entire gun crew killed; the boy to whom he had just given a cigarette had been decapitated.[27] To make the situation worse, the hospital was not in operation, so only emergency medical treatment could be given to the wounded before loading them on a LST for Guadalcanal. (The dead were buried that night in Rendova Lagoon from the upper deck of a LST.) Much personal baggage and supplies still on the beach were destroyed, but the most serious long-term losses were three Seabee bulldozers, medical supplies and equipment, and a quantity of scarce powder for the Marine 155s.[28]

Fighter Command would have to wait until 4 July to exact retribution. The usual navigational difficulties that plagued the Army Air Service in the Southeast Area had cropped up; planes landed at scattered airfields, and three 68th Sentai Ki-61s went missing. It took a day to regroup at Rabaul.[29] Only Zeros were sent out on 3 July, and they were intercepted northwest of Rendova.[30] On 4 July, however, Endō led a second army/navy strike made up of seventeen bombers, seventeen Ki-43s, and forty-nine Zeros. The target was not Rendova but the Roviana Island area, where the Americans were now active. Shortly after Endō left Buin, the Vella Lavella coast watcher called in the warning. Then, as Endō neared Kolombangara, he had to circle for a time because nearly forty SBDs and TBFs were attacking Munda. The early warning and the delay gave the thirty-two navy F4Fs time to get the altitude for a high-side run on the bombers. When the Strike Command aircraft had left the area, Endō made for Roviana Island, but seeing nothing but jungle, he diverted to attack Rendova Harbor. But this would not be a repeat of the 2 July raid. Some of the navy F4Fs took on the fighters while some hit the bomber formation; the 9th Defense Battalion and the twenty or more LCIs in the harbor threw up intense antiaircraft fire. In all, six of Endō's bombers went down, two were damaged but made it to an airfield, and three Ki-43s and one 251st Zero were lost with their pilots. The F4Fs suffered no losses, while at Rendova, five men were killed and fourteen wounded, and two LCIs suffered slight damage.[31]

The 4 July raid marked the end of the air battle attending the Rendova landing. Imamura terminated joint air operations, noting both the need to use the 6th Air Division in the Salamaua area and the arrival of Kusaka's own air reinforcements. For his part, Kusaka was already shifting his targeting to the American landings east of Munda and Rice Anchorage in Kula Gulf. (And we might add, he was rebuilding 1st Base Air Force, with the reinforcements arriving from Carrier Division 2, 12th Air Fleet, and his own 21st Air Flotilla on Saipan. By mid-July, his air strength was up to around 230 aircraft.)[32]

Neither 8th Fleet nor Eighth Area Army was able to interfere at Rendova. Samejima made two attempts that achieved nothing; at Eighth Area Army and Kongō Hill there were continuous discussions regarding a counter-landing, but in the end these amounted to nothing. We will take them up in order.

The landing caught the Reinforcement Force (Destroyer Squadron 3, Rear Admiral Akiyama Teruo) in the midst of the scheduled late June–early July transports. In fact, a run made on the night of 29–30 June turned back to Buin, supposedly because of an air attack, but most likely due to the bombardment Merrill's destroyers carried out at Vila. On 30 June, these four destroyers were at Buin, two more were at Buka, and three others along with Akiyama's flagship, the new 3,000-ton *Niizuki*, were at Rabaul. Samejima, nonetheless, ordered Akiyama to rendezvous with the Bougainville destroyers and attack shipping at Rendova and enemy troops south of the harbor, but not the harbor itself – an order that reflected the Japanese confusion as to the actual situation. In any case, bad weather prevented the rendezvous, and while Akiyama's destroyers arrived off Rendova in two groups at different times, neither saw anything and both returned. On the night of 2 July, Samejima tried again. The plan was for the old *Yūbari*, with two destroyers, to operate south of the Treasuries to act as a diversion, while Akiyama with six destroyers would destroy enemy shipping and shell the harbor. The weather was bad in the afternoon and grew worse as night fell. A PB4Y had spotted the diversion force, but two COMAIRSOLS strike forces, one of PB4Ys and

the other of B-25s, failed to locate the Japanese. The weather at Guadalcanal soon grounded the armed and ready third strike force of SBDs and
TBFs. In the meantime, Akiyama closed the southern tip of Rendova,
circled the island, and opened fire at some point west of the harbor. This
sortie is memorable for three reasons: first, no one – American or Japanese – seemed to know where the shells hit; second, a VP 54 Black Cat
latched on to Akiyama west of Rendova and continually harassed him
on his run around the island, dropping a bomb at intervals; and third,
the PT-boats, alerted by the Black Cat and homing in on the flashes of
gunfire, fought a wild ten-minute action with the destroyers, in which
two of the boats ran aground. Akiyama headed home. Next night, Ainsworth and his task group lay in wait off the west coast of Rendova, but
Akiyama did not show. He was in fact preparing to resume the transport
runs, the first of which was scheduled for the night of 4–5 July – the same
night, as it turned out, that Turner would land the Northern Landing
Force at Rice Anchorage.[33]

While New Georgia Occupation Force (NGOF) thought the Japanese would be capable of landing a substantial force by 3 July and arranged defenses accordingly,[34] Eighth Area Army and Southeast Fleet
had agreed that a counter-landing was not possible. Even if Imamura had
been willing to commit the troops, the air and naval forces required were
simply not available. For Sasaki, who had argued for the counter-landing,
this was extremely frustrating; the shelling of the airfield by the Marine
155s that began that day fueled his desperation. At Kongō Hill there were
some tense moments. At one point, around midnight on 3 July, Sasaki
proposed violating orders to simply defend Munda and make a counter-
landing using Tomonari's 13th Infantry and Ōta's barges. He thought it
would be possible to mix in with the American landing craft that were
making roundtrips to the mainland through Honiavasa Passage; even if
half of his force perished, the attack would be worth it. Ōta objected on
the grounds that the barges would be needed for the transports scheduled for 4 and 5 July, and Sasaki, "visibly upset," adjourned the meeting
and left the room. Ōta went after him and brought him back, agreeing to
work on the plans (these were duly submitted and immediately squashed
at Rabaul). Talk of a counter-landing ended. Already there had been
clashes with American patrols east of Munda, and on the night of 4–5

July American troops landed at Rice Anchorage. Sasaki, who had assumed command of all forces on 2 July, was facing two fronts.[35]

THE EASTERN FORCE – WICKHAM ANCHORAGE, VIRU HARBOR, SEGI POINT

Rear Admiral Fort, who commanded the Eastern Force, was charged with making three separate landings on 30 June. Segi, of course, was already occupied, but Wickham Anchorage and Viru Harbor resulted in sharp engagements. As with Rendova, there is the problem of sources. Fort, like Turner, filed no action report.[36]

Oloana Bay and Wickham Anchorage

A night landing on a 500-yard strip of beach in bad weather, with low clouds, rain, high winds, and heavy seas, created problems. Fort, who was commanding in person, tried to postpone the landing until dawn, but communications failed. The slow LCIs carrying Lieutenant Colonel Lester E. Brown's 2nd Battalion, 103rd Infantry, and a section of the 20th Seabees, had no difficulty in finding the well-marked beach. But the destroyer transports carrying two companies of the 4th Raiders, which were to have landed first, scattered the marines all over the area in a series of mishaps that left six Higgins boats wrecked in the heavy surf and one platoon stranded on a reef 7 miles west of the landing point. But there were no casualties.[37]

The beach party greeted Brown with fresh intelligence. Rather than being concentrated at Vura Village just inland from the entrance to the anchorage, only a small Japanese force was there; the main force was a short distance north at Kearuku Village. Brown detached one company of the 2nd Battalion, with an attached heavy mortar section, to deal with Vura. Then, with the rest of his battalion and the Raiders (all but the platoon that landed 7 miles west had caught up), he set out for Kearuku Village at 0705 along a trail Kennedy's scouts had cut. A driving rain, mud, thick brush, and two streams swollen with water up to the men's shoulders slowed the march.

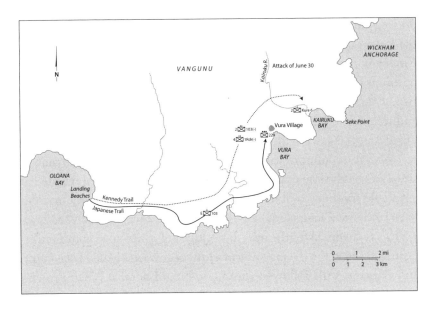

Map 6.2. Wickham Anchorage.

That morning, around 1000, Sasaki had radioed the Wickham Occupation Force – the 2nd Rifle Company, Kure 6th (Lieutenant Yamamoto Kazuo), and one platoon from the 229th – to withdraw around the northern coast of New Georgia. If Yamamoto received the message, and there is no evidence that he did, he was in no position to begin an immediate withdrawal. His barges, along with a substantial number of troops, were scattered in Marovo Lagoon, and preparations would take time. It is also unlikely that he was aware of the American landing at Oloana Bay; otherwise, he would have concentrated his forces. Instead, the naval troops he had on hand were in the bivouac on the south bank of the Kairuku River; the weapons section, made up of a 37mm gun and mortars, was at Seke Point, which overlooked Kairuku Bay from the north; and the army platoon was just south at Vuru.[38]

Brown's attack from the north side of the Kairuku started shortly before 1400. The Japanese met it with rifle and machine-gun fire. Most of the casualties resulted from this fight, twelve marines and ten soldiers killed and many more wounded. By nightfall, the Japanese had been pressed back, and Brown took up a defensive position at the mouth of the Kairuku River, where there was a small beach. In the meantime, E Company had scattered the Japanese at Vura Village and had taken up positions on the beach at the mouth of the Vura River. After midnight, two or three unsuspecting Japanese barges approached Kairuku beach and were met by a hail of machine-gun fire. How many Japanese were killed is uncertain, but after that, the rest of the night was quiet.

With the coming of daylight, Brown was uncertain as to the general situation, but he knew that fire was coming from Seke Point. Unable to get an observation point to direct fire from an artillery battery that had been landed at Oloana Bay, he called for air and naval support. This support was scheduled for the next day, 2 July, but a mix-up in communications delayed it. On the morning of 3 July, destroyers shelled Seke Point, and eighteen SBDs followed with 1,000-pound bombs. When Brown's troops went in, they killed seven dazed Japanese and captured another.[39]

This ended the battle. Raiders searched Gatukai Island, but the Japanese lookouts were gone. In the meantime, 2nd Battalion, 103rd, sent out patrols, but the only contact they made with enemy forces was on 11 July, when an LCT took a reinforced platoon up the coast to Batuna Mission to establish an observation post. The Americans found three barges hidden in the river and sank one in which the Japanese attempted to escape, killing ten men and capturing one. On 19 July, the battalion was withdrawn and sent to join in the fight for Munda.[40]

Viru Harbor

Based on his loading order of 13 June, Turner's original plan for the capture of Viru Harbor appears to be as follows. A coastal transport (APc) would take a detachment from one of the 4th Raider companies and land them at Nono on 29 June. From there, presumably, they would march overland and on the morning of 30 June seize the 100-foot cliffs that formed the entrance to Viru Harbor. At the same time, two destroyer transports would arrive with the rest of the company and a company from the 103rd to complete the capture of the harbor.

The preemptive landing at Segi caused a change in plans. On 25 June, Currin received orders from Fort to send one company of raiders by rubber boat up to the Choi River at the western end of Nono Lagoon on the morning of 28 June, and from there the raiders would go overland and attack the Japanese bivouacs, a small one (Tombe) on the east side of the harbor and the larger one (Tetemara) on the west side. Waiting off the harbor's entrance would be the destroyer transports with the occupation force of the 103rd company and support units. After making his own reconnaissance of the mouth of the Choi River and finding it unsuitable for landing, Currin requested a change in plans. He proposed, and Fort approved, that he take both companies, leave Segi on 27 June, land at a village just west of Nono, and from there go overland to Viru harbor. An estimate of enemy troop strength provided to Currin – at least 30 known to approximately 100 unconfirmed at Tetemara and an unknown number at Tombe – showed American intelligence to have been completely unaware of Hara's presence.

The trip by rubber boat was uneventful, and at dawn the next morning, 28 June, Currin set out by land. Immediately, the raiders found themselves in a mangrove swamp. By 1030, Currin realized that he would not make it by 30 June, and with no working radio, sent two of Kennedy's scouts back to Segi to notify Fort that he would be a day late. But this message did not reach Fort until the 103rd was underway for Viru Harbor on 30 June. On 29 June, the raiders suffered their first casualties when a strong Japanese patrol attacked the rear guard. In the fight that followed, five raiders were killed and one wounded; the Japanese left behind eighteen dead.

That night, as Merrill and Turner were moving northwest, the raiders bivouacked in the rain near the headwaters of the Choi River. The next morning, Currin split his forces. Captain Anthony Walker with two platoons left to attack Tombe; Currin with the rest, set out to circle west of the harbor, cross the Mango River, and attack Tetemara from the southwest. Currin's force had the most difficulty. The Mango River was deep – over the heads of the tallest men in places – but the raiders crossed it by forming a human chain, only to face an all but impassable swamp, with water knee-deep or higher, and the inevitable mud. Darkness overtook the struggling men, so that one could not see the one just in front of him, which threatened a further delay. But the scouts solved the problem by bringing "tree light," chunks of decaying, phosphorescent bark that

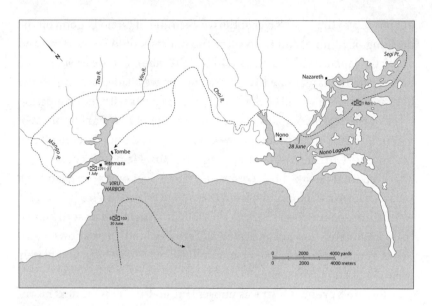

Map 6.3. Viru Harbor.

gave off a luminous glow. With these on their packs, the raiders were able
to reach high ground, where they could bivouac for the night and be in
position to attack the next day.[41]

Meanwhile, at Viru Harbor, Commander Stanley Leith arrived off
the entrance with three destroyer transports at 0530 on 30 June, carrying
B Company, 103rd, and support units. At this point, Leith knew only that
Currin had been delayed. After failing to make radio contact with Currin, Leith then took his ships in closer but came under fire from the Yokosuka 7th's old English-made 8cm gun emplaced on the west side of the
harbor entrance. The destroyers returned fire, but, unable to locate the
gun, moved out of range and cruised about until orders came from Fort
to unload the infantry company at Segi, from where it could make its
way overland. At Segi, the air liaison officer requested an air strike on the
gun, which was approved by Mulcahy and sent on to COMAIRSOLS.[42]

At the same time, Hara received orders from Sasaki to withdraw
overland to Munda. Other than instructing his force to draw rations for
ten days, nothing is known about his plans and preparations for with-

drawal. In any event, the Japanese were still there when the raiders attacked on 1 July.[43]

Currin's raiders began their approach at 0745. An hour later, they heard firing from the east shore, which was correctly thought to be Walker attacking Tombe. At 0900, seventeen SBDS put 1,000-pound bombs on the west side of the harbor. The gun was not hit, but the crew deserted it and headed into the jungle. Fortunately for the raiders, who knew nothing of the scheduled attack, they were still out of range when they saw the planes diving. An hour later, the Japanese opened fire on Currin's point, and at 1030 the Raiders suffered their first casualty. Currin pushed on, and a few minutes after 1100 encountered heavy machine-gun fire on both flanks. At roughly the same time, three LCTS, which made up Fort's second echelon and carried the 20th Seabees' heavy equipment and army antiaircraft guns, nosed into the harbor. Their arrival was the result of another communications mishap. The Seabees heard gunfire on the west shore but found that the east shore had been cleared – Walker's raiders had made short work of the Tombe outpost, killing thirteen, without suffering a single casualty. On the western shore, however, the fight continued. Each machine-gun position had to be destroyed, and it was here that the Raiders suffered most of their casualties. At 1600, Currin launched his final attack, and thirty minutes later Tetemara was occupied. Hara and 160 men – at least this is the number he brought to the Kure 6th Farm on 19 July – slipped into the jungle. The raiders listed their losses as 8 men killed and 15 wounded and gave the Japanese losses as 48 killed.[44]

The raiders returned to Guadalcanal on 10 July and were joined two days later by the two companies from Wickham. Their stay would be short. On the night of 17 July, 4th Raider Battalion was bound for Enogai in four APDS (high speed transports) to take part in the scheduled attack on Bairoko Harbor.

Segi Point

At 1010 on 30 June, the 47th Seabees began landing from a LST, and by 1300 their bulldozers were at work in Markham's plantation. Lights were set up, and the work continued around the clock. Although Japanese reconnaissance planes reported the construction on 6 July, no raid came in until the night of 13 July, when bombers hit the runway and blew up the dynamite dump. The raids continued, forcing the night work to be shut down. By that time, however, the strip was far enough along that fighters were already using it for emergency landings. But the runway was slippery due to the fine clay soil and soft coral mixed with clay that the Seabees had to use, which resulted in accidents. In August, the Seabees surfaced the runway with coral dredged from the bay and created an all-weather strip. Another problem was the short runway length of 3,300 feet, which sorely tried the brakes on the New Zealand P-40Es landing there. In August, the Seabees were able to add an additional 200 feet. Base development of roads, storage, and housing went on apace.[45]

The Eastern Landings Assessed

The effect of the eastern landings on the battle for New Georgia was mixed. On the debit side of the ledger, neither Wickham Anchorage nor Viru proved to be of any use. Moreover, the unexpected resistance, as Turner called it, deprived him of the 4th Raiders for the landing at Rice Anchorage and delayed the movement of the 2nd Battalion, 103rd, to Munda. On the asset side, Segi proved valuable, not just as an emergency strip but as a permanent fighter base. By late July, P-39s and P-40s were basing at Segi. An operations officer with a small staff (Air Command, Segi) controlled tactical operations under orders from NGOF. Fighters on alert were able to intercept Japanese aircraft picked up by radar as they approached Munda/Rendova, a significant advance for Fighter Command, when the departure of the navy F4Fs in August reduced its strength. (At its operational peak, during the air battle of Bougainville, Segi based three squadrons of navy F6Fs.)[46]

THE NORTHERN LANDING FORCE – RICE ANCHORAGE

With Ainsworth's task group delivering a preliminary bombardment of Vila and Bairoko Harbor, Turner's original plan called for Colonel Harry B. Liversedge, Commander, 1st Marine Raider Regiment, to take his 1st

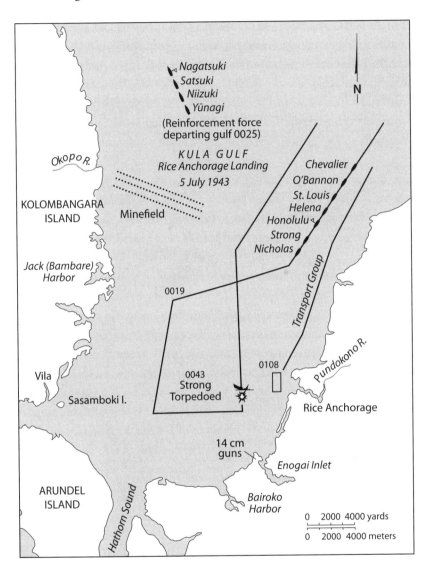

Map 6.4. Rice Anchorage.

and 4th Battalions, with 3rd Battalion, 148th Infantry, 37th Division, and land at Rice Anchorage on the night of 3–4 July. But delays in the previous landings forced last-minute changes in both force composition and timing. In place of the 4th Raiders, which was tied up at Wickham Anchorage and Viru Harbor, Turner substituted the 3rd Battalion, 145th Infantry, also from the 37th Division. Then the 43rd's difficulty in moving troops from Rendova to the mainland caused him to delay the landing. He had counted on the Japanese being unable to send reinforcements north because of having to defend Munda. By 3 July, however, Hester reported that he had found a good beach and the troops were landing. Turner then gave the go-ahead for the night of 4–5 July. As we have noted, this was the same night that Samejima planned his reinforcement run, but by 4 July, Turner had some indication of the run from CINCPAC (ULTRA). He sent the message on to Ainsworth and added, "This may give you a real target."[47]

Ainsworth's task group led the landing force up the Slot; Leith followed with the transport group – seven destroyer transports, two fast minesweepers, two destroyers, and two escort destroyers – carrying 2,600 troops. The sea was calm with no swells, the sky was overcast with occasional showers, and surface visibility was 6,000 yards maximum. Ainsworth entered the gulf around midnight with his ships in column: *Nicholas* and *Strong* in the van, *Honolulu*, *Helena*, and *St. Louis* in the center, and *O'Bannon* and *Chevalier* in the rear. His plan differed from his earlier bombardments in two respects. First, on his initial approach he would have to keep to the New Georgia side of the gulf in order to avoid the minefield laid back in May, turn west once he was clear to close the range, then back south to shell Vila, then east to shell Bairoko, and then back north to exit the gulf. The track chart described a rough rectangle at the bottom of the gulf. The second difference was that the two van destroyers would not shell Vila but concentrate solely on a search for any Japanese ships that might be present.[48]

Nonetheless, they failed to detect the Japanese. With massive Kolombangara looming behind him, Captain Kanaoka Kunizo with four destroyers – *Nagatsuki*, *Satsuki*, *Niizuki*, and *Yūnagi* – was headed south to Vila with 1,300 men and fifteen barge-loads of supplies. His only covering force was submarine *I-38*, which Kusaka had sent to interfere with American attempts against the reinforcement runs.[49]

The American bombardment proceeded as planned, and *Nicholas* and *Strong* had just completed their turns due north when around 0043 *Strong's* gunnery officer "saw a thin phosphorescent wake about 3,000 yards in length strike the port side amidships." The torpedo almost cut the destroyer in two. Ainsworth ordered *Chevalier* and *O'Bannon* to render aid while he cleared the gulf as quickly as possible, and then stood toward Kolombangara to make a radar sweep. But Kanaoka's destroyers were headed back up the Slot. By their account, the Japanese detected Ainsworth at 0015, and ten minutes later, at a range of 16 kilometers (10 miles), fired fourteen torpedoes before retiring. Kanaoka claimed hits on a cruiser and a destroyer. Some have suggested a submarine was responsible; *I-38* did report firing a single torpedo at a destroyer but missing, but this was probably later, at a target in the transport group. At 0249, the *Radford* dropped a full pattern of depth charges on a submarine contact, and then again at 0407, after having picked up prop noises close by. For his part, Ainsworth was certain that it had been a submarine strike, despite the transport group later reporting that they had detected Kanaoka. But then Ainsworth was prone to ignore his destroyers' reports when they differed from his own.[50]

Off Enogai Inlet, *Strong* was settling fast. *Chevalier* and *O'Bannon* carried out the rescue while engaged in a gun duel with the Enogai batteries (Ainsworth had wanted to target these, but Turner insisted they were not there). By 0122, *Chevalier* had 239 men on board out of *Strong's* complement of 325, when its commander decided it was time to go. His ship had suffered considerable damage. Ramming *Strong* to keep it from capsizing had ripped a ten-foot gash in the bow; a near miss from the Enogai guns had opened seams aft; and a jammed shell had exploded, wrecking the No. 3 gun mount. *Chevalier* suffered more. As it was pulling away from *Strong*, which immediately broke in two and sank, three of *Strong's* depth charges exploded under the *Chevalier*, lifted it out of the water, and caused flooding forward.[51]

In the meantime, the transport group had arrived off Rice Anchorage, where a Raider team and coast watcher Corrigan with his natives waited. The Pundokono River, 50 to 70 yards wide, depending on the rains, emptied into the anchorage, and the American plan was to land 200 yards upstream on the south side of the river. Despite the rain, darkness, and intermittent shelling from the Enogai guns, the landing went smoothly enough until the very last. Fearing an air attack, Turner had given orders for the transport group to be clear of the gulf by 0700. (Leith was long gone before the Japanese strike came in at 1300.)[52] At 0600, therefore, Liversedge gave the order to leave, and the remaining transports left hurriedly, with all but a small percentage of the supplies unloaded. But in the cargo still on board was the navy TCS radio that Liversedge had specifically requested because of its long range; this lapse would affect communications later. A second mishap caused by the quick departure was that 200 to 300 men of the 3rd Battalion, 148th, were left in a dozen landing craft milling around in the open sea with the coxswains confused as to the landing area. Since the Enogai gun crews could see them clearly, incoming shells came closer and closer. Captain Charles A. Henne took charge and landed the men about 3,000 yards north of Rice Anchorage. (Henne caught up with the main body on 7 July).[53] A final mishap was that some of *Strong*'s survivors were left in the water. When *Chevalier* left the gulf, it notified the transport destroyers that men were still in the water and requested they be picked up. Some were, but because no thorough search was made, some men were left in the water.[54]

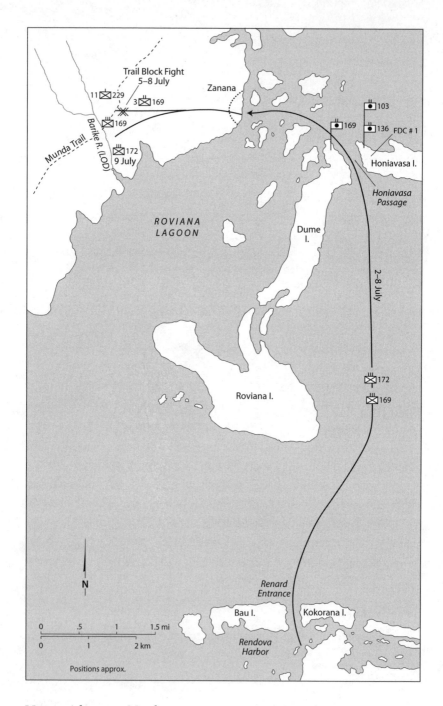

Map 7.1. Advance on Munda.

SEVEN

The First Battle for Munda

COLONEL GEORGE W. MCHENRY MOVED WITH THE TROOPS TO the Barike River on 8 July, and on the thirteenth, he summed up the situation as he saw it in his personal diary:

> Believe advance will bog down due to loss of momentum and drive and that fresh troops will have to be thrown in to keep moving toward Munda. Looks like a week's job at the present rate and believe troops will be exhausted before then. They need a few "first down[s]" to bolster their spirits. Night harassing tactics are taking a lot out of them. They do not regain their nerves until about 0900. Maybe some limited night movement would help and restore confidence. Seems pretty low and haggard. They probably scare each other with their haggard look and tired eyes. Most all losing weight and are tired.[1]

THE 43RD'S OFFENSIVE

The original plan for the quick capture of Munda Field – the 169th and the 172nd Infantry jumping off from the Barike River on 7 July and advancing from the east, and the 3rd Battalion, 103rd Infantry, landing on the west coast at Munda on 9 July – quickly fell by the wayside. On 7 July, Hester postponed the start date to 9 July and canceled the hook around to Munda. On that same day, while the 172nd was in place on the lower Barike, the 169th still had a battalion on Rendova, while its lead battalion on New Georgia, the 3rd (Major William A. Stebbins), lost six men killed and thirty wounded in a failed attempt to reduce a Japanese trail block east of the Barike.[2] For the New Georgia Occupation Force (NGOF), it was a serious logistical failure. Colonel McHenry observed:

"Whole offense set back about two days – can be attributed to amount of gear carried and conditions of roads and also reorganization of staffs due to casualties [from Endō's 2 July air raid]."[3] To this should be added that both Hester's NGOF and Wing's 43rd Division were initially under-staffed. Hester took the senior 43rd staff officers; Wing was left with their assistants. To move two regiments and support units from the morass of mud at Rendova, through the narrow channel of Roviana Lagoon to the Zanana landing zone, and then 3,000 yards through rain forest and mangrove swamps to the Barike, would have required planning of the first order.

But the 43rd's slow and confused movement had served Sasaki well. On the day of the landing, 30 June, he ordered Colonel Tomonari to assume command over all forces at Vila and to begin moving Kojima's 3rd Battalion, 229th, to New Georgia. As Sasaki read the situation at this point, the Americans would attack the airfield directly, using Hopei Island for their artillery, Roviana Island as the staging area, and am-phibious tanks for the assault. Consequently, he moved more 8cm dual-purpose guns and 13mm antiaircraft machine guns to cover the beaches; he also had Hirata's 2nd Battalion (Major Satō) digging antitank ditches along the beach, with orders to destroy the enemy tanks at the water's edge. But on 2 July, when patrols sent east to Zanana reported American activity there, Sasaki shifted his effort to the eastern defense line that ran north from Ilangana Point. Satō's battalion occupied the southern sec-tor that was anchored on Roviana Lagoon and began clearing fields of fire and setting up obstacles forward of the line. By 4 July, Kojima's 11th Company (Lieutenant Yamamoto Yoshio) had arrived and set a block encountered by the 169th. The rest of the battalion followed and was in the line on Satō's left by 6 July.[4]

On 9 July, Wing's advance began. At 0500, Brigadier General Harold R. Barker's three battalions of artillery, emplaced on both shores of the Honiavasa Passage, and the army and marine 155s on Rendova opened fire. Starting at Lambete Plantation and moving back toward the depar-ture line, the artillery put several thousand rounds of 105mm and 155mm high explosives on the area.[5] A few minutes after the artillery opened up, Captain T. J. Ryan in *Farenholt* led *Buchanan*, *McCalla*, and *Ralph Talbot* onto the firing track in Blanche Channel and began the naval bombardment, putting over 2,000 5-inch shells on Munda. The Japanese recorded that the area was lit up as if it were daytime. On the east bank of the Barike, Wing had three battalions abreast: Major William H. Naylor's 1st Battalion, 172nd Infantry, on the left; Major James M. Devine's 3rd Battalion, 172nd, in the center; and Major Joseph E. Zimmer's 1st Battalion, 169th, on the right. Stebbins's 3rd Battalion was on Zimmer's right but to the rear. Patrols from 1st Commando Fiji Guerrillas (Major Charles W. H. Tripp)[6] were out in front across the river. H hour, 0630, came and went, but for unknown reasons no troops moved. At 0830, Strike Command, which had been flying missions daily, hit all three objectives – Munda, Enogai, and Bairoko Harbor – with 107 SBDs and TBFs dropping 79 tons of bombs.[7]

At 0900, the 172nd finally began fording the chest-high Barike, then advanced in columns of companies, stopping every 200 yards for a five-minute break. No enemy opposition was encountered, only the difficult terrain, and by 1400, when the 172nd stopped to dig in for the night, it had advanced 1,100 yards (the Japanese defense line was still 1,000 yards distant). But the 169th had made no progress. Machine-gun fire stopped 1st Battalion, and 3rd Battalion had not moved. The 3rd Battalion was shaken and demoralized. The night before, Yamamoto's 11th Company, which had been harassing 3rd Battalion at night from the time it had arrived, was back the moment the bright quarter moon set. "What a hell last night was," Robert E. Casko of H Company wrote. "I didn't get a bit of sleep. Jap harassing troops filtered into our area, tossed hand grenades, yelled and fired all night."[8] In his unit, one man was killed, another shot, and a third got war neurosis. The next day, 10 July, Wing relieved Stebbins and replaced him with Colonel Frederick G. Reincke.

On 10 July, little progress was made. The 172nd, now far out ahead, moved a few hundred yards, but again the 169th, with Lieutenant Colonel John B. Fowler's 2nd Battalion replacing the 3rd behind Zimmer, made slow progress. After advancing 500 yards, Zimmer's 1st Battalion ran into a block set by Kojima's 9th Company and was stopped by heavy machine-gun fire. Zimmer pulled back, and Barker put a heavy artillery concentration on the Japanese, but the subsequent attack failed. That night Yamamoto's troops were back in force. There were more casualties – many self-inflicted as men shot and stabbed wildly in the night – and the war neurosis cases increased. The next day, 11 July, Wing relieved the 169th's commander, Colonel John D. Eason, and replaced him with Colonel Temple G. Holland from the 145th Infantry. Holland brought his own staff, and so the change at the top was complete. That night, Yamamoto harassed the 169th for the last time.

By 10 July, supply had become a serious problem. Building any type of road in the 172nd's sector was difficult because of the terrain, and the 118th Engineers had to follow the high ground northwest to the upper Barike on a single-lane jeep trail. Their equipment – three little Caterpillar D-4 bulldozers – was woefully inadequate. Where possible, they sidebenched the low ridges with a bulldozer and made a cut when this was impossible; the low areas had to be corduroyed. By 10 July, the jeep trail was approaching the Barike River, but having to swing so far northwest brought an additional problem – the engineers would have to bridge both forks of the Barike, which took until 14 July. A considerable number of infantrymen had to be used to carry supplies in and casualties out over a 1,000-yard trail knee-deep in mud.[9]

To solve the immediate supply problem, on 10 July, Hester decided to swing the 172nd southwest to occupy Laiana Beach, about 500 yards east of the main Japanese defense line at Ilangana. This move would considerably reduce his supply line. To hold the new beachhead, he planned to use Lieutenant Colonel James B. Wells's 3rd Battalion, 103rd Infantry, then at Poko Plantation on Rendova's west coast. The 9th Defense Battalion's eight M3 Stuart light tanks under Captain Robert S. Blake were also to land; anxious to get the tanks into action, Hester had landed three at Zanana, where the terrain was too soft to support them. The landing at Laiana Beach was scheduled for 13 July, while Ross was to begin his advance on 11 July.

The operation went badly at first. The 172nd brushed up against the Japanese "Front Angle" – forward defenses constructed by Kojima's 3rd Battalion to cover the junction of the Munda-Laiana Trail – and the 169th, being reorganized by Colonel Holland, had not yet caught up. After a heavy bombardment of the Lambete-Munda area by the Rendova 155s, which killed or wounded three dozen Japanese and destroyed two heavy antiaircraft guns, Ross got underway at 0900 with his 1st and 3rd Battalions, leaving 2nd Battalion (Major John F. Carrigan) to cover his rear until the 169th caught up. Two parties of Tongans from 1st Commando[10] under their New Zealand commanders were out in front. One under Sergeant Brian W. Ensor had left to scout Laiana the previous afternoon; the other under Lieutenant Ben Masefield had left at 0730 that morning to scout ahead of Ross. An hour later, a single machine gun stopped the advance for two hours while the leading battalion withdrew and waited until the artillery took it out. When the troops were again underway, they came under heavy machine-gun and mortar fire from the high ground to their right, which quickly killed or wounded about twenty men. Again, the troops withdrew and requested artillery fire. When it came in, Masefield and the Tongans were caught near the Japanese lines; Masefield was killed and two of the Tongans were wounded. During the bombardment, Ensor returned to report that his patrol had had to shoot its way out of a Japanese ambush at Laiana. The 172nd made no further progress that day.

For the next day, 12 July, Wing ordered the 169th, which had arrived at the front, to clear the Japanese positions at the trail junction, while the 172nd resumed its march to Laiana. Rear Admiral Merrill, who had known that he would be called on once the 43rd hit the Japanese defense line, would provide a heavy naval bombardment; COMAIRSOLS would make the usual strike, and Barker's artillery would be ready to fire on call.

Merrill led the way in the early morning darkness with his task group – four light cruisers in the main firing section, two destroyers under Ryan in the forward firing section, and eight destroyers in the antisubmarine screen. His formation reflected the restrictions Turner and Hester had put on him. To prevent casualties among the ground troops, they wanted the bombardment to be parallel, which meant that Merrill would have to take his cruisers into the narrow confines of Blanche Channel between Rendova and Roviana Lagoon. With submarines a concern, he sent three destroyers out front to make a radar sweep of the channel but kept five in a close screen. Turner and Hester also wanted Merrill's target grid to start one mile west of the troops, and as Merrill later reported, this negated any support for them. This was simply another bombardment of Munda. But to make it as effective as possible, Merrill sent Ryan far ahead of the cruisers to a point off the Munda Bar, where his destroyers could fire on the area in the rear of Kokenggolo Hill.

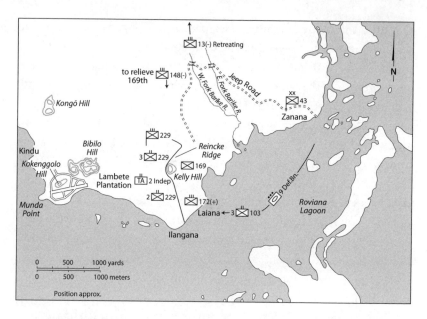

Map 7.2. Initial Engagements at Munda.

The mission was flawlessly executed; at 0257 the cruisers began firing, followed at 0330 by Ryan's destroyers. Ryan hit something behind Kokenggolo Hill, as evidenced by billowing smoke. The destroyers retired without incident.[11]

On the ground, however, the attack bogged down from the start, when the two regiments became entangled as they tried to gain their positions. Most of the morning was spent sorting out the units. Then, at 1120, SCAT (South Pacific Combat Air Transport Command) made the requested airdrop, and troop details were dispatched to retrieve the supplies.[12] Finally, just before noon, Holland sent the 169th forward, 2nd Battalion on the left to frontally assault the Japanese position and 1st Battalion on the right to attempt an envelopment. (3rd Battalion was kept in reserve.) 2nd Battalion advanced 300 yards but then met heavy opposition. 1st Battalion maintained the line but came under considerable fire from its right (north) flank, and the Fiji scouts assigned to the 169th reported at least one Japanese company east of the 1st Battalion.

That afternoon, an attack made behind a rolling barrage from Barker's guns faltered and failed. Holland requested an air strike on the Japanese positions for the next day, which Mulcahy approved. Meanwhile, the 172nd had also run into difficulty. Major Tripp, Lieutenant Henry Taliai, and twenty-five Tongans were leading the American battalions when they ran into heavy machine-gun fire. Taliai, a New Zealand sergeant, and a Tongan private were cut down immediately, and the rest scattered. At the same time, heavy mortar fire fell on the 3rd and 1st Battalions, which were following the scouts. The regimental command post was cut off and had to withdraw back to the 2nd Battalion near the trail junction. The Tongans were able to escape to the east, but after dark Tripp worked his way into the Japanese rear, then shot his way out in a hair-raising escape east, with a map of their positions in his mind. The Japanese were impressed enough by the action to note it in their official history. For his part, Tripp longed for some kerosene to pour into the rice pots cooking in their kitchens. During the day, Hester made his first visit to the front and decided the Laiana landing would have to be delayed a day to the 14th.

The next day, 13 July, the 43rd recorded its first success. At 1000, as Holland had requested, twelve SBDs of VMSB-144 dropped 1,000-pound daisy cutters on the smoke laid on the Japanese positions by the 169th. The dive bombers hit the target squarely, as was usually the case with the 144th, but the smoke marker was 600 yards off the grid coordinates provided by the 169th. How much damage was done is not known.[13] As VMSB-144 departed the scene, Barker's guns opened fire on the ridges – these were not much more than 100 feet in elevation and ran in all directions – and when the barrage began to lift, Holland sent all three battalions to the attack. From right to left, 1st Battalion (Zimmer) had the north spur, 2nd Battalion (Major Harry F. Sellars, who had replaced Fowler the day before)[14] the draw, and 3rd Battalion (Reincke) the south spur. The 1st Battalion gained some ground but sustained so many casualties while attacking the pillboxes that it withdrew to its original position. In the face of heavy machine-gun fire, the 2nd Battalion also made gains up the draw, until its leading elements were hit by an artillery barrage (thought to be friendly), causing what was described as "extreme casualties" that forced its withdrawal. On the south spur of the ridge, however, 3rd Battalion, less K Company, which was guarding the regimental CP, fought its way forward, pillbox by pillbox, for four hours until it secured the south ridge, and Reincke, after whom the troops named the ridge, decided to hold his position. That night, at the cost of two men killed and almost two dozen wounded, 3rd Battalion beat off several determined Japanese counterattacks, and when morning came still held Reincke Hill.

Meanwhile, the 172nd occupied Laiana without opposition. To avoid Japanese fire, Ross had directed Carrigan to swing east with his 2nd Battalion and hack his way through the mangrove swamp. The other two battalions followed and dug in facing the Japanese line.

On 14 July, as the 172nd began probing the Japanese line to the west, 3rd Battalion, 103rd Infantry, and the marine tanks landed at Laiana Beach. The infantry met no opposition, but the LCMs carrying the tanks came under some inaccurate artillery fire. Barker's artillery blanketed the area with phosphorus shells to serve as a smoke screen, along with high explosives for counterbattery fire. The only casualty on either side was a Japanese regimental gun. As this was going on at the beach, in the 169th's sector to the north, 1st and 2nd Battalions were out of action and undergoing reorganization. Casualties and war neurosis cases had depleted the 169th, and Wing stripped the divisional antitank company at Zanana Beach of eighty men and sent them to Holland.

For 3rd Battalion holding Reincke Ridge, however, this was a "dark day." Japanese artillery took the ridge under accurate fire in the morning. A tree burst killed 4, wounded 23, and caused 5 cases of "shell shock" and 7 of "war neurosis."[15] Machine-gun fire during the day killed another 2 and wounded 5. A cemetery was laid out on the ridge. At 2000, another accurate artillery barrage struck the center of the perimeter, killing 8 and wounding 26. No medical officer was with the battalion, but medics did what they could for the wounded. In their first twenty-four hours on the ridge, Reincke's troops had taken 101 casualties, and L Company was left with 51 enlisted men and no officers. But the 3rd Battalion's success forced the Japanese to evacuate the north spur, which was then occupied by 2nd Battalion.

The following day, 15 July (the day Griswold assumed command), saw little action on the ground. But in the air, COMAIRSOLS annihilated Ueno's bombers that were attempting to hit the Zanana area.[16] Nine G4Ms of the 751st, led by the detachment commander Lieutenant Motozu Masao, with an escort of forty-four Zeros from the 253rd and the aircraft carrier *Ryūhō*, came in without much semblance of formation around 1430, a most unfortunate bit of timing because the American fighters that had escorted a raid on Vila were still in the area. Vega directed both the escort fighters and the Rendova Patrol to intercept, and the battle spread over the sky from Honiavasa Passage to Vella Lavella. The 136th gun crews at Honiavasa watched the fight overhead and noted it in their journal; on Kolombangara, Evans reported the number of aircraft that he saw go into the water off Gizo and Vella Lavella. Six of the nine G4Ms were shot down, including Motozu's, leaving the 751st Detachment with three aircraft and no officers higher than warrant officer. Five Zeros went down, and Fighter Command lost three pilots killed. None of the bombers got through to hit a battalion of the 37th Division, which was moving in landing craft to Zanana, a most attractive target; in fact, they did no damage at all. As a result, Kusaka terminated daylight missions against New Georgia for land-based bombers.[17]

During the next two days, 16 and 17 July, the 43rd made its last attacks on the Japanese line before Griswold began reorganizing for the XIV Corps offensive. On the left, the 2nd Battalion, 172nd Infantry, after being hit by a friendly air strike,[18] attacked along the beach road behind Blake's tanks and extended the beachhead toward Ilangana Point. Just to the north, 3rd and 1st Battalions, with L Company, 103rd Infantry, in between, pushed into the high ground and cleared the pillboxes from a small rise. Blake's tanks supported this attack, but the terrain was an obstacle. In fact, the only casualty came when a log penetrated the driver's door into the turret of one tank and broke the tank commander's leg.[19] On the right, Zimmer's 1st Battalion, 169th Infantry, passed over Reincke Hill on 16 July, crossed the draw, and without opposition occupied the ridge some 300 yards to the southwest. Before the troops could dig in, a Japanese artillery barrage hit the hill, killing fourteen men and wounding many more, but Zimmer held the hill (named Kelly Hill for a lieutenant killed in the artillery barrage).

At the end of the 43rd's offensive, the American line ran from just east of Ilangana to Kelly and Reincke Hills, with a gap still between the 172nd and the 169th. The main Japanese defense line still held, but the 169th had driven the first wedge into it.

GRISWOLD TAKES COMMAND

Before the 43rd was even at the line of departure on the Barike River, Halsey's commanders had recognized their forces were inadequate. At a 5 July conference on Guadalcanal convened to consider Hester's request for additional troops, Turner, Harmon, and Griswold agreed to send in the 37th Division, less its 129th Regiment (still in the New Hebrides). Consequently, the 145th Infantry, less its 3rd Battalion, which was with Liversedge, began moving to Rendova, with 2nd Battalion arriving on 8 July, regimental headquarters two days later, and 1st Battalion on 13 July. With two divisions now committed, Harmon wanted NGOF under XIV Corps. He therefore radioed Halsey with a proposal to send in Griswold and a forward echelon of his staff around 8 July to prepare to take over administrative, supply, and planning for NGOF, so that when Munda fell and Hester began moving against Vila, XIV Corps could assume command. Harmon's justification, for the record at least, was that Hester's staff was too small to do the job. Probably another reason was to relegate Turner to a supporting role; the army, like the marines, resented Turner's meddling in ground operations. Turner naturally opposed the move, while Halsey replied that Harmon could increase Hester's staff as he saw fit, but that he wanted to discuss the question of a command change. Harmon lost no time in flying back to COMSOPAC HQ on Nouméa, where he met with Halsey and brought him around. On 9 July, the same day that troops began wading across the Barike River to begin the attack, Halsey told Turner that once Griswold was in the combat area and prepared to assume command, all ground and naval forces of NGOF would pass to Griswold, who would assume the title of commanding general, New Georgia. TF 31 would revert to a supporting role.[20]

Events moved rapidly thereafter. Griswold and his senior staff flew into Rendova on 11 July. The next day, he crossed over to Zanana and spent most of the day at divisional headquarters located up the jeep road. What he found was not encouraging. "Many wounded coming back. Losses heavy. Men look all fagged out. Bewildered look of horror on many faces. Troops impress me as not having been mentally prepared or well trained. Impress me as not doing job very effectively. Enemy resistance however is very stiff."[21] Griswold had arrived at Zanana a few days after the trickle of casualties with mental disorders, commonly called "war neuroses," had grown into a steady stream with dozens of men leaving the line each day. Captain Robert L. Saillant of the 118th Engineers, busy with pushing the jeep road toward the front, watched the men straggle out of the jungle; most he thought simply exhausted, but others a "heartrending spectacle."[22]

Two days after Griswold's visit, Colonel Franklin T. Hallam, XIV Corps surgeon, arrived at Zanana. In his opinion the term "war neurosis" was a misnomer, for at least 50 percent of the cases he saw coming in were the result of physical exhaustion. Another 35 percent showed psychological or physical symptoms that he described as "temporary mental disturbance," and 15 percent "showed manifestations of the various true psychoneurotic complexes." He thought that most of the cases, especially those caused by physical exhaustion, could have been cured by a few days in a combat area rest camp where the men could receive proper medical attention.[23]

But neither was available in New Georgia during most of July. The 43rd went into combat an estimated 30–35 percent understrength in medical personnel and lacking the necessary medical supplies (these had been destroyed at Rendova by either Japanese bombs or the rain and mud, and some had been left behind in the Russells). The casualties overwhelmed the medical battalion; the division hospital (125 beds) at Rendova was no more than a clearing station where the patients were loaded on a LST and shipped to Guadalcanal. Up until 17 July, the 43rd had 636 men wounded in action (not counting those injured in accidents) and 1,000 cases of sickness from diseases such as diarrhea, dysentery, and malaria. The cases of war neuroses, however, were almost equal to the numbers of wounded and sick, estimated at roughly 1,500 for the period 30 June–31 July.[24] With the army providing medical service and the navy handling evacuation, there was no single authority determining which patients needed to be sent to the rear. A man suffering from exhaustion was evacuated with a man with battle wounds. The army's official historians put the blame squarely on the SOPAC planners, writing that "the situation cried out for planning that would not again send one division to do the work of three, or a clearing station to perform the duties of a field hospital."[25]

Back on Rendova on 13 July, Griswold was not impressed as he observed the staff work at NGOF HQ. Before the day was over, he radioed Harmon his opinion that the 43rd could not take Munda – to the contrary, it was about to fold – and that the 25th Division, in addition to the 37th, would be needed. The same day, Turner's acting chief of staff, Colonel Henry D. Linscott, USMC, returned from a stay at the front with a report similar to Griswold's, and as a result, Turner radioed both Griswold and Halsey his agreement that a change of command was now necessary. At Nouméa, Halsey, who was looking ahead to Bougainville (orders to IMAC to begin planning came on 16 July), wasted no time. As early as 11 July, he had queried both Fitch and Turner about bypassing Kolombangara and landing on Vella Lavella. Now, Halsey shelved the planning for Vila and told Harmon to take charge and do what was necessary to take Munda. Orders went out from COMSOPAC on 14 July, directing Griswold to take command of NGOF and ordering Turner to hand over TF 31 to Wilkinson and proceed to Pearl Harbor as Nimitz had requested.[26]

That same day at Rendova, Griswold set up XIV Corps headquarters in the mud. As had been the case on 30 June, everything had to be hand carried. In the midst of all this, Sasaki launched his counterattack.

THE JAPANESE COUNTERATTACK

By 8 July, Sasaki had a clear picture of how NGOF's two-front attack was developing. It was obvious that the main force would advance from the Barike River. By then, he also had an accurate estimate of Liversedge's force – and most importantly, he knew that it had no artillery. Sasaki, therefore, wanted to use the 13th Infantry to launch a counterattack from the headwaters of the Barike, with the objective of destroying the 43rd's rear and taking Zanana. For this, he would need higher approval, since additional troops would have to be sent in for the defense of the Dragons Peninsula and Vila. Both Samejima and Imamura approved the plan. Sasaki then ordered Tomonari, with his 1st and 3rd Battalions (Majors Kinoshita and Takabayashi), to move by barge to Bairoko and overland from there to the Kure 6th Farm. He had already sent two companies of the 13th to reinforce the Kure 6th at Bairoko.[27]

Sasaki hoped to make the counterattack around 13 July. Tomonari moved to Bairoko on the night of the 9th without incident. But then the delays set in. Tomonari ran into the trail block set by 3rd Battalion, 148th Infantry, on 10 July and wasted time and men trying to eliminate it before deciding to bypass it. It was not until 12 July that Tomonari was able to assemble his force at the Kure 6th Farm. The next day, Sasaki's chief of staff, Lieutenant Colonel Kamiya, met Tomonari with orders for the counterattack. Tomonari was to take his forces around the American right flank to the east bridge at the headwaters of the Barike River, and from there he would drive through to Zanana Beach and destroy the American forces east of the river. Sasaki would attach a platoon of engineers, a radio squad, and a reserve artillery detachment to man any captured artillery, and Hirata would send what forces he could from the 229th to join the 13th on the upper Barike River for a counterattack.[28]

With about six companies, Tomonari set out on 14 July on his march to the upper Barike; communication with Sasaki was severed. Two days later, Sasaki sent a patrol to try to make contact. He heard nothing until around 1600 the next day, when a radio message came in declaring that "the regiment is attacking the opponents near Zanana." Then communications failed again. The only account available (the 6th Division history, based largely on the recollections of Major Kinoshita and his orderly, Corporal Kaga Dennosuke) presents a confused picture of what occurred between 14 and 17 July. What emerges with some clarity, however, is that Tomonari's troops had a rough time. While they had no map, they did have a guide from the 229th, who knew the location of the bridges. With men hacking out the trail, the terrain slowed them to 200 to 300 meters an hour. Early on, it appears they either were hit by one of the COMAIRSOLS air strikes or else blundered into one of Barker's firing grids. Both the 1st and 3rd Company commanders were killed. Years later, the frustration with the terrain was fresh in the minds of the division's historians: "If we had to go round and round in circles in the jungle, not having been able to find the enemy, nor having been able to help the 229th Regiment and let them die, it would really hurt the reputation the 13th Infantry Regiment had had for a long time, since the

Sino- and Russo-Japan War. That was why most soldiers were feeling the pressure. Finally meeting the enemy at that point was like meeting Buddha in hell."[29]

The night of 17 July was clear with a full moon rising. Tomonari sent his troops down the jeep road, 1st Battalion on the left and 3rd Battalion on the right (at least this was the plan; in reality 3rd Battalion's whereabouts is a mystery). In their path, about a mile from the beach and completely exposed, were the camps of a medical company, two companies of engineers, and the 43rd Command Post (CP).

The main battle developed at the 43rd CP. Both Wing and Barker were there (Hester was at Laiana), and they had some inkling that something was up from a patrol report of a large number of Japanese moving east. For defense, they had one platoon of the 43rd Reconnaissance Troop and seventy men of the second section of the 1st Commando, which had just landed at Zanana and were rushed up the road to the 43rd perimeter. The fighting was close-in, fierce, and confused. One report said the Japanese briefly penetrated the perimeter and destroyed communications equipment; other accounts claimed the perimeter was not breached. But what saved the night was the 136th Field Artillery Battalion. With no wire cutters, the Japanese hacked and sawed at the thick cables with bayonets and swords, and while they apparently cut the cable to Fire Direction Center (FDC) No. 2 on Rendova, they failed to cut the one to FDC No. 1 on Honiavasa. Barker got through to the 136th, and he and the artillery liaison officer spotted for the 155s. The 136th laid a box of fire around the CP. Colonel McHenry described it as "beautiful"; the Japanese called it so devastating that they feared 1st Battalion would be destroyed.[30]

While the artillery ended any threat to the 43rd CP and sent the surviving Japanese retreating back up the jeep road, fighting elsewhere went on until well after midnight. Some Japanese did make it to Zanana, but Lieutenant John R. Wismer from the 9th Defense Battalion organized a miscellaneous collection of marines and army service personnel, and in a sharp firefight, defended the beach.[31] On the Ilangana front, Hirata launched two counterattacks. Satō made the first attack against the 172nd Infantry along the beach at around 1630. In an hour's fighting, the attack was beaten off, just as Ross received a call from 43rd CP that it was under attack and needed help. Ross replied that he was under attack himself and had no help to send; then he ordered his battalions to firm up their lines, even if they had to fall back. But no further attacks came on the 172nd's front. The fighting moved north to the 169th's sector, where Kojima's 3rd Battalion, attacking after midnight, attempted to recapture Kelly Hill. Zimmer's 1st Battalion, aided by 3rd Battalion mortars firing from Reincke Ridge, threw them back. With this, the fighting died down for the rest of the night.

Tomonari's troops kept the road blocked for the next three days. In response to the Japanese attack, Griswold had sent Colonel Stuart A. Baxter with his 148th Infantry, less 3rd Battalion, moving to Zanana at 0100 on 18 July. With the situation in hand there, Baxter was ordered at 1100 to relieve the 169th. Baxter claimed that he was told that the road was clear, but his advance party, which had set out on that morning, was ambushed. Two men were killed and two badly wounded. That night the Japanese were out in force at the Barike bridges; some were drunk on the whiskey looted from the ration dump located between the bridges. At some point during the night, parties of Japanese moved over the west bridge, where a platoon from the 169th was dug in to protect the new water point and where a party carrying wounded had stopped for protection. What followed is not at all clear, but the Japanese managed to kill most of the litter patients along with two medics and one soldier, so that thereafter the west bridge was called "Butcher's Bridge."[32]

At 0800 on 19 July, Baxter set out with his 1st Battalion and his headquarters back up the jeep road, ready for a fight. The Japanese appeared to have withdrawn, and the troops crossed the east bridge without incident. But the road then made a sharp bend to the west, and as the lead troops rounded the bend, Japanese machine guns opened up with devastating effect. A Company lost more than a dozen men killed or very seriously wounded. Attempts to flank the position failed, and at 1630 Baxter dug in. But the Japanese then withdrew, and by 21 July, Baxter had relieved the 169th.[33]

Tomonari's counterattack had failed to accomplish its objective, and he withdrew back into what the Japanese called the Yahata Highlands. When Sasaki learned the extent of the failure, he ordered Tomonari to keep his forces there and to prepare for another attack on the American northern flank. What he thought of Tomonari's defeat was not recorded, but what the troops who made the attack thought was: "13th Infantry Regiment members realized in the past several days that things were really different from what they were in China."[34]

With that, a relative calm descended over the Munda battlefield until 25 July, when Griswold was ready to open the XIV Corps offensive. We will take advantage of this lull on the ground to go back and bring up to date Liversedge's battles in the Dragons Peninsula (chapter 8) and Ainsworth's and Mitscher's battles with the Tokyo Express (chapter 9).

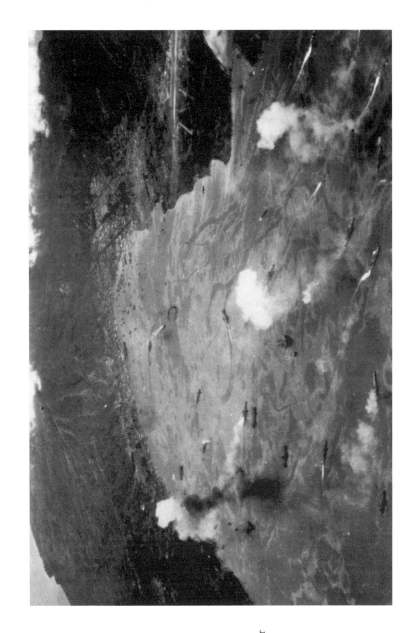

1. Target Rabaul: Simpson Harbor under attack, with Lakunai airstrip visible on the right. *U.S. National Archives: Navy collection 80-G-89098.*

2. Munda Point under Japanese control, early
1943, with visible bomb damage from Allied raids.
U.S. National Archives: Navy collection 80-G-80193.

3. Sunlight fighter airstrip (foreground) and Renard bomber airstrip (background) Russell Islands. *U.S. National Archives: Navy collection 80-G-201311.*

4. US Army 43rd Infantry Division,
172nd Regiment, landing at Rendova 30 June 1943.
U.S. National Archives: Marine Corps collection 127-GR-132 60624.

5. Marine long-range battery height-finder squad at Rendova.
U.S. National Archives: Marine Corps collection 127-GR-132 58005.

6. Tropical climate and muddy terrain provided a
constant challenge to Allied advances on New Georgia.
U.S. National Archives: Marine Corps collection 127-GR-134 60593.

7. Army flamethrower team in action clearing
Japanese pillbox fortifications at Munda.
U.S. National Archives: Signal Corps collection 111-SC-179171.

8. A Marine patrol near Enogai Point, New Georgia Island.
U.S. National Archives: Marine Corps collection 127-GR-132 60166C.

9. Abandoned Japanese G4M Betty bomber at Munda.
U.S. National Archives: Navy collection 80-G-065444.

10. Navy Seabees extending the newly captured Munda aerodrome.
U.S. National Archives: Navy collection 80-G-056597.

11. The Consolidated B-24 Liberator heavy bomber wreaked considerable damage on Japanese positions with its range and payload capacity.
U.S. National Archives: Navy collection 80-G-089725.

12. The Chance Vought "Birdcage" Corsair F4U's introduction in early 1943 was pivotal in gaining air superiority over its Japanese counterparts. *U.S. National Archives: Navy collection 80-G-205932.*

13. SBD dive bombers on newly captured Munda
aerodrome with Rendova in the background.
U.S. National Archives: Navy collection 80-G-056508.

14. Navy Seabee TD18 bulldozer and carryall
collecting coral base for airstrip construction at Segi.
U.S. National Archives: Signal Corps collection 111-SC-181657.

15. Marston matting, an interlocking pieced-steel planking, enabled the Navy Seabees to quickly lay an airstrip on newly captured soil. *U.S. National Archives: Navy collection 80-G-036381.*

16. VS-64 SBD antisubmarine patrol over Segi airstrip.
U.S. National Archives: Navy collection 80-G-225915.

17. Japanese destroyer *Nagatsuki*, a casualty of the Battle of Kula
Gulf, grounded off Bambari Harbor, Kolombangara.
U.S. National Archives: Navy collection 80-G-232154.

18. (*facing*) USS *Honolulu* CL-48 at Tulagi with collapsed bow after
the Battle of Kolombangara, assisted by USS *Vireo* ATO-144.
U.S. National Archives: Navy collection 80-G-259444.

19. USS *Selfridge* DD-357 at Nouméa displaying
torpedo damage from the Battle of Vella Lavella.
U.S. National Archives: Navy collection 80-G-259442.

20. (*facing*) Admiral Bill "Bull" Halsey, Allied naval commander of the
South Pacific Area and principal architect of the New Georgia campaign.
U.S. National Archives: Navy collection 80-G-205279.

21. Rekata Bay, Santa Isabel Island, from where
Japanese float planes harassed Guadalcanal.
U.S. National Archives: Navy collection 80-G-071798.

22. Ballale Island, Shortland Islands, where Betty bombers
and 'Gekkō' night fighters operated from.
U.S. National Archives: Navy collection 80-G-071796.

23. Vila airstrip, Kolombangara Island, was of limited
use to the Japanese due to drainage problems.
U.S. National Archives: Navy collection 80-G-042591.

24. Bonis airstrip at Buka Passage aerodrome, Bougainville Island. A crash strip (Bonis) was later constructed on the opposite side of the Passage. *U.S. National Archives: Navy collection 80-G-071798.*

25. (*facing*) Halavo Bay seaplane base, Florida Island.
U.S. National Archives: Navy collection 80-G-085663.

26. (*above*) Ondonga aerodrome, at the neck of
the Diamond Narrows, New Georgia.
U.S. National Archives: Navy collection 80-G-225914.

27. Barakoma aerodrome, Vella Lavella Island: the last Allied
stepping stone before the assault on Bougainville.
U.S. National Archives: Navy collection 80-G-225912.

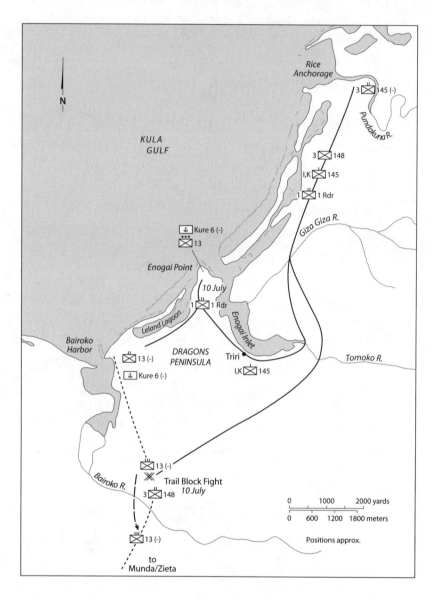

Map 8.1. Dragons Peninsula, 5–18 July 1943.

Battles in the Dragons Peninsula

WHEN ASKED AFTER THE WAR ABOUT THE DEFEAT AT BAIROKO Harbor, Peck replied: "I was against it myself, but they had the raider battalion and they attacked Munda from the rear. It didn't make sense. I've forgotten who made that decision. It must have been Halsey. Turner proposed the thing. I objected to it, but Halsey said, 'All right, we'll go ahead,' and he had them attack from the rear, and they didn't get anywhere."[1] With evident sarcasm, then Colonel Merrill B. Twining, operations officer, IMAC (I Marine Amphibious Corps), wrote of Bairoko Harbor that "this was Kelly Turner's last appearance in the role of soldier/sailor in the Solomons."[2]

So Turner got the blame, perhaps rightly so. But the story is a bit more complicated, as we shall see.

THE APPROACH

At Rice Anchorage on 5 July, as the sun rose and the rain slacked off and then stopped, Colonel Liversedge organized his forces. To secure the base at Rice Anchorage, he left Lieutenant Colonel George G. Freer with I and M Companies of his 3rd Battalion, 145th Infantry. With the rest of his force he set out for the Giza Giza River north of Enogai Inlet. The 1st Raider Battalion (Lieutenant Colonel Samuel B. Griffith II) was on point, followed by K and L Companies, 145th Infantry (Major Marvin D. Giradeau), and the 148th Infantry (Lieutenant Colonel Delbert E. Schultz) in the rear. If things went according to plan, once they crossed the Tomoko River at the head of Enogai Inlet, the 148th would strike off

southwest and establish a block on the Bairoko-Munda Trail; two companies of the 1st Raiders would take Enogai, while the other two would
take Bairoko Harbor. Giradeau's two companies would be in reserve. The
elimination of the estimated 500 Japanese from the Dragons Peninsula
was expected to be quick: Liversedge's troops carried just three days'
rations and one unit of ammunition.[3]

The distance from Rice Anchorage to Enogai is about four miles as
the crow flies, but how many miles Liversedge's force had to cover to get
there is anybody's guess. The first day's march to the Giza Giza River
went well enough, since Corrigan's natives had been able to cut trails.
Even then, Griffith described the going as difficult and the humidity like
a "Turkish bath."[4] That night, Captain Clay A. Boyd, who had led the
June reconnaissance, crossed the river with his D Company, while the
main force bivouacked on the near bank. It rained hard, and next morning the ankle-deep Giza Giza was thigh-deep, with a steep and slippery
ten-foot mud bank to climb on the other side. At 0800, seventeen SBD
Dauntlesses and eighteen TBF Avengers struck Enogai, and the sound
of 43 tons of bombs hitting the Japanese cheered the troops on as they
set off for the Tomoko River. A miserable day lay ahead. While Schultz
with his battalion split off and crossed the river upstream without too
much difficulty, Liversedge planned to cross at the mouth and struck
out through a swamp that in places the rains had turned into knee-deep
mud. When he finally reached the mouth of the Tomoko, it could not be
waded, and the crossing had to be made on a single log that had fallen
across the river. At one point, the toggle ropes linked together to make
a hand rope broke, spilling men into the river; only the quick action
of their comrades saved them from drowning. By 1730, the main force
was able to bivouac on the southern side of Enogai Inlet, but the march
from the Giza Giza had consumed a full day. Liversedge was now behind
schedule.

That night, Sasaki sent the first army reinforcements to Commander
Okumura, whose Kure 6th SNLF (Special Naval Landing Force) had
responsibility for defense of the Dragons Peninsula. They were badly
needed as a result of the loss of the 2nd Rifle Company, most of the weapons company at Wickham Anchorage, and half of the 1st Rifle Company
at Rendova Harbor. Combining the rest of the 1st Rifle Company with

troops from the support units (ninety-nine riflemen at full strength) created a force of about company strength. Sasaki, accordingly, directed Tomonari to send Major Obashi (2nd Battalion, 13th Infantry) to Bairoko Harbor with his own 5th Company, one half of his 2nd Machine Gun Company, and the 9th Company from the 3rd Battalion, which was detached to his command. Although Obashi came under Okumura's overall command, it appears that he assumed tactical command at Bairoko. Intercepted messages to 8th Fleet refer to the command as the "merging" of army-navy forces or the joint army-navy force.[5]

On the morning of 7 July, Schultz's 148th set out southwest on a scout trail, which appeared to the Americans as no trail at all, heading for the Bairoko-Munda Trail. Griffith's 1st Raider Battalion, followed well behind by Giradeau's two 145th companies, took another trail toward Enogai Point. Since the two units fought separate actions on the same day, we will first follow the Raiders to Enogai and then take up the 148th at the trail block.

THE BATTLE OF ENOGAI

It took the Raiders three days to get into position to attack Enogai. Terrain was the biggest problem, compounded somewhat by Japanese harassment. On 7 July, with Boyd's D Company leading, the Raiders followed a tortuous trail at the base of a ridge that gave way to a swamp. Around noon, the advance patrol surprised a small Japanese working party and killed two. One hour later, near Triri, they suffered their first casualties, three killed and four wounded, in a fight with a strong Kure 6th patrol. The Japanese lost almost a dozen killed, including a platoon commander carrying maps of the Bairoko and Enogai defenses. The Raiders occupied Triri, established a perimeter, and buried their dead. The next day, 8 July, was lost altogether. A firefight with the Japanese on the trail thought to lead to Bairoko took up most of the morning, but no casualties were reported. Then, the Raiders moved out along the trail they thought went to Enogai. All went well for 1,500 yards when the trail ended in an impassable mangrove swamp. Griffith called it "one of the disheartening episodes of the operation." Patrols operating on his left (west) flank, however, found what appeared to be a passable trail, and

Griffith decided to take his men back to Triri for the night and try the newly discovered trail in the morning.

As the Raiders moved back along the trail, they could hear the sound of gunfire, which steadily increased in volume, from the direction of Triri. At noon, Liversedge had ordered Giradeau forward with his two companies from the 145th to Triri, and he had also moved his headquarters there. What the Raiders heard was a battle between an estimated company of Japanese, almost certainly from Obashi's 13th Infantry, and K Company, which was trying to dig in. The arrival of a strong raider patrol in the Japanese rear quickly broke up the fight. By raider accounts, the Japanese left behind twenty dead along with two machine guns. K Company had four men wounded, including the company commander.[6] In the midst of the firefight at Triri, the air strike on Enogai came in, seventeen VMSB-144 SBDs that hit the southwest side at 1620.[7]

On 9 July – the same day the 43rd stepped off from the Barike River – the 1st Raiders closed in on Enogai. The battalion moved out at 0730 along the inland trail discovered the previous day to the sound of 1,000-pounders hitting the Japanese positions. As Liversedge had requested, eighteen SBDs of VMSB-132 came in from the southeast, divided, and hit both Enogai and Bairoko Harbor.[8] Compared to the last few days, the march went quickly, and at 1100 Griffith had Leland Lagoon in sight. There, he turned north toward Enogai Point, and by 1500 he was some 750 yards from the objective. About that time, C Company (Captain John P. Salmon) made contact with the first Japanese outpost and came under heavy machine-gun fire. In addition to an undetermined number of Kure 6th troops, Obashi had sent a platoon from the 13th Infantry as reinforcements. Griffith put A Company (Captain Thomas F. Mullahey Jr.) to the left of C Company and B Company (Captain Edwin B. Wheeler) to the right. Boyd's D Company was in reserve, faced toward Bairoko to guard against an attack from that direction. With C and A Companies engaged, the firefight went on until dusk, costing a number of casualties.

The Raiders dug in for the night in what Griffith described as a rain forest with giant trees and little undergrowth. Things were quiet in the line, but a heavy limb from a Banyan tree, perhaps damaged in the air strike, crashed down on the communications area of Griffith's CP, killing one man instantly and injuring five more, one so badly the surgeon had to amputate his arm. At 0100, the four Enogai guns (1st and 2nd heavy gun batteries, Kure 6th)[9] opened up and fired two dozen shells at Rice Anchorage without causing damage. After that, the night was quiet around Enogai. The Raiders got what sleep they could on empty stomachs, since they had run out of rations. At 1540 that afternoon, a marine R4D had made the requested ration drop at Triri, but apparently no attempt was made to carry the rations up to Griffith.[10]

When daylight came on 10 July, the Raiders took Enogai. The night before, Griffith had ordered Wheeler, whose B Company had made no contact on the right, to send out a strong patrol at dawn. This patrol reached Enogai Inlet without opposition and reported that a fairly good route to the point could be had. The foliage was sparser, allowing the 60mm mortars, the heaviest weapons the Raiders had, to be used. At 0700, Griffith ordered Wheeler to begin the assault, supported by a barrage of mortar fire. As the Japanese had not constructed the elaborate pillboxes encountered elsewhere, both on the southern front and later at Bairoko, the mortars fired with good effect.

By 0900, Wheeler was reporting good progress in the assault, which relieved pressure in front of C Company, allowing it to advance, although more slowly. But A Company, in the low ground on the left near Leland Lagoon, was stopped by heavy machine-gun fire from well-concealed positions in the mangrove swamps. Nonetheless, as Griffith wrote, A Company "was giving it as well as taking it" and acted as the "hinge for the 'Swinging Door' which in the form of Baker Company, was steadily moving, pushing the Japs ahead of, and crowding them off the high ground into the low area around Enogai Point."

By 1300, Mullahey reported that the Japanese were evacuating Enogai Point, crossing the shallow passage between the point and the sand spit on the seaward side of Leland Lagoon. His machine guns were in a position to take the retreating Japanese under fire, and did so with good effect. At the same time, Griffith ordered 1st Lieutenant Thomas D. Pollard to take a platoon from Boyd's D Company and attack on the left of C Company. In a swift and determined attack, Pollard's platoon drove through to Kula Gulf and effectively broke the Japanese resistance. With the exception of a single machine-gun pocket in front of A Company, which was sealed off to wait until the next day, when it was reduced, the fight for Enogai was over. Raider casualties were forty-seven killed, eighty wounded, and four missing. The Japanese said that eighty-one Kure 6th and a platoon of army troops died honorably. In addition to the four 14cm guns, for which the buried breech blocks were soon found, the Raiders captured some two dozen machine guns. Around 1500, 145th troops carried up rations and water, and the Raiders finally ate.[11]

The next day, 1st Base Air Force weighed in with two strikes against Enogai. The first, made up of nine G4Ms with forty-seven Zeros, came in around noon. Because of communication problems at VEGA (Rendova Fighter Control) and mechanical difficulties that took three F4Us out of the action, only five VMF-221 F4U Corsairs intercepted. Three Corsairs, which had attained the necessary altitude, dove out of the sun to hit the G4Ms making their run. They downed one bomber, damaged three others, and caused some to drop their bombs short in the water. But others were on target, killing three Raiders and wounding nine more. Zeros from the *Ryūhō* and the 253rd swarmed all over the three Corsairs, which tried to break off in the face of overwhelming odds. One went down with the pilot missing, another made it back to Guadalcanal with the pilot wounded, and the third returned undamaged. The two remaining Corsairs made a second interception of the Japanese formation as it was turning back to the northwest. Neither plane made it home that day. One pilot ditched his shot-up plane off Segi, the other in the Slot; both pilots were rescued.

In addition to the bomber, the Japanese lost two Zeros.[12] By the time the second Japanese strike arrived, made up of eight Zeros carrying bombs and fifteen more flying cover, a number of P-39s, P-40s, and Corsairs were on hand over the gulf, and these made the interception and broke up the attack. Fighter Command lost one P-39 and two F4Us (all pilots were rescued), while the Japanese lost one Zero. Thereafter, the Japanese resorted to dusk- or night-harassing attacks on Enogai, which caused a number of casualties.[13]

At 1600, three PBYs arrived to take out the wounded. Although two F1Ms slipped in and attacked while the wounded were being loaded, ground fire from the Raiders drove them off, and the PBYs took off safely. Liversedge also sent out his communication officer and his air liaison officer from VB-21 to acquaint Turner with the situation and to request that Currin's 4th Raiders be sent in for the attack on Bairoko Harbor, which request was approved.

THE BATTLE AT THE TRAIL BLOCK

Schultz had easier terrain to cross, and by 8 July he had set the block on the Bairoko-Munda Trail, some 4,000 yards from the harbor. Contact was made almost immediately with what Schulz called "a human pack train," protected by approximately a platoon.[14] In three skirmishes that day a number of Japanese were killed. The 148th also lost its first man killed along with three wounded. The next day, 9 July, was quiet at the block, but a patrol sent south on the trail ambushed a twelve-man party of Japanese coming from Munda and killed three. The party had been sent to guide Tomonari's 13th Infantry, which had begun landing at Bairoko, to the Kure 6th Farm. The only map the 13th had been given was a worthless two-page map of New Georgia.

On 10 July, while the Raiders were taking Enogai, Tomonari with 1st Battalion (Kinoshita) and 3rd Battalion (Takabayashi) set out for the Kure 6th Farm. By then, Tomonari knew of Schultz's trail block, but he was determined to eliminate it. Although not stated in so many words, the tone of both the 6th SNLF historians and the official historians was that the 13th Infantry came from an elite division, combat-tested in China, and would easily brush the Americans aside.

The task fell to Takabayashi, and around 0900 he launched a series of well-executed probing attacks, which elicited the admiration of Schulz. Apparently, he found what he was looking for. Around 1600, he struck hard at L Company (Captain Lawrence D. Robertson), which was holding the northern flank. Takabayashi was hit in the leg by grenade fragments but stayed in action. The Americans were driven back, and had Schultz not moved his CP quickly, it would have been overrun. A timely counterattack by K Company (Captain Vernon B. McMillan) stopped any further penetration.

But as night fell, the Japanese held the ridge on the 148th Infantry's northern flank, and M Company (Captain Henne) laid heavy mortar fire on their positions during the night. A series of counterattacks the next day, 11 July, partially restored the original lines, and I Company, 145th Infantry, which Liversedge had sent from Triri to reinforce Schultz, arrived at dusk. That night the Japanese made a final attack on K Company with bayonets and grenades but were repulsed. Next morning they were gone, having skirted the trail block in the night with "tree light" on their backs, much as the 4th Raiders had done in the Mango River swamp near Viru Harbor.

In the fight at the trail block, which they had hoped to brush aside, the Japanese instead took about 100 casualties. And, as we have seen, the unnecessary fight cost Tomonari a two-day delay in making the counterattack on the 43rd. It was a costly test of American combat abilities.[15]

Schultz's main problem was logistical – how to get rations in and his twenty-eight wounded men out. On the tenth, the day of the heaviest fighting, he was down to a fraction of a K ration per man, and the situation got worse. A SCAT air drop on 11 July was largely unsuccessful. Most of what fell in the 148th area was ammunition, much of it faulty. Most of the food fell among the Japanese, who first thought the drops were parachute bombs. When nothing exploded, they opened the packages and soon discovered that "blue" meant "food." The canned meat, biscuits, and coffee were delicacies for the always-hungry Japanese, who ate as much as they could before filling their packs. On 13 July, Schultz got some relief when Corrigan's carriers arrived with 300 pounds of rice, which Schultz's men cooked in their steel helmets, seasoning the rice with salt tablets. On the return trip, the carriers took out the wounded.

Liversedge, with his headquarters and K Company, 145th Infantry, passed the carriers late in the afternoon at the Tomoko River landing while on his way to assess the situation at the trail block, which he reached on 14 July. The next day, Liversedge sent one strong patrol from the 145th on the trail toward Munda in a futile effort to make contact with the 169th. As we know, but Liversedge did not, the 169th was nowhere near Munda, and this incident points out the lack of communications between NLF and NGOF. At the same time, he sent another patrol from the 145th toward Bairoko, which made no contact, and still another, from the 145th and his headquarters, back to carry in rations. A SCAT drop on the 16th helped with the ration situation. But with the 4th Raiders due to arrive on 18 July for the attack on Bairoko, and with no observable activity on the trail, Liversedge abandoned the trail block. All troops moved back to the Enogai and Triri area on 17 July.

THE BATTLE OF BAIROKO HARBOR

Commencing at 0100 on 18 July, four destroyer transports escorted by five destroyers landed Currin's 4th Raider Battalion and forty tons of supplies. The only incident was a clash between the destroyers and PT boats, which were out of their assigned position north of Kolombangara. Both sides missed; as Halsey commented in his report, the destroyers' gunfire and the PTs' torpedo fire were "of a low order."[16] The price was paid, however, a few miles off Vangunu, around the time the 4th Battalion began landing. Submarine *RO-106* sank *LST-342*, which was sailing without escort because of the Enogai run and carrying replacements for the 43rd Division. An estimated 100 men perished; an APc rescued 110.[17]

For the attack on Bairoko set for 20 July, Liversedge planned to use the 1st and 4th Raider Battalions and Shultz's 3rd Battalion, 148th Infantry. All three battalions were understrength. The 1st Raiders was down to about 500 men, reorganized into two full-strength companies, B and D, which would make the attack, and two reduced companies, A and C, which would remain in defense of Enogai. As a result of the operations against Viru Harbor and Wickham Anchorage, Currin's 4th Raiders was down to 700 men, while Shultz's battalion had just over 600 of the 747 men with whom he had started.

Late in the afternoon of 19 July, Liversedge met with his battalion commanders to go over the attack plan. Since the terrain did not allow for maneuver, he intended to take the 1st and 4th Raiders over the Enogai-Bairoko Trail and attack the Japanese frontally, while sending Shultz with 3rd Battalion, 148th Infantry, along the Triri-Bairoko Trail to hit their southern flank. He left Freer's 3rd Battalion, 145th Infantry, behind at Triri. Why he elected not to use the 145th – a quarter of his strength – has never been satisfactory explained. Without artillery or heavy mortars, he seems to have intended to rely on an air strike at 0900, which he requested that night. However, there is no record of the request having been sent to Mulcahy, which would have been standard procedure, and there is no evidence that COMAIRSOLS ever received it.

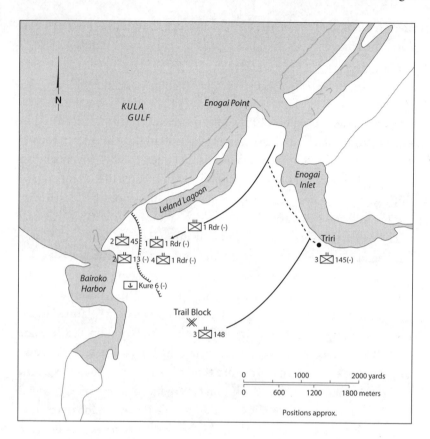

Map 8.2. Battle of Bairoko Harbor, 20 July 1943.

But at least Liversedge thought he would have air support.[18] What good it would have done is a different matter. In a message to 8th Fleet dated 9 July, the Japanese reported that the heavy strikes of that day and the previous day had inflicted no casualties or material damage.[19]

Meanwhile, at Bairoko Harbor, the Japanese had taken advantage of Liversedge's slow progress and Ainsworth's failure to stop the Reinforcement Force (see Battle of Kolombangara, chapter 9). A battalion under Major Yamada Tadaichi and a mountain artillery battery landed at the new barge transfer base at Ariel (now Meresu Cove) on southwest Kolombangara on the night of 12–13 July. From there, Commander

Tokeda (Yokosuka 7th SNLF) oversaw the transfer of both units to Bairoko by barge on the night of 13–14 July. In the spirit of the Sasaki/Ōta agreement, Yamada came under Okumura's command, while the senior officer took command of all army units. From indirect evidence, this seems to have been Yamada, and he likely had tactical command of all units. How many troops is another question. In addition to Tadaichi's battalion, Obashi may have had two companies from the 13th Infantry, but this is just a guess. The Kure 6th would have had few riflemen, although there would have been a number of naval base personnel capable of serving in the line. But the Japanese had a good estimate of American troop strength and, most importantly, knew that Liversedge had no artillery.[20]

While Liversedge lacked intelligence on the Japanese reinforcements, he knew from identification on the bodies at Enogai that army troops were present in the Dragons Peninsula. From 15 July, he knew from patrol reports that the Japanese were working hard on the defense line east of the harbor. On 15, 17, and 19 July, therefore, he had requested air strikes on the eastern side. In response, a total of ninety-eight SBDs, TBFs, and B-25s struck the Japanese defense lines. The extent of damage is not known.[21]

On the morning of 20 July, Liversedge cleared Enogai at 0830, marching along the Bairoko-Enogai Trail in column – Corrigan and his scouts, Griffith's 1st Battalion a (less A and C Companies), Currin's 4th Battalion, and Liversedge's headquarters. One platoon from B Company went down the Leland Lagoon sand spit to cover the extreme right flank. Shultz, who had the greater distance to travel, had started thirty minutes earlier, laying the telephone line by which he was to maintain contact with Liversedge. The expected air strike at 0900 did not materialize. The eighteen SBDs of VMSB-144, the designated ground support squadron, sat idle on the field in the Russells until 1400, another indication that neither Mulcahy nor Strike Command knew anything about a request for air support. Liversedge went on without it. An hour later, the scouts sighted the first of a series of Japanese outposts forward of the main defensive line. The outpost was quickly reduced. Griffith deployed B Company on the right and D Company on the left, and the advance continued against ever-increasing resistance. Griffith then committed his demolitions platoon on the exposed left flank. With this, all of 1st Raider Battalion was in the line.

At noon, Griffith confronted the Japanese main line of resistance, four successive lines of mutually supporting log and coral pillboxes on low, parallel ridges running north–south. Heavy machine-gun fire quickly stopped the 1st Raiders. At 1230, Liversedge then committed the 4th Raiders on Griffith's left, but they made little progress, and two company commanders were badly wounded. In his report, Liversedge noted that an "observer who had participated in the battle of Bloody Ridge on Guadalcanal said that the fire fight at BAIROKO exceeded even that in volume." At the same time, having heard nothing from Schultz and discovering that the telephone line was down, Liversedge sent his executive officer with a patrol to catch up with Schultz. But this took over three hours as the patrol had to go back to Enogai, up to Triri, and then along the trail to Bairoko. Meanwhile, the battle went on, and at around 1430, D Company broke into the first defense lines, but a Japanese counterattack quickly threw it back. An hour later, the Japanese began laying down heavy and accurate mortar fire from the ridges back to the regimental CP, turning the area into a killing field and inflicting heavy casualties. With the issue now in doubt and no reserves to commit, Liversedge finally learned at 1600 that he could expect no help from Schultz, who was stopped by a Japanese trail block several thousand yards from the harbor. Consequently, after consulting his commanders, he decided to withdraw east to high ground.

The withdrawal was made in good order. When the corpsmen and litter bearers had carried all of the wounded back to the aid station in preparation for sending them on to Enogai, the companies disengaged in turn and retired 500 yards to near the south shore of Leland Lagoon, where they dug in for the night. Runners were sent to tell the platoon on the sand spit to hold in place and then withdraw in the morning; orders to withdraw went out to Schultz. (Schultz claimed in his report that he was somewhat surprised, since he had no idea of the situation on the raider front; he was methodically preparing to attack the trail block in order to continue his advance the next morning.)[22] Liversedge ordered a company from the 145th, which had carried supplies to Enogai, to bring medical supplies, water and ammunition, and then join his perimeter defense. To cover the withdrawal to Enogai the next day, he requested heavy air strikes on both sides of Bairoko Harbor.

With the exception of a Japanese probe of 1st Raider Battalion's lines at 0200, which left one marine dead and nine wounded, the night of 20–21 July was quiet. At 0600, the withdrawal to Enogai began. The Japanese made no effort to interfere, which made withdrawal easier. Corrigan's scouts helped carry the litter cases, while Shultz withdrew to Triri without difficulty before being ordered on to Enogai.

For its part, COMAIRSOLS put 250 aircraft over Bairoko Harbor that day. At 0950, the first strike of twenty-four Dauntlesses and twenty-five Avengers came in, followed thirty minutes later by eight B-25s. There was no letup. At noon, thirty-seven TBFs and six B-25s came in and, at 1600, forty-eight SBDs and twenty-two TBFs. Around 130 tons of bombs hit Bairoko, along with an estimated 24,000 rounds of machine-gun fire. When the B-25s dropped their bombs, they came back for a strafing run – the pilots reporting that the .50s cut down trees – and the marine, navy, and New Zealand escort fighters hung around until the bombers had done their job before strafing as well.

The one air battle of the day developed around 1710, when the final mission against Bairoko, consisting of eight B-25s, arrived at almost exactly the same time as a Japanese formation of nine D3A Vals and fifty-eight Zeros bound for Rendova. The outnumbered F4Us and F4Fs intercepted – the men on the ground at Rendova saw a tangle of dogfights overhead – but the details are hazy. None of the Zeros got through to attack the B-25s, but some of the D3As made good their attack on Rendova, one scoring a direct hit on the deckhouse of LST-343, which wounded several men and killed Captain Elphege Alfred M. Gendreau, Nimitz's fleet surgeon.[23] At Enogai, three PBYs were loading wounded personnel, and while two aircraft got away safely, two Zeros shot up an engine of the third, wounding some of the crew and some of the patients, and forcing the PBY to return to Enogai for the night. COMAIRSOLS claimed two Zeros against one F4F lost.[24]

The Battle of Bairoko Harbor was over. The two raider battalions had lost 46 men killed and 190 wounded, while Shultz had 3 killed and 10 wounded. Japanese casualties are more difficult to determine. The list of casualties from 30 June to 23 July that Sasaki sent to Eighth Army recorded the losses in the "Bairoko Area" as one officer and 22 enlisted men killed, and 68 enlisted men and 2 officers wounded. On the other hand, the summary of losses by unit compiled by Colonel Kamiya on the eve of the evacuation listed 40 killed and 116 wounded for 2nd Battalion, 45th. Whatever the exact number the Japanese lost, they held Bairoko, and Liversedge's Northern Landing Force was spent – battle casualties, sickness, and exhaustion from battling the terrain had seen to that. He received orders to hold his positions at Enogai, Triri, and Rice Anchorage, and to sit tight. For their part, the Japanese kept Yamada at Bairoko for the duration of the fighting on New Georgia. Bairoko was an important storage area with tons of supplies that had been brought in by sea trucks,[25] which could be distributed by barge. Reinforcements for the Munda front went in by the Hawthorne Sound–Diamond Narrows route. Sasaki had debated the risk of using Bairoko Harbor to stage the 13th to Munda, but that was before Enogai fell.[26]

Historians have pointed to a number of reasons for the Northern Landing Force's failure to take Bairoko: COMAIRSOLS not making the air strike; Schultz's failure to get into the battle; Liversedge not using the 145th or at least the mortars of its heavy weapons company; the lack of a naval bombardment; the failure to use the captured 14cm guns (although it should be noted, the Raiders had no trained artillerists); and so on.[27] It is doubtful if any or all of these would have altered the outcome. The major factors, it seems to me, are the following. First, the planners put together a mixed force of two very different units, Marine Raiders and army infantry, and this may have had some bearing on Liversedge's ineffective use of the latter. After all, he chose to make the main attack with only six companies of Raiders. Second, the planners totally underestimated the terrain, which put the operation behind schedule from the start. Third, the Japanese defense of Enogai was stronger than expected, which caused another delay while the 4th Raiders came in to reinforce. Fourth, Ainsworth failed to stop the arrival of Yamada's 2nd Battalion, 45th, and given the time provided by the terrain and purchased by their dead at Enogai, the Japanese were able not only to put the battalion in place but also to prepare strong defensive positions. For

Liversedge to have prevailed, he would have needed to have used all four of his battalions – and these might not have been enough – and, above all, he would have needed adequate artillery support. Against the log and coral pillboxes, about all the heavy mortars could do was to uncover their locations.

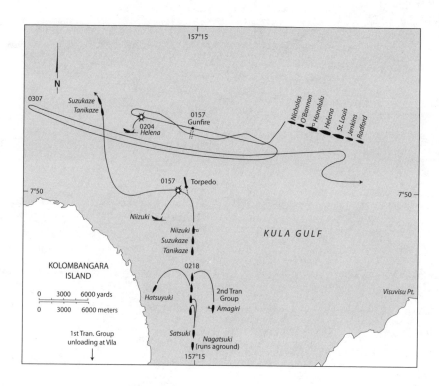

Map 9.1. Naval Battle of Kula Gulf, 6 July 1943.

NINE

Battles with the Tokyo Express

BOTH AINSWORTH, IN TWO NIGHT SURFACE ENGAGEMENTS, AND Mitscher, in a weeklong air campaign, failed to stop the Japanese Reinforcement Force from landing troops during the battle for Munda. Samuel Eliot Morison, author of the Navy's history of World War II, was on the bridge of *Honolulu* with Ainsworth at the battle of Kolombangara and saw with his own eyes what he thought were three Japanese ships burning and exploding. But the Japanese lost only one ship, had no others damaged, and in turn sank an American destroyer and torpedoed all three Allied light cruisers. But Morison, like Ainsworth, could never quite shake the belief that they had at least damaged two other Japanese ships. Consequently, even after his volume that included the New Georgia campaign had been published, he was still trying to find evidence for that belief. "Another delicate subject for you to investigate in Tokyo," he instructed one of his researchers, "is the Battle of Kolombangara, July 1943, won (?) by me and Pug [Ainsworth]." What he wanted was evidence that two of the Japanese destroyers sunk by COMAIRSOLS a few nights later had been damaged in the naval battle. "It would console us a lot if this surmise could be shown to be at least probable."[1] But no evidence was discovered then, or since.

BATTLE OF KULA GULF

As we have seen, the Japanese planned reinforcement runs for the nights of 4–5 and 5–6 July, but the first was aborted because of the naval forces covering the Rice Anchorage landings. As a result, they combined the two transports for the second run, which Kusaka ordered Samejima to carry out at all cost. With a fight a good possibility, Akiyama organized the Reinforcement Force into a covering force and two transport groups. He would personally command the covering force with *Niizuki* (F), *Suzukaze*, and *Tanikaze*. The 1st Transport Group, *Mochizuki*, *Mikazuki*, and *Hamakaze*, under the command of Captain Orita Tsuneo, would unload first and then depart Vila by Blackett Strait. The 2nd Transport Group, *Amagiri*, *Hatsuyuki*, *Nagatsuki*, and *Satsuki*, under the command of Captain Yamashiro Katsumori, would then unload and return via Kula Gulf.[2]

Early in the morning of 5 July, two F5As hit a clear patch of sky over Buin and got 100 percent coverage. Photographs showed eighteen ships present, half of them destroyers, and along with the earlier CINCPAC warning on 4 July that a run was likely, this prompted Halsey to cover all possibilities. He ordered Merrill, who was heading to Guadalcanal, to take his task group west of Rendova in case this was the target, while Turner alerted NGOF that an attack was possible. To deal with either a reinforcement run to Vila or a possible counter-landing at Rice Anchorage, he sent Ainsworth back to Kula Gulf.[3] Low on ammunition and fuel as a result of the Rice Anchorage operation, Ainsworth was between Guadalcanal and San Cristobal, bound for a rendezvous with a tanker, when he received the orders at 1500. Pressed for time, he took the quickest route through Indispensable Strait, round Florida to the north, and then up the Slot. To replace *Strong* and *Chevalier* – the first sunk and the second damaged the night before – *Radford* and *Jenkins* from Turner's TF 31 joined up northwest of Savo Island. The night was dark and overcast, and a storm front between Kolombangara and Manning Strait was solid enough to turn back the B-17s headed for Kahili. Visibility was about 2,000 to 4,000 yards, and the sea slightly choppy.

Akiyama had departed Buin after dark, beating Ainsworth to the gulf by just about thirty minutes. Orita's group split off 20 miles north of Kolombangara and headed for Vila, steering close to the coast. *Mochizuki* badly damaged its port propeller, either on a reef or with an entangled barge tow cable, and so lagged behind the others.[4] Yamashiro in *Amagiri* was leading his group into the gulf, with Akiyama following, when at 0105, *Niizuki's* radar picked up Ainsworth's force. At that time, however, Akiyama had no clear idea as to the type or number of ships he would be facing. At 0118, he turned back north to engage Ainsworth.

Ainsworth was closing fast. At 0136, *Honolulu* made contact with Akiyama's force at 22,000 yards. Ainsworth immediately ordered the destroyers to form in column in the van and the rear of the cruisers so that his formation was as follows: *Nicholas, O'Bannon, Honolulu* (F: Captain Robert W. Hayler), and *Helena* (Captain Charles P. Cecil), *St. Louis* (Captain Colin Campbell), *Jenkins*, and *Radford*. He notified his captains that the battle would be fought according to his Night Battle Plan A, which was based on the assumption that the Americans enjoyed an overwhelming superiority in radar – both for detection (which assumed surprise) and gunnery control (which assumed that the cruisers could sink or disable enemy ships quickly and turn away before torpedoes could be launched). Consequently, the plan called for opening fire beyond the maximum range of visibility, the American ships remaining completely dark, but at the medium range of 8,000 to 10,000 yards to ensure hitting the enemy quickly and effectively. Ainsworth, therefore, immediately ordered a 60° turn to port to close the range and at 0149 brought his column back to a northwesterly heading by a 60° turn to starboard.

By this time, radar not only had a clear contact on Akiyama standing north but also on Yamashiro deeper in the gulf. For just a moment, Ainsworth considered opening on both groups, with the cruisers reaching out to Yamashiro and the destroyers taking on Akiyama, but he quickly dismissed this idea. Instead he notified his captains that they would "blast this group [Akiyama's] first, reach ahead, then make a simultaneous turn and get the others on the reverse course." This is precisely the way Ainsworth fought his battle.

In the meantime, Akiyama was preparing to fight his. His first duty was to get the transports safely into Vila – Kusaka had made this clear – and at 0143 he ordered Yamashiro to make for Vila. Five minutes later, however, it was also clear that he was facing three light cruisers and at least two destroyers, not the most favorable odds. Despite the fact that Yamashiro's transports were crowded with troops, he ordered the latter to rejoin at 0152. The gap between Akiyama and Yamashiro was about 8,000 yards.

The battle commenced at 0157, when Ainsworth's cruisers and van destroyers opened fire at a range of about 7,000 yards – all, it would appear, on *Niizuki*, the newest and largest of the Japanese ships. The concentration of shells hit with devastating effect, quickly reducing the ship to a blazing wreck, and it fell out of line. But because of poor fire distribution, neither *Suzukaze* nor *Tanikaze* received a serious hit; they immediately launched torpedoes, veered sharply to port to avoid *Niizuki*, then turned back north to pass to the west of Ainsworth (unharmed by the six torpedoes *Jenkins* and *O'Bannon* had fired at long range). Behind them, *Niizuki* sank at 0212, carrying Akiyama, Commander Kaneda Kiyoshi, the ship's captain, and most or all of the crew to the bottom.[5]

But before *Niizuki* went down, *Suzukaze*'s and *Tanikaze*'s torpedoes had exacted retribution. Ainsworth was approaching the limits of his northwest reach. Radar indicated that Akiyama's group had been obliterated: the ships had disappeared from the screen and were presumed sunk, and the remaining pips appeared to be dead in the water. At 0203, Ainsworth executed a 180° simultaneous turn to go back and deal with Yamashiro's group, which was coming up out of the gulf. At this instant, the Japanese torpedoes arrived. The first hit *Helena* abreast the No. 1 turret, blowing off the bow and the turret with its crew; the second and third hit amidships and broke the ship's back. The fourth hit *St. Louis* without exploding, and a fifth passed closely by *Honolulu*. In the smoke of battle and the darkness, Ainsworth was unaware that something was amiss with *Helena* until it failed to acknowledge turn orders to close the target at 0207 and 0215. All ships were on an easterly course, firing on Yamashiro's group, but scoring few hits.

This second phase of the battle was a confused affair. At around 0218, *Amagiri* made smoke, turned hard to starboard, launched torpedoes, and headed back to Vila. At the same time, *Hatsuyuki*, which was astern of *Amagiri*, turned to port, opened fire with its guns, was hit in return by a dud, and then turned toward Vila. *Nagatsuki*, which had taken one hit, and *Satsuki* reversed course for Vila, but *Nagatsuki* ran hard aground on the reef at Sulimuni Cove on Kolombangara's eastern coast. *Satsuki* stayed with the ship to try and pull it off the reef. *Amagiri* and *Hatsuyuki* made port safely.

In the meantime, Ainsworth had turned back west, since it was evident something had happened to *Helena*. He sent *Nicholas* ahead to make a radar sweep of Vella Gulf, while *Radford* swept Kula Gulf. At 0330, *Radford* picked up a small pip, which turned out to be *Helena*'s bow. Ainsworth directed Captain Francis X. McInerney in *Nicholas* to take charge of the rescue operations, then turned back onto his retirement course, confident that he had taken the Japanese by surprise and equally certain from radar reports and visual illumination – and an abiding faith in the radar-directed guns of the cruisers – that he had sunk all of the Japanese ships except one or two cripples. The one discordant note for both Ainsworth and McInerney was what they called the "poor" performance of the destroyers. In his report, McInerney recommended that if destroyers had not operated with the task group before, they should be left in port. As we shall see, this advice was not heeded.[6]

Back at Kula Gulf, a square mile of water covered with oil, debris, and survivors marked *Helena*'s passing. The ship sank amidships first, the stern lifting out of the water so that the men in the water could see the propellers, then what was left of the forward section came out of the water, and by 0225 *Helena* was gone. In flashes of gunfire during the battle, the bow with the number 50 was sometimes visible floating in the water. *Helena* had a complement of 1,187 officers and enlisted men, and Captain Cecil thought that all except those killed by the torpedoes made it off. By 0340, both *Radford* and *Nicholas* were working to rescue survivors.[7]

Down in the gulf, the Japanese worked to save *Nagatsuki*, or at least to unload Major Hara Hidetome's 2nd Independent Quick-Fire Battalion before dawn, when COMAIRSOLS planes were certain to come. A heavy downpour at 0400 soaked the laboring men. *Satsuki* attempted to free *Nagatsuki,* but the ship had plowed up onto the reef and sat like a beached whale. The attempt was not abandoned until nearly 0700, when *Satsuki* left for Vila and a return home by way of Blackett Strait. In the meantime, Hara's battalion, equipped with 37mm and some scarce 47mm guns, was unloaded and dispersed in the jungle, while *Hatsuyuki, Amagiri,* and *Mochizuki* unloaded, partially at least, at Vila. Out of 2,600 men and 180 tons of supplies loaded, the Japanese were able to land 1,600 men and half of the supplies. The 1st Battalion, 13th Infantry, which carried out Sasaki's counterattack, was among the units landed.[8]

The Battle of Kula Gulf ended in a series of skirmishes between the opposing destroyers that remained in the area. At 0400, the American destroyers detected ships closing fast from the northwest. McInerney directed *Radford* to continue with the rescue work, while he would block any enemy attack. At 13,000 yards, however, *Tanikaze* and *Suzukaze*, returning to the scene for a look-see, reversed course and disappeared out of range. A few minutes later, *Radford* picked up what was thought to be two large ships in the gulf, but the contact turned out to be false. When Ainsworth received the reports of radar contacts, he reversed course to return and help, then thought better of it and turned again on his retirement course, advising McInerney to try to make the Russell Islands by daybreak. *Nicholas* and *Radford* resumed rescue work until 0517, when *Amagiri* was detected coming out of the gulf. Both *Nicholas* and *Radford* left the survivors and fired torpedoes at the ships, certain that they had scored hits. *Amagiri*, however, was untouched until 0533, when the American destroyers illuminated the ship with star shells and opened fire. *Amagiri* then took several hits before firing five torpedoes of its own, making smoke, and retiring in the direction of the Shortlands. All five torpedoes missed. Rescue work again resumed until 0612, when *Mochizuki* made its breakout, hugging the Kolombangara coast at reduced speed due to its damaged propeller. It was now daylight, and *Mochizuki* suffered one hit in an exchange of gunfire before making its escape.

At this point, McInerney decided that it was time to retire. He cited the arrival of daylight, uncertainty about how many Japanese ships might still be in the gulf, reports that a submarine was in the area, and the probability of an air attack from Buin. Consequently, he broke off rescue operations, but left three manned whaleboats to assist the men still in the water. Between them, *Nicholas* and *Radford* had 739 of *Helena*'s crew on board when they left the gulf at 0621.[9]

With the exception of a few scattered cumulus clouds, 6 July broke clear and sunny over New Georgia. The first COMAIRSOLS aircraft over Kula Gulf at 0743 was a New Zealand Hudson flying the morning X-Ray search, which reported a large number of survivors in the water and on rafts. In actuality, there were two groups of survivors that were separated by a distance too great to be seen by one another. The group reported by the Hudson was the larger, just under 200 men clustered around the bow of *Helena*; the second group, which included Captain Cecil, consisted of three officers, seventy-eight enlisted men, and the seven destroyer men manning the whaleboats. Cecil organized this group and set out for Visuvisu Point, where two destroyers picked them up next morning. The group around *Helena*'s bow stayed in the area for most of the day. Around noon, a VB-101 PB4Y dropped three rafts (only two were recovered) and all its life preservers, and radioed for PBYs to be sent. None were. The men of this group who survived would have a more trying story to tell (to which we will return later).[10]

Despite the excellent flying weather, Japanese bombers made no appearance. At 0800, the scheduled COMAIRSOLS strike hit Enogai, and two hours later SBDs and TBFs arrived to search for the Japanese ships Ainsworth had reported damaged. Finding nothing but *Nagatsuki*, the bomber pilots circled for thirty minutes, debating the identity of the beached destroyer. They finally decided that it was Japanese, and commenced bombing. As the last of the bombers turned for home, four VF-11 F4Fs intercepted incoming Zeros and claimed four. Details are hazy, but both the Rendova Patrol and the men in the water from *Helena* saw the fight. At 1427, three B-25s with a P-38 escort came in to finish off *Nagatsuki*, and when they left, a 3,000-foot column of smoke towered over the wreck.[11]

That same day, Kusaka moved his headquarters to Buin and requested Combined Fleet for reinforcements. In response, Koga sent Rear Admiral Izaki Shunji, commander, Destroyer Squadron 2, with his flagship light cruiser, *Jintsu*, a destroyer, and Rear Admiral Nishimura Shōji with Cruiser Division 7, *Kumano* and *Suzuya*. Izaki arrived at Rabaul on 10 July, and Nishimura the following day.

UNOPPOSED TRANSPORTS

Without waiting for the reinforcements, Samejima planned to send in the personnel and cargo that had not been unloaded because of the naval battle. Captain Aruga Kōsaku in *Chōkai* would be in command, and with the light cruiser *Sendai* and four destroyers, would make up the covering group. Four destroyers, carrying 1,200 men and 85 tons of cargo, would make up the transport group and use the Vella Gulf–Blackett Strait route to Vila. Aruga sailed on the night of 9 July. Submarine *I-38* was in the gulf, and 938th seaplanes scouted ahead. A Black Cat spotted the force off Visuvisu Point, and at 0245, five VB-101 and VB-102 PB4Ys sent off by COMAIRSOLS attacked. While they reported a hit on a light cruiser, none were made. If the Raiders, spending a fitful night before the attack on Enogai, heard the bombing, they did not mention it. The transport group made Vila, unloaded, and returned by the same route.[12]

The following night, 11–12 July, Ainsworth was back in the gulf covering Turner's transport group to Rice Anchorage, made up of three destroyer transports and three escort destroyers. The RNZN light cruiser *Leander* (Captain C. A. L. Mansergh, RN) took *Helena*'s place. The night was bright with a three-quarter moon overhead, and Ainsworth hugged the shore of Santa Isabel to keep from being silhouetted. But Japanese seaplanes spotted him as he cut diagonally across the Slot toward Visuvisu Point, and 6th Air Attack Force prepared for a dawn strike. Samuel Eliot Morison, on the bridge of *Honolulu*, watched Merrill's bombardment of Munda, writing later that "we are too far off to hear the reports, but the sky over New Georgia keeps blinking as if from continuous summer lightning."[13]

Turner's transport group had a more trying time. At Rice, the arrival of the transport was apparently unexpected. Unloading went slowly, since the greater part of the 145th had departed to join Liversedge and manpower was inadequate. At 0430, as the transport group retired, with some boats missing and some cargo still on board, *Taylor*'s radar picked up a contact that turned out to be a submarine on the surface. *Taylor* opened fire at close range, and when the submarine submerged, laid a depth charge pattern. Apparently, this was RO-103, which was seriously damaged but was able to resurface and make emergency repairs off the northwest coast of Kolombangara.[14]

At first light, the Japanese 6th Air Attack Force sent off thirteen D3A "Val" dive bombers and forty-seven Zeros from the 582nd and 251st, which arrived at roughly 0800. In an attempt to protect the vulnerable D3As, the Japanese flight leader tried a new tactic. One group of fighters and the bombers headed for Visuvisu Point, but finding no shipping, they turned to attack Rice Anchorage. The other group of fighters staged a mock dogfight over Vila in an attempt to draw the American fighters away from the carrier bombers. The ruse did not work. Vega told VMF-213 that the dogfight was a phony and to stay on station to intercept any Rendova-bound aircraft, while the Corsairs of VMF-122 and the P-40s of the 44th Fighter Squadron made the interception. As the men on the ground at the anchorage watched, the Corsairs and P-40s shot down four Zeros and damaged a Val so badly that it ditched short of its base at Ballale. One F4U and one P-40 went down.[15]

BATTLE OF KOLOMBANGARA

Less than an hour after the American fighters had cleared Japanese aircraft from the skies over Kula Gulf, Ainsworth made port. But there would be no rest for his task group. At midday, he received orders from Halsey to return immediately to Kula Gulf to intercept an expected "Tokyo Express."[16] At the same time, Turner received orders to block the western end of Blackett Strait with PT boats and to provide all destroyers practicable to Ainsworth. Turner came up with seven from three different squadrons that had never worked together as a unit before, much less as a part of Ainsworth's task group. To further complicate matters, two of these did not have SG radar, two more could make only 30 knots because of engineering problems, and one had just arrived a few days before. Turner's destroyers were under the command of Captain Ryan, who was quickly taken aboard *Honolulu* for a hurried twenty-minute briefing on the battle plan and operating procedures. TBS (talk between ships)[17] call signs and voice codes were a different matter, and Ainsworth decided to use plain English. With his destroyers still scattered, Ryan would have to gather them, brief the commanders, and then catch up with the main group, since Ainsworth intended to get under way as soon as possible. By throwing all the ships he had available at the Japanese, Halsey had saddled Ainsworth with an unwieldy formation, and worse, with destroyers that had no experience working with a cruiser task group.

At 1700, Ainsworth got underway. Making up the vanguard were McInerney in *Nicholas*, followed by *O'Bannon*, *Taylor*, *Jenkins*, and *Rad-*

ford. Honolulu (F), *Leander,* and *St. Louis* followed in the center. Ainsworth placed *Leander* in the middle because of its inferior radar; when he ordered a 180° turn to avoid torpedoes, he wanted *St. Louis* in the lead. Ryan's destroyers would make up the rear when the group caught up, but Ryan had to leave his flagship, *Farenholt,* behind because of engineering problems. Action reports and the subsequent histories are unclear about the positions of the rear destroyers when the battle line was formed. The assigned positions seem to be as follows: *Ralph Talbot* (F), *Buchanan, Maury, Woodworth,* and *Gwin.* However, *Buchanan,* moving from its screen position and limited to 30 knots, could not get into position in the line and was trying to pass *Woodworth* on the engaged side (starboard) as the action began.[18]

Ainsworth's orders were for him to be north of Visuvisu Point by 0100, and if no contact was made by 0230, to retire to Tulagi. Since the three-quarter moon was bright and not due to set until 0215, Ainsworth kept close to the coast of Santa Isabel as he headed up the Slot at 25 knots. Far to the west were rain clouds, and a few scattered rain squalls were over the Slot. As the task group passed the Russells, those on deck saw a G4M going down in a ball of flames before the guns of a P-38 night fighter. In *Maury,* the executive officer and CIC evaluator,[19] Lieutenant Russell Sydnor Crenshaw Jr., wrote, "Men checked and double-checked their equipment, puffed nervously on cigarettes, or just fell silent and waited." In *Honolulu,* Morison read a book to pass the time. Far ahead was a PBY Black Cat with *Honolulu's* spotter on board, searching the sea below for the Japanese.[20]

The Japanese were there. As much as they liked to avoid a transport during the bright moon period, they had to get Yamada's battalion to Bairoko to defend against Liversedge's Northern Landing Force. The covering force – *Mikazuki, Jintsu* (F), *Yukikaze, Hamakaze, Kiyonami,* and *Yūgure* – under the command of Rear Admiral Izaki, which had sailed early that morning from Rabaul, was coming down the Slot at 25 knots. Hanging back some distance was Kanaoka's transport group, *Satsuki, Minazuki, Yūnagi,* and *Matsukaze,* which had sailed from Buin after sunset. The plan was for the covering force to take station off Kula Gulf to block American interference, while the transport group would slip into Vella Gulf and unload at Ariel, the recently established barge base on the southwest coast of Kolombangara.

At 0015, the Black Cat spotted the Japanese, and twenty minutes later it accurately reported the course, speed, and composition of the force to Ainsworth. Ainsworth reckoned Izaki's location at about 20° on the starboard bow at a distance of 26 miles. He ordered battle formation and increased speed to 28 knots, which was *Leander's* maximum. At 0044, a seaplane found Ainsworth, and *Yukikaze* (Captain Shimai Zenjirō) reported that its radar detection gear indicated that it had been detected. At 0050, Ainsworth ordered McInerney to increase speed and reach out ahead. Nine minutes later, *Honolulu's* radar made contact, and at 0106, Ainsworth ordered a 30° simultaneous starboard turn to close the range.

The battle opened at around 0109, when Izaki's destroyers launched their torpedoes and McInerney's destroyers fired theirs. After making two 30° turns to port to bring all batteries to bear, Ainsworth's cruisers opened fire at 0112, and the rear destroyers fired their torpedoes. Although Ainsworth reported that after five minutes the three leading Japanese ships were burning and practically dead in the water, gunfire distribution was again poor; the full weight of his guns fell on *Jintsu*, which had turned on its searchlight to illuminate McInerney. Izaki and Captain Satō Torajirō were killed, and the ship quickly caught fire, but the other destroyers were unscathed. Around 0145, one or more torpedoes from McInerney's destroyers sent *Jintsu* to the bottom with 482 men.[21] *Mikazuki*, which was in the van, apparently tried to go to the aid of *Jintsu*, but Ainsworth's gunfire was too intense, so *Mikazuki* made smoke, turned due north, and cleared the battle area. The rear destroyers under the command of Shimai escaped to the northwest and began reloading torpedoes.

At 0116, Ainsworth ordered the 180° turn away to port, but *Leander* missed the execute signal. All the rear destroyers except *Ralph Talbot* began turning on the order a minute before the execute signal, which left *Ralph Talbot* out of position. Captain Mansergh saw the other cruisers turning and quickly brought *Leander* around; he was just at the completion of his turn when the Japanese torpedoes arrived. The rear destroyers, already bunched in disarray, managed to avoid them, but at about

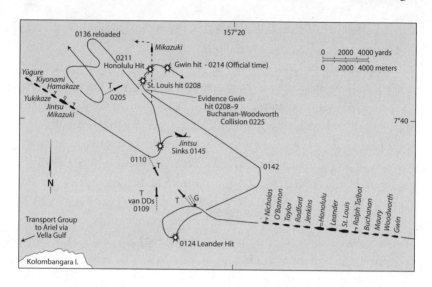

Map 9.2. Naval Battle of Kolombangara, 13 July 1943.

0124, one hit *Leander* on the port side, flooding the forward boiler room. Mansergh ordered engines stopped. Ainsworth's line was now in considerable confusion as *Gwin* and the other scattered rear destroyers put on speed to take up their positions in the van.

At this point, Ainsworth's picture of the battle grew murkier. He was on the reverse course with both cruisers firing on what was thought to be crippled ships. From radar reports, he thought he had accounted for all of the Japanese ships; the Black Cat, however, reported four enemy destroyers making off at high speed. Ainsworth ordered McInerney to pursue these ships, while he worked around northward and up the Slot to finish off any crippled ships. He then ordered a simultaneous 60° turn to port, which put his cruisers on course 300° headed up the Slot. At around 0156, *Honolulu* made radar contact with a group of ships, but the Black Cat reported these as two destroyers trying to get away. Ainsworth set out in pursuit and gradually began to overtake them. As he did so, the two destroyers materialized into four. But Ainsworth was still in some doubt as to their identity, since they could possibly be McInerney's ships with which he had lost contact. At 0203, the four destroyers were seen to be closing fast, and two minutes later, Ainsworth illuminated them with star shells, ordered a simultaneous 60° turn to starboard, and opened fire.

"Then the party really started," Hayler said later. The four destroyers were Shimai's, rejoining the battle with their torpedoes already in the water. At 0208, one hit *St. Louis*, blowing open the bow; a few seconds later, a second hit *Gwin* aft in the No. 2 engine room, while another narrowly missed ahead; Hayler in *Honolulu* managed to dodge the torpedoes seen to port, but could not avoid one that hit the starboard bow at 0211 and another that embedded in the stern without exploding.[22] Almost immediately, he had to do some desperate maneuvering to avoid *Gwin*, which was bearing down on *Honolulu*, ablaze aft with its rudder jammed. It seemed that it would ram squarely amidships, and when Morison went into Hayler's cabin he found everyone lying on the floor awaiting the collision that never came. *Gwin* missed *Honolulu* by about fifty yards. The night was now dark, the moon having set a few minutes early behind the western clouds, and as *Woodworth* and *Buchanan*, the two destroyers that lacked SG radar, headed for *Gwin*, *Woodworth's* stern sideswiped *Buchanan's* bow, but neither ship's speed was hampered.

Ainsworth now had to get his three groups of damaged ships out of the area. A quick inspection showed that both American cruisers had lost their bows, but otherwise were in good shape, able to make 15 knots. Neither had suffered any serious casualties. Four destroyers were assigned as escort. *Leander*, with eighteen men killed and ten missing, had suffered more damage but could make 10 knots.[23] Two destroyers were assigned to the ship. *Gwin*, the heaviest damaged of all, had its No. 2 engine room flooded, the afterdeck house and No. 4 gun mount blown over the side, and fifty-seven officers and men dead or missing. Two would die of wounds later. *Gwin* would have to be towed, and *Ralph Talbot* and *Maury* stood by.[24]

Ainsworth radioed COMAIRSOLS that he had sunk one cruiser and two destroyers and damaged two other destroyers, that all of his cruisers had been hit, and that he would need plenty of air cover. *Honolulu* and *St. Louis* then set off down the Slot, their wakes reminding Hayler of San Francisco ferryboats running abreast. *Leander* group followed.

In the meantime, around 0200, Kanaoka with his transport group arrived at Ariel and by 0400 had unloaded Yamada's battalion and twenty tons of ammunition. He left by way of Vella Gulf, looked over the battle area, saw no sign of *Jintsu*, and headed back to Buin. The Japanese reported no interference from the PT boats blocking the Blackett Strait entrance (expecting Vila to be Kanaoka's destination, the PT boats were too far east).[25]

Dawn broke on a busy day for COMAIRSOLS, especially Fighter Command, which now had to cover the *Gwin* group and the two separate cruiser groups making their way slowly down the Slot. *Gwin* was in the most danger, so the Rendova Patrol of twenty navy F4Fs kept watch. At 0700, eight B-25s with twelve F4U Wildcats came looking for the destroyers that Ainsworth reported he had damaged, searched the coasts of Kolombangara and Vella Lavella, and returned to base. Kosaka sent down six D3A Vals and thirty-two Zeros, which the F4Fs intercepted at 0845 west of the *Gwin* group; the Americans said the D3As jettisoned their bombs and ran for it. The navy pilots claimed four Zeros but lost one; the VF-28 pilot set down by *Maury* and was picked up. Less than an hour later, the attempt to save *Gwin* ended, and *Ralph Talbot* sank the ship. The navy was lavish in its praise for the fighters' performance, which was well-deserved. Operationally, however, the price had been high. At the end of the day, nine aircraft had been lost – three pilots had been picked up but six were still missing – and seven more had made forced landings at either Segi or the Russells.[26]

At Pearl Harbor, Nimitz was giving considerably thought to the costly Kula Gulf battles. The smoke had hardly cleared before he set down his concerns in a letter to Halsey: the damage that Japanese torpedoes continued to inflict, the unwieldy formation Ainsworth had led into the second battle, specifically the addition of Turner's destroyers, and the exaggeration of Japanese losses due to overreliance on radar. Since the primary justification for sending naval units into the confined waters of New Georgia was either the prevention of Japanese reinforcements or the protection of American reinforcements, Nimitz suggested that a well-trained squadron of 2,100-tonners, *Fletcher*-class destroyers, would do the job better than light cruisers.

In his reply, Halsey argued his case. He did submit a more conservative estimate of Japanese losses, but concluded that Ainsworth had inflicted more damage than he had suffered. On the torpedo question, he admitted that Ainsworth had closed too much and got himself into torpedo water in the second phase of the second battle, but he suggested that *Leander* had been hit by American torpedoes. Nonetheless, he was prepared to accept the fact that the Japanese had a torpedo comparable to that of the British (13,000 yards at 31 knots, 11,000 yards at 36 knots), figures he had used in a warning to his task force commanders. But about the use of the *Fletcher*-class destroyers, however, he disagreed with Nimitz entirely and restated the assumptions behind Ainsworth's Night Battle Plan A: the SG radar and radar-directed gunnery were far superior to anything that the Japanese had, and the solution "appears to be the greatest volume and weight of gunfire that can be incorporated into a highly maneuverable unit – and a unit that is certainly not appreciably weaker than the enemy unit."[27] This said, what Halsey actually did was designate two squadrons of 2,100-tonners to alternate in the New Georgia operations, and he never risked more than two of his remaining light cruisers up the Slot on any one mission – and even then, he exercised the greatest caution.[28]

In his assessment of the battles, Morison would characterize such thinking as "over-confidence in 6-inch gunfire, over-confidence in radar, and ignorance both of the Japanese torpedo performance and of Japanese ability to track without radar."[29] We will take these up in order. First, faith in radar-directed gunfire was misplaced. Accuracy was not that good – in the two battles the cruisers had fired 5,630 rounds to sink two ships – while fire distribution was not observed in either battle, the entire weight falling on the largest ship on the screen. Second, the American high command simply could not comprehend that the Japanese had a torpedo with the range, speed, and warhead that the Type 93 ("Long Lance") had. The Type 93 carried a 1,000-pound warhead and could travel 20,000 meters at 48 knots and 40,000 meters at 36 knots. In effect, the Type 93 negated the assumptions of Night Battle Plan A. Third, and finally, the faith in the SG radar was misplaced, especially in the belief that it would guarantee surprising the Japanese force. In neither battle were the Japanese surprised. Even if the Japanese had not begun to install radar – admittedly inferior – or had not developed a radar detection set, their seaplanes were on hand to conduct searches. It was a leap of faith to take surprise as a given. In battle conditions, rain squalls and the close and very high landmass of Kolombangara interfered; Japanese ships disappeared from the screen and were considered sunk, which was responsible for the continual and embarrassing American overestimation of damage inflicted.[30]

THE *HELENA* RESCUE MISSION TO VELLA LAVELLA

We left the nearly 200 survivors in the area around *Helena*'s bow around midday 6 July. The wounded had been placed in the two rubber lifeboats dropped by the PB4Y and waited for rescue that never came. As night set in, Lieutenant Commander John L. Chew, the senior naval officer, and the other ranking officers decided to try to make the Kolombangara coast 6 or 7 miles south. The wind and the current, however, carried them north of the island, and the next morning, they decided to try for Vella Lavella. A case of potatoes floated by and was recovered, which relieved their thirst. One man died in Chew's boat; others just swam away and were not seen again. During the night, the two boat groups became separated. The next morning, 7 July, sixty-one men made landfall in the Paraso Bay area west of Horaniu, and another group of 104 men under Chew reached Lambu Lambu Cove east of Horaniu. Some made it ashore on their own; Josselyn's scouts went out in canoes and brought in the rest. The main Japanese force on the island, Josselyn estimated at around 100, was at the naval relay base at Horaniu, but there were lookout posts on both sides of Lambu Lambu and another near Paraso Bay. Nonetheless, the Japanese made no effort to intervene.

Protecting and feeding 165 men presented Josselyn with a considerable problem. With most of his scouts, he went to Paraso Bay to take charge, gathered the survivors in a camp inland, and set up a defense perimeter. He sent three armed scouts with seven rifles and a shotgun to Chew's group, which armed Major Bernard T. Kelly and his five marines, and asked Reverend Silvester to provide for their medical care and living needs. Only once did a small Japanese party get too close – this at Lambu Lambu – but the scouts killed all four. The men, in poor condition from their ordeal, were fed well. They had stew twice daily made from canned meat and local vegetables, and over 100 pounds of navy coffee washed up on the beach. The wounded were put up in a house of the small Chinese refugee community from Ghanongga.

Josselyn, of course, had been in communication with T F 31 from the start, and an evacuation was arranged for the night of 12 July. But delays, first caused by the Battle of Kolombangara and then one requested by Josselyn to get the Chew party ready, pushed the date back three days. On 15 July, the evacuation force sailed from Port Purvis in two groups. Three destroyer transports and four destroyers under Ryan took the route south of Rendova and through Gizo Strait. Four destroyers under McInerney headed directly up the Slot to a point off Vella Lavella to serve as the covering force. With nightfall, the full moon lit up the night, and while Japanese seaplanes spotted McInerney, they flew on to continue their nightly battle with the P T boats. There were no Japanese warships anywhere in the area.

The greatest problem were the reefs at Paraso, so Josselyn decided to evacuate that party first, going out himself in a canoe to meet the destroyers and guide in the Higgins boats. All went well, and Ryan proceeded to Lambu Lambu and loaded that party, along with some of the Chinese. By 0450, both groups were headed back down the Slot, picking up two *Jintsu* survivors floating in a boat from *Gwin*. Altogether, the destroyers carried 165 men from *Helena*, sixteen Chinese, one Japanese pilot captured at Paraso, and the two *Jintsu* sailors.[31]

COMAIRSOLS AGAINST THE REINFORCEMENT FORCES

In the aftermath of the Battle of Kolombangara, Samejima formed the Night Battle Unit under Nishimura to smash American interference with the transports. This was a formidable force made up of three heavy cruisers (*Chōkai* joined Cruiser Division 7), *Sendai*, now the flagship of Rear Admiral Ijūin Matsuji, who had replaced Akiyama, and four destroyers. The first transport was scheduled for 17 July; Orita with three destroyers would deliver fuel and supplies to Ariel. Two destroyers left Rabaul for Buin on 16 July with supplies for transfer to Orita's destroyers.

But Samejima's plans coincided with Mitscher's to put an end to the Japanese using the Buin naval base without fear of daylight air attacks. On 17 July, an F5A photo reconnaissance aircraft led the way at 0843 taking "before" photographs, so that the F5A following the bombers could take "after" photographs for damage assessment. Off Kahili airfield, *Hatsuyuki* and *Mochizuki* were alongside *Minazuki* and *Satsuki* transferring supplies and fuel drums, and smaller shipping and barges were swarming in the area. Since a high-flying F5A was a routine event for the Japanese, work never ceased. But this morning would be different. Thirty-seven minutes behind the F5A came a formation of seven B-24s with thirty-two P-38s and P-40s, and ten minutes behind the heavy bombers came thirty-six marine and navy SBD Dauntless dive bombers, thirty-six navy TBF Avenger torpedo bombers, and sixty-four navy Wildcats and marine Corsairs.

For the Japanese sailors toiling on the bunched-up ships, the first hint that something was wrong was when Zeros began taking off from Kahili. The B-24s made their run, and while it is possible they set a small cargo ship afire, most of the drops were near misses or wide. Ten minutes later, the SBDs and TBFs attacked the warships off Kahili, but surprise had been lost and all but *Hatsuyuki* and *Minazuki* had gotten underway. *Hatsuyuki* took a direct hit to a magazine that sent it to the bottom, and *Minazuki* and two other destroyers received some minor damage from near misses. It was a poor performance for the SBDs and TBFs. But if the bombing results were meager, the escort fighters did well. Altogether, the Japanese were able to send up forty-eight Zeros; the American fighters shot down thirteen with eight pilots killed, while losing six of their own. (One P-38 pilot was rescued later.) One SBD and one TBF failed to return. Next day, COMAIRSOLS was back again with twenty-one B-24s, thirty-nine SBDs, TBFs, and seventy fighters. But the Japanese had already called off the transport, and the bombers only inflicted minor damage on one destroyer. COMAIRSOLS fighters shot down three Zeros, losing three F4Us of their own, while one TBF was missing. One F4U pilot was recovered. For the effort expended, the results were disappointing; perhaps the continuous missions against land targets had taken the edge off the ship-killing skills of the Dauntless and Avenger pilots.[32]

The battle with the Japanese 8th Fleet resumed on the night of 19–20 July. Nishimura's Night Battle Unit sailed from Rabaul two hours before midnight on 18 July, and at 1920 on 19 July joined Orita's transport force, *Mikazuki*, *Minazuki*, and *Matsukaze*, for the trip down the Slot. The sky was overcast with a storm front pushing southeast between Santa Isabel and Guadalcanal. Just before Orita split off and headed down Vella Gulf for Kolombangara, a Black Cat spotted the Japanese force, tried to report it to Guadalcanal, but failed to get through. Nishimura maintained course to Kula Gulf, encountering no American ships. (Merrill's task group was in the New Hebrides.) In the meantime, the Black Cat finally established contact, and at 0045 Strike Command got off six TBFs armed with 2,000-pound bombs. The TBFs caught up with Nishimura at 0225, after he had turned back. *Yūgure* took a direct hit and sank quickly, while the heavy cruiser *Kumano* received serious damage aft from a near miss (it caused enough damage that one Japanese report thought it was a torpedo). *Chōkai* may also have sustained minor damage from a near miss. Two of the TBFs failed to return and were apparently shot down. Nishimura's ships scattered at high speed, while *Kiyonami* stayed behind to pick up survivors from *Yūgure*. Whether the TBFs also hit *Kiyonami* is not entirely clear. At 0243 eighteen B-24s on their way home, with Japanese night fighters still dogging them, reported seeing one ship explode and another burning steadily. But *Kiyonami*'s last message, sent shortly after 0310, indicated that it had no trouble and that it was on its way to rejoin the other ships.

The time of *Kiyonami*'s report coincided with the arrival of eight B-25s. The Black Cat directed four of these on the main force and the other four on Orita's transports. The B-25s attacked *Kiyonami* at masthead level through heavy antiaircraft fire, and it appears they hit *Kiyonami*, leaving it all but dead in the water. The B-25s attacking Orita's transports only did some minor damage to *Minazuki* and *Matsuzuki*, while the destroyers shot down a B-25 (the crew was recovered). At 0400, two more strikes came in, five Avengers armed with torpedoes and eight B-17s, the first strike attacking ships of the main force, the second Orita's transports. Neither formation claimed any hits. Daylight brought another B-25 strike of eight aircraft, and these sank *Kiyonami* off the Choiseul coast. But on the return home, four of this group were involved in a friendly fire incident with PT boats south of Ferguson Passage in which one boat was sunk, another set on fire, and one B-25 shot down. At 0830, the final formation of thirty-five SBDs and TBFs arrived, bombed the only ship in sight, the stranded *Nagatsuki*, and returned to base. According to the Japanese, Orita delivered 582 men, 102 tons of ammunition and supplies, and 60 drums of fuel. But the cost had been high, and the Japanese abandoned the Night Battle Unit plan.[33]

The air-sea battle was renewed on 22 July when COMAIRSOLS formations intercepted a Combined Fleet reinforcement run to Bougainville. In an agreement brokered at IGHQ, the navy agreed to transport the South Seas 4th Garrison Unit (or Guard Unit) of 630 men, twenty-two tanks, and eight artillery pieces to Bougainville to compensate Imamura for the troops that he was sending to New Georgia from 6th Division. The reinforcement group, under the command of Rear Admiral Ōsugi Morikazu and built around the seaplane carrier *Nisshin*, sailed on 10 July from Kure for Truk with Ozawa's Carrier Division 1. From Truk, the *Nisshin* group sailed to Rabaul and from there for Bougainville. Two destroyers put in at Buka, where the Japanese were building Bonis Airfield on the Bougainville side of Buka Passage; *Nisshin*, with *Hagikaze*, *Arashi*, and *Isokaze*, proceeded on to Buin.

Acting on ULTRA intelligence from CINCPAC, the COMAIRSOLS formation intercepted off Cape Friendship, just as the group neared the eastern entrance to the Buin anchorages. Twelve B-24s with an escort of sixty-six army, marine, and New Zealand fighters led the formation, followed closely by sixteen navy SBDs and eighteen marine and navy TBFs, escorted by sixty-eight navy F4Fs. Incredibly, given the recent daylight attacks on Buin, Kosaka had no fighter cover over the ships; the COMAIRSOLS pilots reported dust clouds rising at Kahili as the Zeros began taking off. The B-24s began dropping at 1550, but scored no hits on *Nisshin*. But five minutes later, the dive bombers scored multiple hits, one of which went through *Nisshin*'s open hanger and exploded in the bowels of the ship. *Nisshin*'s steering was wrecked, and Captain Itō Jōtarō could only proceed on a straight course. This made things easier for the Avengers, and they made three more hits, two of them deep in the ship. The F4Fs fended off the Zeros now on the scene, and no bombers were lost. But three F4Fs turned up missing (five Zeros were claimed shot down). Scarcely had COMAIRSOLS aircraft turned for home than *Nisshin* sank bow first. The loss was a serious blow not only for the Imperial Navy but also for the Buin defenses.[34]

The next night, Captain Shimai, whose destroyers had inflicted the losses on Ainsworth at Kolombangara, led a successful reinforcement run to Kolombangara. With the 13th Regiment at Munda and Yamada's battalion at Bairoko Harbor, Samejima was concerned about the defense of Vila. Once again Imamura provided troops, Lieutenant Colonel Yano Keiji's 2nd Battalion, 230th Regiment, from the 38th Division at Rabaul. With *Yukikaze* (F), *Mikazuki*, and *Hamakaze*, Shimai departed Rabaul an hour before dawn on 23 July. He set a course southeast that skirted the Treasury Islands to the west of Buin and avoided the Slot by using Wilson Strait to make port at Ariel. Having learned a tough lesson with the sinking of *Nisshin*, the Japanese naval historians record, this time there was air cover over Shimai's destroyers. However, it was the course change that was all-important, for Merrill was coming up the Slot with a powerful task group to supply Liversedge at Enogai. Merrill's covering force was made up of two cruisers and five destroyers; the transport group (Commander Arleigh Burke) consisted of four destroyer transports with 200 tons of supplies and an escort of four destroyers.

All went well for Shimai until a Black Cat spotted him 30 miles west of Vella Lavella. The Black Cat tried but failed to contact Merrill; the report got through to Guadalcanal, however, and four Avengers and four B-25s were sent off. Meanwhile, Shimai made for Ariel. The Black Cat then dropped a flare over Blackett Strait, receiving a protest from the PT boats that it was illuminating them. Shimai began unloading at 2330, but alerted by the patrolling seaplanes that the PT boats were just east of him, stopped after little more than an hour (the Japanese say they were nearly finished), and retired the way he had come. By this time Avengers were in the area. They spotted Shimai, but were uncertain of his identity. The pilots thought it was possible that Merrill was operating in Vella Gulf and that they had not been notified. Merrill arrived at around 0100 and searched west of Kolombangara, finding only empty seas. Meanwhile Burke's group unloaded at Enogai, and two of the destroyers briefly bombarded Bairoko Harbor. To the south in Blackett Strait, the PT boats, evading the Japanese seaplanes that were bombing them, attacked the barges now running from Ariel to Vila. The Black Cat overheard a PT boat accuse a TBF pilot of a near miss on it and the Avenger pilot deny that he had dropped. It was an altogether confusing night for all involved.[35]

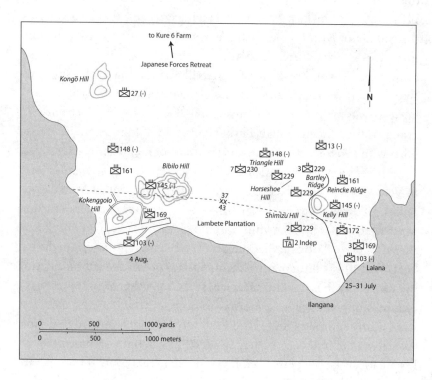

to Kure 6 Farm

Japanese Forces Retreat

Kongō Hill

27 (-)

N

148 (-)

13 (-)

161

148 (-)

Bibilo Hill

Triangle Hill

7 230

3 229

161

145 (-)

Bartley Ridge

Reincke Ridge

Kokenggolo Hill

229

Horseshoe Hill

229

37 XX 43

145 (-)

169

Shimizu Hill

Kelly Hill

103 (-)

Lambete Plantation

229

172

4 Aug.

2 Indep

3 169

103 (-)

Laiana

25–31 July

Ilangana

0   500   1000 yards

0   500   1000 meters

Map 10.1. Munda, 25 July–5 August 1943.

194

TEN

The Second Battle of Munda

ON 5 AUGUST, GRISWOLD TELEGRAPHED HALSEY THAT AFTER twelve days of fighting, Munda had fallen, and the troops "present it to you, as of 1500 Love, as the sole owner.... This operation to date has seen the integrated use of naval bombardment, all forms of air bombardment, the use of tanks, flame throwers and superb artillery – all used in direct support of the infantry, which still had to close and physically wrest the ground from a determined foe. Thus, our Munda operation is the finest example in all my experience of an all-service, All-American Team."[1]

PLANS AND PREPARATIONS

Griswold's plan was simple enough. Following a naval bombardment and a heavy bombing, infantry, supported by marine tanks and Barker's artillery, would make a frontal attack on the Japanese line. The 43rd Division on the left would take Lambete Plantation and the airfield, and the 37th Division on the right would take Bilbilo Hill and envelop the Japanese north of the airfield. Forming his battle line of two divisions would take time, however, so Griswold set the attack date for 25 July.

On the right, Major General Robert S. Beightler, commander, 37th Division, and the only National Guard general to lead his division from start to finish in the war,[2] set up his headquarters on 22 July. He planned to put Baxter's 148th Infantry on his right, the attached 161st Infantry from the 25th Division (Colonel James E. Dalton II) in the center, and Holland's 145th Infantry on his left. The 145th had already relieved the

169th, which was on Rendova for rest and rehabilitation, with 2nd Battalion (Lieutenant Colonel Theodore L. Parker) on Reincke Ridge, and 1st Battalion (Lieutenant Colonel Richard D. Crooks) on Kelly Hill. Japanese positions were on both flanks and the strongly fortified Horseshoe Hill to the immediate front. The 148th's sector outflanked the Japanese line and faced no opposition on its front. Beightler's trouble developed in the center, on the ridge east of Horseshoe Hill, which had been designated as the 161st's assembly area. Unknown to intelligence, Kojima's battalion held it in some force. After Dalton's advance party was hit by machine-gun fire, a probe by a company on 24 July found strong double-logged pillboxes before withdrawing. Beightler then ordered Dalton to take the salient on the morning that the offensive began.[3]

In the 43rd's sector, the reorganization went more smoothly. Ross's 172nd Infantry sidestepped north to make room for 2nd Battalion (103rd Infantry, from Wickham Anchorage), which gave two battalions to Lieutenant Colonel Brown, now regimental commander. In order to give Hester a sixth battalion for the opening of the offensive, Major Ignatius M. Ramsey's 3rd Battalion, 169th Infantry, (Reincke had moved up to regimental executive officer) was given priority on replacements, 203 officers and men, and sent to Laiana on 24 July to go into reserve.

With the new battalions came additional artillery, engineering, and medical support. Barker, now XIV Corps artillery commander, received four additional 105mm battalions, three of which he placed on Dume and Roviana Islands west of Honiavasa Passage. The other he put on Kokorana, freeing up the 192nd, with its 155s, to move to Roviana. Altogether, Barker now had eight battalions of artillery and the two marine 155mm gun batteries.[4] Engineer strength increased by four companies, three from the 37th Division's 117th Engineer Battalion and one from the 25th Division's 65th. Like the 118th, the 117th was equipped with the little Caterpillar D-4 bulldozers, but A Company, 65th, brought in one D-7, a larger dozer that could do the job. Japanese respect for the engineers stood second only to that for the artillery. With some exaggeration, the Kumamato Division historians wrote that the "engineers that led the infantry cleared the jungle and also fought with the infantry with guns and grenades."[5] Finally, the inadequate medical support that had plagued the first attack was partially addressed on July 28 by bringing in the 17th Field

Hospital to set up on Kokorana Island, while the 37th Division brought in its 112th Medical Battalion, less one company, and the 161st brought in one company of the 25th Medical Battalion.[6]

On Kongō Hill, Sasaki did what he could with what he had – he pressed Tomonari to quickly make a second counterattack with whatever troops he could muster on the American northern flank; he wanted to bring over the Guadalcanal veteran Major Yano Keiji with his 2nd Battalion (230th) from Kolombangara when it landed, and use it to reinforce Hirata's 229th on the left of the line.[7] Obstacles bedeviled both. First, Tomonari, who had suffered heavy casualties, was still trying to regroup his forces scattered in the rugged highlands as a result of the counterattack on Zanana. The terrain was as much of an obstacle for him as it was for the Americans, a fact that Sasaki did not seem to appreciate. Not until 27 July would Tomonari start west to attack the 148th on the northern flank. Second, Samejima refused to release Yano's battalion because that would violate the agreement with Eighth Army and would leave Kolombangara vulnerable. Finally, Samejima relented somewhat and gave Sasaki one company, the 7th, which took up a position on 25 July northwest of Kojima's 3rd Battalion at Sankaku (Triangle) Hill.

To reinforce Hirata, who had lost 239 men and 14 officers killed and wounded from the 229th, and 90 men and 3 officers in Major Hara Hidetome's 2nd Independent Quick-Fire Battalion, Sasaki had only Major Hara Masao's depleted 1st Battalion, which had arrived at the Kure 6th Farm from Viru Harbor on 19 July, and some troops retained at Munda Beach and Kokenggolo Hill. Hirata put these into the line between Satō's 2nd Battalion and Kojima's 3rd on Horseshoe Hill, the key position in the Japanese line. With this, Sasaki had his 2nd Battalion facing the American 43rd Division; his 1st and 3rd Battalions and 7th Company (230th Regiment) in the path of the American 37th Division; and his 13th Infantry, less at least one battalion, moving into position on the 37th's northern flank. For good reason, Sasaki was worried about his left.[8]

THE XIV CORPS OFFENSIVE

With seven destroyers, Burke opened the attack at first light on 25 July, with a bombardment of Lambete Plantation from Blanche Channel. Like

Merrill's before him, his group was organized into three sections, each opening fire in succession as they passed through the channel. The light was still dim and visibility made worse by the morning haze over New Georgia, so the aiming points Burke had noted on his reconnaissance the day before were obscured. No shells hit close to the troops, but by 0644, the destroyers had put 4,000 rounds of five-inch shells on Lambete.[9] The destroyers were still firing when the bombs began falling. B-24s and B-17s led the attack, followed by the B-25s, then followed by the SBDs and TBFs. Altogether, 171 bombers with over 100 fighters struck Munda, the largest air attack COMAIRSOLS had ever mounted. All the staff officers who could talk themselves into a ride went along to see what the 23rd Squadron (H) called the "greatest show on earth."[10] The only attempt by the Japanese to interfere was at 0940, when fifty-seven Zeros came in. The bombers had departed, and twenty-nine fighters of the Rendova Patrol intercepted, shooting down six Zeros and losing four. Great clouds of smoke-laced dust hung over Munda, but for all the ordnance dropped, Japanese losses were comparatively light.[11]

On the ground, the attack began before the last bombers turned for home. Griswold fully expected to break the Japanese line. His orders to the battalion commanders stressed maintaining the momentum: "Centers of resistance will be contained, bi-passed, and reduced without impeding the impetus of the attack. Attack briskly." He was to be disappointed. In the 43rd's sector, the artillery lifted at 0700, and the 103rd Infantry on the left and the 172nd on the right moved forward. The 103rd's objective was Ilangana Point, and briefly it appeared the attack would succeed. On the right, E Company found a gap and advanced quickly, reaching the beach behind the Japanese fortifications. Hester, who was at the 103rd CP, immediately ordered Ramsey's 3rd Battalion, 169th Infantry, into the breach to exploit the breakthrough, but the attempt failed when the Japanese opened intense fire from both flanks. E Company was now cut off, but made its way back to the lines, raising the possibility that it might be possible to outflank Ilangana. The 172nd's attack – 2nd and 3rd Battalions supported by five tanks and aimed at enveloping the strong Japanese position on Shimizu Hill (Pure Water Mountain) – failed completely. The hill on the approach was steep with large trees at the crest, making it impossible for the tanks to overrun it. Then three tanks stopped dead with vapor lock, and much time and trouble was spent in extricating them.

On the 37th Division's front, the Japanese positions were still not clearly identified. On his left, Beightler kept the 145th in place on Reincke Ridge and Kelly Hill until the advance cleared its flanks of Japanese. In the center, the 161st had the task of reducing the ridge that jutted east into its sector (named before the day was over for 2nd Lieutenant Martin E. Bartley, who was killed there). Dalton attempted to envelop the ridge with two battalions, but he met with only limited success. On the north, Lieutenant Colonel Slaftcho Katsarsky's 1st Battalion advanced several hundred yards without significant opposition and reached what was to have been the departure line. But on the east and south, Lieutenant Colonel David H. Buchanan's 3rd Battalion was stopped by heavy machine-gun fire. On the 37th's northern flank, Baxter, under strict orders from Beightler to maintain contact with the 161st, reported an advance of 600 yards.

When the fighting ended that Sunday, 25 July, the lines on the map had not moved, with the exception of the 148th's advance. Griswold was both disappointed and frustrated, especially with the failure in the 43rd Division's sector. He blamed Hester. "I am afraid Hester is too nice for a battle soldier. He is sick and all done in," he wrote in his diary. "Tonight I am requesting his relief from the division."[12]

To force the Japanese to withdraw would take six more days of fighting. On most of these days, the line on the G-3 and Strike Command maps showed little or no change. But the line on the maps does not tell the whole story. The badly outnumbered Japanese could not long withstand the terrific punishment being inflicted. The American attacks were continual, and while an attacking battalion, after destroying a number of pillboxes, often had to withdraw due to a withering fire from other well-sited Japanese pillboxes, every attack weakened the Japanese defenses a little more. Barker's artillery took a daily toll of officers and men. Tanks and flamethrowers (used for the first time in the Solomons) had some success in the 43rd's sector but little in the 37th's, where the terrain was impassable for tanks and the dense foliage hampered the flamethrowers. The air strikes on the Munda–Bilbilo Hill areas killed and wounded men in the antiaircraft units – ninety was the count on 23 July – but had little effect on the front. Despite all the enormous firepower on the American side, it was infantry against infantry – two or three Americans attacking a pillbox defended by two or three Japanese.

The American line was only loosely connected. The irregular terrain, the Japanese defensive positions that made skillful use of that terrain, and the disposition of the American forces all saw to this. As army historian John Miller pointed out, there were in fact three separate battles: the 43rd Division's along the Roviana beach and extending north to Shimizu Hill; the 37th Division's (less the 148th Infantry) on Bartley Ridge and Horseshoe Hill; and the 148th's on the northern flank.

The 43rd Division Sector

The 43rd made some gains but failed to break through the main Japanese line. On 26 July, the 103rd Regiment, supported by tanks and 118th Engineers manning flamethrowers, took Ilangana and in the following days advanced a few hundred yards along the beach. In these attacks Blake's eight tanks were knocked out of action (he thought four could be repaired), either by antitank guns or by the magnetic mines that the Japanese attached, often at the cost of their lives. On the right, the 172nd and 169th (Zimmer's 1st Battalion was now in the line with the 3rd), supported by four tanks from the 10th Defense Battalion, and engineers with flamethrowers, pressed the Japanese back until they held only the crest of Shimizu Hill. While the details are not clear, Naylor's 1st Battalion was involved in some heavy fighting on 29 July, during which the first Medal of Honor was earned at New Georgia.[13]

On 31 July, the 43rd made no attack, probably to give Major General John Hodge,[14] who had relieved Hester on the 29th, a chance to acquaint himself with the situation. As the 43rd G-3 Periodic Report put it, "Today's operation for our entire front consist[ed] of vigorous patrol action determining enemy dispositions and strengths prior to a coordinated attack on August 1st." Hodge, Wing, and Ross went up to the 145th forward observation post, from where they saw signs that the Japanese were making a general withdrawal from the 43rd's sector, covered by fire from Horseshoe Hill. For 1 August, Hodge directed that the main attack be made against Shimizu Hill. (The Americans would find it empty.)

The 37th Division Sector – Bartley Ridge and Horseshoe Hill

Believing that a single misstep could cost him command of the division,[15] Beightler fought a cautious battle in the unfamiliar terrain of the ridges. Including the opening day of the offensive, he spent two days attacking the Bartley Ridge salient with two battalions of the 161st, while the 145th and one battalion of the 161st stood in place. On 26 July, with the support of six marine tanks but without an artillery preparation, due to the irregular configuration of the American positions, Dalton attacked the ridge from the south. A five-hour battle ensued in which Buchanan's 3rd Battalion lost twenty-nine men killed or wounded and three of the tanks disabled – one lodged on the trunk of a tree – before the Americans withdrew.

Still preoccupied with Bartley Ridge (the Japanese were in fact withdrawing), on 27 July Beightler ordered Holland to send Parker's 2nd Battalion eastward to round Bartley Ridge and attack the Japanese positions known to be to the southwest in the rear of the ridge. As it turned out, these were the forward defense of Horseshoe Hill. After a brief artillery preparation, Parker launched his attack at 1000 with two companies against the knob (Wing Hill)[16] connected to Horseshoe Hill by a low saddle, and took it after four hours of fighting. But 2nd Battalion did not hold it long. The Japanese opened up from Horseshoe Hill with everything they had, pinning down the two companies. When the orders came to withdraw, the troops had to crawl on their bellies off the hill. In the meantime, Holland had requested that Crooks's 1st Battalion be brought in on his left the next day, which Beightler approved. With this, Beightler had inadvertently opened the attack on the key position in the Japanese line.[17]

On 28 July, while Beightler kept the 161st Infantry taking mostly empty pillboxes on Bartley Ridge, Holland's two battalions attacked Horseshoe Hill. Barker laid a short but heavy barrage on the hill, and the attack began on the right, where 2nd Battalion reoccupied Wing Hill, and from there made the approach by creeping along the defiladed side of the saddle that connected the two hills. Advancing pillbox by pillbox, F and G Companies fought their way to the crest of the hill. But they were immediately pinned down by machine-gun fire from the front and from both flanks. In the meantime, to their left Crooks's B Company attacked the hill from the southeast at 1000 and was met by the same heavy fire. At 1530, Crooks committed A Company to the left of B Company, and the attack continued, coming within fifteen yards of the crest before being stopped. At 1730, Parker ordered 2nd Battalion to withdraw back to the foot of the hill, but Crooks's two companies dug in where they were. Twenty-four men and the observer for the 169th Field Artillery were killed and forty-four men wounded.

North of Parker's 2nd Battalion, Katsarsky's 1st Battalion, 161st Infantry, which had been kept on a short leash due to the Japanese positions in its rear on Bartley Ridge, advanced so that at nightfall it was even with Parker. But to its north, the only contact with the 148th was by patrol. In mid-afternoon, Tomonari's forces finally began moving into the rear of the 148th, and while the situation was still confused, Beightler was soon to be preoccupied with his northern flank.

On Kongō Hill that day, Sasaki's attention was on the same area. The Detachment Field Log recorded that "Enemy troops are surrounding and putting pressure on us from the left side, but we are still holding our position." This pessimistic entry was offset somewhat by a wildly exaggerated report from Tomonari that he had obliterated the Americans at a place the Japanese called Bochi kōchi (Highland Cemetery), killing 150 Americans and destroying fifteen tractors and four antitank guns and that he was now attacking at Sugiura Hill, the Japanese located just northeast of the supply dump (Tōgeno chaya).[18]

As if on cue, the good weather that had held since 25 July ended as a strong front moved in from the northwest. The rain fell off and on for the rest of the week, usually at night. The engineers, trying to keep the roads passable, felled trees in an attempt to let the sunlight through and dry the roads during the day.

On the 29th, while Beightler kept Katsarsky's 1st Battalion in place because of the unsettled situation. Baxter's 148th and the rest of the 161st Infantry were again occupied with Bartley Ridge, and Holland had renewed the attack on Horseshoe Hill. Parker's F and G Companies again reached the crest, while E Company, supported by the heavy machine guns of H Company, attacked the north side. The fighting on the north side was hand to hand, and E Company made little progress. By night-fall, 2nd Battalion had been withdrawn to the foot of the ridge. Crooks's attack never got started. The Japanese laid down such heavy fire that the two assault companies had to withdraw, and Holland ordered 1st Battalion back to Kelly Hill. He was concerned about reports that the Japanese had infiltrated between his two battalions as well as the failure of the 43rd to advance and close the gap on his southern flank.

The next day marked a lull in the American attacks on the ridges. Beightler planned to begin withdrawing the 161st that evening, begin a heavy artillery barrage on Bartley Ridge on 31 July, launch a general attack, and clear the salient once and for all.[19] But in the afternoon, patrol reports from Bartley Ridge finally convinced him that resistance was negligible, and this, along with uncertainty as to the 148th's where-abouts, led him to call it off. Instead, on 31 July, 2nd Battalion, 161st Infantry, would clear Bartley Ridge and Parker's 2nd Battalion, 145th Infantry, would attack Horseshoe Hill. The rest of the 161st would remain in place until the 148th's situation was clear.

On 31 July, Major Francis P. Carberry's 2nd Battalion, 161st, advanced across Bartley Ridge without meeting resistance and at 1645 made contact with Parker's CP at Horseshoe Hill. Two hours before, after a four-hour mortar barrage followed by the 135th Field Artillery firing ahead of the assault troops, Parker's battalion had taken the crest, and by 1745 it held about one-third of the hill before intense mortar fire forced a withdrawal back to the foot of the hill. All accounts from the 37th Division agree that this was the bitterest fighting yet encountered, as the Japanese fought doggedly to keep their line from collapsing before their scheduled withdrawal. Out of the fighting that day came a second Medal of Honor.[20]

37th Division Sector – the Northern Flank

With no organized opposition in his front, Baxter steadily advanced. While he had orders to maintain contact with Katsarsky's 1st Battalion, 161st Infantry, on his left, this soon became possible only by patrol. Lieu-tenant Colonel Herbert W. Radcliffe's 2nd Battalion led the first three days of Baxter's advance, with the 117th Engineers, Baxter's headquarters, Lieutenant Colonel Vernon F. Hydaker's 1st Battalion, and service troops strung out behind. Patrols fanned out south, west, and north, and on 26 July, one of these ran into an ambush, losing three killed and three wounded. The next day, a machine-gun detachment, which Sasaki had organized from antiaircraft troops, ambushed a platoon of the 117th Engineers working with a bulldozer at the head of the road just west of the ration dump. Three engineers were killed, three wounded, and a 1st Commando section leader killed while engaging a machine gun. Baxter left A Company and machine-gun and mortar sections from D Company to protect both the dump and the engineers (who had armored their bulldozers with steel plates from a wrecked Japanese barge).[21]

On the morning of 28 July, Hydaker leapfrogged Radcliffe and took the lead. With Hydaker some 1,500 yards from the departure line and patrols approaching Bilbilo Hill, Baxter received that afternoon the first reports of Japanese troops in his rear on the road east of the supply dump. Tomonari had finally arrived. Baxter immediately sent his S-4, Major Laurence Hipp, with troops from his antitank company and a platoon of infantry, to reinforce the troops at the supply dump. Late in the afternoon, an undetermined number of Tomonari's troops attacked the dump, but Hipp and his assortment of troops held firm (contrary to Tomonari's report of considerable success). During the night, Tomonari's main force of between 300 and 400 men arrived, and by dawn it was astride the road east of the supply dump.

At 0655, Beightler radioed Baxter the belief that good numbers of Japanese were coming through the gap between the 148th and the 1st Battalion, 161st Infantry, and ordered Baxter to close up his battalions. Fifteen minutes later, Beightler radioed Baxter instructions to withdraw both battalions to the east, make contact with the 161st, and protect his supply route. In this confused situation, messages flew back and forth between Beightler, who was convinced he was about to be hit by a major Japanese force coming from the west through the gap between the 148th and the 161st, and Baxter, who argued, "There is no gap. Enemy came from NE." Baxter correctly concluded that they were the same group—the Japanese 13th Infantry—that had harassed the 148th on 19 and 20 July. The argument continued almost to the point of insubordination by Baxter before Beightler told Griswold to give his regimental commander a direct order to withdraw and make contact with the 161st.[22]

Early the next morning, 30 July, Baxter began the breakout. The sky was overcast, and a fine mist saturated the forest. Baxter planned for Radcliffe's 2nd Battalion to lead, while Hydaker's 1st Battalion, the engineers with their bulldozer, and regimental headquarters would follow. "That was the plan," Baxter reported, "but the Japs messed it up a bit." As disorganized as Tomonari's troops were, the withdrawal played into their hands, allowing them to move about, set random ambushes, and inflict heavy casualties. Radcliffe with two companies got through to the 161st, but two companies ran into ambushes and had to rejoin Baxter's force. Meanwhile, Baxter's force started its advance at 0925 but ran into heavy machine-gun fire east of the supply dump. While the fighting went on for most of the afternoon, it became apparent that the attack along the trail was going nowhere. With darkness near, Baxter dug in at the supply dump. That night the mist turned into a downpour, and the men, who were short on water, used their helmets and any other contraptions available to catch rainwater.

Baxter needed two more days to reach the 161st Infantry. On 31 July, the skies cleared, and Baxter followed the route that Radcliffe had successfully taken the day before. Baxter's force made some 400 yards before being stopped again by heavy machine-gun and mortar fire. Beightler sent an improvised force to try and break through to Baxter from the east, but the attempt failed. At 1555, he directed Baxter to destroy all heavy equipment and "suggested that he break up into small groups for the break-out attempt in the morning." With night coming on, Baxter withdrew to the defense perimeter at the supply dump.[23] During the night, however, Tomonari began withdrawing, in line with Sasaki's orders. Baxter's forces met no opposition on 1 August and by 1300 had rejoined the division. For the three days of fighting, Baxter gave his casualties as 43 killed and 147 wounded, a steep price for an unnecessary operation. The 37th later admitted "that a roving band of an estimated 200 Japanese, caromed off our several units in such a manner as to keep alive in our minds at all times the possibility of reinforcements from the north" over unknown trails.[24] At 1500, Beightler learned from Griswold that the Japanese had apparently withdrawn from the entire front.

THE JAPANESE WITHDRAWAL AND THE FALL OF MUNDA

As the pressure on his left grew more intense, especially at Horseshoe Hill, Sasaki notified Samejima that the line could not hold much longer and requested new instructions. Samejima sent 8th Fleet staff officer Commander Kisaka Yoshitane, who arrived at Kongō Hill around 0100 on the morning of 30 July. But the response he brought contained no new instructions. As recorded in Sasaki's Confidential Log, the response merely read: "Our air strength shall gradually become dominant from mid-August. The Combined Fleet shall carry out a full-scale offensive in early or mid-September with all its power. Therefore, retain Kolombangara and Munda." Kusaka's chief of staff, Rear Admiral Nakahara, however, recorded a more specific version to the effect that the new goal was to prevent the use of the airfield, keep the supply lines to Kolombangara secure, and prevent a breakdown in the overall plan – even if that meant enduring a temporary setback. In light of the actions Sasaki took, this version seems accurate. Also, Kisaka probably brought the news that Imamura was sending reinforcements, a battalion of the 23rd Infantry on the night of 1 August, and six companies of replacements for the 13th and 229th on the night of 5 August.

Sasaki made his plans accordingly. Hirata and Tomonari would withdraw on the evening and night of 31 July. The new defense line would be anchored on Kokenggolo Hill on the right, run east of Bilbilo Hill to protect the Munda–Bairoko Trail, and then north to what the Japanese called Hachiman Hill. Yano was ordered over from Kolombangara with the rest of his battalion, so that the planned troop disposition was that Hirata's 229th would hold the right at Kokenggolo Hill;[25] Yano (under Hirata's command) would hold the center at Sankaku Hill, and Tomonari the left at Hachiman Hill. At this point, Sasaki had slightly over 2,000 men, including over 200 headquarters personnel. Kisaka, who had remained at Kongō Hill with Sasaki, returned to Buin to report to Samejima.[26]

Late in afternoon of 31 July, Hirata's units on the right began withdrawing, followed after darkness by the units on the left. Much equipment was left behind. By dawn of 1 August, all of Hirata's units had safely withdrawn. Satō's 2nd Battalion and Hara's Quick-Fire Battalion were in the elaborate tunnels of Kokenggolo Hill, while the remnants of 1st and 3rd Battalions were at Bilbilo Hill. Tomonari, as we have seen, was disengaging on the northern flank.

On the ground on 1 August, the 43rd Division's attack faced no opposition; the troops walked across Shimizu Hill, and by 1500 they had advanced 700 yards and linked up with the 145th. On the American right, as we have seen, XIV Corps notified 37th Division at 1500 that a general withdrawal had been made. Beightler ordered forward Katsarsky's 1st Battalion, 161st Infantry, and Parker's 2nd Battalion, 145th. By 1600, both forces had moved across Horseshoe Hill and beyond without firing a shot. As darkness fell over the battleground, XIV Corps's G-3 was on the telephone to Hodge and Beightler with instructions for a general and "aggressive" advance on 2 August. The left of the 37th and the right of the 43rd were to maintain contact, and if solid resistance was met, they were to develop the location, strength, and composition of enemy forces. Baxter's 148th Regiment was to remain as corps reserve, with the mission of protecting the northern flank, since the 27th Infantry RCT, 25th Division, which had come in the night of the 31st, was not expected to be in position on Beightler's right until 3 August. But this order was quickly modified, and Baxter was also ordered to advance.[27]

On 2 August, XIV Corps moved on Munda with a line that stretched from 3rd Battalion, 103rd Infantry, on the left, to 2nd Battalion, 148th Infantry, on the right. Progress was so rapid that an air strike on Kokenggolo Hill requested by the 43rd was canceled due to the close proximity of American troops. Yano, who had taken up his position east of Bilbilo Hill, recalled that the American troops just swept by his headquarters so quickly he thought they failed to notice they had overrun a battalion CP. The Japanese had been unable to form the line Sasaki had planned, and Hirata's troops were in the tunnels of Kokenggolo and Bilbilo Hills. Sasaki blamed Hirata, but in fact, Barker's artillery was turning the area into an inferno. On August 1st, almost 2,000 rounds were fired; on the 2nd another 2,000 rounds; on the 3rd a relentless barrage of 7,300 rounds; and 3,600 on the 4th.

Yano lost the commander and all of the platoon leaders of 8th Company; Kojima and four of his officers were killed when a shell made a direct hit on their dugout on Bilbilo Hill; Hara Masao was killed, and what remained of his 1st Battalion was placed under Satō's command early on 2 August. Not even the tunnels in Kokenggolo Hill were safe; a direct hit collapsed the entrance to Satō's tunnel, burying him along with sixty men, and it took the next day to dig them out. Tomonari escaped only by a hairsbreadth as he retreated across what was described as a valley. After a T B F spotter swooped low overhead, the expected artillery quickly came in and on target. One shell hit Tomonari's headquarters and killed a number of staff, but Tomonari escaped unharmed.[28] By the end of the day, 2 August, the Japanese line was in effect Kokenggolo–Bilbilo Hill with American troops closing on both. The 103rd and 169th Regiments held the dispersal areas at the eastern end of the airfield (the 169th dug in among the wrecked Japanese aircraft); the 145th and 161st were up against the eastern ridges of Bilbilo Hill; and the 148th was in position to cut the Munda–Bairoko Trail.

The issue was decided on 3 August. By nightfall, the 103rd had advanced several hundred yards along the southern edge of the airfield. The 169th was up against the eastern end of Kokenggolo Hill. To the north, the 145th had taken the first of the eastern ridges of Bilbilo Hill, the 161st had broken through on its right, and the 148th was astride the Munda–Bairoko Trail. At Kongō Hill, Sasaki was in an unenviable position. He had just received vague orders from Samejima to secure a part of New Georgia and the airfield on Kolombangara. Requests for clarification – "what area?" – received no reply. At the same time, Sasaki had no clear grasp of the precarious situation on the battlefield, which he blamed on Hirata's optimistic and misleading reports. But a messenger from Yano, who had regained the lines, acquainted him with the reality of the situation. Rightly or wrongly, Sasaki was clearly put out with Hirata.[29] At any rate, at 0300 on 4 August, Sasaki ordered a general withdrawal to the Kure 6th Farm. Hirata was to hold his positions until sundown – in effect to serve as the rearguard – and then withdraw to Kongō Hill, where he would join with Ōta's units. Sasaki would move his headquarters to the Kure 6th Farm at 1300.

At about 0720 on 4 August, twenty-five S B D s, twenty-four T B F s, and twenty-four B-25s hit Gurasai–Kindu Point northwest of the airfield, where the Japanese had elaborate fortifications and antiaircraft guns. The 1st Battalion, 145th Infantry, described it as "the most severe bombing and strafing attack in our memory. . . . The big one-tonners shook the earth and vibrated the landscape before our eyes." Griswold's battalions began moving forward around 0800. In Hodge's sector, tanks supported the effort against Kokenggolo Hill. In Beightler's sector, the 27th Infantry took over the northern flank, which freed up the 148th to push alongside the 161st toward the western beach. The heaviest fighting was in the Bilbilo Hill area, where Holland's 145th was up against Satō's dug-in troops, and in the 27th's area, where troops defending Kongō Hill put up stubborn resistance. By the end of the day, both the 148th and the 161st had broken through to the sea north of Kokenggolo Hill, and the 145th had almost cleared Bilbilo Hill. But the Japanese had escaped and were on the trail to the Kure 6th Farm. (It is worth noting that just before noon, the ground troops got to witness their first fighter battle overhead when the Rendova Patrol intercepted thirty-one Zeros chasing marine F4Us, which had pulled off a sneak raid on the seaplane base at Poporang.)[30]

The next day, XIV Corps occupied Munda with little opposition. The only fight was at Kongō Hill between the 27th and the last elements of Hirata's rear guard. That morning, Sasaki ordered Hirata to abandon Kongō Hill and withdraw to a position 2 kilometers east of the Kure 6th Farm; Tomonari was to proceed to Kolombangara and take charge of the defenses; Major Nagakari Miyoshi was to stay at Baanga Island with his 3rd Battalion, 23rd Infantry; and Ōta was to defend southern Arundel Island. With the rest, which included almost 1,000 antiaircraft troops and construction personnel, Sasaki would arrange the defenses of the Kure 6th Farm and await the arrival of the replacement companies.[31]

THE TOKYO EXPRESS BATTLES

The Blackett Strait PT Boat Action

In separate runs, the Japanese planned to send a battalion from 6th Division and six companies of replacement troops to Sasaki in early August. The first run was scheduled for the night of 1–2 August. With Munda now in jeopardy, the course was set directly to Vila through Vella Gulf and Blackett Strait rather than unloading at Ariel. To deal with the PT boats certain to be waiting off the Ferguson Passage, Buin sent down a strike of six D3As with an escort of Zeros to hit the base at Lumbaria in the midafternoon of 1 August. Rendova picked up the formation at 105 miles, but for whatever reason, no COMAIRSOLS fighters were in the area. Twelve P-39s that had been scrambled from Segi took station overhead, just as the D3A Vals and a dozen Zeros came in low beneath them. 9th Defense Battalion gunners sent one Zero plowing into the water near the Lumbaria, but a second made a direct hit on a nest of PT boats, wrecking *PT-164* and *PT-117*. Lieutenant (jg) Richard E. Keresey, firing from his own *PT-105*, saw the bow of one of the boats blown fifty feet into the air. The damage could have been much worse.[32]

Captain Sugiura Kaju commanded the Reinforcement Force of three destroyers. He brought down 799 men, most for the 7th Combined and 8th Combined Special Naval Landing Forces (SNLF), to Erventa, where he loaded Nagakari's 3rd Battalion, 23rd, and supplies, fuel, and equipment. East of Bougainville, he met up with Captain Yamashiro in *Amagiri* (Lieutenant Commander Hanami Kōhei), who had come down from Rabaul to serve as the guard for the run to Kolombangara. The sky was overcast with rain squalls over the Slot; there was no moon and the night was pitch dark. Japanese seaplanes were out searching in force, and at 2225 one reported Burke's five destroyers 45 miles off Visuvisu Point, hurrying to take up station off Kula Gulf. As the Japanese entered Vella Gulf, two seaplanes reported attacking PT boats in Ferguson Passage.

All fifteen available boats were out. Wilkinson certainly knew that the "Tokyo Express" was running. Crenshaw in *Maury*, who personally handed the orders to Burke, recalled that they offered detailed information concerning the Japanese force. But because of Sugiura's course, the interception of the Reinforcement Force would be made by the Rendova PT boats.[33] The boats, in four divisions, were strung out in Blackett Strait from Vanga Vanga on southwest Kolombangara east to Ferguson Passage. Only the four boats of the division commanders had radar.

At 2400, the westernmost division made radar and then visual contact with what was thought to be large barges. The division commander, with one other boat, closed to make a strafing attack, at which time the Japanese destroyers settled the identification question by opening fire. The two boats then fired six torpedoes, which all missed, and the division commander, who had fired all four of his torpedoes, returned to base – and with him his radar. As the destroyers passed, two more division commanders duplicated this attack: fired torpedoes, missed, and returned to base, leaving only PT boats without radar on station in the western strait. At 0010, Yamashiro broke off from Sugiura and took up station off Ferguson Passage. Hanami turned on his searchlight in order to fire at the boats to his west, which along with the gunfire, illuminated *Amagiri*. The three boats stationed fired ten torpedoes at the lit-up target at 0025, but none struck the target. Two of these boats returned home, leaving *PT-105* with two torpedoes remaining on station in Ferguson Passage. Five minutes later, Sugiura arrived off Webster Cove and began unloading. With only twenty-five of the forty-eight transfer barges operable, unloading was slower than expected, and at 0200, with a few tons still on board, Sugiura headed back through Blackett Strait.[34]

Only five boats, four in the strait and *PT-105* at the northern end of Ferguson Passage, were in any position to make an attack. Five had gone home and five were south of the Ferguson Passage. At 0224, *Amagiri* began putting on speed to catch up with Sugiura, and was making thirty knots when it hit Lieutenant (jg) John F. Kennedy's *PT-109*. *Amagiri* suffered some damage to its bottom, which caused minor flooding, and to one of the propellers, which reduced its speed to thirty knots. *PT-109* was sliced in two, and two men were killed. Kennedy and ten other survivors, three of them with serious burns, made it to Plum Pudding Island, one of the string of islands that dotted the reefs from Gizo to the Ferguson Passage. The small islands were unoccupied, but a company of Sasebo 6th SNLF troops was on nearby Gizo. From Plum Pudding, the survivors worked their way east to an island nearer Ferguson Passage. With the aid of coast watcher Evans and some of his scouts, the survivors were rescued on the night of 7–8 August.[35]

Because Kennedy came from one of America's elite families, and later was elected president of the United States, *PT-109*'s collision with *Amagiri* has taken its place as an iconic event in the popular memory of the Pacific War.[36] The *PT-109* incident, however, has overshadowed the action itself, which was poorly executed and a complete failure. For this, 43rd Division infantrymen would pay the price when facing Nagakari's battalion on Baanga Island.[37]

Battle of Vella Gulf

The second reinforcement run had been originally scheduled for 5 August but was moved back a day due to equipment changes. Captain Mikami Kisaburō was temporary commander (he would join Sasaki's staff) of the eight replacement companies, six of which were to go to Sasaki, while two would be retained at Buin (they would later fight on Vella Lavella). Each was made up of three rifle platoons, one infantry gun, one trench mortar, two heavy and nine light machine guns, and twelve grenade launchers (knee mortars). While they were well equipped, the replacements were mostly reservists called up in December 1942 and shipped to Rabaul. There, they seemed to have been used more for labor rather than given additional training.[38]

Rear Admiral Ijūin in *Sendai* would make the transport to Buin with the two replacement companies, other units, and supplies. Sugiura would again command the transport to Kolombangara in *Hagikaze* (F), with *Arashi* and *Kawakaze*. To replace the damaged *Amagiri* as the guard, Ijūin selected Captain Hara Tameichi in *Shigure*, but when Hara objected because his ship could make only 30 knots, Ijūin put him in the rear. Sugiura would serve as both guard and troop carrier. He intended to take the same route he had taken on the 1–2 August transport. Hara claimed he objected to this, too, as a grave mistake.[39]

At Guadalcanal, Wilkinson had specific intelligence that the Express was running. On the afternoon of 5 August, he ordered his new destroyer commander, Commander Frederick Moosbrugger, to depart Tulagi the next day at 1236 with the six available destroyers, take the route south of Rendova to the Gizo Strait entrance to Vella Gulf by 2200, and sweep the gulf until 0200 on 7 August. The Rendova PT boats would remain tied up and the Lever Harbor PT boats would operate at the base of Kula Gulf.[40] COMAIRSOLS would provide the usual air cover, and Black Cats would be on station. The fleet tugs *Rail* and *Pawnee* would be on station to tow any damaged ships. In a meeting with Wilkinson later that evening, Moosbrugger received the detailed information that the Reinforcement Force was expected around midnight and would most likely be made up of destroyers, although there was a possibility that a cruiser might be involved (*Sendai*). The intelligence was so accurate it had to have come from CINPAC.[41]

Moosbrugger based his plan on one that Burke had drawn up and practiced before leaving Guadalcanal to take command of a squadron. The plan called for dividing his force into two divisions, a torpedo division (a-1) and a gun division (a-2), a plan that later kept the CINPAC staff in a tizzy as to whether this violated the principle of concentration.[42] When contact was made, the torpedo group would go in and attack, while the gun group would cut across the bows of the enemy and open fire when the torpedoes hit.[43] Although the Japanese had given Burke no opportunity to test the plan in battle, all of Wilkinson's destroyer commanders were familiar with it. On the run-up to Honiavasa with the 27th Infantry convoy on 31 July–1 August, Burke had practiced maneuvers and signals for his new plan, and during the run-up on the night of 1–2 August to intercept Sugiura, he had the destroyers organized in the torpedo and gun divisions.

For the Vella Gulf interception, Moosbrugger would command Division a-1 – *Dunlap* (F), *Craven*, and *Maury* – since his ships carried the greater torpedo complement, and Commander Roger W. Simpson would command Division a-2 – *Lang* (F), *Sterett*, and *Stack*. He would enter Vella Gulf through Gizo Strait at moon set, make a sweep east a mile or two off the Gizo reefs at 15 knots so as to create little wake for the Japanese seaplanes to spot, then turn north to be off the northwest coast of Kolombangara at 2325. When contact was made, Division a-1 would dash in, make a close torpedo attack, then "haul tail" to about 10,000 yards (still thought to be the effective range of the Japanese torpedoes) and await the results. The effectiveness of the torpedo attack would determine whether to attack again with guns or torpedoes. Over breakfast on 6 August, Moosbrugger discussed the plan with Simpson. At 0930, the destroyer commanders convened in *Dunlop*, the plan was distributed, and every detail discussed. The commanders then returned to their ships, called their officers together, and went over the plan again.[44]

An hour before schedule, due to feed-pump problems that limited *Maury*'s speed to 27 knots, Moosbrugger led his ships out of Port Purvis for what was to be an uneventful trip up. Of any force yet sent up, his was the best prepared for a successful engagement with the Reinforcement Force. Burke's tactics were excellent, and Moosbrugger's plan to utilize them equally so. The intelligence was 100 percent accurate, and as it so happened, at 1730 a message was received that earlier in the day a search plane had spotted Sugiura as he passed Buka Passage and that he should arrive on time.

All six destroyers were fitted with sg radar, and all had a working cic. Unlike the formations thrown together on the spur of the moment, with which Ainsworth had been forced to fight his battles, the ships of the two divisions had worked together as a team. Finally, but most importantly, something had been done about the two problems afflicting the torpedoes – a defective magnetic exploder and torpedoes running much deeper than their settings. Admiral King's order to deactivate the magnetic exploder had arrived in time for this to be done, while Moosbrugger, on his own, had ordered the torpedoes set to run at the minimum possible depth setting of 5 feet, alternating with 9 feet. Crenshaw wrote that Moosbrugger's depth settings were a "radical departure from previous practice"; nonetheless, he convinced his commander to set all of *Maury's* sixteen torpedoes at 5 feet.

Precisely at 2200, Moosbrugger began passing through Gizo Strait at fifteen knots, turning southeast in a sweep of the Gizo reefs toward the approaches to Blackett Strait. The moon had set at 2226, the sky was overcast with a ceiling of 4,000 feet, and surface visibility was reckoned at 3,000 yards. A light breeze was blowing from the southeast, and the sea was calm. The destroyers passed in and out of frequent rain squalls.

At 2256, Moosbrugger turned due north up the gulf, his division taking the lead, with Simpson's 4,000 yards off his starboard quarter, roughly 2 miles off the Kolombangara shore. The volcanic mass in the background cloaked the American destroyers; Hara recollected later that all he could see in that direction was blackness. At around 2330, contact was made and verified; Sugiura was coming straight down the middle. Moosbrugger immediately changed course to close the range and ordered his division to prepare a full port broadside of twenty-four torpedoes. At 2341, at a range of between 4,800 and 4,300 yards, Division A-1's torpedoes began hitting the water. At 2346, Moosbrugger ordered a 90° ships' turn to starboard so that the three destroyers were in line abreast and headed east. In the meantime, with guns locked on target and ready, Simpson had changed course so that his division could cross Sugiura's bows. Then "three terrific explosions were observed from left to right followed by successive violent explosions totaling between seven

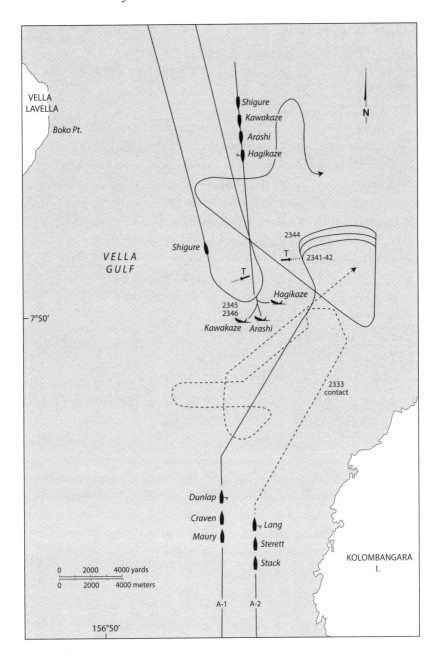

Map 10.2. Naval Battle of Vella Gulf, 6 August 1943.

and ten." Simpson immediately opened fire, adding to the conflagration. On Kolombangara, Evans's scouts saw the fires spread over the water and reported ships burning; both the PT boat crews deep in Kula Gulf and the crew of *Pawnee* waiting off Ferguson Passage saw the bloom of the explosions.[45]

The Japanese had been taken by surprise. At 2342, just as Sugiura ordered a course change to port to make Blackett Strait, lookouts spotted the white waves and black shapes of Moosbrugger's destroyers emerging out of the darkness. Only Hara's *Shigure*, which was lagging behind, was able to fire torpedoes and make a hard turn to starboard. Two torpedoes hit *Hagikaze*, three hit *Arashi*, and two *Kawakaze*. *Shigure* barely escaped. Hara later wrote that three torpedoes passed the bow, which was swinging to starboard, by less than 20 meters, while one passed through the rudder but did not explode. None of Hara's torpedoes hit.[46]

Simpson's job was to finish off the stricken ships with gunfire, and he led Division A-2 back and forth across the Japanese bows. "The firing was slow and deliberate," Simpson reported. "Salvos got on and stayed on." *Kawakaze*, hit directly under the bridge, went first, jackknifing at 2352. *Arashi* followed about twenty minutes later. *Hagikaze* was the last to go. Describing the ship's last moments, Moosbrugger said Simpson's "5-inch fire gave the appearance of machine-gunfire sweeping across the deck obliterating the topside as it progressed and culminating in a large explosion aft."

The Japanese navy historians said that 820 out of 940 troops on board the three destroyers perished, while the navy lost somewhat over 400 men. Vila ordered the base at Horaniu to rescue survivors and sent four large barges for that purpose, which picked up some of the survivors, while other survivors drifted ashore on Vella Lavella.[47]

JAPANESE DECISIONS

At the Kure 6th Farm on 7 August, Sasaki received the news of the Mikami Battalion's destruction; he wasted no time in ordering a general withdrawal to Kolombangara by way of Baanga Island. He ordered the 96th Shore Duty Company, which had come in with the Yano Battalion, to Baanga and gave it the responsibility for handling the boat transport over the narrow Lulu Channel that separated Baanga and New Georgia. "To stall the enemy advance," Yano was to remain in position east of the Kure 6th Farm, Nagakari was to put one company of the 23rd under Yano and secure Baanga with the rest of his battalion, while Yamada was to remain at Bairoko Harbor. But when Sasaki radioed his plans to 8th Fleet, he was told to hold a part of New Georgia and a staff officer would be dispatched with instructions. As a result, Sasaki moved only his headquarters to Vila and instructed the 229th to remain on Baanga. When the staff officer arrived on 9 August, Sasaki read the letter the officer carried with amazement. Samejima simply reiterated that a part of New Georgia must be held for future operations, and Sasaki would be notified when these had been decided. The official army historians wrote that Sasaki actually felt sorry for Samejima, who was trying to direct a land battle for which he had no experience, and in any case his air and naval strength was too diminished to support it.[48]

Actually, Samejima's instructions were in line with the decisions being made at IGHQ. On 7 August, the army and navy operations sections agreed to withdraw from the Central Solomons and to cooperate in strengthening the Bougainville defenses. The Army/Navy Central Agreement needed to be revised, which was done by 13 August. New directives were issued to Koga, Kusaka, and Imamura on the same day. These were delivered to Rabaul by staff officers from IGHQ and Combined Fleet on 21 August, since the agreement was not put before the emperor until the 20th. By these, Koga, Kusaka, and Imamura were instructed to hold as much of New Georgia as possible; both services were to cooperate in strengthening the defenses at Bougainville; and at the right time, between late September and early October, the forces in New Georgia would be evacuated. The specific dates for the evacuation depended on the progress of strengthening the Bougainville defenses, but the local commanders would be responsible for the operation. Sasaki, in effect, was to fight a delaying action.[49]

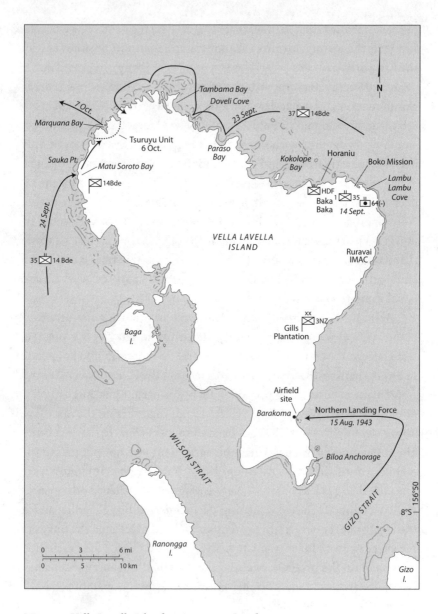

Map 11.1. Vella Lavella Island, 15 August–7 October 1943.

ELEVEN

The Vella Lavella Occupation

ON THE NIGHT OF 22 JULY, GENERAL HARMON'S CHIEF ENGINEER, Colonel F. L. Beadle, took a party of six to Vella Lavella in a PT boat. Aerial photographs had identified two possible airfield locations, and Beadle's mission was to inspect these sites. If they proved unfeasible, he was to look for others. Scouts in canoes met them off Barakoma, and with Josselyn as guide, an inspection quickly showed both sites to be unfeasible. But back at Barakoma, Beadle determined that a 4,000-foot field could be built and that the landing beaches were adequate for LSTs. His report established the first prerequisite for a move to Vella Lavella.[1]

The second prerequisite was the ability to provide effective air cover. Vella Lavella in Allied hands would cut the Japanese supply line to Kolombangara, which by this time was heavily dependent on the fishing boats and barges based at Buin. The Japanese could be expected to throw their available air forces against the beachhead, especially against the slow LSTs that constituted the bulk of Wilkinson's shipping. Since significant changes in command structure and force composition occurred in both air forces during late July and early August, we will take up these next.

THE AIR COMMANDS

1st Base Air Force

In mid-July, significant reinforcements arrived in the Solomons: the 201st Kōkūtai (Aerial Bomb Group) and the rest of Carrier Division

2's aircraft. The overall strength of 1st Base Air Force was estimated at between 220 and 230 aircraft of all types. On 20 July, Rear Admiral Sakamaki Munetake, commander, Carrier Division 2, arrived. At Buin, Kusaka reorganized 1st Base Air Force along lines similar to COMAIRSOLS. All land-based bombers would remain under Ueno's 25th Air Flotilla at Rabaul; fighters at Buin would be under Kosaka's 26th Air Flotilla, with the 204th Kōkūtai absorbing Carrier Division 2's fighters; and all D3A Val dive bombers and B5N Kate torpedo bombers would be merged into the 582nd Kōkūtai under Sakamaki in what was called the 2nd Mobile Air Attack Force. (The fighter unit of the 582nd Kōkūtai had already been dissolved with most of the pilots going to either the 204th or the 201st.)

Ueno's mission was the night bombing of Guadalcanal and New Georgia bases; Kosaka's mission was to conduct interceptions over Munda and Buin; and Sakamaki's mission was the destruction of enemy shipping in New Georgia. But Kusaka was not satisfied with the Buin command structure, and just before he returned to Rabaul on 1 August, he unified the command under Sakamaki in what was called the 1st Combined Air Attack Force. This changed on 1 September when Kosaka and his staff went home and all aircraft at Buin were placed in the 26th Air Flotilla under Sakamaki. Carrier Division 2 would be rebuilt.[2]

COMAIRSOLS

On 25 July, Mitscher turned over command of COMAIRSOLS to Twining. Thus, a proponent of air power delivered by heavy bombers took over from one who was a proponent of air power launched from carrier decks. With Twining's arrival, the top subordinate commanders, with the exception of Hansen (Photographic Command), also changed as scheduled. Captain Charles Coe, USN, took over as chief of staff, Lieutenant Colonel D. F. O'Neill, USMC, took over Strike Command, Brigadier General Don Strother (AAF) took over Fighter Command, and Colonel William A. Matheny moved up from command of the 307th to Bomber Command.[3]

For much of August, Twining faced a reduction in fighters. This was due to the scheduled departure of the navy carrier groups in early August, and with them the Grumman F4Fs from the skies over the Solomons. Both Halsey and Harmon lobbied unsuccessfully for additional fighters. Nimitz replied that the most Halsey could expect were three marine replacement squadrons, the first scheduled to arrive in early August, and two carrier groups due to arrive in late August.[4] Arnold's reply to Harmon was identical. Twining would get no more than the forty-seven P-38s previously allocated, seventeen of which were then being prepared for shipment.[5] This meant that COMAIRSOLS, which had 161 fighters available on 31 July, now would have 129 for 18 August. Twining had sufficient strength in bombers. The number of light and medium bombers dropped by less than a dozen to 129, while the number of heavy bombers increased from 48 to 61.[6]

Under these circumstances, getting Munda Field operational by the occupation date, 15 August, was critical. The day after Munda fell, Commander K. P. Doane, whose 73rd Seabees would have that job, was looking over the field. Fitch's master plan for Munda Field called for a 6,000-foot runway with a minimum 8-inch coral surface and taxiways and revetments ready for 200 fighters by 25 September (and eventually 48 heavy bombers). The immediate objective, however, was a fighter strip. While he had just a week to have the field operational, Doane had two critical assets. First, Munda was by far the best airfield site in the Solomons. Beneath one to three feet of topsoil was solid coral, while a plentiful supply of live coral, which hardened like concrete, was available for surfacing. Second, the 73rd was the best-equipped battalion yet to arrive in the Solomons, with D-7 and D-8 bulldozers, ¾-yard power shovels, 8-yard carryalls, and 7-ton rollers. The 73rd set to work under fair weather and a bright moon, waxing gibbous to full, which permitted the work to go on at night without lights. It was also a "bomber's moon," but the two raids that came in from Rabaul were ineffective. For whatever reason, the 12cm of Yokosuka's 7th Division at Baanga, which could have brought the field under fire, remained silent.[7]

By 14 August, the Seabees had a 3,600-by-120-foot runway ready, with two rough but usable taxi loops, and the field was declared operational. Mulcahy flew over and set up his headquarters, and VMF-123 and VMF-124 flew into base, with a R4D carrying their gear and personnel. The pilots lived in tents on Bilbilo Hill, notorious for its flies. Reverend Metcalfe had complained about them when he was hiding from the Japanese, and so had Suhō when the Cactus Air Force was destroying his Ze-ros. The Americans added their complaints. "During the daylight hours, flies swarmed over everyone trying to catch up on sleep," 1st Lieuten-ant John M. Foster of VMF-222 wrote. "And before the sun went down, mosquitoes buzzed out to relieve the flies and gnats patrolling over us."[8]

As had the Japanese before them, the Americans had to confront logistical problems. Landing craft brought fuel and supplies up Roviana Lagoon to Ilangana, and then by truck the rest of the way. To fuel the planes, the 73rd had mounted pontoon tanks on coconut logs. A ramp for the trucks hauling barrels of fuel allowed the barrels to be emptied by hand, while fuel trucks could pull under and load. Around 15 August, the 73rd began blasting a passage 15 feet deep and 300 feet wide through the Munda Bar for LSTs and small tankers, while the 24th built an 800-foot causeway carrying a pipeline from Munda Point. The first LSTs used the passage on 12 September. (Eventually, the Munda channel had to be dredged.)[9]

THE OCCUPATION OF VELLA LAVELLA

Following Beadle's reconnaissance, Wilkinson recommended that 15 August be set as D-Day, and Halsey concurred. The forces allocated were the 35th RCT, 25th Division, the 4th Marine Defense Battalion, the 58th Naval Construction Battalion, and the Naval Base Group. The force was designated the Northern Landing Force, with Brigadier General Robert B. McClure, assistant commander, 25th Division, in command. For the initial landing, Wilkinson would use twelve destroyers, six destroyer transports, twelve LCIs, three LSTs, and two subchasers. COMAIRSOLS would furnish air support (a request to MacArthur for an attack on Ra-baul was rejected). Wilkinson planned to put in five echelons during the amphibious phase and then turn over command to Griswold on 3 September.[10]

The operation started on the night of 12 August, when Captain George C. Kriner, commander, Naval Base, took in the advance party by PT boats to mark the landing beaches. Two companies from the 103rd went along to deal with bands of Japanese, survivors of the Vella Gulf battle that were reported in the area. The sky was clear, the moon bright, and the Japanese seaplanes of the 938th were out in force. The party had one boat seriously damaged and four men wounded in an attack. As it turned out, the Japanese on Vella Lavella posed no threat, although six were captured and others killed.[11]

The night of 14–15 August was quiet at Barakoma. The sky was again clear, and a full moon hung overhead. The PT boats lying to in picket lines in the western approaches, the Lever Harbor boats off Vella Gulf, and the Rendova boats off Wilson Strait and between Ghanongga and Simbo all reported visibility to the horizon. Japanese seaplanes of the 938th were out, and a small convoy consisting of an APc, two LSTs, and two PT boats en route to Enogai had attracted their attention.

In the Solomon Sea southeast of Gizo, the three groups of TF 31 making up the 1st Echelon were approaching the Gizo Strait. At 0305, 1st Transport Group, made up of the destroyer transports with an escort of six destroyers, and carrying two battalions of the 35th RCT (Colonel Everett E. Brown)[12] to make the initial landing, passed first. Captain Ryan was in command of the group in *Nicholas*, while Wilkinson rode in *Cony*. Second Transport Group, made up of the LCIs with the rest of the troops, the Seabees, and support personnel, followed one hour behind, with four destroyers (Captain William R. Cooke) as escort. Transport Group 3 (Captain Grayson B. Carter, LST Flotilla 5) carried the construction equipment, heavy guns, and fuel and supplies. The Caterpillar D-8s of the 58th were loaded last to roll off first.

With a few exceptions, the landing went off as planned. At 0620, the troops began landing from the destroyer transports, which headed back to Guadalcanal. The LCIs of Group 2 were already nosing into the landing beaches when the first problem arose; rather than accommodating all twelve LCIs, as the reconnaissance party had reported, the beaches had room for only eight. Even as the LSTs were arriving as scheduled at 0800, the final four LCIs were still unloading.

This was the situation when the first Japanese air attack came in. Sakamaki sent down forty-eight Zeros and six D3A dive bombers. Flying under Mulcahy's NGAF, the usual assortment of fighters – P-40s from No. 16 and 44th Squadrons from Segi, VMF-123 and VMF-124 Corsairs from Munda – intercepted the Japanese. The D3As came in under the fighters but scored only a few near misses that did no major damage. The 2nd Transport Group left at 0900, leaving the three LSTs, guarded by two destroyers, to complete what was an all-day job. The LSTs found the beaches even more difficult, since they could not approach near enough to land the loaded vehicles; the D-8s, however, plowed through the water to shore and began constructing landing ramps to the LSTs, which took just less than an hour.

Buin got off two more strikes before the LSTs retracted at 1800 and headed for Gizo Strait. The first strike came in around 1230, made up of forty-eight Zeros and eleven D3As. Again no damage was done. Seven Zeros that came in low to strafe the beach turned away after running into the fire of sixty-five automatic weapons from the LSTs. To remedy the lack of antiaircraft protection on these early LSTs, Carter had borrowed twenty-one 20mm guns from Guadalcanal and had also set up the automatic weapons of the 4th Marine Defense Battalion's Special Weapons Section on the upper decks.[13] The final attack by thirty-two Zeros and eight D3A Vals materialized at 1730, but the NGAF fighters broke up the attack.

Fighter Command had a surprise waiting for the Japanese formation when it returned to base. While the Vals were having no success at Barakoma, two divisions of VMF-214 Corsairs were headed to Kahili. When they swept over the field at treetop level, some twenty planes were in the landing circle, gas trucks were just off the field refueling aircraft, and personnel were everywhere. The marines claimed three Vals shot down and four destroyed on the ground.[14]

For the day, the Japanese reported their losses as nine Zeros and eight D3As. COMAIRSOLS reported one Corsair downed, with the pilot rescued, and one P-40 lost, with the pilot killed. Operational losses evened the score somewhat, for it was a hectic day at Munda. Two F4U Corsairs from VMF-124, for example, collided head-on when they attempted to take off from opposite ends of the airfield; both planes were write-offs, and one of the pilots suffered serious injuries. Altogether, five aircraft were lost on the field, with two pilots injured. And while no shipping was damaged at Barakoma, twelve men were killed on the beach and forty wounded.[15]

After darkness fell, Ueno's 5th Air Attack Force at Rabaul made the final attempt on the retiring American convoys. At around 1530 that afternoon, three G4M tracking planes were sent off from Vunakanau; these sighted both the LCIs southeast of Gatukai and the LSTs as they entered Gizo Strait. The 5th sent three chūtai, totaling twenty-three G4Ms, one chūtai armed with torpedoes, the other two with bombs. The torpedo-armed chūtai of seven aircraft made the first attack on the LCIs, an attack met by heavy antiaircraft fire from the destroyers. The torpedo planes inflicted no damage. The other two chūtai bombed the LSTs but scored no hits. For this futile effort, four of the torpedo planes were damaged, one making a forced landing, while one of the tracking planes was shot up badly enough that it made a water landing (the crew was rescued).[16]

THE JAPANESE REACTION

The immediate reaction at Buin was an unrealistic plan to wipe out the American invaders. Hyakutake would provide a battalion from 6th Division that would move by barge, Samejima would provide the destroyer escort, and Sakamaki would provide air support. The operation would take place the night of 16–17 August. Imamura immediately rejected this plan, since three to four battalions would be required to have any chance of success, but these could not be spared from the defense of Bougainville.[17]

The main threat posed by the Vella Lavella landing was the severance of the supply route to Kolombangara (and the elimination of Vella Lavella in the planning for the main evacuation). Consequently, Imamura and Kusaka planned to hold Horaniu for as long as possible and to establish a new supply route along the west coast of Choiseul. Horaniu would be reinforced with a unit made up of two companies of the Mikami Battalion and a detachment from the Yokosuka 7th Division. Rekata Bay would be evacuated, and part of these troops, the 7th Combined SNLF (Rear Admiral Katsuno Minoru), would set up relay bases on Choiseul.

The Horaniu operation was scheduled for the night of 17–18 August. Lieutenant Commander Niwa Toshio commanded the Transport Unit of thirteen barges and three torpedo boats in three groups, with a guard of two subchasers, one torpedo boat, and three armored barges. Ijūin in *Sazanami*, with *Shigure, Hamakaze,* and *Isokaze,* was to come down from Rabaul to provide the covering force. Ijūin departed Rabaul just before dawn so as to rendezvous southeast of the Shortlands, with Niwa's convoy scheduled to leave around noon. But less than 100 miles out of Rabaul, a search plane spotted Ijūin; Wilkinson correctly anticipated that he was headed for Kolombangara or Barakoma.

At 0830 Wilkinson radioed Barakoma that four Japanese destroyers were headed down and that he was sending four destroyers to intercept. Ryan in *Nicholas*, with *O'Bannon, Taylor,* and *Chevalier,* departed Tulagi around 1500 for Vella Lavella. At about the same time Ryan was getting underway, Ijūin learned from the 938th seaplanes that Wilkinson's 2nd Echelon under Cooke, which had been delayed by bad weather at Guadalcanal, was approaching Gizo Strait with three destroyers in the group. Wilkinson had in fact ordered two of these to join Ryan at 2300. Three LSTs beached at Barakoma by 1635, but a series of air attacks that began around 1830 finally forced the LSTs to retract at 2030 and retire toward Rendova. At the same time, Ryan ordered Cooke to rejoin the convoy, doubting that he could join him in time. It was a decision Ryan later regretted.

Ryan's destroyers came up the Slot in column at 32 knots. Out ahead, two Black Cats were searching for the Japanese, while seven TBFs from VMTB-143 were on their way. At 2255, one of the Black Cats spotted Ijūin's destroyers and Niwa's convoy. No report got through to Ryan for some time, but the Black Cats were able to direct four TBFs onto the Japanese; between 2310 and 2330, the Avengers made their attacks but failed to score a hit. But Ijūin's antiaircraft fire alerted Ryan, and at 2335, he received the first report regarding the makeup of the Japanese forces. At roughly the same time, the approaching Ijūin reversed course to the west, which put him just over 11 miles north of Ryan on a parallel course.

At 0029, *O'Bannon* made radar contact, and a few minutes later the Japanese ships were visible. Although both the Americans and the Japanese had run through rain squalls, the sky was now clear with a bright full moon and a calm sea. The Japanese spotted Ryan at 0032 and promptly ordered a 45° turn northwest. According to Hara, Ijūin later told him that his intention was to draw Ryan away from Niwa's convoy. If so, the ruse succeeded. From 0032 to 0121, there was some ineffective long-range gun and torpedo fire from both sides, but Ryan failed to close with Ijūin, then gave up the chase to go after the convoy. But Ijūin had bought time for Niwa; the tows were cut, and the barges were making for the security of the coast. An unnamed soldier of the Mikami Battalion, riding over rough water in one of the towed barges, wrote in his diary, "This was the first time in my life I knew what fear was. . . . In our dizzy condition we awaited the hour wearing our life jackets, the only thing we could depend on."[18] Ryan managed to sink both subchasers and a large barge, while one torpedo boat ran aground and had to be destroyed. But the rest of the convoy made Horaniu. Ryan, on the other hand, was satisfied that by preventing the destroyers from getting through, he had foiled the reinforcement.[19]

Meanwhile, Cooke had his own problems south of Gizo. The seaplane attacks had ceased after midnight, when they were drawn north by the destroyer action, and at 0141, Cooke reversed course back toward Gizo Strait. At 0210, LST-396 reported a fire in the tank deck (thought to have been started by gasoline vapor igniting), and ten minutes later flames were shooting through the ventilators. At 0232, a heavy explosion blew off the aft deck, and the rest of the ship was engulfed in flames and torn apart by further explosions. LST-396 sank at 0320, taking with it tons of fuel, supplies, and ammunition. One man was killed, but the rest of the crew was rescued. By 0700, Cooke was back at Barakoma, with the two remaining LSTs beached.

The expected Japanese air strike soon arrived in scattered groups, in all forty-eight Zeros and ten Val D3A dive bombers, and P-39s and F4Us intercepted. One D3A scored near misses on LST-339, which lifted the bow and drove the ship onto the coral ledge. With the unloading completed, LST-339 reported that it could not retract. Its commander did some quick thinking and requested that the destroyers make a high-speed wake as near shore as possible; the surf rocked LST-339 sufficiently to allow it to slide off the beach. Shortly thereafter, the second Japanese air attack of forty-one Zeros and six D3As arrived, but by that time heavy weather had set in and prevented an attack. Aircraft losses for the day were one P-39 shot down and one F4U Corsair lost. Both pilots were killed. In addition, the marine batteries shot down a VMF-123 Corsair. (The pilot was picked up.) The Japanese had one D3A severely damaged.[20]

The Japanese scheduled the Rekata Bay evacuation for 22 August; Captain Miyazaki Toshio left Rabaul with three destroyers to carry out the operation. But harassment by a PB4Y off Bougainville and an erroneous report of American cruisers and destroyers in the area caused him to abort the mission. On 25 August, the Japanese tried again. This time, Ijūin led a "diversion" force made up of *Sendai* and two destroyers, while Miyazaki with three destroyers went in to bring out the troops. In response to the coast watcher's report, Bomber Command sent off at least ten PB4Ys, which caught up with Miyazaki in the Bougainville Strait and scored one hit on the *Hamakaze*'s forecastle, killing or wounding thirty-six men. Rather than try to make Buin, which was reported to be under air attack, Miyazaki returned to Rabaul. On 28 August, *Sendai* and a destroyer returned the troops to Buin. In the meantime, six flying boats and one submarine took off the rest of the personnel.[21]

XIV CORPS TAKES OVER

The final three echelons of the amphibious phase went in to Barakoma during the last week of August without further loss in shipping. The air battles continued but without serious loss on either side – one F4U against one Zero and three D3As. Altogether, Wilkinson had landed 6,505 men, 1,097 tons of rations, 843 tons of drummed petroleum products, 2,247 tons of ammunition, 2,528 tons of vehicles (this included the 58th's construction equipment, artillery, 4th Defense Battalion's tank platoon, and trucks), and 1,911 tons of other materiel. This gave the NLF a forty-day supply of rations, five units of fire, and thirty days of fuel, medical, and other supplies.[22] At the airfield site, the 58th's bulldozers had cleared forty acres of rain forest, and the shovels were biting into the first of the 75,000 cubic yards of coral and earth that had to be removed. The 4,000-by-300-foot runway had to be wedged in between the sea and the steep hills a few hundred yards inland. To do this, the dispersal areas had to be located at each end of the strip, while the taxiways ran parallel to the runway. As at Munda, solid coral beneath the topsoil made for an excellent runway. The 58th had the field operational by 27 September.[23]

On 3 September, Wilkinson turned over command to XIV Corps and assumed his support role.[24] This marked the end of the amphibious phase and the beginning of operations to occupy all of Vella Lavella, a task Halsey had assigned Major General Harold E. Barrowclough's 3rd New Zealand Division, which was scheduled to arrive in mid-September.[25] No organized resistance was expected, since American intelligence was unaware that Niwa had landed reinforcements on the night of 17–18, but the search for a suitable radar site proved otherwise. The site of the mobile long-range radar (SCR-270-D), just south of Biloa, proved unsatisfactory, since the radar could provide only high-altitude coverage in the critical sector of 310° to 10°. This created all but insurmountable difficulties for both NGAF Fighter Command at Munda and the Vella Lavella Fighter Director.[26] A 25th Reconnaissance Troop patrol had found a suitable site on the northeast coast, and Griswold sent in 1st Battalion, 145th Infantry, to relieve Major Delbert Munson's 1st Battalion, 35th, in the perimeter. Munson would go up the east coast and secure the Boko Mission/Horaniu Kokolope Bay area.

Given the nature of trails in the Solomons, the beach trail was a good one as far as Orete Cove, and 1st Battalion made good progress, reaching Lambu Lambu Cove on 4 September. Supplies arrived by boat, while C Company, 65th Engineers, worked on the trail and put in bridges.[27] A and C Companies, with Tripp and his Fijians, followed the maze of trails to Boko Mission, where A Company ran into a strong Japanese patrol. In the firefight that followed, twelve Japanese were killed, including an officer with a sketch map of the Japanese positions in his possession. An examination of the sketch map, the weapons, and the bodies told Munson that he was up against healthy, well-equipped troops with prepared positions, not the underfed stragglers roaming the jungle he had been told to expect.

The dead troops were from the Horaniu Defense Force under the temporary command of Yokosuka 7th Lieutenant (jg) Sawayama Tatsuji. In addition to the troops Niwa had brought in on the night of 17–18 August, a detachment from the barge relay base at Supato on the southwest coast had marched overland to join up on 25 August. Three days before, an air strike of twenty-five VMTB-143 Avengers and eight 70th Squadron B-25s had left the installations "blown to hell," as the Avenger pilots reported. While Sawayama had roughly the equivalent of an understrength battalion, he realized that both he and his troops were ill-trained and inexperienced. "We are at a disadvantage in ground combat," he told his troops on taking command, "but I have confidence in the accomplishment of our purpose through your cooperation and courageous fighting."[28]

On the morning of 5 September, 4th Company, Mikami Battalion, attacked A Company, which was dug in near Boko Mission. A Company beat off the Japanese at the cost of two killed and two wounded. Mullen now requested artillery, and C Battery, followed by A Battery, 64th FA Battalion, was soon on the trail north to firing positions at Ruravai. The engineers had done their job, and by 7 September, C Battery was firing harassment missions. In addition to the artillery, Brown started moving his 3rd Battalion to Orete. In the meantime, Munson had cleared the Boko Mission area, which allowed supplies to come in by boat, and he was starting his troops toward the main Japanese defenses at Baka Baka. The main strongpoint was a steep ridge studded with machine-gun positions, and Tripp and his Fijians circled around to the west to determine the depth of the defenses. The terrain was difficult, in a heavy rain forest laced by a confusing maze of trails leading in all directions. On 10 September, C Company, following a trail toward Baka Baka, ran into an ambush and lost three men killed and eight wounded.

But on the same day, the engineers pushed the beach trail to Lambu Lambu, and the next day, C Battery moved there from Orete Cove. From this point on the battle of Horaniu was fought between Sawayama's green troops, who had never faced artillery fire, and Lieutenant Colonel William H. Allen Jr.'s 105s. As the artillery concentrations began to fall with unerring accuracy, the Japanese realized that the American gunners knew exactly where they were, which in fact they did. By transposing Captain John Burden's translation of the Japanese sketch onto their maps and filling in details from Munson's patrol reports, A and C Batteries had created accurate firing grids. When Munson launched his attack on 14 September, his battalion occupied the Horaniu area without opposition. The abandoned Japanese positions showed the effects of shellfire: dugouts that had suffered direct hits, corpses holding picks and shovels in their hands, and equipment scattered everywhere. Sawayama began the retreat to the northwest coast with Tripp's Fijians following, 1st Battalion moved back to Lambu Lambu, while 3rd Battalion occupied the Horaniu area. A and C Batteries went back to Biloa.

For the 35th, the Vella Lavella operation was over. On 18 September, Wilkinson brought in the first units of Barrowclough's 3rd Division, the 35th and 37th Battalions of 14th Brigade (Brigadier General Leslie Potter), and landed them at Les Gill's plantation at Joroveto north of Barakoma.[29] Gill owned Lambete Plantation at Munda and from Rendova had watched COMAIRSOLS and Barker's guns destroy it; now he was with the New Zealanders hoping to see what was in store for his other plantation.

Unloading was almost completed, and the escort destroyers were herding most of the ships offshore, when Sakamaki's attack came in. Twenty-seven fighters – seventeen F4US from VMF-213 and VMF-214, six F6FS from VF-38, and four P-40s from 44th Squadron – intercepted the forty-eight Zeros and twelve D3AS over Baga Island, and the battle spread eastward over the landing area and Vella Gulf. VMF-213 lost three planes and two pilots, one shot down by the rear gunner of a D3A, while the F4US and P-40s claimed fifteen aircraft (not confirmed). Shipping suffered no damage. Once ashore, Barrowclough assumed command of the NLF.[30]

With Allied bases now being established up the east coast of Vella Lavella, Wilkinson was forced to scatter his LSTs. This cost him the protection of the Barakoma antiaircraft guns and spread thin the fighter cover. He soon paid the price. On 25 September, a large convoy arrived, with 14th Brigade's 30th Battalion and USMC and Seabee units, to establish an advanced IMAC base at Ruravai for the upcoming Bougainville operation. Sakamaki sent down eight D3AS covered by forty Zeros. NGAF (now under the command of Brigadier General James T. Moore, USMC)[31] had twenty fighters covering the convoy. Twelve F6FS of VF-12 intercepted the Zeros at 1113 (and claimed to have downed one), but two minutes later the D3AS came out of the sun to attack the IMAC landing site at Ruravai. The 77th Seabees had cleared the beach area, and the marine 40mm guns were set up, but two bombs hit *LST-167* and the rest hit the beach, killing thirty-two men and wounding fifty-eight. *LST-167* was beached and later towed to the Russells. The 30th Battalion escaped attack as it unloaded farther down the coast at Joroveto.[32]

On 1 October, the Japanese repeated their success at the IMAC base, when Wilkinson's 9th Echelon arrived with Lieutenant Colonel Victor H. Krulak's 1st Marine Parachute Battalion. At 0925, an estimated eight D3AS with a dozen Zeros evaded both radar and the fighter patrol and went after the LSTs. With only a few seconds of warning, the gunners on *LST-334* at Ruravai saw four D3AS coming out of the glare of the morning sun. Two veered off to attack *LST-448* a few hundred yards south, and the other two, in a glide bombing attack, scored one hit and a near miss on *LST-334*, causing some damage but no casualties. *LST-448* was not so fortunate. Two direct hits wiped out the New Zealand Bofors crew to a man, ignited fuel and ammunition, and left the ship in flames. Fifty-two men were killed and many more wounded.[33] With all the men he could muster, the LST group commander had the fires under control and was preparing to tow the damaged LST when the second air raid came in. The fighter patrol intercepted, but not before a single D3A got through to make a direct hit on *LST-448*, which in effect finished it; *LST-448* sank under tow.[34]

The 1 October raid marked the last attack on Vella Lavella shipping. By then, the Japanese were in the midst of evacuating their troops from New Georgia, while the 26th Air Flotilla was beginning to withdraw from Buin.

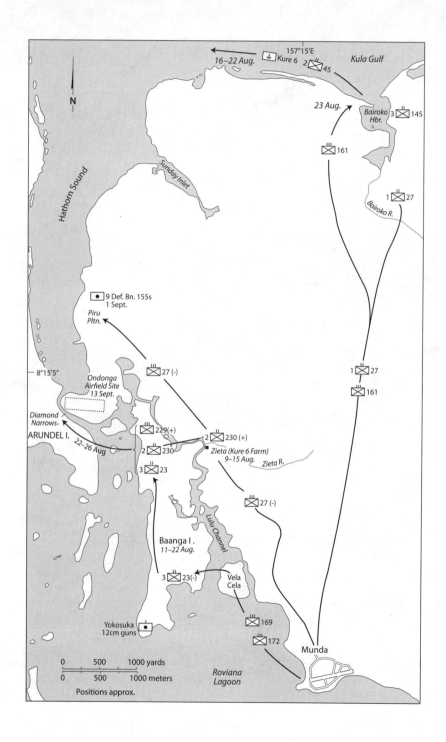

N

16–22 Aug.

157°15′E
↓ Kure 6

Kula Gulf

2 ⊠ 45

23 Aug.

Bairoko
Hbr.

3 ⊠ 145

⊠ 161

1 ⊠ 27

Bairoko R.

Hathorn Sound

Sunday Inlet

● 9 Def. Bn. 155s
1 Sept.

Piru
Pltn.

Ondonga
Airfield Site
13 Sept.

⊠ 27 (-)

1 ⊠ 27

⊠ 161

— 8°15′5″

Diamond
Narrows.

ARUNDEL I.

22–26 Aug

⊠ 229(+)

2 ⊠ 230

3 ⊠ 23

2 ⊠ 230 (+)

■ Zieta (Kure 6 Farm)
9–15 Aug.

Zieta R.

⊠ 27 (-)

Baanga I .
11–22 Aug.

Lulu Channel

3 ⊠ 23(-)

Vela
Cela

Yokosuka
12cm guns ●

⊠ 169

⊠ 172

Munda

0   500   1000 yards
0   500   1000 meters

Positions approx.

Roviana
Lagoon

TWELVE

The "Cleanup" in New Georgia

AFTER THE CAPTURE OF MUNDA, MAJOR GENERAL OSCAR W. Griswold's next objective was to clear the Japanese from New Georgia Island and the Diamond Narrows/Hawthorne Sound area. Operations went much more slowly than he had expected. Around 25 August, he wrote in his diary, "I am not happy. This clean-up is almost as bad as the _big_ battle." He noted the terrain: "Very difficult supply problem and much rain. Air drops used extensively for supply. Operations over almost unbelievably difficult terrain – moved very slowly."[1] But there were problems he did not mention. Intelligence had little knowledge of the topography, so that the maps prepared for the operations were of little use; often the combat units had no idea where they were in relation to each other or to reference points on the maps. Nor, with the exception of Bairoko Harbor, did intelligence have any knowledge of the location or composition of the Japanese forces. While intelligence was aware that the Japanese forces were withdrawing over the Zieta Trail rather than the Bairoko Trail, it was assumed that they were headed for the Sunday Inlet on the coast of Hawthorne Sound. The strong Japanese resistance at Zieta (Yano) and Baanga (Nagakari) would come as an unpleasant surprise.

For the "cleanup" operations, Griswold divided responsibility between the 25th Division (27th and 161st Infantry), now under its commander, Major General J. Lawton Collins, and the 43rd Division (commanded by Hodge until 11 August, then Barker to 20 August, then

Map 12.1. New Georgia and Baanga Island "Cleanup" Operations, August 1943.

Wing).[2] Griswold assigned New Georgia Island (Piru Plantation near Sunday Inlet and Bairoko Harbor) to the 25th Division and the contiguous islands of Baanga and Arundel to the 43rd.

BATTLE OF ZIETA (KURE 6TH FARM)

With his headquarters just north of Kongō Hill, Collins started 1st Battalion, 27th Infantry, (Major Joseph F. Ryneska) and Dalton's 161st up the Bairoko Trail, and the rest of the 27th (Colonel Douglas Sugg)[3] along the Zieta Trail toward Piru Plantation. A company of the 65th Engineers and the 89th FA were in support of the 27th. On the afternoon of 8 August, the leading 2nd Battalion (Lieutenant Colonel Benjamin F. Evans) entered a deep ravine roughly 2 miles up the trail and immediately came under heavy machine-gun fire. An attempt to outflank the Japanese failed in the face of intense fire, while patrols reported the positions to be in depth.[4]

Major Yano Keiji, the veteran from Guadalcanal, had selected an area of rough terrain east and south of Zieta Village and the Kure 6th Farm – the Americans later called it the Zieta Garden – with his first line of defense across the Zieta River. A patch of high ground just north of Zieta Village would have been more defensible, but he had to be in position to protect the trail running to Lulu Channel and Baanga, which was his sole line of communications. Yano had 330 troops from the 2nd Battalion, 230th Regiment, and the 12th Company, 23rd Regiment, with a critical shortage of ammunition. The problem was the tortuous supply route. Barges made the run to the west coast of Baanga, from where the transport troops carried the supplies through thick jungle and mangrove swamp to Lulu Channel. Fearing air attack, they waited there for night to cross the channel in rubber boats, and then the troops shouldered their packs for the trip up the trail.

The battle for Zieta began in earnest on 9 August. For three days, the Japanese held off the 27th, which attempted to envelop their positions. But these attacks gradually confined the Japanese into a smaller and smaller area. During the night of 11–12 August, therefore, Yano ordered the frontline troops to withdraw back across the river, moved all his forces several hundred yards back, and formed a defense perimeter. With the opposing lines very close, the Japanese yelled and threw stones at the

Americans throughout the night to cover their withdrawal. The deception worked. On the morning of the 12th, the 27th pulled back, and the 89th laid 2,700 rounds, the heaviest concentration of the operation, on the empty Japanese positions. At 1300, both battalions moved forward, crossed the river, and continued their advance into the late afternoon before hitting Yano's perimeter. Here they dug in for the night. The next day, Sugg sent 3rd Battalion, with E Company attached, to make the attack, keeping the rest of 2nd Battalion in reserve. Again, the objective was to envelop the Japanese, but the right flanking attack was stopped by heavy fire, while the left ran into a swamp that forced it to swing too far left to make contact with the Japanese. No gain was made.

But 13 August was the turning point in the battle, for a patrol from H Company finally stumbled on the trail to Lulu Channel. Realizing that the trail was heavily used, the machine-gun platoon set up a roadblock. That night, H Company gunners killed all seven men of a carrying party coming up the trail, convincing Yano that he was about to be cut off. Sasaki, who had considered sending the 13th Infantry to reinforce Zieta, issued orders for Yano to withdraw to Baanga. Yano set the withdrawal for the night of 14–15 August, and during the day his forces held fast against the 3rd Battalion, stopping an attack in the morning and another in the afternoon. Late in the afternoon, the Japanese threw back an attack led by four marine tanks, which had crossed the river on a bridge the engineers had built. Accounts of the withdrawal that began that night are conflicting. Yano described an elaborate maneuver by which they avoided the Americans; H company machine gunners described a battle with a large number at the trail block – both are probably correct up to a point. Whatever happened, Yano and his force were on Baanga by the fifteenth, while the 27th occupied Zieta and made contact with Schultz's 3rd Battalion, 148th Infantry, on Zieta Hill north of the village. Schultz had arrived on the 13th but had made no attempt to join the battle.[5] At the end of the Zieta operation, the 27th reported the casualties suffered to date on New Georgia as forty-two men killed and three times that number wounded, nearly all in the battle for Zieta.

The 27th set out for Piru Plantation and Sunday Inlet and ran into a deep swamp that the aerial photographs had interpreted as high ground. It took until 23 August to get there. "Crossing that swamp was the toughest physical test I underwent during the war," Collins later wrote.[6] On the other hand, the Japanese were relieved that the 27th had not pursued Yano and cut off Nagakari on Baanga, where fighting was now in progress.

At Vila, Sasaki learned before dawn that Yano had safely withdrawn, but this was followed shortly by a report of the American landing on Vella Lavella. As the Japanese official historians observed, Vella Lavella finally ended the long back-and-forth deployment issue between Sasaki and Samejima. Shortly after noon, 8th Fleet sent a message simply advising Sasaki to do what he thought was best. Sasaki replied that he intended to do what he had advised all along – concentrate all his forces on Kolombangara. The evacuation of Bairoko posed some problems, since the loss of Zieta had cut off the escape route by land for the troops, and both the troops and considerable supplies would have to be evacuated by barge. Ōta had less than a dozen operable barges, which complicated the situation. The one factor in Sasaki's favor was the terrain, which had slowed the advance of the American troops from the south to a snail's pace. As for his southern forces, he intended to make a fighting withdrawal on both Baanga and Arundel.[7]

BATTLE OF BAANGA ISLAND

The 43rd Division made no move against Baanga until 10 August, when Hodge ordered the 169th Infantry Regiment to reconnoiter the island. The next day, patrols from Ramsey's 3rd Battalion located the Japanese strongpoint on the southwest tip near the Yokosuka 7th guns. The following day, Ramsey sent L Company (sixty-six men) to occupy Baanga. "For some reason," read the 43rd's report, "they were not ordered to land where the patrol had experienced no opposition, but in a cove in the Island which had not been reconnoitered" – which was in fact right into the teeth of Japanese strength. The Japanese waited until the first tank barge had unloaded before opening fire. Both barges pulled away, leaving thirty-four men on the beach. (Six apparently survived.)[8]

With the Japanese presence on Baanga established at a costly price, Barker on 13 August committed all of 3rd Battalion, using Vela Cela, a small island at the mouth of Lulu Channel, as a base. Ramsey's battalion moved there the next morning. The landing on Baanga was made late in the day. L Company raced ahead toward the point where the men had been abandoned on the beach and promptly found itself cut off and surrounded. The fight went on all night. On the morning of 15 August, I Company attempted to break through but was stopped by heavy fire. The attack, however, allowed L Company to escape, leaving behind six badly wounded men. L Company was now reduced to sixteen men. For the rest of the day, 3rd Battalion held what little ground it had gained and waited for reinforcements. Realizing that he had a fight on his hands, Barker committed 2nd Battalion, 169th Infantry, and 1st and 3rd Battalions, 172nd Infantry. Two battalions of artillery and an engineer company were in support. But the terrain defeated the engineers. While the west side of the island was suitable for a plantation (the Methodists had one there), the east side where the fighting took place was as the 172nd described it, "Thick, dense, mangrove swamps . . . with water usually ankle-deep and often knee-deep."

While Barker was getting his troops in position, the Yokosuka 7th 12cm guns and two mountain guns began firing on Munda Field, causing slight casualties and damage. But they had the potential to be more than a nuisance. On 16 August, the 136th opened counter-battery fire, which continued through the night. "If the Japanese fired one," the official historians observed, "there would be hundreds returned, along with relentless bombing." Nonetheless, the guns escaped damage. But just as they opened fire at dawn the next morning, a P-39 sent up from Munda spotted the flashes, and the call went to COMAIRSOLS. At 1320, thirteen VMTB-233 TBFs hit the area, followed a few minutes later by seventeen VMSB-141 SBDs; the amount of ordnance placed on the small target area had the effect of carpet bombing. The Yokosuka 7th guns did not fire again.

The ground fighting, which lasted until 20 August, was heaviest in the area of the 2nd Battalion, 169th Infantry. The battalion, which correctly believed that it faced the strongest Japanese pocket, planned to push the defenders west where 3rd Battalion, 172nd, could join in the attack. But 2nd Battalion made little progress. On 18 August, Naylor landed his 1st Battalion, 172nd Infantry, and tied in with 3rd Battalion; Barker came with him, relieved Ramsey on the beach, and put 1st Lieutenant

John M. Haffner, S-3 of the 172nd, in command of the battalion. On 19 August, Naylor's patrols reached the coast at the coconut plantation, and the battalion followed, turning south where they found the abandoned 12cm guns. That night, caught between 2nd Battalion, 169th, and 1st Battalion, 172nd, the Japanese began slipping through the swamp and the American positions, making their way north. By nightfall the next day, all had escaped. The Japanese withdrawal to Arundel began on the night of 20 August and continued until the 22nd. Hirata's 229th, Yano's battalion, and Nagakari's battalion all got away. The Japanese recorded that in the darkness and continual rain, this was a difficult operation, but by 26 August, Hirata's forces were at Vila.

The cost of "cleaning up" Baanga had been considerable. The 169th recorded 44 killed, 74 wounded, and 300 nonbattle casualties; the 172nd lost 8 killed, 36 wounded, and almost 200 evacuated with disease. No count or estimate of Japanese casualties is available.

THE JAPANESE EVACUATION OF BAIROKO HARBOR

Collins expected a battle at Bairoko Harbor, unlike Zieta. As it evolved, his plan was to send the 161st and 1st Battalion, 27th Infantry, supported by engineers and artillery up the Bairoko Trail to a point known as Mt. Bao. About 2,500 yards south of the Bairoko River at the junction of the Munda and Zieta Trails, this was just a spot of high ground that has never been precisely located. There, the 161st with an artillery battalion would turn west on the Zieta Trail to another point known as Mt. Tirokiambo (which the troops called "Turkey Hill"). There the artillery would be emplaced, and the 161st would turn north to attack the west side of Bairoko Harbor in conjunction with 3rd Battalion, 145th Infantry; 1st Battalion, 27th Infantry, would attack the east side. Two 47th Seabee bulldozers were brought around from Segi in LCTs to cut a road from Enogai to Bairoko Harbor.[9]

The terrain gave the advantage to Sasaki. The engineers cut the road up to the Zieta Trail junction, but the road could not be maintained for heavy traffic. The 73rd Seabees lent the army two D-7 bulldozers, which simply bogged down and got stuck. When the engineers turned west to cut a road to Mt. Tirokiambo, they ran into an impassable swamp. Any hope vanished of getting the 140th FA Battalion in position to place Bairoko under fire. With great effort, on 21 August, Marine Defense Battalion tractors pulled the 155s of the 136th FA Battalion over the soft road to emplace on Zieta Hill, but by the time the 136th began targeting Bairoko, the Japanese had completed their evacuation. Supplies were carried by hand and dropped by SCAT (South Pacific Combat Air Transport Command). For the 161st alone, SCAT flew six missions from 15 to 24 August.

In the meantime, Ōta's barges, usually five to eight in a group, were running every night, taking off the supplies and troops from Bairoko. The barges hugged the coast, where they blended in and shot it out with the attacking PT boats. The guns on Kolombangara kept the PT boats under fire, since they were operating in open water and silhouetted by a bright moon. Usually, the 938th seaplanes joined in.[10] Unable to stop what American intelligence thought was the reinforcement of Bairoko, the American command came up with a plan for a daylight raid to blow up the barges in their bases. Rendova would furnish the PT boats, XIV Corps the demolition teams of volunteers from the 117th Engineer Battalion, and NGAF the fighter cover. Consequently, on the morning of 22 August, two groups of three boats, two to carry the engineers and the other to cover, made for Ringgi and Vavohe Coves. Mulcahy had twelve fighters overhead. One group nosed in to Ringgi Cove, saw Japanese all around, and beat a hasty retreat. The second group entered Vavohe Cove with *PT-108* leading. Machine-gun fire immediately riddled *PT-108*; a seaman brought the boat out on one engine, with its commander and two others dead and six wounded. The boats beat a retreat down Blackett Strait, covered by smoke from *PT-105*. That night the Japanese barges made their final run, completing the evacuation. On the next day, the 161st entered a deserted base. The 161st occupied the area, and the Raiders went back to Espíritu Santo.[11]

THE JAPANESE REORGANIZE

On 23 August, Samejima ordered Sasaki to hold the Gizo–Kolombangara–Arundel line and to wait to be notified when the evacuation date was set. Accordingly, on 26 August, Sasaki sent Kinoshita with his 1st and 4th Companies to Arundel to hold the north coast. Kinoshita put 4th

Company (1st Lieutenant Itō Saburō) at the base of the Stima Peninsula on the northeast coast, while with the reinforced 1st Company Kinoshita occupied the high ground on Arundel to the west. Sasaki sent Yamada with two companies of the 45th Infantry Regiment to Gizo on 28 August and ordered Hirata with his forces to Jack Harbor (Bambare), the largest inlet on the east coast, some 6 miles north of Vila, to defend against an indirect attack. To defend the Vila area, Sasaki created Base Force under Tomonari, made up of the 13th Infantry, Hara's 2nd Independent Quick-Fire Battalion, Takeda's Yokosuka 7th land defense units, and the remaining mountain artillery units. Kure 6th detachments held the west coast. As a reserve, Sasaki retained 5th and 8th Companies, 45th Regiment, and 3rd Company, 13th Regiment, under his direct command.[12]

Sasaki had adequate food supplies, provided the evacuation was carried out in a timely fashion. On 23 August, he reported that he had forty days of rice and twenty days of vegetables, fish, salt, soy sauce, miso, and other "subsidiary" food. But his stock of antiaircraft ammunition was low, the troops from Munda were in desperate need of clothing and shoes, and while not mentioned, medical supplies were probably needed for the 1,500 patients in the hospitals. He had been notified on 20 August that he would begin receiving 220 tons of supplies at the end of the month during the dark of the moon period. But Sasaki reported that by the first week of September he had received only 14 tons, which in light of the Japanese shipping records for the period seems incredibly low.[13] By the first week of September, Sasaki was revising his food supply downward, but the Japanese never ran out of rations.

The Japanese used fishing boats, barges, submarines, and air drops. The fishing boats had arrived in early July and were placed under Itagaki's 1st Transport Group. They had an armored pilot house and cargo hold, mounted a heavy machine gun and a 20mm cannon, and could carry up to 30 tons at 6 knots. Before the occupation of Vella Lavella shut down their relay bases in mid-September, the fishing boats and PT boats fought it out as they made for Vila. In two separate fights that can be documented, the PT boats drove one fishing boat hard aground off the tip of Vella Lavella, but the other, which was carrying wounded from Vila, made it back to Buin, so badly shot up and burned that the Japanese were amazed the vessel could still float.[14] On the other hand, on the night of 6–7 September, two PT boats were lost when they made their run on a fishing boat – at high speed, in low visibility – and ran completely onto a reef.[15] The Japanese submarine *I-38* made two supply runs to Vila, and in early September, Bettys from the 702nd began air drops, coming in so low over the airfield that one crashed and burned at the end of the strip.[16]

THE BATTLE OF ARUNDEL ISLAND

Wing had responsibility for clearing the Japanese from Arundel, with the objectives of bringing Vila under heavy artillery fire while at the same time protecting the airfield site at Ondonga on the Diamond Narrows. On 29 August he gave Ross's 172nd the job, and 2nd Battalion began moving up the east coast while 1st Battalion moved up the west. Foot patrols led the way, and the main body followed in landing craft. The terrain was some of the worst in New Georgia – shorelines of hard coral and a tangle of mangroves; the interior rain forest with dense underbrush – and movement was slow. But by 5 September, Carrigan's 2nd Battalion had located the general area of Kinoshita's two positions. On the same day, Naylor's 1st Battalion landed at Bustling Point on the west coast and occupied the tip of the Bomboe Peninsula. These were to be the key positions for American operations: Bustling Point for the artillery site and Bomboe Peninsula as the axis of the main attack against the Japanese.[17]

On Arundel, meanwhile, little fighting occurred; the 172nd made no attack on either Japanese position. As a result, Kinoshita was reporting great success; this and the desire to eliminate the artillery at Piru Plantation led Sasaki to counterattack. Shortly after midnight on 9 September, the first elements of Takabayashi's 3rd Battalion, less 11th Company, and a platoon of the 6th Engineers began crossing to the western end of Sagekarasa Island, the largest of the fringe islands that ran west from Stima Peninsula. The objective was to drive the Americans from north Arundel and if possible, take the Piru Plantation–Ondonga area. Sasaki's biggest worry was his lack of barges. The eight or so that Ōta had would have to make round trips across Blackett Strait, which was 1,200 yards wide at that point, with the trip taking about twenty minutes each way.

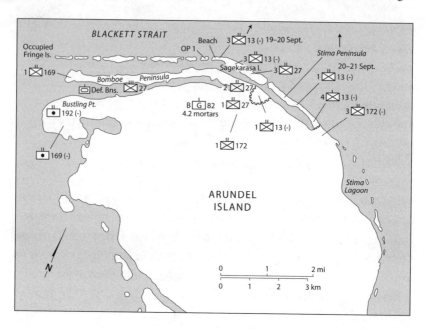

Map 12.2. Arundel Island, 29 August–21 September 1943.

A few hours after Takabayashi's troops landed on Sagekarasa, Griswold, who was unaware of the Japanese buildup but aware that the 43rd "had more than it could handle,"[18] ordered Sugg with his 2nd and 3rd Battalions, 27th Infantry, to move to Bomboe Village and attack from the west. Barker was to put artillery in Piru Plantation and at Bustling Point. The first 4.2-inch mortars to be used in the Solomons (B Company, 82nd Chemical Battalion), which were to do horrific damage to the Japanese, were sent in. Although the 27th was attached to the 43rd, Sugg was given operational control.

Sugg advanced east on Bomboe Peninsula on 12 September. Evans's 2nd Battalion would deal with Kinoshita; Davis's 3rd Battalion would deal with Takabayashi. The advance went quickly that day, but the next day Evans ran into Kinoshita's position, and heavy machine-gun fire stopped the battalion. At the same time, Davis's 3rd Battalion forded Bomboe Lagoon, using a small islet called Stepping Stone Island, and landed on Sagekarasa very near the middle of the island. The move took the Japanese by surprise, and no defenses were in place. 3rd Battalion was now in position to contain the main Japanese beachhead and cut that line of communication with Kinoshita. For the next four days, in extremely close fighting, Davis beat back repeated attempts to break his block by Takabayashi from the west and Itō from the east.

Meanwhile, a killing field was being prepared for the Japanese at their Sagekarasa beachhead. Crews from M Company and B Company, 82nd, were chopping trees and clearing underbrush on Bomboe to set up their mortars to hit any place on Sagekarasa Island. At the same time, 1st Battalion, 169th, completed setting up outposts on the chain of small islands running west from Sagekarasa numbered 1–8, Island No. 1 being nearest Sagekarasa. From this outpost, OP1, observers could track the Japanese barges in the moonlight from the time they left Vila until they approached the landing area. This was the moment when the shells would begin to rain down. The mortar crews had plotted a "barge zone" that was based on a captured Japanese map, while the 192nd had an observer with Davis's battalion to adjust fire. On the night of 15 September, Tomonari brought his headquarters across; ten minutes later while he was sitting on a log listening to a company commander report, he was killed instantly when a mortar shell landed at his feet. Takabayashi assumed command of the 13th Infantry, and Moriya took over 3rd Battalion. A day or two later, mortar fire killed Takabayashi, and Kinoshita took command.

On Arundel on 15 August, Evans, now with Naylor's troops attached, attacked Kinoshita's positions around noon but was beaten back. Meanwhile, on Griswold's orders, LCTs were bringing Ryneska's 1st Battalion around from Enogai, and LCMs were on the way with five 11th Defense Battalion tanks. By the early afternoon of the sixteenth, Ryneska and the tanks had arrived, a heavy rain muffling the sound of the tanks as they moved up. At 0745 on 17 August, behind a heavy artillery and mortar concentration the tanks moved forward, followed by three rifle companies lined abreast. The appearance of the tanks surprised the Japanese, and they fell back. But the following day, when two tanks supported by infantry attacked two machine-gun positions, Kinoshita had his anti-tank gun ready, which knocked out the first tank, and the second caught on fire. The Japanese charged the disabled tanks, and in the firefight that followed, the tank crews escaped. The Americans beat back the attack, and the tank that had suffered the fire was recovered. Seven more marine tanks were on the way for an attack on Kinoshita the following day.

But Kinoshita was withdrawing to the Stima Peninsula. Sasaki, having received the details of the evacuation plan on the night of 15 August, had halted the movement of the rest of the 13th Infantry to Arundel on 17 August. Two days later, he ordered the withdrawal to begin that night. At around 2200, the 3rd Battalion evacuated under heavy mortar and artillery fire while the Yokosuka 7th guns opened covering fire, which caused several casualties on the American side. Moriya had given the rearguard assignment to 1st Lieutenant Kajima Gorō's 12th Company. Kajima was killed by shellfire, and the platoon commander, who lived to tell the story, had his leg blown off. Moriya, who left in the last barge, died when a mortar shell hit his barge. The following night, 20 September, the barges took off Kinoshita's troops. Barker's artillery fired blindly all night, since the evacuation point was not known. When the first barge arrived, the troops made a rush for it – panicked, the Japanese said – until the officers quickly restored order. After that, the evacuation went smoothly.

For the 13th Infantry, Arundel had been costly. The numbers in the Japanese sources are difficult to reconcile, but the 6th Division historians gave the casualties as 233 killed (177 from shellfire) and 363 wounded, and 10 killed from the 6th Engineers. No numbers are given for barge crews and other support units. On the American side, only 43rd Division and 2nd Battalion, 27th Infantry, reported casualties; the former had 26 men killed and 200 wounded and the latter had 5 killed and 25 wounded.

THE BOMBARDMENT OF VILA

On the last day of August, the 9th Defense Battalion's 155s that had emplaced at Piru Plantation opened fire on Kolombangara; that night a Black Cat dropped leaflets on Vila describing the misery and death the American artillery had in store for the Japanese. Ask the survivors from the 229th what it was like on Bakudan Hill, the message suggested. But the drop was, of course, a waste of paper and gasoline. The next morning, Takabayashi simply told 3rd Battalion that "enemy shelling and firing will be intensified in the future," and ordered that "any rambling activity must be avoided and everyone must always be on the alert."[19]

Barker and COMAIRSOLS did their best to fulfill the promise. Barker moved up more artillery – another battery of the 192nd to Bustling Point, the 103rd FA to south of the point, and the 89th FA to a small island in Vonavona Lagoon. Battery B of the 11th Defense Battalion was brought around to Enogai to join the 9th Defense Battalion in the duel with the Yokosuka 7th.[20] The latter landed a few shells near where the 37th and 82nd Seabees were building the twin-runway fighter field at Ondonga but did no damage. For its part, COMAIRSOLS flew twenty-two missions from 24 August to 2 October, with the heaviest strike on 28 September carried out by ninety-two SBDS, TBFS, and B-25S. There was no fighter opposition; Sakamaki had his hands full with Vella Lavella. On one occasion SBDS approaching Vila could see the D3AS diving on American shipping off Barakoma. A few planes were lost to light antiaircraft fire, or in the case of the TBFS, to the explosions of their own bombs since they went in so low.[21]

A case in point happened on 11 September, when Strike Command operations officer Lieutenant Commander Harold H. Larsen, a veteran TBF pilot, apparently fell victim to his own doctrine of going in low. Major J. S. Flickinger (VMSB-236), leading the third division of SBDS in a heavy strike of twenty-four Dauntlesses, fifteen Avengers, and eighteen B-25S, had dropped his bombs and was on a strafing run when he saw a TBF coming in, extremely low, to drop on targets at Jack Harbor (Bambere). "The release was made at such a low altitude," he reported, "that the flame of the explosion and the debris reached a greater height than that of the plane." When he recovered from the strafing run, he saw a TBF on his starboard side and slightly ahead "turn from a near vertical nose high position and dive toward the water at a 70° angle. . . . Immediately before striking the water, the nose of the plane whipped up sharply and the plane made an excellent water landing, slightly nose low." Flickinger soon had his own problem, when his gunner threw out a raft for a man standing on the wing of the downed aircraft. The raft caught on the tail of Flickinger's plane, sending it into downward spiral before he recovered at 300 feet. Neither he nor his gunner had seen Larsen's parachute. He landed at Munda, picked up another raft, and returned to the scene, where his gunner spotted Larsen in the water. After some delay, Larsen and Sergeant G. E. Wood, Strike Command photographer, were picked up early the next morning. The other two men, an intelligence officer and a radio-gunner, were lost.[22]

The Japanese historians made no mention of the casualties or damage from the heavy bombardment. At any rate, in preparation for the evacuation, the Japanese were using both bomb and shell explosions to mask the sound of the demolition of their installations.

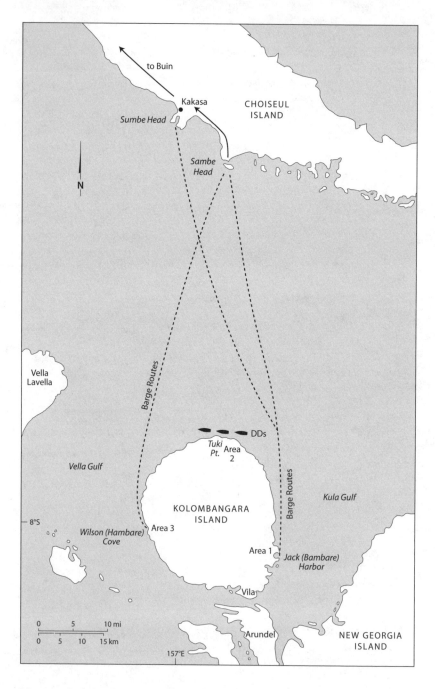

Map 13.1. Japanese Retreat to Choiseul Island – Operation Se-gō.

THIRTEEN

The Japanese Evacuation

"THE ENEMY WAS GUARDING THE KOLOMBANGARA AREA VERY cautiously," wrote Lieutenant Commander Imai, 8th Combined chief of staff. "Forty sea miles from Kolombangara to Choiseul, they had surrounded the area with torpedo bombers, destroyers, and cruisers. We had to go through the siege, close to being unarmed, with twice as many passengers as we should have, on slow motor barges. It was like sending the troops to sea just so they could get sunk. At worst, we all could have died. Even if we were successful, we thought we would probably lose half the troops. It was a miracle that 90% of the troops were actually transported."[1]

Perhaps it was a miracle, but the close cooperation between the army and the navy in planning and executing the operation, the bravery of the barge commanders and their crews, and Terai's 938th seaplanes, which scouted for the barges and harassed the American destroyers, all played their part.

KOLOMBANGARA

Samejima was responsible for the planning and execution of the operation. For guidance, he had a general memorandum of understanding between Kusaka and Imamura, issued on 30 August. The main points were: (1) the evacuation would be carried out using only small boats, either via Vella Lavella or Choiseul, and would take place from late September to late October, and (2) the army would contribute Major General Yoshimura Masayoshi's 2nd Shipping Engineer Group, less the 1st Regiment, with at least thirty barges.[2]

In early September, Samejima began work, able assisted by Yoshimura and Ijūin. Yoshimura proposed carrying out the operation quickly in two stages between 28 September and 20 October via the Choiseul route; Ijūin proposed using the 8th Fleet destroyers for both transport and cover. Kusaka approved the timetable and the use of the destroyers, and he obtained six additional destroyers for Ijūin from Combined Fleet. In addition, Kusaka sent submarine RO-109 to the area (it arrived on 25 September) and arranged for Sakamaki and Ueno to provide limited air cover over Choiseul by day, with the 938th carrying the main burden at night. For the movement to Choiseul, Yoshimura would come under Samejima's command, and in turn would command all army and navy small boats, his own 2nd Shipping Engineer Group, and Tanegashima's 1st Transport Group. (Tanegashima had commanded *Murasame*, which had been sunk in Kula Gulf.) The Japanese called Yoshimura's force the "17th Army Sea Battle Unit."

By 15 September, the plan for the operation, now called Se-gō, was mostly complete. That night, Kisaka flew into Vila to discuss the details with Sasaki and Ōta. He no doubt landed in the midst of exploding shells, since the American artillery opened fire the moment a seaplane was heard landing or taking off. Kisaka stayed until the following night while he went over the plans with Sasaki and Ōta. Preparations for withdrawal would begin 20 September. In a two-stage operation during the dark of the moon, 28 September and 2 October, Ijūin's destroyers and Yoshimura's small boats would take off the Southeast Detachment. The Choiseul staging bases would be Sumbe Head and Sambe Head, while Tuki Point on north Kolombangara would be the boarding point. Sasaki was leery of using the destroyers in the first stage for fear of alerting the Americans and provoking a landing at Vila, but eventually he agreed. He won his argument, however, that a single boarding point would be logistically difficult, and 8th Fleet modified the plan to use three major locations: Jack Harbor (Area 1), Tuki Point (Area 2), and Wilson (or Hambare) Harbor on the west coast (Area 3).

Kisaka flew back to Buin, and the preparations began as scheduled. Yoshimura had already begun arming the barges, usually with a heavy machine guns, training the crews for their expected confrontation with American destroyers and PT boats, and arranging for the necessary tools to establish temporary repair shops. But his biggest problem was to move the approximately seventy barges and nine small naval launches (vedettes) to the forward bases and keep them hidden from air attack. NGAF immediately confirmed his apprehension 20 September, when eight F4Us from VMF-215 on an alert from Waddell destroyed five of the eight barges that made up the first group. This was an "inauspicious start to the operation," Yoshimura recalled, but he carried on, leaving Buin 23 September and arriving at Sumbe Head on 25 September, where Eighth Fleet had sent in a detachment of the Kure 7th to establish his base of operations.[3] By that time, Waddell already had a copy of Yoshimura's preliminary plan of 10 September, but what appears to have been an intelligence turf fight at Guadalcanal prevented NGAF from getting it in time.[4]

At Nouméa, Halsey had intelligence that the Japanese were planning either to reinforce or to evacuate Kolombangara. He sent Merrill's cruisers (TF 39) back up to Port Purvis, split into two task groups (TG 39.1 and TG 39.2).[5] From the night of 22–23 September to the night of 25–26 September, he sent powerful forces north, a cruiser group up the Slot and a destroyer group swinging south and up Vella Gulf, with the objective of catching Ijūin between them. Halsey called his plans "Mousetrap" and "Birdcage." No trap was sprung, of course, because the Japanese did not come down. But on the night of 25–26 September, both *Columbia* and *Cleveland* reported torpedo wakes, and a possible contact was made on a surfaced submarine, most likely *RO-109*. This was enough for Halsey. He returned one cruiser task group to Espíritu Santo and kept the other at Tulagi for use only if Japanese heavy units came down. Wilkinson's destroyers would have to interdict the Japanese evacuation, which Halsey's intelligence now had pinned down as 29 September to 2 October. As a result, he ordered Wilkinson to retain four destroyers that were due to return for convoy duty.[6]

In the meantime, Sasaki made his preparations at Vila. Concealing his intentions was a major concern. Until the last minute, he kept the Yokosuka 7th guns firing and ordered increased patrolling to eliminate the native scouts (the heavy presence of the Japanese following the withdrawal to Kolombangara had already forced out the coast watchers). He began moving patients and 38th Division units to the north shore, since he intended to load them on the first destroyers. Demolition teams blew up all airfield installations, their explosions mingling with those of Barker's artillery, leaving the Americans none the wiser, and construction units began cutting trails to Jack Harbor and Wilson Harbor (Hambare). Ōta was in charge of all matters relating to the embarkation – communications, locating hiding places for the barges, and loading – in accordance with a detailed loading chart that assigned units by transport and area number. Each unit was responsible for its supply and was to carry enough rations to last to 5 October. All troops were to take their personal weapons and as much ammunition as they could carry, with medical supplies divided among them. Weapons that could be disassembled – mountain guns, quick-fire guns and heavy machine guns – could be taken if there was room. All else was to be destroyed, right down to the street signs, on the night before the unit left for the embarkation point.[7]

Se-gō began as scheduled. On the night of 27 September, Yoshimura's barges headed for Kolombangara in separate groups, a trip of about six hours. Wilkinson had five destroyers under the command of Captain Martin J. Gillan Jr. up the Slot that night, and around midnight these made contact with a group of seventeen barges under Tanegashima that were headed for Kolombangara. The night was clear with only a few clouds, and four barges were sunk, with considerable loss of life. With his remaining barges, Tanegashima made it to Kolombangara; none of the other barge groups ran into trouble.

During the daylight hours of 28 September, the barges and vedettes successfully hid out at various points on Kolombangara. Tight security prevented COMAIRSOLS from receiving intelligence from Kolombangara.[8] But at 1305, just northeast of Green Island, a VB-102 PB4Y flying the westernmost long-range search spotted Ijūin coming south, counting eight destroyers before being driven off by Zeros. In fact, there were eleven, four in the transport group under Kanaoka and seven in the strike force under Ijūin. Once spotted, the Japanese knew what to expect. As Ijūin approached the Bougainville Strait at 1920, his column came under attack by radar-equipped 394th SB-24 "Snoopers" sent off from Carney

Field to intercept.[9] Over the next hour, five SB-24s made their individual runs, but none of the ships were hit.

As the first SB-24 made its bombing run on Ijūin's destroyers, the Japanese barges and vedettes at Kolombangara were getting underway, some moving troops to the destroyer boarding point, others to make the trip across the Slot. Thirty minutes before the destroyers arrived, the groups destined for Choiseul set out across the open water on what was another clear night. But for whatever reason, Wilkinson had no destroyers in the Slot.[10] At Tuki Point, the barges were waiting when Kanaoka brought in his destroyers and boarding began. Here the only major mishap occurred, when the commander of the barges carrying 735 men from Jack Harbor to board *Amagiri* steered wide, missed the signal light from the destroyers, and headed for Vella Lavella. By the time the mistake was discovered and the barges had returned, the destroyers were gone, with 1,950 men on board. At Guadalcanal, Wilkinson made one last attempt against Ijūin. At his request, Bomber Command canceled the scheduled Kahili mission and at 0547 on 29 September began sending off twenty-seven B-24s without escort to search for Ijūin. But bad weather and an attack by Zeros (beaten off without loss) intervened. Around the same time, a PB4Y spotted Ijūin rounding the northern tip of Buka Island.[11]

Over the next two days and nights, 29–30 September, the Japanese completed Stage 1 of Se-gō against the now fully alerted American forces. At 0915 on 29 September, Strike Command hit Kakasa near Sambe Head with seventeen SBDs and twelve TBFs with fifty-six fighters as escort, but the Japanese records make no mention of damage. That night at 2000, Tanegashima, who had been on stand-by after loading the destroyers the night before, headed for Choiseul with eleven barges carrying 1,100 men. Captain Frank R. Walker with four destroyers was in the Slot searching for him and made contact at 2230.

There was no moon, and frequent rain squalls dotted the Slot. Even in clear patches surface visibility was 3,000 feet. Tanegashima ordered the barges to scatter, and Walker detached *McCalla* to deal with a small group while he went after a larger group. Yano, whose battalion was part of the transport, recalled his barge running at full speed, shells landing all around them, and the engine so hot that it was burning red. No barges were sunk or seriously damaged, but as *McCalla* rejoined Walker's group off Sambe Head the ship lost steering control and sliced off *Patterson's* bow, with *McCalla* losing its own bow as it backed away. With the damage-control parties hard at work, it was near dawn when Walker's force set out down the Slot at 10 knots.[12]

With his convoy headed for Vella Lavella, Wilkinson could spare only three destroyers under Commander Alvin D. Chandler for barge interdiction on the night of 30 September. On Kolombangara, the Japanese readied four barges that had been undergoing mechanical repair for the final run of Stage 1, with 375 troops on board. Chandler made contact with the barges at 2107, 13 miles northwest of Tuki Point. Visibility was so poor that *Radford* illuminated the area with star shells, and then the destroyers opened fire. A direct hit destroyed one barge that carried troops of the 3rd Battalion, 23rd; ninety men were lost, including Nagakari and his headquarters. The other three made it, but one was so badly hit that it sank after unloading sixty-five troops west of Sambe Head. The second unloaded ninety-one men but had lost six men killed. The third, the only one to make it through undamaged, unloaded seventy-three. Chandler thought he had destroyed six.[13]

Earlier that same day, Samejima had ordered the execution of the 2nd Stage. The loss of a considerable number of barges worried the Japanese, and some adjustments were made to the plan. The remaining forty-three barges and five vedettes would depart Choiseul on the night of 1 October as originally scheduled, but these would be reinforced by three torpedo boats and two armed boats of some type. Ijūin would send down three destroyers to decoy the American forces that were certain to be waiting; then on the night of 2 October, Ijūin would bring down his main force. As on the 28th, three destroyers would take off troops from Tuki Point, and the small boats would head for Choiseul.

On 1 October, COMAIRSOLS hit Kusaka with another heavy strike in the afternoon, while Wilkinson sent two task groups up the Slot. Chandler with four destroyers was in the lead, followed by Merrill with two cruisers and eight destroyers. The three Japanese destroyers coming southeast to serve as the decoy were not spotted until 2120 off northwest Choiseul by a VP-54 Black Cat, which began tailing the force as it headed in the direction of Vella Lavella. At 2204, off Visuvisu Point, in accordance with orders not to risk the cruisers unless Japanese heavy units were present, Merrill turned back. Gillan with his four destroyers formed up with the cruisers, and Cooke hurried on ahead to join Chandler, who was already engaged with Yoshimura's barges that were headed for Kolombangara. But Cooke himself ran into barges, and so the two groups acted independently.

The moonless night was exceedingly dark, the sky overcast with frequent lightning flashes, and the sea was smooth. Gun flashes, star shells, and flares from the Japanese seaplanes marked the location of the American destroyers and lit up the darkness. Watching from Sambe Head, Yoshimura recalled that he was so absorbed by the spectacle he could neither sit nor stand, only pray to the gods. But the decoy worked. At 2304, the Black Cat reported the three Japanese destroyers were stopped off Vella Lavella, and Cook and Chandler took the bait, allowing the barges to go on their way. The Japanese mentioned only two barges lost, while a near miss from a 938th seaplane on *Saufley* inflicted over a dozen casualties.[14]

On 2 October, Ijūin left Rabaul at 0500 with nine destroyers. At noon, Cooke began refueling for a return trip up the Slot. For some reason, *Renshaw* had to be left behind. Commander Harold O. Larson with three destroyers replaced Chandler's division. On Kolombangara, Sasaki and Ōta readied the remaining units. Okumura's Kure 6th and Kinoshita's 1st Battalion (13th Infantry) were at Wilson Harbor, and Takeda's Yokosuka 7th and Hara's 2nd Independent Quick-Fire Battalion were at Vila. Sasaki worried that the Americans might land in his rear, that the destroyers might be prevented from arriving, and that even with a plan to load the remaining barges far beyond their maximum capacity, there would still not be enough room for all the men. At Vila, the Yokosuka 7th guns fired their last rounds at 0605; at 1100 Barker began an artillery shoot for the benefit of some visitors, Harmon and his staff. The bombardment continued for the rest of the day as the Japanese moved to Jack Harbor to embark. At Wilson Harbor, between 1620 and 1720, twelve TBFS, twenty-five SBDS, and six B-25s avoided the nearby thunderstorm and went in low to attack. The Japanese reported some damage to barges but none knocked out. The tip-off to COMAIRSOLS was the rough road that had been cut from Vila to Wilson Harbor, which could not be kept hidden from the scouts.

The Japanese successfully completed the evacuation that night, but not without considerable casualties among the barges and a very close call for the destroyers. The barges began moving as darkness settled in, and like the previous night, there was no moon, a low overcast, and even more frequent lightning flashes. Tanegashima was waiting with 2,100 men for the three destroyers. He managed to load 1,450 men by around 2235, when the destroyers were forced to pull away because the Americans were in the Slot. Tanegashima, nonetheless, headed for Sumbe Head with the rest, more than 600 men, on a night already lit by gunfire. Larson's division was firing on barges, when Cooke in *Waller* made contact with the destroyers at 2242. But failed communications with his other two destroyers, *Cony* and *Eaton*, and so he ordered Larson to make the attack while he re-formed. Closing with the Japanese, who were putting on speed, Larson fired torpedoes at 2325 but scored no hits. He then opened with his guns, but only three shells struck *Minazuki*, none of which exploded. Cooke then took up the chase but called it off after midnight. Both groups returned to barge hunting, sinking five of Tanegashima's barges.[15]

Sasaki and Ōta landed at Sambe at 0400 on 3 October and waited out the day in the forest because of the risk from the air. With darkness, they made their way to Sambe Head, where they met Yoshimura for the first time. From there Sasaki, Ōta, and their staffs went on to Buin, arriving on 5 October. Southeast Detachment was dissolved, the various units returning to either the 38th Division at Rabaul or the Seventeenth Army at Buin. Sasaki was assigned to Eighth Army Headquarters and Kamiya to the 38th Division staff. Ōta left the theater and died on Okinawa, where he was in command of all naval personnel.[16]

Exactly how many men the Japanese evacuated is problematical. The navy did not provide numbers for those on Kolombangara or for those who made it to Choiseul. The army gave a total of 7,543 on Kolombangara as of 20 September but did not take a muster on Choiseul.[17] Whatever the exact number, it was far above the Japanese expectations.

The American destroyer commanders found the operation frustrating. They came to the conclusion that if they had been able to slow to the speed of the barges, turn on searchlights, and use the 40mm guns, more barges would have been destroyed. But the submarine threat and constant presence of the Japanese seaplanes forced them to maintain a speed of no less than 20 knots and keep their searchlights switched off.[18]

THE VELLA LAVELLA EVACUATION

Following the battle at Baka Baka on 14 September, the survivors of the Horaniu Defense Force retreated to the northwest coast of Vella Lavella. Tripp's Fijians found them scattered in the area from Tambala Bay in the north to Marquana Bay in the south. This intelligence was reported to Barrowclough, who had taken command on Vella on 18 September.

The task of locating and eliminating what was thought to be scattered groups of Japanese fell to Potter's 14th Brigade. Accordingly, Potter planned to take 35th Battalion (Lieutenant Colonel C. F. Seward), a battery of artillery, and 14th Brigade Headquarters up the west coast to Matu Soroto Bay, and send 37th Battalion (Colonel A. H. L. Sugden) around the north coast to land at Doveli Cove, east of Tambala Bay. Seward would then work his way north and Sugden south, trapping the Japanese between them. All movement would be by landing craft along a jagged coastline with innumerable inlets and bays that were fringed with almost unbroken reefs. On 25 September, both the 35th and 37th battalions were at their starting points.[19]

By then, however, the Japanese situation had changed. On 21 September, Buin had sent in Captain Tsuruya Yoshio, IJA, to take command on Vella Lavella. He concentrated all troops at Marquana Bay, where a radio station was located, and established a defensive perimeter. The dense rain forest aided in the concealment of his positions. Tsuruya's pressing concern, however, was food, ammunition, and medical supplies. On 27 September, the fishing boat *Hinode Maru*, with a cargo of 10 tons of supplies and a radio set, put in at Tambala Bay, and after a brief firefight, the boat was captured by a New Zealand patrol at a cost of two killed. All indications are that the radio station at Marquana Bay was not operating – hence the radio set in the cargo – and that Tsuruya had sent a small party up to Tambala Bay to guide the *Hinode Maru*. The loss was a major blow. As a result, starting on the night of 28 September, the 938th began dropping food, ammunition, medical supplies, and batteries for the Tsuruya Unit.[20]

Nonetheless, Seward's 35th Battalion, which was closing on the Marquana Bay area by the 26th, was in for an unpleasant surprise. Two platoons sent ahead that day to scout the head of the bay were cut off, surrounded, and engaged in a fight for their lives until their rescue on 2 October. (Total casualties were twelve killed and ten wounded.) In the meantime, on 28 September, Potter ordered Seward to clear the Japanese from the dense rain forest south of the bay. Seward sent three companies up the trail to do the job. As Seward put it, these ran into a "hornets' nest." Machine-gun fire stopped the New Zealanders cold. A second attack the next day met with the same results. What the New Zealanders now called "Machine Gully" had cost eighteen dead and ten wounded. Potter now ordered Seward to keep up patrol action, while he sent every landing craft he could muster to bring Sugden's 37th Battalion down from Tambala Bay as quickly as possible for an attack from the other side. But the movement of the 37th down the rugged coast was slow going.

At Buin, meanwhile, Samejima was well aware of the situation. The "Tsuruya Unit was now cornered all the way with its back against Marquana Bay," the official historians wrote. "Supplies were not reaching them. There was little food and ammunition. The troops were hanging by a thread." Samejima was determined to get the troops off, and on 3 October, without consulting Kusaka, he notified Tsuruya that his force would be evacuated on the night of 5 October. Kusaka immediately ordered the evacuation postponed for a time, but Samejima persisted until Kusaka relented. The operation was rescheduled for the night of 6 October.[21]

Before dawn that morning, Ijūin left Rabaul with nine destroyers divided into three groups. Ijūin in *Akigumo*, with *Isokaze, Kazagumo,* and *Yūgumo,* led the strike unit. Kanaoka in *Fumizuki*, with *Yūnagi* and *Matsukaze,* had the transport unit, which carried six small barges and thirty folding boats from the depot ship *Usaka Maru*. Hara in *Shigure* with *Samidare* served as the guard unit. At 1700 the fourth group, the collection unit of five subchasers, three vedettes, and one barge under Commander Nakayama Shigoroku, left from Buin. Eighth Fleet's evacuation plan (or a plausible reconstruction) was for Kanaoka to stand off Marquana Bay and launch the barges for Nakayama to use in taking off the Tsuruya Unit. Eight 938th seaplanes were assigned to bomb the New

Zealand positions during the evacuation. Sakamaki would have twelve Zeros over the area in the morning.[22]

The complicated plan began to unravel around 2200. Ijūin, who had scouted Vella Lavella and found it clear, ordered Hara and Kanaoka, who had been lagging behind, to proceed to the staging point. But minutes later, a scout plane reported four cruisers and three destroyers northeast of Vella Lavella and headed west. Ijūin then ordered Hara to join him, and Kanaoka to retire west toward the Shortlands (and eventually to return to Rabaul). Ijūin himself turned back on a north-northeast course. What the plane had seen was Walker in *Selfridge* with *Chevalier* and *O'Bannon* coming up the Slot. But the erroneous report of cruisers influenced Ijūin's subsequent actions to the point that he would report engaging them.

Wilkinson had received warning that morning that the Japanese might attempt to take off the evacuees on Choiseul. With his 10th Echelon underway carrying the IMAC Advance Base to Vella Lavella, the only force he had available was Walker's, which was returning from a run up the Slot and was passing the Russells en route home. Wilkinson ordered him to reverse course and head back up the Slot, and to pay particular attention to the Choiseul coast. But around 1830, Wilkinson began receiving specific information from Halsey that the Tokyo Express would definitely be running, but to Marquana Bay instead of Choiseul. At this time, 10th Echelon was off Blanche Channel; Wilkinson immediately reversed course and at 1900 detached Larson in *Ralph Talbot* with *Taylor* and *LaVallette* to rendezvous with Walker at 2300 off Sauka Point, just south of Marquana Bay. Shortly, Walker received more intelligence on the Japanese force composition that was both clarifying and confusing. Around 1930, he learned that an undetermined number of destroyers, three torpedo boats (incorrect, but this lodged in the minds of the American commanders), and six subchasers were expected at 2230, with embarkation at 2330. At 2102, he was told that possibly nine destroyers were in the Japanese force. A few minutes later, a report was passed on to him that B-25s going in to attack Buin had spotted four destroyers or possibly *Jintsu*-class cruisers. Worst of all, Walker learned that Larson could not make the rendezvous point until 2340 (*Ralph Talbot* had prob-

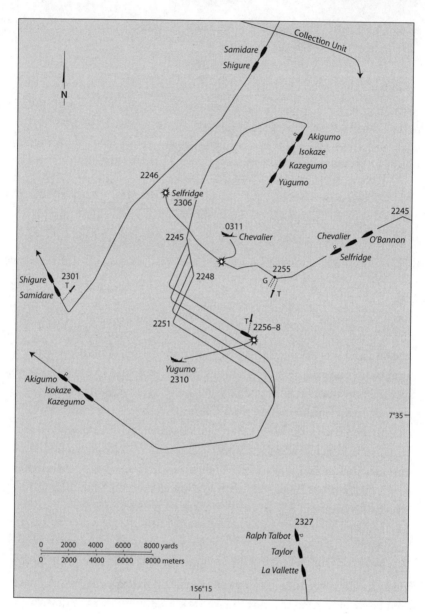

Map 13.2. Naval Battle of Vella Lavella, 6–7 October 1943.

lems with bearings in the port shaft). Not quite certain what to expect, Walker's crews went to General Quarters at 1900, and forty minutes later the 938th seaplanes began dogging them.

At 2150 Walker announced over TBS, "When we round the corner close the gap and be ready for anything. I want to get the fish off without guns if possible." A bright first-quarter moon due to set at 0045 made for excellent visibility of up to 15,000 yards. Scattered clouds were overhead, and on the surface a few squalls and areas of heavy mist. The sea was calm with a long swell running, and a light wind blew out of the west. Radar contact was made at 2230.

Ijūin was still on a course north-northeast at 2235, when *Kazagumo* sighted Walker to the south. Ijūin turned to port and headed southwest to cross Walker's bows, but he misjudged the distance and opened the range. At 2240, Hara, who was west of Ijūin and having difficulty in joining up because of mist and a lack of visibility, sighted Walker. After attempting unsuccessfully to contact Larson over TBS, Walker had just increased his speed to 30 knots to head off Ijūin, At this point, Ijūin began a series of maneuvers that cost him what advantage he had. At 2245, he altered his course to south-southeast to close the range and at 2248 ordered a simultaneous 45° turn south. Then, realizing the target he was presenting, he ordered another simultaneous turn to port, which staggered his ships in line abreast on a course opposite to and almost parallel to Walker, with the range rapidly closing. At 2257, he tried to correct what he later conceded was a major mistake by making yet another starboard turn into column, south, continuing around until he was headed west – but with only three of his destroyers, for at 2255 Walker's destroyers had launched half-salvos of torpedoes and then opened fire with their main batteries. *Yūgumo,* which was closest and thought to be a cruiser, was the main target; Commander Ōsako Higashi veered the ship to port, fired eight torpedoes, and opened gunfire before *Yūgumo* was reduced to a wreck, engulfed in flames and drifting south.

The next five minutes decided the battle. At 2301, Walker made contact with Hara to his southwest (Hara had just turned northwest) and veered to the right to engage, which put Hara ahead and parallel to him. At the same time, one of *Yūgumo*'s torpedoes hit *Chevalier* in the No. 2 Gun magazine and blew the ship in two, its bridge and aft section swing-

ing across *O'Bannon*'s path. *O'Bannon* rammed *Chevalier* in its starboard
engine room, the force of the collision mitigated by Commander Donald
J. MacDonald's immediately ordering emergency full speed astern when
he saw the explosion on *Chevalier*. Two minutes later, at 2305, at least one
torpedo, thought to have come from *Chevalier*, hit *Yūgumo*, and the ship
was finished. At 2306, a torpedo fired from either *Samidare* or *Shigure* hit
Selfridge, shearing off the bow and wrecking everything from the bridge
forward. In those five minutes, 104 American seamen died and 66 were
wounded.

Both sides engaged ghost ships. At 2317, Ijūin who was still on his
westerly course fired torpedoes at "cruisers" (*O'Bannon* and *Chevalier*),
claimed one sunk, but broke off the battle and headed for home. On the
other hand, *Selfridge*'s commander, George E. Peckham, was absolutely
certain that they had been hit by torpedo boats and faulted the CICs for
not keeping track of Nakayama's subchasers, which had been picked up
intermittently to the north-northeast. Walker was highly skeptical, but
the "torpedo question" remained open for a time at COMINCH.

Meanwhile the two other groups were approaching, Larson from the
south and Nakayama from the north. At 2255, when Larson was slightly
southwest of Baga Island, Walker's order to execute William (code name
for torpedoes) and Dog (gunfire) was intercepted. Five minutes later,
gunfire could be seen over the horizon. Larson's group passed *Yūgumo* in
its death throes, and by 2340 the group was in the battle area. He could
make no contact with enemy ships and at midnight headed toward Marquana Bay; seeing nothing, he returned to the crippled ships. *Chevalier*
was beyond saving and had to be torpedoed, but by 0315, the damage-
control teams on *Selfridge* had the ship ready to begin the slow voyage
home. Walker waved off *Pawnee*, which had put to sea from Rendova
Harbor, but notified COMAIRSOLS that air cover would be needed at
dawn. In the meantime, Nakayama's group had passed to the east of the
battle area, witnessing the gunfire as they passed, and arrived at Marquana Bay undetected. The Japanese began loading at 0150, while the
938th seaplanes kept the New Zealand artillery quiet. The New Zealanders heard the naval gunfire and later what sounded like barges scraping
against the reefs. At 0310, Nakayama left for Buin with all the 589 men
in the Tsuruya Unit.[23]

At dawn on 7 October, sixteen P-39s covered the destroyers now off Ghanongga Island, while twelve more fighters were in the area, six F4US high and six P-38s low over the water searching for a B-25 crew down from the evening before (the crew was safe with the New Zealanders on Vella Lavella). Sakamaki's twelve Zeros arrived around 0720. In the fight that followed one 204th pilot was killed and two 339th P-38s badly damaged. For the rest of the day, NGAF kept fighters over the damaged destroyers, and by 1930, they were in heavy rain, maneuvering to pass Wilkinson's 10th Echelon coming west near the entrance to Blanche Channel.[24]

Meanwhile the search continued for survivors that were reported to be in the water. A Rendova-based VP-23 PBY picked up eight men from *Selfridge*. The Rendova PT boats picked up seventy-eight men from *Yūgumo*, but shot four who refused rescue. One American and four POWs were killed in an incident on PT-163 as the boats were unloading at Biloa. Along with the seventy-four POWs at Biloa, twenty-seven other men from *Yūgumo* made their way to Buin in motorized whaleboats, for a total of 101 men surviving out of a crew of 280.[25]

The next day, 8 October, 14th Brigade determined that the Japanese were indeed gone, while on the other side of the island Wilkinson's 10th Echelon unloaded without incident. At 1510, *O'Bannon* and *Selfridge* moored alongside *Argonne* at Port Purvis, joining *McCalla* and *Patterson* moored on the other side – all casualties of the evacuation. The naval action off Sauka Point received the American official name of Battle of Vella Lavella, and historians who have written about it since have levied criticism at all concerned.[26]

FOURTEEN

The Bomber Offensive against Buin

"BY MID-OCTOBER THE ENEMY AIR RAIDS AGAINST THE 26TH AIR Flotilla at Buin had become intolerable," Okumiya Masatake wrote after the war. "With its base constantly subjected to enemy bombs and strafing attacks, with living facilities reduced to the lowest possible level, and with a mounting loss of supply ships, the navy pulled out, moving its air strength directly to Rabaul." As chief of staff to Sakamaki at Buin, Okumiya wrote from firsthand experience, but there were other factors, especially events in New Guinea, that affected the Japanese air war in the Solomons.[1]

The air offensive against Buin can be broken down into two phases. The first, which corresponded to the height of the fighting for Munda in July and August, saw mainly nighttime missions. There were exceptions, the shipping strikes in mid-July, which we have covered in regard to the Tokyo Express battles, and four daylight missions in August, which we will cover here. The second phase, September and October, saw a daylight formation bombing campaign against both airfields and base installations.

FIRST PHASE – MAINLY NIGHT BOMBING

By July, the AAF's three groups, 5th (H), 307th (H), and 42nd (M), had reached full strength. In addition, the navy kept at least two squadrons of PB4YS at Carney Field. While the latter had the primary responsibility for long-range searches that required ten aircraft, on occasion they also flew bombing missions against Buin. Bomber Command was thus able to put a much larger number of aircraft over the targets, which in order of priority were Kahili, Ballale, and Buka. With the 5th and 307th alternating, Bomber Command usually put two squadrons over the target almost nightly, but this was not a hard rule; sometimes one squadron was sent, but sometimes three, especially when Buka was on the target list. Weather and mechanical difficulties often interfered, reducing the number of planes over the target, drastically in extreme cases. When runways were targeted, the bomb loadings were 500-pound bombs, while loadings for the dispersal areas were fragmentation clusters, but with at least two aircraft carrying 500-pounders. In night attacks – the timing could vary from dusk, to after midnight, to predawn – the planes made their runs individually at ten-minute intervals, which kept the Japanese awake for two to three hours. The extent of damage is difficult to assess. But in a 5th Group mission of two squadrons on 16 July, the B-17s of 23rd Squadron were assigned the dispersal areas at the north end of the Kahili strip, and when they left, two intense fires were burning on the parking apron, and numerous small fires were observed under the trees. This attack corresponded to a Japanese report that in a mid-July raid, twenty-three Zeros were damaged.[2]

To counter COMAIRSOLS, Kusaka arranged with Imamura for the army to take over the night defense of Rabaul, allowing him to send two or three twin-engine J1N1s of the 251st to Ballale on 6 July. Named Gekkō ("Moonlight"), this was an extremely dangerous night fighter, armed with two fixed 20mm cannon mounted to fire upward and two mounted to fire downward at an oblique angle. The most successful method of attack was to approach a bomber from the stern and below and concentrate fire into the engines or the wing roots to explode the gas tanks.[3]

How many Allied aircraft the Gekkō accounted for over Buin is problematical: lack of records on the Japanese side, the tendency on the American side to report the night fighters as elliptical-wing Zeros. But on the night of 6 July, two B-24s of the 307th failed to return. When last seen, they were straggling behind and under attack with the fire coming from above and below. Nonetheless, intelligence decided that the losses operational. But the next night, a Gekkō definitely shot down a New Zealand Hudson that was dropping flares for bombers over Tonolei Harbor.

On the night of 17 July, a VB-101 crew almost certainly witnessed a classic Gekkō attack on a VB-102 PB4Y over Kahili. In the bright moonlight, the crew saw tracers at about 11,000 feet in the location of Lieutenant (jg) John B. Haskett's plane. Then, "a small ball of fire appeared, dropped and burst into a large ball which began to disintegrate and plunged into the sea." On the night of 20 July, there was no question that night fighters were in the air. Seven out of eighteen 307th crews reported attacks, one by a twin-engine fighter. A B-24 burst into flames and was last seen burning on the water just south of Shortland Island. On 27 September, Major Berton Burns, commander, 23rd Squadron, suddenly saw his wingman's plane explode. He immediately dove away, six 20mm shells stitching his B-17 on the port side from the radio compartment to the tail. While Burns's crew reported that it was "definitely" a single engine radial plane, it is likely that a Gekkō was the shooter.[4]

After July, the night fighter threat declined drastically. This was due in large part to the reduced number of night missions as well as the difficulty of keeping the few Gekkō aircraft at Ballale operational. While some have suggested that the arrival of the SB-24s ("Snooper") in mid-August forced Kusaka to use the night fighters for convoy protection, this does not seem to be the case. The first SB-24 mission was not flown until 28 August in the Solomons area, and it was well into September when the Snoopers began to hunt in the waters off the Bismarck Islands. Over Buin, no more aircraft were lost to night fighters, although a 31st Squadron mission on 14 August reported two B-24s attacked by twin-engine night fighters.[5]

The August daylight missions gave both sides a preview of what was to come. On 1 August, three squadrons of B-24s from the 5th and 307th Bomb Groups under Colonel Marion D. Unruh, commander, 5th Group, led the attack, followed by the VMSB-141 SBDs and VMTB-143 TBFs. Sixty fighters provided the escort. The B-24s began dropping on Kahili at 1455 with good results – photographs showed it to be one of the most successful raids yet – while the dive-bombers and torpedo planes went after shipping, possibly sinking at least two small sea trucks. No interception was made, for the Zeros were escorting the D3As for the Rendova PT base attack that had destroyed two boats. But six P-40s returning the short way from Kahili ran into twenty or so Zeros over Gizo, losing one plane and its pilot, while another was shot up badly enough to be forced to land at Segi.[6]

The 12 August raid struck the heaviest blow. Three squadrons of B-24s were over Kahili a few minutes after noon. While a heavy front lay just to the south, the weather over the target was good, with only a few scattered cumulus clouds in the sky. Japanese fighters made no attempt to interfere when the bombers made their run, with the squadrons flying in a V formation and each squadron javelin down.[7] The squadrons flew from north to south along the axis of the runway, the first bombs striking at mid-center and marching south. As they headed for home, the bomber crews and escort pilots observed heavy explosions at the south end of the runway. When the film from the cameras of the F5A that had followed the bombers by about two minutes was developed and studied, the interpreters counted twenty fighters burning on the south end of the runway, while the southwest dispersal area was cloaked in flames and smoke. A Japanese source put the number destroyed on the ground at twenty-four. As the bombers turned for home, Japanese fighters attacked in two groups (mainly Zeros, but the bombers reported three to five army K-61s),[8] and a fight began that continued all the way to Segi. Of the forty-eight fighters Fighter Command had allocated, only thirty-one showed up, and of these it appears that only twenty-one made contact. Some of the bombers were shot up, and although none were seriously damaged, a radio operator was killed. The small fighter escort stuck close to the bombers, earning the praise of the crews. One P-40 (whose pilot was rescued by Waddell) and one Zero went down.[9]

The 12 August raid set the bar higher than the rest of the August missions would reach. On 24 August, three squadrons set off but were forced to turn back by weather, the bombers unloading over the tertiary targets of Vila and Rekata Bay. The mission was rescheduled for the next day, but Bomber Command canceled the two squadrons from the 307th – most likely because the 371st was relieving the 424th that day. The nine B-24s of the 31st Squadron, 5th Group flew the mission, with twenty-four assigned fighters. Planes forced to turn back with mechanical problems depleted the formation and in the end only six bombers, with nine marine F4Us and four 16th Squadron P-40s, reached the target. A few minutes after 1500, the B-24s turned onto the bombing run from north to south. There were broken clouds at 10,000 feet around the target area, but visual sighting could be made; nevertheless, five bombers missed the runway, and the sixth, with rack problems, dropped its bombs into the sea. The Japanese interception was just as ineffective; the New Zealanders broke up the first group and the marines the second.[10]

The following day, 26 August, three squadrons took off for Kahili, but only fifteen of the twenty-seven B-24s reached the target. A number of the two dozen escort fighters also turned back. Little went right over the target. Low clouds obscured the runway, and the lead bombardier's bombs would not drop, throwing off the timing of the following planes. Antiaircraft fire was intense and accurate, and inflicted some damage. The Japanese fighters, estimated at between thirty and thirty-five, attacked just as the last bombs were released, but they were as ineffective as the bombing. The 307th was not happy with the mission and in its report stressed the need for a better means of signaling the formation when the lead bombardier was in trouble. The report also requested that the S-2 and S-3 officers brief the crews against shooting at their own planes and lecture the new crews on formation flying.[11]

During the final mission of the month, flown on 30 August, twenty-four B-24s loaded with fragmentation clusters reached the target. This time the southern route was taken, with the formation making a turn east over southern Bougainville and then a right turn onto the target. Forty-three fighters provided the escort – thirty-two F4Us, nine P-39s, and six P-40s. They were to have their hands full; thirty minutes from the target, the pilots could see a great cloud of dust rising at Kahili as the Japanese fighters took off. Visibility over the airfield was excellent, and some of the aircraft ran into heavy and accurate antiaircraft fire. At 1558, the bombers made their right turn and began their run from northwest to southeast, but the bombing results were difficult to determine because the Zeros, estimated at between thirty and forty, attacked as the run was being made.

"Tojo's boys were on their toes today," the 307th reported. The Zeros that evaded the escorts persistently pressed home their attacks, sometimes to within seventy-five feet. Over the target, a Zero hit Lieutenant H. L. McDonald's B-24, setting an engine afire, with the flames spreading over the left wing. For whatever reason, a New Zealand pilot ducked under the bombers during the run – low-cover fighters were supposed to move out to either side when the bomb bays opened – and a cluster bomb blew him out of the air. A Zero shot down a VMF-123 F4U, and a heavy antiaircraft burst between two 12th Squadron P-39s damaged one so badly that despite the best effort of the wingman to protect it, six Zeros sent it flaming into the sea, where it exploded. The B-24s, including two with an engine shot out and McDonald's badly hit aircraft, swung southeast for home, followed by the Zeros. McDonald and his crew did not make it. About twenty miles northwest of Vella Lavella, with several P-39s and F4Us protecting it, the B-24 fell out of formation with its left wing blazing. Then the wing crumpled, and the bomber spun into the sea. Just west of Ghanongga in the final phase of the battle, two more American planes went down, one of them flown by the great Marine Corps fighter pilot Lieutenant Kenneth A. Walsh. Both pilots were rescued. In addition to the crew of the B-24, three American pilots were killed; the Japanese lost three pilots as well.[12]

KUSAKA AND NEW GUINEA

The Japanese 4th Air Army (6th Division and part of the 7th) had been concentrating at Wewak on four newly built airfields. Beginning in the early morning darkness of 17 August, Lieutenant General George C. Kenny's 5th Air Force caught the Japanese by surprise and destroyed or badly damaged over 100 aircraft, at one blow reducing 4th Air Army's strength by almost half.[13] Perhaps it was no coincidence – although the Japanese official historians drew no connecting line – that on 21 August, Kusaka appealed to Koga to send Carrier Division 1's air group to Rabaul. Ozawa was steadfastly against it, and Koga refused. A few days later, Kusaka requested that they be sent in temporarily, and again Koga refused.[14] Given the navy's agreement with the army to provide air support in New Guinea when needed, 1st Base Air Force, which had been able to concentrate almost solely on the Solomons, now faced a two-front war. And it would not be long in coming. For on the last night of August, the troops of the Australian 9th Division were preparing to embark in the morning on the LSTs, LCIs, and LCTs that would carry them to a landing point just north of Lae. The battle for the Huon Peninsula had begun.[15]

To face the full weight of Kenny's and Twining's air forces, Kusaka could expect little in the way of reinforcements. For September, only two reorganized kōkūtai, the 253rd and the 751st, both with a large number of inexperienced pilots and crews, were scheduled to come in. While he had been assigned the newly formed 501st Kōkūtai equipped with the new Type 2 D4Y2 *Suisei* ("Comet")[16] carrier bombers, the 501st would not arrive until mid-October. The sixty-three Zeros of the 253rd and the thirty-four G4Ms of the 751st were scheduled to begin arriving on 3 September. On 1 September, Kusaka reorganized 11th Air Fleet. The 751st and the 253rd went to Ueno's 25th Air Flotilla, which allowed the rest of the 201st to move to the 26th Air Flotilla, now under Sakamaki's command. In addition, Sakamaki was to get the 501st when it arrived.

The official Japanese naval historians estimated 1st Base Air Force's strength in September as: 160 to 200 Zeros, of which 100–150 were operational; 80 G4M Bettys, of which 50 to 60 were operational; 30 D3A Vals, of which 10 to 20 were operational; 20 B5N Kates, of which 10 were operational; and 10 J1N1 Gekkōs, of which 2 to 5 were operational.[17]

Twining's situation, on the other hand, was the reverse of Kusaka's. He complained to Arnold that the navy has "averaged only one fighter squadron in the combat area during August and September" from carrier groups that were "in and out." While this struck a chord with Arnold, who replied that he had concluded "that your 'unsinkable carrier' has been abandoned by the Navy for more comfortable surroundings,"[18] Twining was not being exactly fair to the navy. For August he was correct, but for September he was not. On 1 September, the first Grumman F6F-3 "Hellcats" of VF-33 sat on the field at Guadalcanal, and by midmonth VF-38 and VF-40 had come in with their composite bomber squadrons.

Twining was on firmer ground when he complained about the navy squadrons being "in and out." *Saratoga's* Air Group 12, which arrived in late September, stayed only long enough for each of its squadrons to fly a few missions before they rejoined the carrier. The other three navy squadrons – VF-33, VF-38, and VF-40 – were withdrawn at the end of September for intensive training at Espíritu Santo, but these returned in mid-October for the duration of the Solomons air war. From a planning point of view, Twining's frustration is understandable, but he was not starved for fighters from mid-September on. Arriving with VF-38 and VF-40 was what amounted to a new marine squadron – Major Gregory "Pappy" Boyington's VMF-214 "Black Sheep"[19] – and a fresh New Zealand Squadron, No. 17, in addition to No. 15 rotating back in. On 23 September, the P-38-equipped 339th arrived, fully rested, reequipped, and reorganized.

SECOND PHASE – DAYLIGHT FORMATION BOMBING

During the first two weeks of September, Bomber Command flew five missions against the Buin bases. The number of intercepting Zeros was noticeably fewer, for on the day of the first American raid, 2 September, Kusaka ordered all fighters, except three chūtai, along with the D3As, to Rabaul to be attached to Ueno's 5th for operations against the Lae invasion convoys.[20] For three days straight, 2–4 September, Allied bombers struck the Buin bases. Mechanical failure plagued the 2 September mission. Of thirty-six AAF and navy B-24s that set off, nine turned back, as did a number of fighters, including ten of the twenty-four F6Fs of VF-33,[21] which were making their debut over Kahili. Seventy-four fighters were with the bombers over the target, Kahili Airfield, at 1555. Zeros were in the air but none attempted to intercept; rather they used aerial bombs to no effect. The F4Us claimed five. The next day seventeen B-24s, covered by sixty-one fighters, reached Kahili at 1240. Again the interception was feeble, ten or so Zeros, none of which pressed their attack against the bombers, except against a straggler with an engine out. Low-cover fighters dropped back and drove them off. A New Zealand P-40 was shot up and went into the water off Vella Lavella, where the pilot was picked up, and the wounded pilot of a P-39 crash-landed at Segi. On 4 September, nine 307th B-24s bombed Ballale with no interference.[22]

For the last two missions of early September, Bomber Command changed its targeting from the Kahili runways to the revetment and dispersal areas in what was left of the forest cover. Bomb loadings were changed to fragmentation clusters, with at least one aircraft carrying

500-pound general-purpose bombs with delayed-action fuses. On 9 September, eighteen B-24s with twenty-eight fighters were over the target at 0949. There was no interception, for the approximately twenty Zeros in the air were fully engaged with twenty-nine F6F Hellcats and F4U Corsairs that had trailed the bombers to break up any attack as the bombers retired. Nevertheless, photographs showed a great many bombs going into the sea. One VMF-213 pilot and one 201st pilot were killed; four pilots from VMF-222 went down and were rescued (three of these crashes were operational). On 11 September, twenty-five B-24s with forty-seven fighters were over the target at 1215 with no interference with the bombers; most bombs fell in the target area. The fighters claimed five Zeros and three Ki-61s, with one F6F missing.[23]

The Japanese got a two-day respite as Twining's new squadrons – VF-38 and VF-40, VMF-214, and No. 17 New Zealand – came in. Then, in a three-day campaign, Bomber Command put 241 tons of bombs on the Bougainville bases. On the first day, 14 September, Twining sent off six formations, three in the morning and three in the afternoon. The first formation of twelve B-25s, with six assigned to Kahili and six to Kara, which was nearing completion, took off at 0245, but was turned back by weather over Kula Gulf. The second formation of ten 372nd Squadron B-24s was over the target at 0900 but without their escort of twenty F4Us. As the bomber pilots soon realized, in the turn left onto the target at Kieta, Zeros had hit the F4Us, and the single fighter division that had been assigned close cover became separated from the bombers. As a result, a number of Zeros attacked the B-24s during the bombing run, and one B-24 had an engine shot out. In their fight, the F4Us claimed four Zeros plus one Ki-61 "Tony," but they returned with five aircraft so badly shot up that they would be out of commission indefinitely. At 1031, the third formation of twelve 371st B-24s and twenty-three F4Us was over the target. The crews saw Zeros taking off, but there was no interception.

The afternoon strikes began at 1202, with the fourth formation of ten 31st Squadron B-24s with twenty-four fighters over the target. Ten to twelve Zeros intercepted. The American P-40s claimed one Zero but lost three planes and their pilots. Two planes were lost over Kahili, and one crashed at Segi when the pilot, attempting a belly landing at considerable speed in a badly shot up plane, went into the water and was lost.

The fifth and sixth formations were over the target just minutes apart. The fifth formation, with four F4US strafing as they led the way, thirty marine and navy SBDS with 1,000-pounders, and twenty-four marine and navy TBFS carrying 2,000-pounders, struck Ballale around 1300. Forty-one P-39s and F6FS made up the escort. The F6FS claimed nine of the estimated fifteen intercepting Zeros and lost two of their own. One plane crash-landed at Munda and the other in Roviana Lagoon; both pilots were seriously injured. As the fight over Ballale was in progress, the sixth and final formation, nine VB-102 PB4YS with ten F4US, bombed Kahili without interference.

For the day, fighter losses in combat were nearly equal: COMAIR-SOLS lost five planes, with three pilots killed and two wounded; 6th Air Attack Force, with some pilots flying three missions that day, lost five planes with four pilots killed, two men each from the 201st and the 204th. But the bombers destroyed nine aircraft on the ground. "So severe was the damage to the field, and so great was the number of planes either damaged or wrecked by the enemy bombs," Okumiya wrote, "that every single officer and enlisted man worked more than twelve hours without rest or food" and by nightfall again had Kahili partially operational.[24]

With darkness, the Japanese retaliated. An undetermined number of seaplanes and B5NS were over Barakoma seven times, killing one man dead and wounding fifteen; at Munda, ten raids by Kates and Bettys left six men killed and thirteen wounded, one bulldozer destroyed, and seven F6FS hit, one burned and six badly damaged, three of which were write-offs. At Guadalcanal, three G4MS destroyed one SBD, but lost one of their own to antiaircraft fire.[25]

On the next day, 15 September, the B-25s initiated a series of attacks at 0455. Six bombed Kara – the first attack on the new airfield – and six Kahili. At 1115, thirty-one SBDS and twenty-four TBFS, with forty-two F6FS, twelve P-39s and seven F4US, struck Ballale. More Zeros were in the air (the Lae operation had ended the day before), but in small groups of six or seven. The escort fighters kept them clear of the bombers, claiming fourteen shot down for a loss of two F6FS and a P-39 that crash-landed at Segi. Fifteen minutes later, sixteen B-24s with twenty-six fighters bombed Kahili with no interception, and at roughly the same time, eight unescorted 31st Squadron B-24s dropped on Buka, after flying a long circuitous route to the target. There was no interception. The rest of the day was quiet until the sun went down, then at 2334, nine B-25s caught the Japanese with the lights on at Kahili, while at the same time five Lockheed PV-1 Venturas of VB-140 made their maiden run on Ballale. (One Ventura went down, perhaps a victim of the Gekkō seen in the air.)[26]

On 16 September, seven B-25s struck Kahili at 0155. One bomber failed to return, apparently the victim of antiaircraft fire. At 0400, ten B-24s took off, but bad weather from Savo Island to Visuvisu aborted the mission. Then at 1450, in the final mission of the three-day operation, thirty SBDs and twenty-four TBFs with seventy-three fighters hit Ballale. The SBDs and TBFs, accompanied by sixteen American and New Zealand P-40s, met no opposition from the Zeros, but the TBFs lost two planes, possibly to antiaircraft fire but more likely to their own exploding bombs. (A VC-40 TBF was clearly seen to have a wing blown off by an explosion as it passed low over the island.) The thirty-three F6F Hellcats (from VF-33, VF-38, and VF-40) and twenty-four F4Us (VMF-214) took on the estimated thirty to forty Zeros of the 204th and the 201st. The F6Fs claimed three Zeros but lost four of their own; three pilots were picked up, but a VF-38 pilot was missing. The Corsairs claimed eleven, with Boyington getting credit for five of them. (Boyington's biographer, Bruce Gamble, citing Henry Sakaida, put the number of Japanese pilots killed at six.)[27]

For a week, there was a lull in the Buin offensive, but no lull in the air war that ranged from Cape Cretin to Nauru Island. On 19 September, twenty-four B-24s, with five PBYs as pathfinders, flew a long mission out of the Solomons to bomb the airstrip and phosphate plants on Nauru Island. Two days later, three unescorted squadrons of B-24s went after the 702nd G4Ms at Buka Passage, which had been harassing Guadalcanal. But this time a chūtai from the 253rd, which Kusaka had ordered there, intercepted. The inexperience of the 253rd pilots showed, for in the long fight down the Bougainville coast, the B-24s escaped. One of the B-24s, with an engine shot out, became the first four-engine plane to land at Munda; a nose gunner was killed in another.[28] Bad weather at Guadalcanal grounded the COMAIRSOLS mission to Kahili, which otherwise would have met little opposition.[29] For his part, Kusaka again had to withdraw fighters from Buin on 22 September to attack the Allied convoy loaded with troops to make a landing at Finschhafen. During the attack, the Japanese lost six G4Ms and eight Zeros, with four pilots from the 201st and 204th killed.

During the last week of September, Twining hit Buin with four heavy strikes. On the 23rd, twenty-three B-24s, with sixteen P-38s as escort, and twenty-two SBDs and twelve TBFs were sent off with twenty-seven F4Us, sixteen New Zealand P-40s, and sixteen P-39s. The mission was only partially successful. Heavy cloud cover from 15,000 to 20,000 feet blanketed the airfield, so the B-24s returned and dropped on Vila. The SBDs and TBFs went in, bombing the gun positions at Jakohina, southwest of the airstrip. None of the intercepting Zeros got through to attack the bombers, but VMF-213 lost two planes, with one pilot rescued, while No. 17 Squadron lost two panes, with both pilots missing. The Japanese lost at least one 204th pilot killed.[30]

For the last three missions, and much to the satisfaction of the heavy bomber crews, who were tired of making run after run over the airfield, targeting was changed to the installations at Ebery's Lease, just north-east of Kahili. On 26 September, twenty-one B-24s with fourteen P-38s were first over the target and were intercepted by an estimated twenty to thirty Zeros from Kahili and Kara (the 204th had moved there on 24 September). In the fight, a 339th pilot was wounded, and, with an engine shot out, was forced to ditch off the Russells. The bombers left the target area with several large fires burning, but with Zeros trailing them. The F4Us flying high cover for the SBDs and TBFs, just arriving, scattered the Zeros, losing one F4U when the wounded pilot crashed his shot-up plane into a bulldozer at the end of Munda Field. The pilot suffered no further injuries, but the plane was a wreck. In the meantime, the twenty-four SBDs and twelve TBFs with the remaining fighters, twenty of *Saratoga's* F6Fs, sixteen New Zealand P-40s, and fourteen P-39s, went in unmolested against the gun positions at Jakohina and Kangu Hill.[31]

At 1220 on 27 September, twenty-seven B-24s bombed the Ebery's Lease installations. On this mission there was a mix-up at Fighter Command. The bombers left Guadalcanal with twelve New Zealand P-40s and eight P-39s for low and medium cover, but the F6Fs intended to provide high cover were apparently not notified of the mission. Orders were quickly sent to Munda to get F4Us in the air, but with just fifteen minutes notice the four divisions took off as they could and never formed up. Consequently, as the bombers approached the target, only six F4Us were above them, and these were met by twenty or so Zeros. Nevertheless, the bombers again left the area with large fires burning. One B-24 was hit and soon lagged behind with a smoking engine, while the bombers headed toward Vella Lavella. The Zeros followed, but the P-40s and three VMF-214 Corsairs kept them off the straggling bomber. One F4U pilot was killed and three P-40s were shot up.[32]

As we have seen, the mission scheduled for 29 September was canceled in order for the B-24s to attempt to catch Ijūin, who was headed for Rabaul with evacuees from Kolombangara. The mission was rescheduled for the next day, and fifteen B-24s dropped on the installations. Weather prevented eight Munda-based F4Us from joining up, so that the escort consisted of fourteen P-38s and eight New Zealand P-40s. Just after the bombs dropped, about twenty Zeros attacked the rear of the B-24 formation, and in turn, the Zeros were caught by surprise and scattered by P-38s diving down on them from high altitude. One P-38 failed to return, and the wounded pilot of another landed his plane at Munda.[33]

Aircraft losses in combat for September were about equal. The Japanese summary for September listed twenty-three Zeros, sixteen G4Ms, four D3As, and one B5N lost in combat. COMAIRSOLS lost thirty fighters, give or take one, and ten bombers, nearly all to antiaircraft fire.[34]

THE 26TH AIR FLOTILLA'S WITHDRAWAL FROM BUIN

At an Imperial Conference in Tokyo on 30 September, the emperor gave his approval to the new IGHQ defense policy, which had been worked out since mid-September. The policy established an "absolute defense sphere," a line running from Saipan through Truk and western New Guinea and on around the East Indies. While Rabaul was not included in the absolute defense sphere, it was to be held along with northeast New Guinea in order to slow down the Allied offensive and gain time to build up defenses in the absolute sphere. The Southeast Area commanders were expected to accomplish this mission mainly with their own resources.

In late September, as IGHQ worked on the plan, the army section approached the navy section one last time for help from Ozawa's Carrier Division 1 but was rebuffed. (In November Ozawa's planes would be sent along with the 17th Division for the army.) After the conference, Kusaka and Imamura simply received instructions to do what they were already doing. Since early September, they had been trying to stem MacArthur's offensive, which threatened to kick open the doors to the Vitiaz and Dampier Straits. An attack on Bougainville was inevitable, but the immediate flash point was at Finschhafen. Kusaka and Imamura would also have been influenced if they had known of the emperor's displeasure over the Australian landing at Finschhafen. At any rate, as the official historians pointed out, Kusaka intended to concentrate 1st Base Air Force at Rabaul to deal with the threat to the Huon Peninsula. On the other hand, Kusaka could no longer defend the Buin bases. At the time of the withdrawal, the 204th had twenty-four Zeros, the 201st had twenty-nine, and the 582nd had fifteen D3As and ten B5Ns. Ballale was already inoperable, and it was just a matter of days before COMAIRSOLS put Kahili and Kara out of commission.[35]

Consequently, the 582nd's B5N Unit left Buin on 3 October, and from then until the Bougainville landing, the unit would shuttle back and forth between Kavieng and Buka. Five days later, the 204th (headquarters at least) and the 582nd's D3A Unit left for Lakunai. (The D3A Unit would be annihilated over Oro Bay on 15 October, losing thirteen out of fifteen planes.) Ueno's 253rd moved from Lakunai to the newly operational airfield at Tobera, which was inland from the army's airfield at Rapopo. On 11 October, 26th Air Flotilla Headquarters moved to Rabaul for the operation against Finschhafen, which was scheduled to begin the next day. (Coincidently, this marked the beginning of Kenny's offensive against Rabaul with some 350 aircraft.) The 201st (or part of it) was left at Buin, but Twining's attacks drove it to Buka on 22 October, and from there on to Rabaul a few days later. Thereafter, COMAIRSOLS ranged over Buin at will, with the B-24s soon flying without escort.[36]

As was their custom, the Japanese left fighting. On 10 October, Twining renewed the attack on Buin. At 1120, with the skies clear and visibility unlimited, twenty-four B-24s with sixteen P-38s and six F4Us hit Kahili Field; eighteen Dauntlesses, twelve Avengers with fifteen Corsairs, twenty four P-40s, and fifteen P-39s hit the installations and antiaircraft guns. No enemy aircraft opposed the SBDs and TBFs; for the B-24s, however, it was a different matter. The B-24s had made a good run and had turned for home when a single 201st Zero attacked the formation head-on. It passed through the first element of the leading 72nd Squadron, 5th Group, to attack the lead plane in the second element and sent it spinning into the sea. Parachutes were seen, and a 307th Group B-24, piloted by Lieutenant Walter Galyon, dropped out of formation to drop rafts; his plane was immediately attacked by a dozen or so Zeros. The F4Us and P-38s drove off the Zeros, claiming five destroyed (two 201st pilots were killed), but not before the Zeros had inflicted heavy damage on Galyon's plane. He tried to reach Munda, but over Kula Gulf, at an altitude of no more than 100 feet over the water, he was directed to land at Ondonga. A P-38 buzzed the field to clear off a bulldozer that was working, but as Galyon reached the edge of the strip, the B-24 stalled and spun in, killing him and his copilot, and injuring six more men, one of whom later died. It had been a bad day: the 339th was critical of Galyon for dropping out of formation; VMF-214 was critical of the 339th for not showing up in time.

And the sun had not yet set. A P-38, returning from covering a PBY in a fruitless search for the B-24 crew, went into the water short of Munda Field and was lost.[37] Darkness brought no end to misfortune. Shortly after midnight, six Kates from Buka came in undetected and torpedoed *John H. Couch* and *George H. Hines*, which were unloading at Koli Point. *Couch*, with a load of aviation gasoline, was immediately set ablaze and ultimately lost, while *Hines* was towed and beached farther up the coast.[38]

But the actions of 10–11 October actually marked another milestone in the Solomons air war. The two B-24s lost were the last in the campaign against Buin. The B5N raid was the last on Guadalcanal. And at Guadalcanal, Koli Field had just become operational – the 307th moved to Koli and the 5th moved from Henderson to Carney. Two heavy bomber fields would support the air war as it moved on northwest.

Epilogue

TOENAILS CONCLUDED

AFTER 1ST BATTALION, FIJI INFANTRY, WHICH WAS SENT IN ON 12 October to occupy Kolombangara, had scoured the island and reported no Japanese, Halsey on 15 October 1943 declared TOENAILS terminated. Two days before, the Japanese had similarly called an end to Se-gō as they ferried the last of the evacuated troops on Choiseul across the Bougainville Straits to Buin. The 13th Infantry described the trek up Choiseul as being as bad as the Slot crossing, with a shortage of food and with harassment by COMAIRSOLS aircraft the entire way.

TOENAILS had as its objective the securing of airfield sites from which to cover the invasion of Bougainville. This objective was fully achieved. When the landings went in at Torokina on Empress Augusta Bay on 1 November 1943, bypassing the Japanese stronghold at Buin, four New Georgia airfields – Munda, Segi, Ondonga, and Barakoma – based 350 planes.[1] Of these, 200 were fighters. In the Bougainville air battles, fought from 1 to 11 November, the New Georgia–based fighters were instrumental in the destruction of the Japanese naval air forces. Ozawa's Carrier Division 1, which Koga finally committed, lost 70 percent of its aircraft and 47 percent of its crews, according to the official historians, who also estimated that Kusaka lost 125 of 175 planes.[2] New Georgia's role in furthering the war effort against Rabaul did not end with Bougainville. After the Joint Chiefs made the decision to bypass Rabaul and neutralize the base from the air, the single-engine bombers advanced to the newly built airfields at Torokina, while all of the heavy bombers moved to Munda, where they based for the duration of the air campaign against Rabaul. When the 5th and 307th Bomb Groups (H) departed Munda in the spring of 1944, they flew over an isolated and devastated Rabaul, where the Japanese were reduced to living in hundreds of kilometers of tunnels, to base in the Admiralties and support the Allied offensive westward. Thus, unlike some Pacific War battles, New Georgia furthered the war effort against Japan.

On the other hand, historians are mostly agreed that TOENAILS was poorly planned and badly executed. Morison set the tone that has prevailed to this day, writing that "the strategy and tactics of the New Georgia campaign were among the least successful of any Allied campaign in the Pacific."[3] At New Georgia, Halsey found himself in the position of the Japanese at Guadalcanal and Torokina – attacking a well-defended perimeter. He and his commanders made two fundamental misjudgments: (1) they underestimated the terrain; and (2) they underestimated the Japanese. But even as the battle was being fought, they realized their mistake. "Munda is a tough nut – much tougher in terrain, organization of the ground and determination of the Jap than we had thought," Harmon wrote his chief of staff in late July.[4] The Japanese agreed; an intelligence report dated 11 August stated that the "reasons for the slow advance of the enemy in Munda, etc, are due to the courage of our forces and the difficult fighting in the jungle."[5]

That both sides conducted joint operations rather smoothly has not attracted much attention among historians. To say the least, the command structures on both sides were unique. Halsey had an army commander, and in turn, he commanded large army forces. His friendship with MacArthur and the team effort on Harmon's part ensured that differences were settled within the theater. Likewise, the friendship between Kusaka and Imamura was a major factor, with differences worked out within the theater. While Halsey had gained some experience with joint operations on Guadalcanal, New Georgia was a first for the Japanese in that Sasaki was directly under the command of Samejima but in turn commanded navy SNLF units in operations.

The local commanders in New Georgia agreed that joint operations had been a success. Griswold, as we have seen (chapter 10), called his forces an All-American team, and in his appreciation, which I did not quote, he included the 1st Commando, Fiji Guerillas. Had this been written after Vella Lavella, 3rd New Zealand Division undoubtedly would have also been included. While expressing muted criticism of the army for not committing sufficient troops in time (in Imamura's defense, he ended up fighting the battle for the navy), Samejima was lavish in his praise of his field commanders. "The relations between the Army and Navy units in this area were extremely harmonious and satisfactory, and the foregoing is due to the character and judgment of Maj-Gen. Sasaki and Rear Admiral Ōta." He took full responsibility for the defeat: "However, because of my inexperience in commanding land operations, there were times when I failed to dispatch appropriate orders to Maj-Gen. Sasaki in conducting our operations. And the fact that there is evidence that I left the operations up to the arbitrary decisions of Maj-Gen. Sasaki to some degree clearly reveals the folly of placing a Naval Commander like me in charge of land operations involving Army and Navy units."[6] But on Samejima's behalf, it should be noted that he got all but one Reinforcement Force through, and with equal determination, he took off all of the Japanese personnel.

Lessons were learned on the Allied side. The most important among many were: the provision of adequate medical support and the implementation of effective evacuation procedures; close air support of ground troops; the effectiveness of naval gunfire support (or lack thereof); and the triad of weaponry most effective against the Japanese – the 155mm howitzer or gun, the tank (preferably the medium), and the dive-bomber. Some of these were put into effect immediately on Bougainville.[7]

Several thousand men died in the battle for New Georgia. NGOF 972 army dead, 23 missing in action, and 3,873 wounded. Rentz puts the Marine Corps casualties at 192 killed and 534 wounded. Somewhere around 500 navy personnel were lost; New Zealand and Fiji dead and wounded were at least 100, while aircrew would add a few hundred more.[8] For the Japanese, NGOF claims 2,483 dead counted; this excludes Vella Lavella, where the estimate is 200–250 killed. The only Japanese count is for the army on 20 September and probably does not include the Arundel casualties, or all of them, and lists 1,725 dead, 33 dead from wounds, 34 from sickness, and 1,762 wounded in action. To this would be added the 820 men from the Mikami Battalion killed at Vella Gulf, several hundreds more lost in the Kolombangara evacuation, and a hundred or more on Vella Lavella. The Japanese official naval historians give no casualties for the 8th Combined or for the naval actions; however, the Kure 6th suffered heavy casualties, and this, plus the number of ships that went down with their crews, would put the total at somewhere between 2,000 and 3,000 men.[9]

Notes

1. The Japanese Occupation

1. For the Japanese selection of Munda over Rekata Bay as the airfield site, see Bōeichō Bōei kenshūjō senshishitsu, *Senshi sōsho*, vol. 28: *Minami Taiheiyō rikugun sakusen (2): Gadarukanaru Buna sakusen* [Self Defense Research Center, Department of War History, *War History Series*, vol. 28: *Army Operations in the South Pacific (2): Operations at Guadalcanal and Buna*] (Tokyo: Asagumo shinbunsha, 1969), 282, hereafter *Senshi sōsho*, 28:page number(s). For the 13 November landing, see Bōeichō Bōei kenshūjō senshishitsu, *Senshi sōsho*, vol. 83: *Nantō hōmen kaigun sakusen (2): Gadarukanaru tou tesshu made* [Self Defense Research Center, Department of War History, *War History Series*, Vol. 83, *Naval Operations in the Southeast Area (2): Before the Guadalcanal Withdrawal*] (Tokyo: Asagumo shinbunsha, 1971), 337, hereafter *Senshi sōsho*, 83:page number(s).

2. An edited version of Metcalfe's diary is in Elizabeth Corben, *My Father's Journey* (Alstonville, New South Wales: Privately published, 2001),

350–59, 368. Metcalfe made his way to Kennedy's station at Segi Point and was flown out to Guadalcanal, where he provided intelligence to the Americans.

3. Richard B. Frank, *Guadalcanal* (New York: Random House, 1990), 491. Also see Stanley Coleman Jersey, *Hell's Islands: The Untold Story of Guadalcanal* (College Station: Texas A&M Press, 2008), 306–307.

4. Frank, *Guadalcanal*, 497–98; Imperial General Headquarters Navy Directives, vol. I, Washington Document Center (WDC) in Records of the Japanese Navy (RJN), Box 41, Naval History and Heritage Command (NHHC).

5. For the navigation of the Munda Bar, see SWPA, Area Study of New Georgia Group (2nd Revision), Terrain Study No. 54, Box 243, RG 127, National Archives and Records Administration (NARA). The coast watching network and the Guadalcanal air force will be taken up in chapter 2.

6. As a result of either antiaircraft fire or pilot misjudgment, the second attacking SBD plunged into the sea. See VMSB-142, War Diary, USMC,

Aviation Unit Files, RG 127, NARA, hereafter simply Squadron Number, War Diary.

7. *Senshi sōsho,* 83:430, 453–54; *Senshi sōsho,* 28:406.

8. *Kamo* Transport Order, 15 November, 1942, RJN, Item #863, NHHC. Two nights were required due to the lack of enough barges. By day, *Kamo Maru* hid out on the Vella Lavella coast. *Senshi sōsho,* 83:452. Bōeichō Bōei kenshūjō senshishitsu, *Senshi sōsho,* vol. 7: *Tōbu Nyuginia hōmen rikugun kōkū sakusen* [Self Defense Research Center, Department of War History, *War History Series,* vol. 7: *Army Air Operations in Eastern New Guinea*] (Tokyo: Asagumo shinbunsha, 1967), 75, hereafter *Senshi sōsho,* 7:page number(s). Narrative of 72nd Squadron History, SQ-Bomb-72-HI, Air Force Historical Research Agency (AFHRA).

9. A full account of the air battles, especially the fighter combat, is in Roger Letourneau and Dennis Letourneau, *Operation Ke: The Cactus Air Force and the Japanese Withdrawal from Guadalcanal* (Annapolis: Naval Institute Press, 2012), 60–69. Also see Marine Fighter Squadron VMF-121 and the VMSB-142 War Diaries. Suhō's account is in Okumiya Masatake, *Rabauru kaigun kōkūtai* [*Naval Air Groups at Rabaul*] (Tokyo: Asahi sonorama, 1976), 149–51.

10. Levers Pacific Plantations, Pty. Ltd., part of the Lever Brothers (Unilever) group that had extensive holdings in the Solomons.

11. Terrain Study No. 54. A sketch map of the piers and road network is in Kolombangara Defense Operational Order No. 32, 11 July 1943, RJN, Item #752, NHHC.

12. Ugaki Matome, *Fading Victory: The Diary of Admiral Matome Ugaki, 1941–1945,* trans. Masataka Chiaya, with Donald M. Goldstein and Katherine V. Dillon (Pittsburgh: University of Pittsburgh Press, 1991), 313. Three B-17s from the 11th Bomb Group (H) flying from Guadalcanal were over Simpson Harbor at the time *Kagu Maru* was first damaged. See Joint HQ, 5th and 11th Bomb Groups (H), Periodic Intelligence Report, 1 December to 31 December 1942, 1 January 1943, GP-5-SU OP (Bomb), AFHRA. For the rest of the events, see Records of 2nd Destroyer Squadron, RJN, WDC, Box 39, NHHC.

13. *Senshi sōsho,* 83:451. A map showing the sea truck route is in *Senshi sōsho,* 28:401.

14. Donald Kennedy, District Officer's Report on Coast Watching, 19, BSIP 1/III, F. 5/45, Solomon Islands National Archives (SINA), citation by paragraph number. Also see Diary and Papers of 2nd Lieutenant Adachi Harumasa, Item #598, Box 243, RG 127, NARA.

15. *Senshi sōsho,* 83:451; Records of the 2nd Destroyer Squadron; Camp Diary, 1st Battalion, 229th Infantry, RJN, Item #856, NHHC. The 1st Battalion was aboard the convoy annihilated in the Naval Battle of Guadalcanal. At least one company, probably the 2nd, was on a transport that beached at Guadalcanal, while headquarters and part of the battalion were on the only transport, *Sado Maru,* to survive and return to Buin. The battalion commander and most of his staff were seriously

wounded, and at Wickham the battalion was under the temporary command of the communications officer. POWs from both 1st and 2nd Companies were taken on Guadalcanal.

16. *Senshi sōsho*, 83:451. First Lieutenant Tagaki Masao, Notebook (telegrams sent and received by Wickham Occupation Butai), RJN, Item #794, NHHC. I am also indebted to Ewan Stevenson of Auckland for information on *Azusa Maru* and *Kiku Maru*.

17. Tagaki, Notebook.

18. Frank, *Guadalcanal*, 534–39; Edward J. Drea, *Japan's Imperial Army: Its Rise and Fall, 1853–1945* (Lawrence: University Press of Kansas, 2009), 193 (for Imperial Conferences at IGHQ); and Bōeichō Bōei kenshūjō senshishitsu, *Senshi sōsho*, vol. 96: *Nantō hōmen kaigun sakusen (3): Gadarukanaru tou tesshu go* [Self Defense Research Center, Department of War History, *War History Series*, vol. 96: *Southeast Area Naval Operations (3): After the Guadalcanal Withdrawal*] (Tokyo: Asagumo shinbunsha, 1976), 4–5, hereafter *Senshi sōsho*, 96:page number(s).

19. Sanagi's eavesdropping is taken from some handwritten notes of an interview with him in Samuel Eliot Morison, Office Files, Box 32, NHHC.

20. *Senshi sōsho*, 96:6.

21. Frank, *Guadalcanal*, 548–49; Office of Naval Intelligence (ONI), *Combat Narratives, Solomon Islands Campaign, IX, Bombardments of Munda and Vila-Stanmore, January-May 1943* (Washington, D.C., 1944), 5–17.

22. *Senshi sōsho*, 83:515–16.

23. "We call this going up the Slot. It is like going up an alley at night in the tough section of any big city. You have to be on your guard at all times." James H. Fahey, *Pacific War Diary, 1943–1943* (Boston: Houghton Mifflin, 1963), 36–37.

24. Kojima Jisuke, Interrogation Report, RJN, Item #117, NHHC.

25. ONI, *Combat Narrative, IX*, 18–32; Frank, *Guadalcanal*, 572–73; Kolombangara Airfield Construction Unit Orders, RJN, Item #796, NHHC. The Army Air Service units that used Munda off and on were the 1st and 11th Sentai (fighters) and the 45th Sentai (light bombers), all from Lieutenant Colonel Okomoto Shuichi's 12th Hikōdan, 6th Air Division. See *Senshi sōsho*, 7:140–44.

26. See RJN, Item #642, NHHC.

27. Ōta commanded the SNLF during the Shanghai Incident of 1932 and was in command of the 2nd Combined, which was to have made the landing at Midway. Strength and Composition of the Japanese 8th Combined Special Naval Landing Force, RJN, Item #679, NHHC. SNLF troops were not trained for amphibious assault operations; if any comparison can be made to the USMC it would be to a defense battalion. The 35th Infantry's G-2 on Vella Lavella actually made the comparison.

28. See Letourneau, *Operation Ke*, 141–42.

29. Tamura Yozo, *Okinawa kenmin kaku tatakaeri* [*How the Okinawans Fought*], (Tokyo: Kodansha, 1997), 240. This is a biography of Ōta; the title comes from his famous last message from Okinawa. Also see No. 3 Bomber Squadron, War Diary, A 139/2, National Archives of New Zealand (NANZ).

30. Jefferson DeBlanc, *The Guadal-canal Air War* (Gretna, La.: Pelican, 2008), 85. DeBlanc would be awarded the Medal of Honor for his action in the battle.

31. The fullest account of the air battle is in Letourneau, *Operation Ke,* 165–74. Also see: VMF-112, VMSB-234, and VBSB-131 (TBFs), War Diaries; *Senshi sōsho,* 7:143; and Ikuhiko Hata, Yasuho Izawa, and Christopher Shores, *Japanese Army Air Force Fighter Units and Their Aces, 1931–1945* (London: Grub Street, 2002), 262.

32. For *No. 2 Tōa Maru*'s cargo, see Unloading Plan of the 8th Combined SNLF and Kure 6th, RJN, Item 878, NHHC. Ewan Stevenson provided me with a diagram of the visible cargo in the wreck, and Peter Woodbury of Sydney provided me a photograph of the hole in the bow.

33. *Senshi sōsho,* 96:39 says Iwabuchi was to command units and prepare bases in the rest of the Central Solomons except Wickham (this left only Rekata Bay), and this is the last mention of him. As a rear admiral, he went on to command the 31st Special Naval Base Force defending Manila, where he died.

34. *Senshi sōsho,* 96:42–43.

35. For Ōta's barge unit as well as the variety of barge types, see Mark P. Parillo, *The Japanese Merchant Marine in World War II* (Annapolis: Naval Institute Press, 1993), 180–86. Boat unit orders and barge movements through 15 June are in a captured diary of a Kure 6th soldier assigned to the unit. See RJN, Item #836, NHHC.

36. A complete table of organization for both New Georgia and Rekata Bay is in Bōeichō Bōoei kenshūjō sensh-ishitsu, *Senshi sōsho,* vol. 40: *Minami Taiheiyō rikugun sakusen (3): Munda-Saramao* [Self Defense Research Center, Department of War History, *War History Series,* Vol. 40, *Army Operations in the South Pacific (3): Munda and Sala-maua*] (Tokyo: Asagumo shinbunsha, 1970), 172–73, hereafter *Senshi sōsho,* 40:page number(s).

37. Transport Order, Yokosuka 7th SNLF, 10 February 1943, RJN, Item #859, NHHC.

38. The boundary between Sopac and SWPA was 159° E just west of the Russell Islands.

39. For Cincpac, see Survey of Solomons, 15 January 1943, Gray Book. (The Gray Book is the Cincpac war diary in the Nimitz papers, NHHC. I have used an online copy published by the American Naval Records Society, www.ibiblio.org/anrs/graybook). Citations are by date, Oahu time. For Comsopac, see Halsey to Nimitz, 11 January 1943, Halsey Papers, Box 15, Library of Congress (LC). Halsey did not specifically mention the LCIs; I have included them here as a matter of organizational convenience.

40. Comsowespac to Cincpac, Comsopac, 13 January 1943 and Cominch to Cincpac, 9 February 1943, Gray Book.

2. SOPAC

1. Benis M. Frank, Interview with Major General DeWitt Peck, USMC (ret.), 40, Marine Corps University Research Archives.

2. Gray Book, 15 January 1943.

3. Notes on a Conference held at Nouméa, 23 January 1943, Gray Book.

4. Marine defense battalions played a significant role in the Solomon Islands campaign. For a good introduction to this unit, see David J. Ulbrich, "The Long-Lost Tentative Manual for Defense of Advanced Bases (1936)," *Journal of Military History* 71 (July 2007): 889–901.

5. George Carroll Dyer, *The Amphibians Came to Conquer: The Story of Admiral Richmond Kelly Turner* (Washington, D.C.: Government Printing Office, 1969), 1:460–67.

6. Destroyer Division 9, Action Report – Japanese Night Torpedo Attack on Task Unit 62.7.2, Northeast of San Cristobal Island Solomon Islands on February 17, 1943; Destroyer Division 11, Report of Action between Japanese Torpedo Planes and Task Unit 62.7.2, Box 628, RG 38, NARA; *Senshi sōsho*, 96:24.

7. Jim Lucas, *Combat Correspondent* (New York: Reynal & Hitchcock, 1944), 92; Dyer, *Amphibians*, 1:466–70.

8. Commander, Amphibious Force, South Pacific, Report of Occupation of Russell Islands, 21 February to 17 April 1943, Box 539, RG 38, NARA; *Senshi sōsho*, 96:24.

9. USN Bureau of Yards and Docks, *Building the Navy's Bases in World War II: History of the Bureau of Yards and Docks and the Civil Engineer Corps, 1940–1946* (Washington, D.C.: Government Printing Office, 1947), 1:257–62.

10. COMSOPAC to CINCPAC, 2 March 1943, Gray Book. William F. Halsey and J. Bryan, *Admiral Halsey's Story* (New York: McGraw-Hill, 1947), 153.

11. Worrall Reed Carter, *Beans, Bullets, and Black Oil: The Story of Fleet Logistics Afloat in the Pacific during World War II* (Washington, D.C.: Department of the Navy, 1953), 55–57. Calvertville was named after Commander Allen P. Calvert, MTB Squadron 2 and Carter City most probably after Captain Grayson B. Carter, Commander, LST Flotilla 5.

12. Bureau of Yards and Docks, *Building the Navy's Bases*, 1:249.

13. Carney Field was named for the commander of the 14th Seabees, Captain James V. Carney, who was killed when the SBD he had borrowed to test the crash strip went down off Koli Point.

14. COMAIRSOPAC to COMSOPAC, Airfield and Seaplane Base Construction, South Pacific Area, 7 January 1943, Flag Files (Blue 242), Box 8, RG 313, NARA. Benjamin E. Lippincott, et al., eds., Activation History of the XIII Bomber Command, 13 January 1943 to 1 January 1944, 62, 752.01–1, AFHRA.

15. COMSOPAC, Airfield and Seaplane Base Construction and Administration, 15 April 1943, Flag Files (Blue 242), Box 8, RG 313, NARA.

16. Dyer, *Amphibians*, 1:498.

17. Report on Coast Watching by Lieutenant Commander I. Pryce-Jones, RANVR, DSIO, Solomon Islands, April 1943–January 1944, 26, Administrative History Appendices (AHA), Box 40, NHHC (reference is to paragraph number).

18. 1st Battalion, 1st Fiji Infantry Regiment, War Diary, the National

Archives (TNA): Public Record Office (PRO): WO 176/121.

19. Correspondence on Koli Terminal, March–May 1943 is in Flag Files (Blue 242), Box 8, RG 313, NARA.

20. See Commander Third Fleet, South Pacific Campaign – Narrative Account, Box 37, Halsey Papers; John Miller Jr., *Cartwheel: The Reduction of Rabaul* (Washington, D.C.: Center of Military History, 1959), 72–73; Halsey to Nimitz, 14 May 1943, Box 15, Halsey Papers; Dyer, *Amphibians*, 1:498–99.

21. W. H. Goodman, Notes of an Interview with Colonel W. O. Brice on the Command Set-up in the Early Days of Guadalcanal, 30 January 1945, USMC, Shore Commands, Box 22, RG 127, NARA.

22. W. H. Goodman, Notes of an Interview with Colonel J. C. Munn on the Command Set-up in the Early Days of Guadalcanal, 27 January 1945, USMC, Shore Commands, Box 22, RG 127, NARA.

23. The issues are laid out in an exchange of memoranda between Arnold (17 December 1942) and King (30 January 1943) in Flag Files (Blue 242), Box 7, RG 313, NARA. Also see Oral History 3634, Historical Documentation of General Nathan F. Twining, AFHRA.

24. The 13th was the smallest of the army air forces with two heavy bomber groups, the 5th and 307th; one medium group, the 42nd; and two fighter groups, the 18th and the 347th. In addition, the 17th Photo Reconnaissance Squadron, the 13th Troop Carrier Squadron, which along with three squadrons from MAG-25 made up the South Pacific Combat Air Transport

Command (SCAT), and a detachment of the 6th Night Fighter Squadron all played significant roles.

25. Major Kramer J. Rohfleisch, the Thirteenth Air Force, March–October, 1943, U. S. Air Force Historical Study No. 120, September 1946, 20, AFHRA.

26. Ibid., 36. In early March when the RNZAF established No. 1 (Islands) Group to exercise administrative control over its units under Air Commodore Sidney Wallingford, he established his headquarters near Fitch's. See J. M. S. Ross, *Royal New Zealand Air Force* (Wellington, New Zealand: War History Branch, 1955), 160–61.

27. Major Victor Dykes (AAF), Narrative Account of the Air Comd., Solomon Is., 11 May 1944, 750.309–8, AFHRA.

28. Report by Lieutenant Commander H. A. Mackenzie, RAN, on Coast-Watching in the South Pacific Area, 1 June 1942 to 21 April 1943, Appendix A, AHA, NHHC (citation is to page numbers). Eric A. Feldt, *The Coast Watchers* (New York: Nelson Doubleday, 1946, 1979), 136–37. Feldt had the title of senior intelligence officer (SIO) while Mackenzie and Pryce-Jones held the title of deputy supervising intelligence officer (DSIO), North Eastern Area.

29. Mackenzie, Report, 32. Bougainville was part of the German New Guinea territories mandated to Australia at the end of World War II.

30. Sub-lieutenant Paul Mason, RANVR, was at Buin; Lieutenant W. J. Reed, RANVR, at Teop. For their stories, see A. B. Feuer, ed., *Coast Watching in the Solomon Islands: The Bougainville*

Reports, December 1941–July 1943 (Westport, Conn.: Praeger, 1992), 84, 102, 155–57.

31. For Choiseul, see the following: A. N. A. Waddell, Report on the Coast Watching Organization and Related Matters in Choiseul Island, 1942–1943, Australian War Memorial (AWM), PR 00715 (reference is to paragraph number); C. W. Seton, Report of Coast Watching Activity on Choiseul, 1942–1944, AWM PR 00715 (reference is to topic number).

32. John Robert Keenan, Diary of a Coast Watcher from October 1942 to February 1943, AWM PR 00881 (reference is to page number); R. E. Josselyn, Report with Three Appendices, AHA, Box 40, NHHC (reference is to paragraph number).

33. D. C. Horton, Report on the Coast Watching Organization and Associated Matters in the British Solomon Islands Protectorate, 64–82, TNA: PRO: ADM 1/14785 (reference is to paragraph number). Also see D. C. Horton, *Fire over the Islands: The Coast Watchers of the Solomons* (London: Leo Cooper, 1975).

34. A. R. Evans, Report on Coast-watching Experience on Kolombangara and Komu Island, Flag Files (Red, 182), Box 6782, RG 313, NARA (reference is to page number); Papers of Arthur "Reg" Evans, AWM PR 90/011.

35. Walter Lord, *Lonely Vigil: Coast-watchers of the Solomons* (New York: Viking, 1977), 176–77.

36. Feldt, *Coast Watchers*, 109.

37. Adachi, Diary. See also, *Senshi sōsho*, 96:197.

38. On the other hand, and over the objections of an American army intelligence officer who suggested they be shot, Kennedy sent out eleven captured Japanese airmen by PBY. COMAIRSOLS sided with Kennedy since they wanted to interrogate the POWs. See Horton, Report, 57.

39. William Bennett, "Behind Japanese Lines in the Western Solomons," in *The Big Death: Solomon Islanders Remember World War II*, ed. Geoffrey White et al. (Honiara & Suva: Solomon Islands College of Higher Education & University of the South Pacific, 1988), 142. Bennett was awarded the Military Medal after the war.

40. Data for New Georgia is taken from J. K. Brownlee, District Officer's Report, Gizo District, 6 January 1941, BSIP/III/F. 14/19 (E), SINA. The extent of the Methodist mission's establishment (which also includes Kahili) is in Methodist Missionary Society of New Zealand, War Damage – British Solomon Islands, Box A 120, Methodist Church of New Zealand Archives (MCNZA).

41. RNZAF, Operation Intelligence, February 1943, TNA: PRO: AIR 23/5304.

42. John Prados, *Islands of Destiny: The Solomons Campaign and the Eclipse of the Rising Sun* (New York: New American Library, 2012), 353–54.

43. For the number of Allied airmen rescued, see Lord, *Lonely Vigil*, 245–57. Feldt, *Coast Watchers*, 144, gives the number of airmen killed on Vella Lavella alone as twenty-two, but implies they resisted capture.

3. SOPAC's Air and Naval Offensive

1. At the conclusion of the Pacific Military Conference on 28 March, the Joint Chiefs issued a new directive. Now the objective was to maintain the initiative by operations designed to lead to the capture of the Bismarck Archipelago. The operations consisted of three tasks: (1) establish airfields on Kiriwina and Woodlark Islands, (2) capture the Huon Peninsula (Salamaua, Lae, and Madang) and western New Britain, and (3) occupy the Solomon Islands up to and including southern Bougainville. See Louis Morton, *Strategy and Command: The First Two Years, War in the Pacific Series* (Washington, D.C.: Center of Military History, 1962), 387–99.

2. The IGHQ was working on new strategy and operational guidelines, when the army raised the issue of the Solomons. The army had come to the conclusion that New Georgia should be abandoned. The navy insisted that New Georgia (and Rekata Bay) be held and would not bulge. Events in the Southeast Area helped settle the issue. The Bismarck Sea disaster was a major blow for both army and navy. The army charged that the navy had been more focused on the Solomons than on New Guinea and requested more naval aircraft to protect the supply lines. The navy criticized the army's air force for its inability to carry out missions over water, then asked for even more troops for New Georgia.

Under these circumstances, a coordinated plan could be delayed no longer. A Southeast Area Army/Navy Agreement was negotiated, stating that the army and navy would operate "as one unit" and that the "primary operation of the two forces will be directed against New Guinea," while operations in the Solomons and Bismarcks were to be strictly defensive. The army would defend the Northern Solomons and the navy the Central Solomons, but – and this is the key wording in regard to New Georgia – some army units would be placed under navy command. In the all-important matter of gaining some parity in the air, the two air forces were to operate in both areas, the army air force mainly in New Guinea and Base Air Force mainly in the Bismarcks and Solomons. The key provision with respect to the defense of New Georgia was that the local commanders – Kusaka and Imamura – would decide which army units would be placed under navy command. *Senshi sōsho*, 40:169; 96:89–91, 97–101.

3. Joint Headquarters 5th and 11th Bombardment Groups (H), Office of the Intelligence Officer, 1 March 1943, GP-5-SU OP (Bomb), Dec. 42–Dec. 43, AFHRA.

4. *Senshi sōsho*, 96:25. COMAIR-SOLS, Strike Command, Daily Intelligence Summaries, 749.606, AFHRA. VT-11, Mission Report, Box 515, RG 38, NARA. Carrier Group 11 had been due to operate from *Hornet* but it was sunk in the Battle of the Santa Cruz Islands.

5. *Senshi sōsho*, 96:29. "Spring Offensives: New and More Powerful Allied Air Force Helps Make Them Successful," *Life*, 12 April 1943.

6. 12th AAF Photo Intelligence Det., Munda Airfield Area: Notes on

Japanese Military Installations, October, 1943, AWM, 355.413 M963.

7. 347th Fighter Group, Mission Reports, GP-347-Su-OP-S (F), January–March 1943, AFHRA. *Senshi sōsho*, 96:44. VMSB-144, War Diary. Japanese medical officer's account is from a captured document in COMAIRSOLS, Daily Intelligence Summary, 17 September 1943, 749.606, AFHRA. Waddell, Report, 39.

8. *Senshi sōsho*, 96:74. For Bismarck Sea, see Drea, *MacArthur's ULTRA*, 68–70, and Les McAuley, *Battle of the Bismarck Sea* (South Australia: Burbank's, 1999).

9. Commander, TF 68, Action Report – Battle of Kula Gulf and Bombardment of Munda and Vila-Stanmore Areas, Night of 5–6 March 1943, 9 March 1943, Box 29, RG 38, NARA. Allyn D. Nevitt, *Long Lancers*, www .combinedfleet.com/lancers.htm.

10. The *Grampus* did not return from this patrol, and there has been speculation that the ship was lost to *Murasame* and *Minegumo*. But the Japanese commander made no mention of an encounter with a submarine in his report, nor is there evidence that the *Grampus* was on station in Vella Gulf. 938th seaplanes reported attacks on submarines 15 and 16 March while covering a sea truck en route to Bairoko Harbor. *Senshi sōsho*, 96:78.

11. World War II Interviews, Commodore Arleigh Burke, No. 1, 31 July 1945, Box 4, NHHC.

12. *Senshi sōsho*, 40:199.

13. By 5 March, the Japanese had become aware of American activity in the Russells, and Kosaka planned the attack

for the next day. When search planes were looking for Merrill southeast of San Cristobal, however, they apparently sighted Ainsworth's task force, which was operating there, and sent back conflicting reports, one of which had four destroyers headed northwest. Kosaka then ordered the strike force to search southeast of Guadalcanal and if nothing was found to then attack the Russells. The result was the attack that confused both sides. See *Senshi sōsho*, 96:77, 80–81. For the 67th Squadron P-39s, see 347th Fighter Group, Mission Reports. For Merrill on the significance of the action, see Morison, Office Files, Box 30.

14. Kayama Homare, *Hosen nisshi* [*Memoir of the Pacific War*], (N.p.: Privately published, 1987), 215–26. *Senshi sōsho*, 96:74–76.

15. Commander, Task Group 18.6, bombardment of Vila Stanmore Area, Kolombangara, 18 March 1943, Box 29, RG 38, NARA.

16. Japanese transportation is in *Senshi sōsho*, 96:77–78, 132–33, 159–63. The sinking of *Gishō Maru* is in Record of Events, Fighter Command, Guadalcanal, Shore Commands, Box 27, RG 127, NARA.

17. COMINCH, Battle Experience: Solomon Islands and Alaskan Areas Bombardments, May & July 1943, Flag Files (Red 179), Box 6398, RG 313, NARA.

18. Evans, Report, 6.

19. *Senshi sōsho*, 96:160–62 (includes map of sinking locations). VB-11, Action Report, Box 389, RG 38, NARA. Also see Ross, *Royal New Zealand Air Force*, 180–82.

20. Transport for the period is in *Senshi sōsho*, 96:163, 188–91.

21. ONI, *Combat Narrative, IX*, 54–74.

22. *Senshi sōsho*, 96:163, 194–96; *Senshi sōsho*, 40:203. The Kure 6th Farm is in Tamura, *Okinawa kenmin kaku tatakaeri*, 274.

23. The R-Area Air Force that fought in the Guadalcanal campaign. See John B. Lundstrum, *The First Team and the Guadalcanal Campaign: Naval Fighter Combat from August to November 1942* (Annapolis: Naval Institute Press, 1994), 192, 284–85.

24. *Senshi sōsho*, 96:11, for February 1943 forces; Intelligence Reports of the 1st Base Force since November 1943, Morison, Office Files, Box 28 (gives composition for 1 November); for the 938th see *Senshi sōsho*, 96:136. Itagaki's naval forces were referred to as the Solomon Islands Defense Force.

25. Some at Eighth Area Army wanted to dissolve Seventeenth Army but after a long discussion, Imamura decided against it. His reasons were: (1) 8th Fleet had a headquarters at Buin so a parallel headquarters was necessary; (2) Hyakutake might commit suicide; and (3) Hyakutake had a brother who was an admiral in the navy. See *Senshi sōsho*, 40:80–81. Also see History of the Japanese Occupation of Bougainville, March, 1942–August, 1945, AWM 54 492/4/4/Part 1.

26. 72nd Squadron Narrative History; Statistical data comes from Benjamin E. Lippincott, XIII Bomber Command.

27. *Senshi sōsho*, 96:10.

28. 347th Fighter Group, Mission Reports; Sam S. Britt Jr., *The Long Rangers: A Diary of the 307th Bombardment Group (H)* (Baton Rouge: Privately published, 2002), 19–23; *Senshi sōsho*, 96:25.

29. 347th Fighter Group, Mission Reports; *Senshi sōsho*, 96:10; Alan C. Carey, *We Flew Alone: United States Navy B-24 Squadrons in the Pacific, February 1943–September 1944* (Atglen, Pa.: Schiffer, 2000), 13–14; Sam Walker, *Up the Slot* (Oklahoma City: Walker Publishers, 1984), 85–110. For a discussion of operational losses see Eric M. Bergerud, *Fire in the Sky: The Air War in the South Pacific* (Boulder, Colo.: Westview, 2000), 102–109, 429–33.

30. One man from this crew survived the war to tell the story. See Robert Sherrod, *History of Marine Corps Aviation in World War II* (Washington, D.C.: Combat Forces Press, 1952), 142–43.

31. The air groups of Carrier Division 22 played a significant role in the air war until their withdrawal from the Solomons in early August 1943, but the surviving records are scarce. VC denotes a composite squadron of SBDs and TBFs. See William T. Y'Blood, *The Little Giants: U. S. Escort Carriers against Japan* (Annapolis: Naval Institute Press, 1987), 24–27.

32. SOPAC, TBF Night Bombing and Minelaying, Solomon Islands, February–March, 1943, Flag Files (Blue 242), Box 9, RG 313, NARA; COMAIRSOLS to COMAIRSOPAC, Mine Laying Operations by Aircraft in the Buin-Tonolei Area, Shore Commands, Box 22, RG 127, NARA; *Senshi sōsho*, 96:83.

33. *Senshi sōsho*, 96:83–84. XIII
Fighter Command, Mission Reports,
751.333, AFHRA. Five P-38s and one
F4U made the attack; seven F4Us and
three P-38s turned back.

34. COMAIRSOLS, Weekly Intelligence Summaries, 749, 607, AFHRA.
Plots of the mine fields are in Minelaying Ops & and Misc. Reports, Shore
Commands, Box 24, RG 127, NARA.

35. Technical details are in Strike
Command, Summary of SBD Activity,
1 June–30 September 1943, Shore Commands, Box 27, RG 127, NARA.

36. Strike Command, Daily Intel-
ligence Summary; XIII Fighter Com-
mand, Mission Reports; Fighter Com-
mand, Guadalcanal, Mission Reports;
VT-11, Mission Reports. Japanese losses
come from Ikuhiko Hata and Yasuho
Izawa, *Japanese Naval Aces and Fighter
Units in World War II*, trans. Don Cyril
Gorham (Annapolis: Naval Institute
Press, 1989), 383.

37. 5th Bomb Group (H), Con-
solidated Mission Reports, GP-5-OP
(Bomb), 14 May–24 October 1943,
AFHRA.

4. The Japanese Air
Counteroffensives

1. Ugaki Matome, *Fading Victory: The Diary of Admiral Matome
Ugaki, 1941–1945*, trans. Masatuka
Chiyaya with Donald M. Goldstein
and Katherine V. Dillon (Pittsburgh,
Pa.: University of Pittsburgh Press,
1991), 320–28. During his first night in
Rabaul, 5th Air Force badly damaged
the heavy cruiser *Aoba* at Kavieng. The
ship had been badly damaged in the
Guadalcanal campaign and now after

a lengthy repair was to have replaced
Chōkai as flagship of 8th Fleet.

2. *Senshi sōsho*, 96:103–107.

3. *Senshi sōsho*, 96:107–10.

4. *Senshi sōsho*, 96:109–10. Hata,
Japanese Naval Aces and Fighter Units,
382. COMAIRSOLS, Intelligence
Report, Interception of Enemy Fighters
over the Russell Islands, Flag Files
(Blue 242), Box 9, RG 313, NARA. This
was the first interception for the F4Us
as opposed to escort duty.. For his part,
Nimitz was furious that 5th Air Force
made no follow-up mission and allowed
the ship to escape under tow.

5. Bob Hackett and Sander Kingsepp, *Sensuikan!*, www.combinedfleet
.com. This valuable site contains the
Tabular Record of Movement (TROM)
for Japanese submarines.

6. COMINCH, Chart Room
Dispatches, South Pacific, Box 117, RG
38, NARA.

7. CINCPAC to COMINCH,
Operations in the Pacific Ocean Area,
April, 1943, Flag Files (Blue 242), Box 3,
RG 313, NARA.

8. Afterward Mitscher sent the New
Zealanders a letter of commendation.
See Ross, *Royal New Zealand Air Force*,
320–21. Halsey's dependence on New
Zealand for radar (similar sets were
being manufactured in the U. S. but
Sopac was not a high priority) is in Ross
Galbreath, "Dr. Marsden and Admiral
Halsey: New Zealand Radar Scientists
in the Pacific War," in *Kia Kaha: New
Zealand in the Second World War*, ed.
John Crawford (Auckland: Oxford,
2000), 252–63.

9. One officer and eighteen men
were killed or missing. Two were saved

at 1800 when the crew of the LCT, which was helping in the attempted salvage, heard men rapping in the bunker pump room and got the trapped men out. U.S.S. *Kanawha*, Report of Action, 7 April 1943, Box 1079, RG 38, NARA.

10. Twenty-seven men were lost in *Aaron Ward,* and *Sterett* had one officer and five men wounded. Of the cargo ships, *Adhara,* which took three near misses, suffered the most damage and all of the casualties, one killed and eight wounded. See Task Unit 32.4.4, Action Report, 7 April 1943, Box 133, RG 38, NARA. Also see C. Raymond Calhoun, *Tin Can Sailor: Life aboard the USS Sterett, 1939–1945* (Annapolis: Naval Institute Press, 1993), 112–13.

11. *Senshi sōsho,* 96:111–16; Interception of Enemy Dive Bombing Attack against Shipping, Tulagi Harbor and Vicinity, Fighter Command, Guadalcanal. For the loss of the TBFs, see COMAIRSOLS, Mission Reports, Box 325, RG 38, NARA.

12. Ugaki, *Diary,* 328–29. There was no shipping in the Huon Gulf area because 3rd Australian Division fighting in the Markham Valley was being supplied by air drop.

13. Carroll V. Glines, *Attack on Yamamoto* (New York: Orion, 1990).

14. Donald A. Davis, *Lightning Strike: The Secret Mission to Kill Admiral Yamamoto and Avenge Pearl Harbor* (New York: St. Martin's, 2005), 267. A full bibliography of works on the mission can be found in Davis or Glines.

15. Mack Morriss, *South Pacific Diary, 1942–1943,* ed. Ronnie Day (Lexington: University Press of Kentucky, 1995), 156, 183.

16. See William K. Wyant, *Sandy Patch: A Biography of Lt. Gen. Alexander M. Patch* (Westport, Conn.: Praeger, 1991), 77–80. Patch got into trouble for remarks he made at a National Geographic Society luncheon in Washington during which the Japanese broadcast on Yamamoto's death was announced.

17. *Senshi sōsho,* 96:138. For Koga, see Okumiya, *Rabauru kaigun kōkūtai,* 229–30.

18. *Senshi sōsho,* 96:138. The one exception was two heavy Japanese raids on 25 and 26 April against Gatukai, where the Japanese mistakenly believed American troops had landed. G4Ms and Zeros made the first strike, D3As and Zeros the second. The first raid ran into American fighters returning from a mission to Vila. Two F4Us went down with one pilot rescued; five Zeros were claimed (which I cannot confirm from my sources). See SOPAC, Air Combat Intelligence, Shore Commands, Box 7, RG 127, NARA.

19. *Senshi sōsho,* 96:144.

20. *Senshi sōsho,* 96:150; SOPAC, Air Combat Intelligence.

21. *Senshi sōsho,* 96:153; SOPAC, Air Combat Intelligence; Gray Book, 23 May 1943.

22. *Senshi sōsho,* 96:153; SOPAC, Air Combat Intelligence; COMAIRSOLS, Weekly Intelligence Summary. The night fighter action is in XIII Fighter Command, Mission Reports. A detachment of radar-equipped P-70s (converted Douglas A-20 medium bombers) from the 6th Night Fighter Squadron was based at Carney Field, but the P-70

lacked the altitude and speed to catch the G4Ms.

23. *Senshi sōsho,* 96:176.

24. *Senshi sōsho,* 96:142.

25. *Senshi sōsho,* 96:176.

26. VF-11 Mission Reports, Box 439, RG 38, NARA.

27. *Senshi sōsho,* 96:179; COMAIR-SOLS, Weekly Intelligence Summary. The Japanese reported four planes severely damaged. One of these landed at Munda with the pilot, Warrant Officer Yanagiya Kenji, badly wounded. His right arm was amputated (without anesthetic), and as a result he was the only pilot from Yamamoto's escort to Buin to survive the war. See Henry Sakaida, *Aces of the Rising Sun, 1937–1945* (Oxford: Osprey, 2002), 126–27.

28. *Senshi sōsho,* 96:181–182; SOPAC, Air Combat Intelligence, 6–12 June 1943. VMF-121, which was just completing its move to Guadalcanal, got into the 12 June fight. See VMF-121, War Diary.

29. XIII Fighter Command, Mission Reports; VF-11, Action Report; VMF-121, War Diary; No. 14 Squadron, War Diary, Air 149/1, NANZ; COMAIR-SOLS, Weekly Intelligence Summary; SOPAC, Air Combat Intelligence.

30. Action Report, *LST-340,* 23 June 1943, Box 31, RG 38, NARA. *LST-340* was taking part in training exercises for the New Georgia landing and was loaded with fully fueled trucks.

31. *Senshi sōsho,* 96:182–84.

32. *Senshi sōsho,* 96:185; COMAIR-SOLS, Weekly Intelligence Summary, 11 June 1943. The three G4Ms made one half-hearted attack then stayed in the area until they were engaged. See

President Hayes After Action Report, Convoy Action 10–11 June 1943, Box 31, RG 38, NARA. Also see Four [*sic*] Bettys shot down in Interception, Fighter Command, Guadalcanal.

33. *Senshi sōsho,* 96:187–88.

34. COMAIRSOLS, Weekly Intelligence Summary.

5. Plans and Preparations

1. Halsey, *Halsey,* 154–55. MacArthur put Halsey in the class of John Paul Jones, David Farragut, and George Dewey. Douglas MacArthur, *Reminiscences* (New York: McGraw-Hill, 1964), 173–74.

2. Drea, *MacArthur's ULTRA,* 63. Imamura had studied in England, had been resident officer in India, and in the 1930s had been commandant, Narashino Army School and Army Infantry School. Kusaka relieved an ailing Vice Admiral Tsukahara Nishizō, who had commanded 11th Air Fleet since its activation.

3. Kusaka Jinichi, *Rabauru sensen ijo nashi: warera kaku iki kaku tatakaeri* [*The War in Rabaul: The Record of How We Fought and Survived*] (Tokyo: Kowado, 1958), 24–26.

4. For the Pacific Conference, see Morton, *Strategy and Command,* 387–99.

5. As agreed, Halsey sent considerable forces to SWPA for the operation, including the 67th Fighter Squadron.

6. Morton, *Strategy and Command,* Appendix V; Halsey to Nimitz, 14 May 1943, Halsey Papers, Box 15.

7. Captain Edwin Wheeler, 1st Raider Battalion, made a thorough reconnaissance of Kolombangara and

reported that the few landing beaches would make the cost prohibitive in the face of strong opposition, and most important, the Vila airfield site could not be expanded to meet COMAIRSOPAC's requirements. See Joseph H. Alexander, *Edson's Raiders: The 1st Marine Raider Battalion in World War II* (Annapolis: Naval Institute Press, 2001), 147–48. Halsey said that his operations officer, Captain Harry Raymond Thurber, USN, was the main opponent of the bypass. See Halsey's long letter of recommendation for Thurber's award of the Distinguished Service Medal, 7 February 1947, Morison, Office Files, Box 31. But also see Peck to COMSOPAC, New Georgia Operation, 27 April 1943, Memos on Operations, 750.312-2, AFHRA.

8. Fitch wanted a forward emergency strip in operation as soon as possible and sent his chief engineer, Commander Wilfred L. Painter, to scout out the Viru Harbor area. No site there was possible, and Painter settled on Markham's plantation, where he determined a 3,500-foot strip could be built quickly since slightly decayed coral was just beneath the topsoil, drainage was good, and there was a good LST landing beach. See W. L. Painter, Report on Trip to New Georgia Island, 23 May 1943, Flag Files (Blue 242), Box 8, RG 313, NARA.

9. COMSOPAC, Operation Plan No. 14–43, Box 241, RG 127, NARA. "Infiltration and staging" description is in Halsey to Nimitz, 14 May 1943, Halsey Papers, Box 15.

10. An Acorn was a self-sustained, self-supporting airfield operational unit with the mission of immediately establishing the facilities for air operations.

11. COMSOPAC, Operation Plan No. 14–43.

12. Turner's memorandum to Halsey is cited in John N. Rentz, *Marines in the Central Solomons* (Washington, D.C.: USMC Historical Branch, 1952), 31.

13. For the Vogel affair, see Merrill B. Twining, *No Bended Knee: The Memoir of Gen. Merrill B. Twining, USMC (Ret)*, ed. Neil Carey (Novato, Calif.: Presidio, 1996), 181–89, and Alan P. Rems, "Halsey Knows the Straight Story," *Naval History* 22, no. 4 (August 2008): 40–46.

14. Nimitz to Halsey, 14 May 1943, Halsey Papers, Box 15.

15. See Dyer, *Amphibians*, 1:501–28.

16. TF 33, Operation Plan No. 43, 18 June 1943, Box 242, RG 127, NARA. Commanding General, 2nd MAW, Plans for Air Support Missions for Ground Operations and for Fighter Direction in the New Georgia Area, 24 June 1943, Shore Commands, Box 27, RG 127, NARA.

17. Operation Plan 1–43, 23 June 1943, Flag Files (Blue 242), Box 1, RG 313, NARA. Halsey considered using the battleship *North Carolina* to bombard Munda but dropped the plan.

18. 43rd Division, Field Order No. 3, Annex 1, 27 June 1943, Field Orders, Munda Campaign, 16 June–25 August 1943, 343–3.9, RG 407, NARA.

19. *Senshi sōsho*, 96:97–101, *Senshi sōsho*, 40:169–70.

20. *Senshi sōsho*, 40:192–93; *Senshi sōsho*, 96:189.

21. *Senshi sōsho*, 40:195.

22. In early April, the navy estimated that over 30% of the troops at Vila and Munda were suffering from malaria, while at Wickham the rate was 50%. A replacement plan was drawn up but never carried out. See *Senshi sōsho*, 96:159.

23. Interrogation Report, No. 172, Superior Private Kano Saburō, Translation Files, 25th Division, 325–2.9, RG 407, NARA.

24. *Senshi sōsho*, 40:198–204.

25. 8th Combined/Southeast Detachment Intelligence Reports, April–June 1943, RJN, Item #753, NHHC.

26. Joseph E. Zimmer, *The History of the 43rd Infantry Division, 1941–1945* (Nashville, Tenn.: Battery Press, 1982), 18–20. 147th Inf. Orientation Conference, Guadalcanal, 10–12 April 1943, ENRG-147-3, RG 407, NARA. The 147th was detached from the 37th Division and sent to Tonga in May 1942 and from there to Guadalcanal in November. It remained an independent RCT for the rest of the war, seeing its last action in the mop-up of Iwo Jima.

27. Strike Command, Daily Intelligence Summary.

28. Alexander, *Edson's Raiders*, 232.

29. A captured table of organization dated 1 June 1943 shows the battalion at full strength. See RJN, Item #721, NHHC. But nowhere for the duration of the campaign are 1st and 2nd Companies mentioned, and when the remnants of the battalion came under command of 2nd Battalion, 2 August 1943, only 3rd and 4th Companies and 1st Machine-Gun Company are listed in the order. See Field Orders, 229th, RJN, Item #822, NHHC.

30. For the rebuilding of the battalion see Temporary Independent 229th BN Operational Order No. 1, 10 January 1943, RJN, Item #760, NHHC. For Japanese training, see chapter 6: "Trained in the Hardest School," Edward J. Drea, *In the Service of the Emperor: Essays on the Imperial Japanese Army* (Lincoln: University of Nebraska Press, 1998).

31. Kumamoto hei dan senshi hensan iinkai, *Kumamoto heidan senshi: Taiheiyō senso hen* [Committee of the Military History of the Kumamoto Soldiers Group Compilation, *Military History of the Kumamoto Soldiers Group: Pacific War Series*] (Kumamoto, Japan: Kumamoto nichi nichi shinbunsha, 1965), 77–80, 84.

32. Kumamoto hei dan, *Taiheiyō senso hen*, 78. On Japanese armament see Gordon L. Rottman, *Japanese Army in World War II: The South Pacific and New Guinea, 1942–1943* (Oxford: Osprey, 2005), and U.S. War Department, *Handbook on Japanese Military Forces* (Novato, Calif.: Presidio, 1991).

33. COMAIRSOLS, Weekly Intelligence Summary, 9 July 1943. Search and Patrol Command, also under the command of Schilt, had the PBYs, Black Cats, and RNZAF Hudsons. Photographic Command (Colonel G. W. Hanson, AAF) had the 17th Reconnaissance Squadron (F-5A) and VD-1 (PB4Y-1).

34. *Senshi sōsho*, 96:210, 225. The records of the 26th Air Flotilla for this period have not survived, and the official historians approximate its strength from the individual unit records that exist. I was not able to use the Kōkūtai

action reports (Kōdōchōsho), an obvious weakness for Japanese air operations.

35. *Senshi sōsho*, 7:308. *Sokyu banri: Rikugun hikō sentaishi [Blue Sky Very Long Way: History of Army Air Force Hikō Sentais]* (Tokyo: Rikugun hikō sentaishi kanko iinkai, 1976), 1, 33–34, 43, 94–96, 149–51, 170–72, National Institute of Defense Studies (NIDS) Military Archives Reading Room, Reference No. 392.9S.

36. Carl Boyd and Akihiko Yoshida, *The Japanese Submarine Force and World War II* (Annapolis: Naval Institute Press, 1995), 115; Hackett, *Sensuikan!*

37. ONI, Organization of the Japanese Navy, 1 June 1943, Flag Files (Red, 182), Box 6550, RG 313, NARA.

6. The Landings

1. Nimitz to Halsey, 26 June 1943, Halsey Papers, Box 15.

2. Commander, Amphibious Force, SOPAC, Report of Reconnaissance Missions into New Georgia, 15–23 June 1943, 37th Division Intelligence File, 337–1.0, RG 407, NARA.

3. *Senshi sōsho*, 40:203; Hara Butai Dispensary, Combat Diary, 17 June 1943, RJN, Item #691, NHHC.

4. Kennedy, Report, 26–28; Price-Jones, Report, 104.

5. 4th Raider Battalion, Special Actions Report (SAR), Segi Point and Viru Harbor, 14 September 1943, Box 241, RG 127, NARA; 103rd Infantry, Operations Report, New Georgia Islands Campaign, 343-INF (103)-0.3. RG 407, NARA; 47th Naval Construction Battalion (NCB), Monthly Reports,

Box 1, RG 1, Naval Facilities Command (NAVFAC).

6. *Senshi sōsho*, 96:203.

7. Western Force (31.1), Loading Order, 13 June 1943, Flag Files (Blue, 242), Box 1, RG 313, NARA. This includes all landings except the Northern Landing Force at Rice Anchorage.

8. David Dexter, *The New Guinea Offensives* (Canberra: Australian War Memorial, 1961), 55–58.

9. Commander Task Group 36.2, Action Report – Minelaying and Bombardment conducted in the Shortland-Faisi-Kolombangara Areas, Night of 29–30 June 1943, 16 July 1943, Box 141, RG 38, NARA. Action Report, Mining Detachment Commander Third Fleet Operation Plan 12–43, Box 141, RG 38, NARA. Waller, Action Report, Bombardment of Vila-Stanmore, Kolombangara Island, and Shortland Islands, Night of June 29–30 1943, Box 31, RG 38, NARA. There is some evidence that the commander at Ballale, fearing a landing, executed the surviving British POWs who had been brought from Singapore to build the airfield. See Ballale Island Case, Investigation into the Fate of 300 Europeans, Interrogations of Senior Japanese Officers with a View of Ascertaining the Unit and Its Responsibility for the Custody of Europeans, AWM 54 1010/9/65.

10. Orange Intercepts, 8th Fleet, Box 1089, RG 38, NARA. For naval intelligence organizations, see John Prados, *Combined Fleet Decoded: The Secret History of American Intelligence and the Japanese Navy in World War II* (New York: Random House, 1995), 408–11.

11. *Senshi sōsho*, 96:206–207; *Senshi sōsho*, 40:256.

12. *Zane* had to be towed back to Tulagi. *Zane*, Deck Log, courtesy of Joseph E. Gunterman, a member of the crew, who also sent me other information.

13. Miller, *Cartwheel*, 86. A detailed account of the Rendova Barracudas is in F. H. Rhoades, "Diary of a Coastwatcher in the Solomons," copyright Admiral Nimitz Foundation, 1982, AWM F 940.5485935. Also notes of a conversation with the late Martin Clemens at his home, June, 2001. Clemens with his Malaita police boys was also with the Rendova Barracudas.

14. Operations Report, 172nd Inf. Regt. – New Georgia, 343-INF (172)-0.3, RG 407, NARA. Also, information provided by the late Edgar N. Jaynes, Ross's adjutant. *Senshi sōsho*, 40:252–53. Petty Officer 2nd Class Yada Nobutaro, Kure 6th, Interrogation Report #134, N 2 11(a), PW Interrogation Reports 120–83, Box 16a, NANZ; Sergeant Totsuka Kyoichi, Signal Company, 229th, Interrogation Report, RJN, Item #105, NHHC.

15. Despite the target-rich area, Harada's submarines turned in a dismal performance during the campaign. The one contribution was in picking up and returning pilots who had been shot down and stranded on islands such as Simbo. See Hackett, *Sensuikan!*

16. For the gunnery: Kamiya's statement in *Senshi sōsho*, 40:253. For the air action: *Senshi sōsho*, 96:223; VC-28, Intelligence Report, Box 414, RG 38, NARA; VMF-121, War Dairy.

17. Commander H. Roy Whittaker to Chief of the Bureau of Yards and Docks, 24th Naval Construction Battalion Activities during First Six Days of Battle of Munda, 6 July 1943, Records of the 24th NCB, Box 1, RG 1, NAVFAC; Lieutenant Colonel W. J. McNenny to IMAC, Observer Report, New Georgia Operation, 17 July 1943, Box 241, RG 127, NARA; Colonel George W. McHenry, USMC, Notes and Comments, Box 241, RG 127, NARA. Major General O. W. Griswold, Lessons Learned from Joint Operations, 21 January 1944, 214-0.4, RG 407, NARA.

18. Peck, Interview, 104.

19. VMF-221, War Diary; *Senshi sōsho*, 96:223; Hata, *Japanese Naval Aces*, 141, 383; and Tagaya Osamu, *Mitsubishi Type 1 Rikko "Betty" Units of World War 2* (Oxford: Osprey, 2001), 74.

20. Petty Officer 2nd Class Fujino Mamoru, Interrogation Report, RJN, Item #121, NHHC; *President Hayes*, *President Jackson*, Action Reports, 30 June 1943, Box 72, RG 38, NARA.

21. See the following: Dyer, *Amphibians*, 1:559–62; Samuel Eliot Morison, *Breaking the Bismarcks Barrier, 22 July 1942–1 May 1944* (Boston: Little, Brown, 1950), 150–52; ONI, *Combat Narratives, Solomon Islands Campaign, X, Operations in the New Georgia Area, 21 June–5 August 1943* (Washington, D.C., 1944), 10–13.

22. Kosaka had put the force together and is responsible for the suicidal use of the 938th F1Ms. As one of his emergency measures that morning, Kusaka had put the 938th under the 6th Air Strike Force. Thereafter, the 938th

was attached to 8th Fleet. *Senshi sōsho,* 96:212.

23. XIII Fighter Command, Mission Reports; *Senshi sōsho,* 96:224.

24. COMAIRSOLS, Weekly Intelligence Summary; *Senshi sōsho,* 96:223–24; SOPAC, Air Combat Intelligence.

25. Theodore C. Mason, *"We Will Stand by You": Serving in the* Pawnee, *1942–1945* (Annapolis: Naval Institute Press, 1996), 70–77. As a result of the mix-up, command of the Rendova-based boats was transferred from Naval Base, Rendova to TF 31, which would have the best intelligence on ship movements. See Robert J. Bulkley Jr., *At Close Quarters: PT Boats in the United States Navy* (Washington, D.C.: Naval History Division, 1962), 114–16.

26. 103rd Infantry, Operations Report; *Senshi sōsho,* 96:224; XIII Fighter Command, Mission Reports, (No. 14 Squadron Report is attached); VF-21, Mission Reports, Box 444, RG 38, NARA; 307th Bomb Group (H), Consolidated Mission Reports, July–September, GP-107-HI, AFHRA. The bombers did not drop due to cloud cover; one B-24 was lost to engine trouble, but the crew was rescued.

27. Report of Lieutenant Milton N. Vedder, 4 July 1943, VMF-221, War Diary.

28. Rentz, *Marines in the Central Solomons,* 63, puts the number at 153 killed and wounded in the main target area, and 200 casualties altogether. Also see 118th Medical Battalion, Operations Report, Munda Campaign, 343-MED-0.3, RG 407, NARA; Task Unit C,

155mm Group, Work Sheet, Box 241, RG 127, NARA.

29. *Senshi sōsho,* 7:308–309; *Senshi sōsho,* 96:225.

30. Sixteen 339th P-38s took on forty-eight Zeros. The Japanese reported no losses; three P-38s failed to return. XIII Fighter Command, Pilots' Reports; *Senshi sōsho,* 96:225.

31. *Senshi sōsho,* 7:310; *Senshi sōsho,* 96:225; VF-21, Mission Reports; COMAIRSOLS, Weekly Intelligence Summary; Headquarters, New Georgia Air Force (NGAF), Special Action Report (SAR), Shore Commands, Box 27, RG 127, NARA.

32. *Senshi sōsho,* 96:225, 240; *Senshi sōsho,* 40:269.

33. *Senshi sōsho,* 96:226; COMAIR-SOLS, Mission Reports; Bulkley, *At Close Quarters,* 118–19; Commander, South Pacific, War Diary, Box 49, RG 38, NARA. The *Yūbari* hit a mine on 5 July, 29 miles off Buin, 119°, which took it out of action until late October. The location would put the ship in the area of the minefield laid by Merrill's task group on 29–30 June.

34. NGOF, G-2 Intelligence Summaries and Periodic Reports, Rendova Island–New Georgia Campaign, 1 July–31 October 1943, 343-INF (172)-2-1, RG 407, NARA.

35. *Senshi sōsho,* 40:260–66; *Senshi sōsho,* 96:217–22. The official historians discuss the messages that flew back and forth in detail. Some are very interesting. The Army General Staff sent messages that could be interpreted as supporting Sasaki in the argument over Rendova, but Eighth Army ignored these. Samejima proposed that once

the 4 and 5 July transports had been completed, he would take the *Chōkai* and lead 8th Fleet to attack Rendova in support of a counter-landing. Kusaka ordered him to drop such a reckless plan. Sugiyama sent on a message from the emperor for the Munda commanders to do their utmost to thwart the enemy.

36. For their account, the Japanese historians had practically no records of their own and thus used American works, primarily John N. Rentz's *Marines in the Central Solomons*.

37. Dyer, *Amphibians*, 1:572–76.

38. *Senshi sōsho*, 40:259.

39. The best account is in Rentz, *Marines in the Central Solomons*, 44–51. I also used 103rd Infantry, Operations Report; 4th Marine Raider Battalion, SAR, Vura Bay, Vangunu Island Operation, Box 241, RG 127, NARA; and Strike Command, Daily Intelligence Summary.

40. As late as December, 1943, Japanese survivors were being tracked down and killed or captured. See Chief Petty Officer Uchimura Genji, Interrogation Report, RJN, Item #212, NHHC.

41. Maj. Roy J. Batterton Jr., "You Fight by the Book," *Marine Corps Gazette* 33 (July 1949): 19.

42. Dyer, *Amphibians*, 1:569. NGAF, SAR.

43. Leading Seaman Matsushita Isao, Interrogation Report, RJN, Item #115, NHHC; *Senshi sōsho*, 40:254.

44. Rentz, *Marines in the Central Solomons*, 41–43; 4th Raider Battalion, SAR, Segi Point and Viru Harbor; *Senshi sōsho*, 40:257–258; COMAIRSOLS, Weekly Intelligence Summary; 20th

NCB, Monthly Reports, Box 1, RG 1, NAVFAC.

45. 47th NCB, Monthly Reports. For technical aspects of construction, I have relied on Joseph C. Zimmerman, "The Construction of Airfields in during the New Georgia Campaign of 1943–1944: Lessons learned by the United States Naval Construction Battalions," MA thesis, East Tennessee State University, 2008

46. The first surviving report from Air Command, Segi, dates from 10 August. See Air Command, Segi Intelligence Section, Box 324, RG 38, NARA.

47. COMINCH, Chart Room Collection of Dispatches and Related Records, South Pacific, Box 116, RG 38, NARA.

48. CTG 36.1, Action Report, Night Bombardment of Vila-Stanmore and Bairoko Harbor, Kula Gulf, 4–5 July 1943, Box 134, RG 38, NARA.

49. Hackett, *Sensuikan!* Carl Boyd and Akihiko Yoshida, in *The Japanese Submarine Force and World War II*, 122, write that the *RO-108* "sank an escort vessel, possibly the *USS Strong* (DD-467) on 5 July." Hackett and Kingsepp have the *RO-108* making its first and only patrol to the Solomons 23 August.

50. Action Report of Bombardment of Kula Gulf Area and Circumstances of Sinking of *U.S.S. Strong*, 10 July 1943, Flag Files (Blue 347), Box 75, RG 313, NARA. Two minutes before the torpedo hit *Strong*, *Radford*, which was entering the gulf with the transport group, picked up the Japanese retiring at high speed. *Niizuki*'s radar contact was used to launch torpedoes at 0015 at a range of 11 miles. For an analysis

of the action based on the facts known at the time, see COMINCH, Battle Experience, No. 10, Naval Operations Solomon Island Area, 30 June–12 July 1943, Command File, World War II, Box 261, NHHC. For the Japanese destroyers, see *Senshi sōsho,* 96:227. Paul S. Dull, *A Battle History of the Imperial Japanese Navy (1941–1945)* (Annapolis: Naval Institute Press, 1978), 274.

51. *Chevalier,* Action Report – Shore Bombardment Kula Gulf Area, Night of 4–5 July 1943, Box 910, RG 38, NARA.

52. Forty-seven Zeros and seven D3As made up the formation. With the gulf clear of shipping, the D3As and some Zeros returned; the 44th Fighter Squadron intercepted the rest. *Senshi sōsho,* 96:226; XIII Fighter Command, Mission Reports.

53. Details of the 148th mishap are in Colonel Charles A. Henne, USA (ret.), "History of the 148th Infantry," part 2, 15–18, unpublished manuscript. Two Higgins boats with Raiders also got lost and did not land until after daybreak. See Alexander, *Edson's Raiders,* 262.

54. Survivor's stories are in Brian Altobello, *Into the Shadows Furious: The Brutal Battle for New Georgia* (Novato, Calif.: Presidio, 2000), 124–35.

7. The First Battle for Munda

1. George W. McHenry, Personal Diary, Box 243, RG 127, NARA (not to be confused with his Notes and Comments previously cited). McHenry made this diary available to marine historian Rentz, who put it in the file with a note requesting that it not be used until after McHenry's death.

2. Unless otherwise noted, the 43rd's operations are based on: Miller, *Cartwheel*; 43rd Division, Operations Report, 343–3, RG 407, NARA; 169th Infantry Regiment, Operations Report, 343-INF (169)-0-3, RG 407, NARA; 172nd Infantry, Operations Report; 103rd Infantry, Operations Report.

3. McHenry, Notes and Comments.

4. Unless otherwise noted, Japanese operations are based on: *Senshi sōsho,* 40:272–92; New Georgia Defense Unit [IJA], Operation Orders, RJN, Item #702, NHHC; 2nd Battalion, 229th, Operational Orders, RJN, Item #785, NHHC; 3rd Battalion, 229th, Operational Orders, RJN, Item #705, NHHC.

5. For the artillery, the following have been used: Task Unit C, 155mm Group, Work Sheet; 43rd Artillery, Operations Report, 343-ART-0.3, RG 407, NARA; Harold B. Barker, *History of the 43rd Division Artillery, 1941–1945* (Providence, R.I.: John F. Green, 1960).

6. Unless otherwise noted, all material comes from 1st Commando Fiji Guerrillas, War Dairy, TNA: PRO: WO 176/134. For its creation and history, see R. A. Howlett, *History of the Fiji Military Forces* (Suva, Fiji: Government Printer, 1948), 55–64, 221–22.

7. ONI, *Combat Narrative, X,* 31; Strike Command, Daily Intelligence Summary.

8. Diary of Robert E. Casko, Telling of Wartime in the South Pacific Battle for Munda, courtesy of Richard F. Potter.

9. Captain Joseph A. Lieberman, "Road Construction on New Georgia," *Military Engineer* 36 (March 1944): 75–78; 118th Engineer Battalion, Operation

Journal, 343-ENG-0.3, RG 407, NARA. Captain Richard L. Saillant, Journal, courtesy Joseph M. Carey; Saillant was commander of B Company, 118th Engineers.

10. Queen Salote of Tonga had declared war on Imperial Japan, and her contribution to the war effort was a platoon under Lieutenant Henry Taliai, which was attached to 1st Commando. Also attached were two dozen Solomon Islanders from the BSIPDF "Dukwasi" (Solomon Island for "first into the bush").

11. TG 36.9, Report of Night Bombardment of Munda Point, New Georgia Island and Enemy Installations on and Adjacent Thereto, 12 July 1943, Box 141, RG 38, NARA.

12. SCAT was made up of three squadrons of MAG 25 and the AAF 13th Troop Carrier Squadron, later a part of the 403rd Troop Carrier Group. They flew DC-3s.

13. NGAF, SAR; VMSB-144, War Diary.

14. Nothing is mentioned about this change in the 169th Infantry reports, so the circumstances are not known. I have used Commanders of Units, 20 June–25 August 1943, Box 243, RG 127, NARA.

15. No explanation is given for distinguishing between "shell shock" and "war neurosis." A guess would be severity.

16. The only other Japanese attempt on Zanana had been on 7 July when Ueno sent six G4Ms with forty-three Zeros. The Rendova Patrol intercepted before the formation could reach the target, shot down two of the bombers

and two of the Zeros, and damaged three more of the bombers. One F4U was shot down, but the pilot was rescued. *Senshi sōsho,* 96:242; VMF-221, War Diary; Fighter Command, Guadalcanal.

17. Strike Command, Daily Intelligence Summary; XII Fighter Command, Mission Reports; VMF-213, War Diary; VMF-121, War Diary; VMF-112, War Dairy; COMAIRSOLS, Weekly Intelligence Summary; *Senshi sōsho,* 96:243; 25th Air Flotilla Reports. RJN, WDC, Item #35D, NHHC; Tagaya, *Mitsubishi Type 1,* 75.

18. A single TBF in a large strike dropped far short of the target – small islets in the lagoon west of Ilangana – and killed three men and wounded ten. NGAF, SAR.

19. 9th Defense Battalion, Task Unit D, Tank Platoon, Operations Report, Box 241, RG 127, NARA.

20. Lieutenant General O. W. Griswold, Diary, April 1943–October 1945, 6 July 1943, Oscar Griswold Papers, Military History Institute (MHI); Miller, *Cartwheel,* 122–24; Dyer, *Amphibians,* 1:584–86.

21. Griswold, Diary.

22. Saillant, Journal.

23. Hallam's letter is quoted in Miller, *Cartwheel,* 121. Eric M. Bergerud, *Touched with Fire: The Land War in the South Pacific* (New York: Viking, 1996), 446–48, sets the 43rd's experience in perspective, and Albert E. Cowdrey, *Fighting for Life: American Military Medicine in World War II* (New York: Free Press, 1994), ch. 7, deals with the army's attempts to find a solution to the problem. It was not confined to the

ground troops. See Operations Analysis Section, Neuropsychiatric Cases from the Thirteen Air Force Treated at APO 715 during 1943, 750.3101–12, AFHRA.

24. From 30 June to 30 September, NGOF had 2,500 cases termed "war neurosis." Miller, *Cartwheel*, 121n27, gives the cases per unit as follows: 43rd Division, about 1,950; 37th Division, 200; Marine/Navy, 200; and 25th Division, 150. Seventy percent of the cases occurred in July.

25. Mary Ellen Condon-Rall and Albert E. Cowdrey, *The Medical Department: Medical Services in the War against Japan* (Washington, D.C.: Center of Military History, 1998), 190.

26. Griswold, Diary; Miller, *Cartwheel*, 124–26; COMSOPAC, War Diary, Box 49, RG 38, NARA; Dyer, *Amphibians*, 1:584–87.

27. *Senshi sōsho*, 40:277; *Senshi sōsho*, 96:245; Orange Intercepts, 8th Fleet, Box 1089, RG 38, NARA.

28. *Senshi sōsho*, 40:279; New Georgia Defense Unit [IJA], Operation Orders; Kumamoto hei dan, *Taiheiyō sensō hen*, 97.

29. Kumamoto hei dan, *Taiheiyō sensō hen*, 100.

30. 43rd Cavalry Reconnaissance Troop, Operations Report, 343-CAV-0.3, RG 407, NARA. Barker made a personal visit to the 136th to congratulate them for their fine work. See 136th Field Artillery Battalion, Action Report, 337-FA (136)-0.1, RG 407, NARA.

31. Rentz, *Marines in the Central Solomons*, 83–84; McHenry, Notes and Comments. Wismer commanded 3rd Platoon, Special Weapons Group (Task Unit A), 9th Defense Battalion.

32. Altobello, *Into the Shadows*, 290–301, describes the incident in more detail.

33. Operations of the 148th Infantry (-3Bn) in New Georgia, Box 243, RG 127, NARA.

34. Kumamoto hei dan, *Taiheiyō sensō hen*, 98.

8. Battles in the Dragons Peninsula

1. Peck, Interview, 122.

2. Twining, *No Bended Knee*, 185.

3. Unless otherwise noted, action of the 1st Marine Raider Regiment is based on the following: 1st Marine Raider Regiment, Journal, New Georgia Campaign; 1st Raider Battalion, Operation Order; 1st Marine Raider Regiment, SAR; 4th Marine Raider Battalion, SAR – all documents found in Box 241, RG 127, NARA.

4. Lieutenant Colonel Samuel B. Griffith, "Action at Enogai: Operations of the First Raider Battalion in the New Georgia Campaign," *Marine Corps Gazette* 28 (March 1944): 14–19. Unless otherwise noted, all statements attributed to Griffith come from this article.

5. Kolombangara Defense Operational Order A No. 10, 6 July 1943, RJN, Item #743, NHHC. *Senshi sōsho*, 40:294, 306. Orange Intercepts, 8th Fleet, Box 1089, RG 38, NARA.

6. Accounts of the attack on the 145th vary. I have followed 3rd Battalion, 145th, Unit Journal, 337-INF (145th)-0.7, RG 407, NARA.

7. VMSB-144, War Diary.

8. VMSB-132, War Diary; NGAF, SAR.

9. At full strength, the batteries of the heavy gun companies were made

up of four 14cm guns each. Two of the guns went down on a transport sunk by COMAIRSOLS, and this was probably the fate of the other two. Lieutenant Yanagibayashi Tadateru was the senior officer. Table of Organization and Equipment, 8th Combined.

10. A VMJ-153 R4D (marine designation for the DC-3) made the drop at 1540, 9 July. See VMJ-153, War Diary. The 145th at Triri and VMF-112, which flew escort, both confirm this.

11. In addition to the sources already cited, Alexander, *Edson's Raiders*, 266–75, and Rentz, *Marines in the Central Solomons*, 100–109, cover this action in greater detail.

12. *Senshi sōsho*, 96:242; 25th Air Flotilla Reports; VMF-221, War Diary; NGAF, SAR; Hata and Izawa, *Japanese Naval Aces and Fighter Units*, 384.

13. *Senshi sōsho*, 96:242; VMF-213, War Diary; 18th Fighter Group, Combat Reports, GP-18-OP (F), AFHRA.

14. All statements or decisions attributed to Schultz are from the action report that he wrote. See Report After Action, 3rd Battalion, 148th Inf.®, 137-INF (148)-0.3, RG 407, NARA.

15. Kumamoto hei dan, *Taiheiyō sensō hen*, 96; *Senshi sōsho*, 40:278.

16. COMSOPAC, Action Report, Night of 17–18 July 1943, Box 73, RG 38, NARA.

17. CTF 31 to COMSOPAC, 19 July 1943, COMINCH, Chart Room Dispatches, South Pacific, Box 117.

18. Two different versions, neither conclusive, of what happened to the message requesting the 20 July strike exist. One is in Rentz, *Marines in the Central Solomons*, 111n36; the other

is in Miller, *Cartwheel*, 130n4. I find it strange that every other strike Liversedge requested is in Mulcahy's log and was carried out.

19. Orange Intercepts, 8th Fleet, Box 1088.

20. New Georgia Defense Unit [IJA], Operation Orders.

21. NGAF, SAR; Strike Command, Daily Intelligence Summary.

22. In their reports, the Raiders make no comment whatsoever on Schultz's failure to get into the battle.

23. Captain Gendreau was at Guadalcanal – probably at Nimitz's behest – to see how the wounded were cared for and asked specifically to go to Rendova and return on a LST loaded with wounded to see firsthand the care the patients were given. His death was a personal blow to Nimitz, with whom he shared living quarters. See Wilkinson to Nimitz (copy to Halsey), 22 July 1943, Halsey Papers, Box 15.

24. COMAIRSOLS, Weekly Intelligence Summary; NGAF, SAR.

25. On 2 July, F4Us and B-25s caught the *Kasi Maru* in Bairoko Harbor and sank it. After that, the Japanese ceased using sea trucks for transport to New Georgia.

26. *Senshi sōsho*, 40:292–94, 507.

27. Rentz, *Marines in the Central Solomons*, 109–21; Miller, *Cartwheel*, 127–31; Alexander, *Edson's Raiders*, 278–91.

9. Battles with the Tokyo Express

1. Morison, Office Files, Box 30.

2. *Senshi sōsho*, 96:227–30.

3. Halsey was not absolutely certain the Japanese would show; he ordered

Ainsworth to refuel at Tulagi after the threat had been dealt with and be prepared "for northern dash against Tokyo gents night of July 6–7." COMINCH, Chart Room Dispatches, South Pacific, Box 117.

4. Orange Intercepts, 8th Fleet, Box 1089, says a reef at Jack Harbor; *Senshi sōsho* (96:228) says that a barge tow cable became entangled with the propeller.

5. Some sources have *Amagiri* stopping to pick up survivors on the way out of the gulf before being driven off by gunfire from the American destroyers picking up survivors from *Helena*; others make no mention of it. *I-38*, which was in the Kula Gulf area, likewise makes no mention of picking up survivors.

6. Task Group 36.1, Action Report, Kula Gulf, 1 August 1943, Box 140, RG 38, NARA. TU 31.1.4, Action Report, Kula Gulf, 20 August 1943, Flag Files (Blue 347), Box 29, RG 313, NARA. The commander of *Jenkins* was especially criticized, and since he was detached from command a few days later, his executive officer, who assumed command, wrote the action report dated 11 July 1943. See Box 1071, RG 38, NARA.

7. Conversation with the late Allen Jackson, 1–2 August 1992, at his home at Pensacola Beach. Jackson was a Hearst INP photographer rescued by the destroyers. *Helena*, After Action Report, Kula Gulf, 1 August 1943, Box 1025, RG 38, NARA.

8. In addition to artillery, engineer, and medical units, part of the 2nd Shipping Engineer Regiment landed with fifteen large barges and one small barge.

8th Army Operational Order A No. 351, 3 July 1943, RJN, Item #740, NHHC.

9. TU 36.1.4, Action Report, 5–6 July 1943. Morison's account is in *Breaking the Bismarcks Barrier*, 160–75. Dull, *Imperial Japanese Navy*, 274–76, is much briefer. The Japanese account is in *Senshi sōsho*, 96:227–30.

10. For Cecil's party, see *Helena*, Action Report.

11. VF-11, Action Report. COMAIRSOLS, Weekly Intelligence Summary.

12. *Senshi sōsho*, 96:245; Outer South Seas Force Plan for Strike in New Georgia Area on the Night of 9 July 1943 (JICOPA Item #5060) in Orange Intercepts, 8th Fleet, Box 1088; COMAIRSOLS, Weekly Intelligence Summary; VB-101, Action Report, Box 394, RG 38, NARA. Aruga's last command was *Yamato* on its doomed mission to Okinawa.

13. Samuel Eliot Morison, "Battle of Kolombangara," Morison, Office Files, Box 30.

14. Dyer, *Amphibians*, 1:582–83. Hackett and Kingsepp, *Sensuikan!* On the other hand, *RO-107*, which had been sent to Rendova 30 June, last reported 6 July, and Boyd and Yoshida, *Japanese Submarine Force*, 122, as well as Hackett and Kingsepp, include the sub as the possible victim.

15. COMAIRSOLS, Weekly Intelligence Summary; *Senshi sōsho*, 96:243; VMF-213, War Diary; XIII Fighter Command, Mission Reports; Hata, *Japanese Naval Aces and Fighter Units*, 384.

16. Halsey's intelligence was not specific. An Orange Intercept, 8th Fleet, 12

July 1943, Box 1088, from Commander Reinforcement Force to Commander 8th Fleet, stated that he was "ready to sortie." Buin was closed in, and photo intelligence came up blank.

17. TBS was a high-frequency short range radio used for tactical maneuvering in a naval formation.

18. I have followed Russell Sydnor Crenshaw Jr., *South Pacific Destroyer: The Battle for the Solomons from Savo Island to Vella Gulf* (Annapolis: Naval Institute Press, 1998), 165, 177.

19. The CIC was the nerve center of the ship. At this stage of the war, it was improvised in whatever space could be made available, and there the information from radars and sounding was plotted, evaluated, and sent to the bridge. See Commander Destroyers, Pacific Fleet, C.I.C. Information Bulletin, No. 2–43, 15 December 1943, WWII Command File, Despac Reports, Box 340, NHHC.

20. Morison, "Battle of Kolombangara"; Crenshaw, *South Pacific Destroyer*, 164.

21. Submarine *I-180* rescued twenty-one men.

22. Ainsworth gave the sequence as *St. Louis*, 0208, *Honolulu*, 0211, and *Gwin*, 0214, and Morison followed suit. Crenshaw, however, without giving a specific time, has *Gwin* hit moments after *St. Louis. Gwin* has the torpedo hitting it immediately after *St. Louis* was hit, and *Woodwood* has it ten or fifteen seconds later. See Night Action Report off Kula Gulf on 12–13 July, Loss of USS *Gwin*, Box 1009, RG 38, NARA; *Woodworth*, Action Report, Flag Files (Blue 347), Box 78, RG 313, NARA.

23. HMNZS *Leander*, Report of Action against Japanese Naval Forces, 13 July 1943, N 16/8143, NANZ. One of the injured, Commander Stephen W. Roskill, later wrote the official history of the Royal Navy in the war. *Leander's* history is in S. D. Waters, *The Royal New Zealand Navy* (Wellington, New Zealand: War History Branch, 1956).

24. Morison, *Breaking the Bismarcks Barrier*, 180–91 (account mainly from the perspective of the cruisers); Crenshaw, *South Pacific Destroyer*, 162–79 (account mainly from the perspective of the destroyers); TG 36.1, Action Report – Night Engagement off Kolombangara during the Night of 12–13 July 1943, 3 August 1943, Box 140, RG 38, NARA; Action Report – USS *Honolulu* – Night of 12–13 July 1943, 29 July 1943; and Narrative by Captain R. W. Hayler, U.S.N., USS *Honolulu*, 31 August 1943, Box 140, RG 38, NARA; *Senshi sōsho*, 96:245–48.

25. *Senshi sōsho*, 96:247.

26. Strike Command, Daily Intelligence Summary.

27. Nimitz to Halsey, 13 July 1943 and Halsey to Nimitz, 28 July 1943, Halsey Papers, Box 15.

28. 3rd Fleet to CINCPAC, 30 July 1943, COMINCH, Chart Room Dispatches, South Pacific, Box 117.

29. Morison, *Breaking the Bismarcks Barrier*, 195.

30. For the Type 93 and the tactical thinking behind its development, see David C. Evans and Mark R. Peattie, *Kaigun: Strategy, Tactics, and Technology in the Imperial Japanese Navy, 1887–1941* (Annapolis: Naval Institute Press, 1997), 269–70. The US Mark 15

had an effective range under 10,000
yards and was plagued by a tendency to
run deeper than the setting.

31. Josselyn, Report, 26–27; Chew's
Report in *Helena*, Action Report;
Report of Marine Detachment, USS
Helena, Box 241, RG 127, NARA; Cren-
shaw, *South Pacific Destroyer*, 186–87.

32. COMAIRSOLS, Weekly Intel-
ligence Summary; Strike Command,
Daily Intelligence Summary; VT-11,
VT-21, Mission Report; VB-11, VMSB-
132, War Diary; 307th Bomb Group
(H), Consolidated Mission Reports:
XIII Fighter Command, Mission Re-
ports; VMF-213, VMF-121, War Diaries;
Senshi sōsho, 96:243; Hata, *Japanese
Naval Aces and Fighter Units*, 384.

33. Strike Command, Daily Intel-
ligence Summary; 42nd Bombardment
Group (M), Consolidated Mission
Reports, GP-42-SU-OP, AFHRA.
Japanese losses and data on reinforce-
ment are in *Senshi sōsho*, 96:248. See
COMAIRSOPAC to COMSOPAC,
Boards of Investigation into PT Boat-
B-25 Action on July 20, 1943, Flag Files
(Blue 242), Box 2, RG 313, NARA.

34. Andrew P. Tully, "Neglected
Disaster: *Nisshin*," http://www
.combinedfleet.com/atully10.htm;
SOPAC, Air Combat Intelligence;
Senshi sōsho, 96:249.

35. *Senshi sōsho*, 96:250, 254; PT
Action Reports, Box 72, RG 38, NARA;
Strike Command, Daily Intelligence
Summary; ONI, *Combat Narrative, X*,
49–51. *Mikazuki* along with *Ariake* was
lost a few days later to MacArthur's
Fifth Air Force.

10. The Second Battle of Munda

1. Griswold, Diary.

2. Beightler had solid professional
credentials: service in the 42nd Division (Rainbow) in World War I; graduate of the Command and General Staff
School at Fort Leavenworth, and the
Army War College; active duty from
1932 to 1936 in the War Plans Division
of the General Staff in Washington.
See John Kennedy Ohl, *Minuteman:
The Military Career of General Robert S.
Beightler* (Boulder, Colo.: Lynne Rein-
ner, 2001), 43–54.

3. 37th Division, After Action
Report, New Georgia (BSI) Campaign,
337-0.3, RG 407; 37th Division, G-3
Journal, New Georgia Island, 337-3.2,
RG 407, NARA; After Action Report,
Operations of the 25th Infantry Divi-
sion in the Central Solomons, New
Georgia-Arundel-Vella Lavella, 325-0.3,
RG 407, NARA; 161st Infantry, Staff
Journal, 325-INF (161)-6.1, RG 407,
NARA.

4. The fire of the 9th Defense
Battalion 155s was curtailed due to lack
of powder; one battery was assigned
to coastal defense and the other to
counter-battery fire against Baanga.

5. 117th Engineer Battalion, Operations Report-Technical, New Georgia,
337-ENG-0.3, RG 407, NARA. William
E. Eubank, "Combat Engineers in the
Solomon Islands," *Military Engineer*
36 (August 1944). Kumamoto hei dan,
Taiheiyō sensō hen, 105.

6. Casualties were moved to the
collection station at Laiana Beach and
then by landing craft through Honiavasa Passage to the 17th Field Hospital on
Kokorana, and then, if severe, by LST

to the 20th Station Hospital on Guadalcanal. A map showing the evacuation setup is in Office of the Surgeon, 37th Division, Medical Service of the 37th Infantry Division – New Georgia, 337-0.3, RG 407, NARA.

7. 2nd Battalion, 230th, had a strength of approximately 600 men, organized in three rifle companies, one machine-gun company, and an infantry gun platoon with three light howitzers. See Kolombangara Transportation Schedule Chart, 22 July 1943, Item #821, RJN, NHHC. Yano's battalion that fought on Guadalcanal as the rearguard for the retreating Japanese Seventeenth Army was made up largely of reservists and after being evacuated was disbanded at Erventa. At the time, a veteran gave its effective strength as around 30%. Lieutenant Matsumoto Toraji, Diary, courtesy of Tom McLeod, author of *Always Ready: The Story of the United States 147th Infantry Regiment* (Texarkana, Tex.: Privately published, 1996). It seems safe to assume, however, that a number of Guadalcanal veterans were in 2nd Battalion, 230th.

8. Sasaki – New Georgia Defense unit [IJA], Operational Orders – gives Hara's force as 160 men, of which 48 were naval personnel (and returned to the 8th Combined); *Senshi sōsho,* 40:258 gives it as 170 men.

9. Details of the bombardment and track chart are in are in USS *Taylor,* Action Report for the Morning of July 25, 1943 – Bombardment of Munda, Flag Files (Blue 242), Box 1, RG 313, NARA. Also see ONI, *Combat Narrative X,* 51–55.

10. 23rd Bombardment Squadron (H), Historical Data, SQ-Bomb-23-HI, AFHRA.

11. COMAIRSOLS, Weekly Intelligence Summary; COMAIRSOLS, Mission Reports. The 307th Bomb Group (H) and VMSB-132 reports both give good general descriptions. Japanese fighter losses are in *Senshi sōsho,* 96:284. Some bombs fell far enough east to kill one man and wound four others in the 148th. At Munda, Sasaki's forward headquarters was destroyed; two men were killed and eight wounded. See *Senshi sōsho,* 40:298.

12. Griswold, Diary, 25 July 1943.

13. First Lieutenant Robert Sheldon Scott, Commander C Company. More details on Scott are in Altobello, *Into the Shadows,* 316–17.

14. Commander Americal Division, Hodge was on temporary loan. Griswold requested and Harmon approved Hester's relief, so it was an army matter. Nevertheless, Nimitz was put out when he heard about it later by rumor and told Halsey that if in the future a flag or general officer was relieved, he wanted to know about it immediately and the full circumstances surrounding it. Later a big flap occurred on Saipan when a marine general relieved an army general. Nimitz to Halsey, 8 August 1943 and Halsey to Nimitz, 19 August 1943, Halsey Papers, Box 15.

15. See Ohl, *Minuteman,* 103, 123–24. Fortunately for Beightler – and for Wing – Griswold did not share the pervasive Regular Army contempt for National Guard officers. By the Luzon campaign, he was one of the most

aggressive divisional commanders in MacArthur's armies.

16. Named for Captain Gardner B. Wing, Commander, E Company, who was killed there.

17. Report After Action, 145th Infantry Regiment, New Georgia Campaign [Unit Journal and Narrative History], 337-INF (145)-0.3, RG 407, NARA; 145th Infantry, Battalion Journal-1st & 3rd Bns-New Georgia Islands, 337-INF-0.7, RG 407, NARA.

18. *Senshi sōsho*, 40:296, 300.

19. For this, see 161st Infantry, Staff Journal.

20. Private Frank Petrarca, 145th medic, posthumous award; Stanley A. Frankel, *The 37th Infantry Division in World War II* (Washington, D.C.: Infantry Journal Press, 1948), 103–15.

21. 148th Infantry (-3Bn), Operations Report; 148th Infantry, Journal File, New Georgia Islands, 337-INF (148)-0.8, RG 407, NARA; 1st Battalion, 148th, Narrative Report, Box 243, RG 127, NARA.

22. Statements from or attributed to Beightler or his staff members come from 37th Division, G-3 Journal; likewise, those of Baxter come from 148th Infantry, Journal File. Despite a long friendship, Beightler would have relieved Baxter, but the officer he wanted was not immediately available. When the 37th went into reserve following the fall of Munda, health problems sent Baxter to the hospital in Nouméa and saved Beightler the task of having to relieve him. See Ohl, *Minuteman*, 118, 123.

23. During the withdrawal, Private Rodger Young was killed taking out a machine gun, for which he was awarded the Medal of Honor posthumously. In 1945, Frank Loesser chose Young's citation for his song "The Ballad of Rodger Young," commissioned by the War Department, which became popular around the country.

24. 37th Division, Jungle Tactics and Operations, 337-3.0, RG 407, NARA.

25. One perplexing question I cannot answer from my sources concerns 6th Company, 228th Infantry (Lieutenant Matsubayashi Masaharu). The *Senshi sōsho* 40 Situation Map (endpaper) shows it in the Kokenggolo Hill line, but this is the only reference to the unit in the entire volume. I would be inclined to dismiss it as a mistake were it not for a single document captured at Munda, listing the officers of the 228th. See List of Officers, 228th Inf. Regt., RJN, Item #704, NHHC.

26. *Senshi sōsho*, 40:301–305. There was apparently some talk of a counterattack by Hirata, to which Sasaki briefly agreed, but the sources seem thin.

27. Combat Report 27th Infantry, Campaign against the Japanese, New Georgia, 325-INF (27)-0.3, RG 407, NARA.

28. For Yano, see *Senshi sōsho*, 40:309. The 136th recorded that it began firing on "moving Jap troops" at Munda at 0745 1 August. See 136th Field Artillery Battalion, Unit Journal, New Georgia Island, 337-FA (136)-0-7. For Kojima, see Interrogation Report, Prisoner #11, Private 1st Class Masuda Takeo, 9 August 1943, AWM 54 423/4/68. For Hara Masao, see Satō to 1st Lieutenant Nakao Takichi, Commander 3rd Company, 2 August 1943,

Item #822, RJN, NHHC. For Satō, see *Senshi sōsho*, 40:312. For Tomonari, see Kumamoto hei dan, *Taiheiyō senso hen*, 105.

29. The Japanese historians are uncomfortable with leaving Hirata to shoulder the blame, but lacking the documentation to show his side, simply write that Sasaki's entry "shows a glimpse of the emotion they must have been feeling then." *Senshi sōsho*, 40:313.

30. COMAIRSOLS, Daily Intelligence Summary; VMF-124, War Diary; VMF-214, War Diary; XIII Fighter Command, Mission Reports; *Senshi sōsho*, 96:259. The Japanese lost five Zeros. Two F4Fs were lost escorting a PBY to Enogai in the same action.

31. *Senshi sōsho*, 40:315–316.

32. NGAF, SAR; *Senshi sōsho*, 96:258; Dick Keresey, *PT 105* (Annapolis: Naval Institute Press, 1996), 74. Because of the reef, the boats moored offshore, two or three together in a "nest."

33. Crenshaw, *South Pacific Destroyer*, 198–99; *Senshi sōsho*, 96:258; Keresey, *PT 105*, 78.

34. For the army, Sugiura unloaded 871 men and 53 tons of equipment and supplies; for the navy, he unloaded one man, 30 tons of supplies, which included 12 tons of provisions lent from the destroyers, and 60 tons of fuel. Orange Intercepts, 8th Fleet, Box 1089.

35. PT Operations Night 1–2 August 1943 (revised), 21 August 1943; *Senshi sōsho*, 96:259–260; Orange Intercepts, 8th Fleet, Box 1090; Evans, Report, 11; Strike Command, Daily Intelligence Summary. (COMAIRSOLS had planes looking for survivors.) I also talked

with Biuku Gasa at his home on Vona-vona Island, with Alfred Bisili translating, as well as John Kari at Munda in May 1992. Both were involved in the rescue.

36. Publicity began in the *New York Times*, 20 August 1943. Of the books and articles that have followed, the best is Robert J. Donovan, *PT 109: John F. Kennedy in World War II* (New York: McGraw-Hill, 1961).

37. Keresey, *PT 105*, 91; Bulkley, *At Close Quarters*, 123.

38. *Senshi sōsho*, 40:309, 449. The replacements had originally been intended for the 41st Regiment destroyed at Buna. Superior Private Matsuo, Diary, 25th Division, Translation Files.

39. Hara Tameichi with Fred Saito and Roger Pineau, *Japanese Destroyer Captain* (Annapolis: Naval Institute Press, 1961), 172–83.

40. The Lever Harbor base just east of Visuvisu Point was established 24 July with four boats and an APc in order to attack barges in Kula Gulf.

41. A 2 August intercept identifies the troops as the Mikami Battalion, which was scheduled to advance 6 August; another, dated 3 August, says a reinforcement run to the Solomons was a definite possibility. But Wilkinson knew not only that *Sendai* was involved but also its exact time of arrival. Orange Intercepts, 8th Fleet, Box 1090.

42. Morison, Office Files, Box 31.

43. Crenshaw, *South Pacific Destroyer*, 197 (and for the battle, pages 202–19).

44. Task Force 31, Action Reports, Battle of Vella Gulf, 6 October 1943, Box 73, RG 38, NARA (includes Moosbrugger's report, Simpson's report,

Wilkinson's endorsement, and Halsey's endorsement).

45. Times are from Moosbrugger's report.

46. Hara reloaded and turned back to rejoin the battle but thought better of it; he radioed 8th Fleet for instructions and was told to return to Rabaul. He joined up with *Sendai* off Bougainville.

47. Orange Intercepts, 8th Fleet, 6 August 1943, Box 1090. Sugiura survived and went on to command a heavy cruiser.

48. *Senshi sōsho,* 40:450–53.

49. *Senshi sōsho,* 96:262–64; *Senshi sōsho,* 40:463–64, 475.

11. The Vella Lavella Occupation

1. Interview with Colonel F. L. Beadle (Engineer for General Harmon) – USAFISPA, 23 November 1943, in PRO Materials, Diaries, Memoirs, Articles, 750.309-8, AFHRA.

2. *Senshi sōsho,* 96:240, 243, 253, 258.

3. Dykes, Air Comd., Solomon Islands; Fitch (TF 33) to Twining (CG, 13th AF), Tentative Organization and Personnel Requirements for Comtaskgroup 33.1 (Comair Solomons), 18 June 1943; COMAIRSOLS, Task Organization, 21 August 1943, Shore Commands, Box 22, RG 127, NARA.

4. COMSOPAC to CINCPAC, 11 July 1943, and CINCPAC to COMSOPAC, 12 July 1943, Chart Room Dispatches, Sopac, Box 117.

5. Kramer J. Rohfleisch, *Guadalcanal and the Origins of the Thirteenth Air Force,* USAAF Historical Study No. 35 (Washington, D.C.: Air Force Historical Research Agency, 1945), 91–93.

6. Availability figures are from COMAIRSOLS, Daily Intelligence Summary. After 18 August, these were no longer reported.

7. Master Plan for the Construction of Airfields and Seaplane Bases, Munda Area, 12 July 1943, Flag Files (Blue 242), Box 8, RG 313, NARA; 73rd NCB, Monthly Reports, Box 36, RG 1, NAVFAC. The 24th was brought over and worked on roads and installations.

8. John M. Foster, *Hell in the Heavens: The True Combat Adventures of a Marine Fighter Pilot in World War Two* (Washington, D.C.: Zanger Publishing, 1961), 30.

9. By the end of the month a detachment of the 47th Seabees from Segi and the 13th Air Force's 828th Aviation Engineer Battalion with D-7s came in. XIII Air Force Service Command, Historical Monograph No. 17, Operations of Aviation Engineers in the South Pacific, 753.01-1, January 1942–August 1944, AFHRA.

10. Unless otherwise noted, material for amphibious phase is from Commander TF-31, Report on Occupation of Vella Lavella 12 August–3 September 1943, Box 539, RG 38, NARA.

11. Report of Trip to Vella Lavella, 103rd Infantry, Operations Report; PT Operations [Rendova].

12. The 35th RCT was made up of the 35th Infantry, the 64th FA Battalion, C Company, 65th Engineers, B Company, 25th Division Medical Battalion, and detachments from other divisional support units.

13. VMF-215, War Diary; Commander TU-31.5, Third Transport Group, Action Reports, 13–16 August

1943, Box 128, RG 38, NARA. Carter recommended arming the LSTs with quad-40mm mounts; on 1 October 1943 SOPAC proposed putting three single 40mm mounts in the bow, removing the 3-inch gun aft (which Carter had found useless against the dive bombers), and putting three single 40mm mounts there. One 20mm would be placed on the main deck center line just forward of the deckhouse and six to each side. COMINCH, Chart Room Dispatches, South Pacific, Box 118.

14. VMF-214, War Diary.

15. NGAF, SAR; *Senshi sōsho*, 96:265–266; Hata, *Japanese Naval Aces*, 384, 429.

16. 25th Air Flotilla Reports.

17. *Senshi sōsho*, 96:262–63.

18. 25th Division, Translation Files.

19. Destroyer Squadron 21, After Action Report, Night Action North of Vella Lavella by Desdiv 41, Box 910, RG 38, NARA; *Nicholas*, Action Report, Flag Files (Blue 347), Box 66, RG 313, NARA; *O'Bannon*, Action Report, Flag Files (Blue 347), Box 66, RG 313, NARA; *Taylor*, Action Report, Flag Files (Blue 347), Box 69, RG 313, NARA; *Chevalier*, Action Report, Flag Files (Blue 347), Box 66, RG 313, NARA; *Senshi sōsho*, 96:267–68; Hara, *Japanese Destroyer Captain*, 184–89.

20. LST Group 14, Flotilla 5, War Diary, 12–22 August 1943, Box 358, RG 127, NARA; VMF-123, War Diary; XIII Fighter Command, Mission Reports; *Senshi sōsho*, 96:266.

21. *Senshi sōsho*, 96:269; Hara, *Japanese Destroyer Captain*, 193–96; Carey, *We Flew Alone*, 23–24; A. M. Andresen, Report, AHA, Box 40, NHHC.

22. TF 31, Action Report, Vella Lavella.

23. 58th Naval Construction Battalion, Monthly Reports, Box 1, RG 1, NAVFAC.

24. Unless otherwise noted material for XIV Corps comes from XIV Corps, NLF, G-3 Periodic Reports and Summaries of Operations, 14 August–4 November, 214-NLF-3.1, RG 407, NARA.

25. See John Crawford, "A Campaign on Two Fronts: Barrowclough in the Pacific," in *Kia Kaha*, 140–62.

26. NGAF, SAR; "Daily Digest" in COMAIRSOLS, Daily Intelligence Summary, 28 September 1943.

27. In addition to 25th Division, Operations Report, the ground action is based on the following: 35th Infantry, Unit Journal, 325-INF (35)-0.7, RG 407, NARA; 35th Infantry, S-2 Periodic Reports, 325-INF (35)-2.1, RG 407, NARA; and 4th Marine Defense Battalion, SAR, Box 358, RG 127, NARA.

28. 25th Division, Translation Files; RJN, Item #745, NHHC; 25th Division, Summary of Japanese Operations on Vella Lavella Island, 325-2.6, RG 407, NARA; COMAIRSOLS, Daily Intelligence Summary; VMTB-143, War Diary; 42nd Bomb Group (M), Consolidated Mission Reports.

29. New Zealand 3rd Division had only two brigades (a brigade was equivalent to an American regiment). For the history of the 3rd Division see Oliver A. Gillespie, *The Pacific* (Wellington, New Zealand: War History Branch, 1952), 71–124. The loading chart for the 7th Echelon is in 14 Bde HQ, War Diary, WA II/1 Z155/1/2, NANZ.

30. NGAF, SAR; VMF-213, War Diary; VMF-214, War Diary; *Senshi sōsho*, 96:303.

31. Moore, assistant commander 1st MAW, relieved Mulcahy on 23 September.

32. TF 31.1, Northern Force Loading Order, 21 September 1943, Flag Files (Blue 242), Box 1, RG 313, NARA; NGAF, SAR; VMF-213, War Diary; Major Donald M. Smuck, Narrative Report Covering Operations and Duty as Commanding Officer, Corps Troops and Staging Area, Vella Lavella, 19 September 1943 to 9 October 1943, Box 358, RG 127, NARA; Lieutenant John G. Clark, Report of First Wave of 77th Battalion's Expedition to Vella Lavella, 12 October 1943, Box 1, RG 1, NAVFAC.

33. 18th Fighter Group, Combat Reports; LST Group 15, Action Reports, 12 October 1943, Box 358, RG 127, NARA.

34. COMAIRSOLS, Mission Reports; COMAIRSOLS, Daily Intelligence Summary; VMF-213, War Dairy; No. 15 Squadron, Combat Report, A 150/5, NANZ. A PT-boat base set up at Lambu Lambu Cove on 25 September completed the Allied bases. Bulkley, *At Close Quarters*, 135; PT Operations.

12. The "Cleanup" in New Georgia

1. Griswold, Diary 6 August–25 August 1943.

2. When Hodge returned to the American, Griswold put Barker in command. But Wing was senior to Barker, and the War Department intervened. Wing led the division for the rest of the war, and Barker the artillery.

3. Lieutenant Colonel George E. Bush commanded the regiment until 12 August, when Sugg, who had been recovering from illness on Guadalcanal, arrived to resume command of his regiment.

4. The Zieta operation is based on: 27th Infantry, Combat Report; 25th Division, After Action Report; *Senshi sōsho*, 40:457–60.

5. On 10 August, Collins had ordered Schultz south to join the 27th at Zieta. His reasons for not joining in the battle are in 3rd Battalion, 148th, Operations Report. The 27th Combat Report simply says that apparently he had been on the hill for some time.

6. J. Lawton Collins, *Lightning Joe: An Autobiography* (Baton Rouge: Louisiana State University Press, 1979), 172. Collins went on to command VII Corps, First Army, from Normandy to the end of the European War.

7. *Senshi sōsho*, 40:460–61.

8. Baanga Island operation is based on: 43rd Division, Operations Report; 169th Infantry, Operations Report; 172nd Infantry, Operations Report; and *Senshi sōsho*, 40:461–62.

9. Bairoko operation is based on: 161st Infantry, Staff Journal; 25th Division, After Action Report; 27th Infantry, Combat Report; 3rd Battalion, 145th Infantry, Unit Journal; 136th FA, Unit Journal; 117th Engineer Combat Battalion, Battalion History, New Georgia Island, 137-ENG-0.1, RG 407, NARA; 140th FA Battalion, Report After Action, New Georgia Island, 337-FA (140)-0.3, RG 407, NARA; 1st Marine Raider Regt., Journal; 1st Marine Raider Regt., SAR.

10. PT Operations [Lever Harbor], 16–23 August 1943; 4th Raider

Battalion, SAR, Bairoko Harbor; *Senshi sōsho*, 40:462.

11. PT Operations, Daylight Mission, 22 August 1943; 117th Engineers, Special Engineer Report on Boat Operations against Jap Barges, 21–22 August 1943, 337-ENG-0.30, RG 407, NARA; Keresey, *PT 105*, 115–29; NGAF, SAR.

12. Sasaki's defense plan is in *Senshi sōsho*, 40:468–69; Tomonari's dispositions are in Base Sector Operational Order No. 1, 25 August 1943, RJN, Item #861, NHHC.

13. *Senshi sōsho*, 40:472 gives the transport missions from 23 August to 8 September. These are eight fishing boats, of which four got through, and sixty barges, of which forty-seven got through. Some were sunk, but mechanical problems and navigational errors accounted for about half of the failures.

14. For the fishing boats, see 8th Fleet, Operational Order No. 23, Item #738, RJN, NHHC, and Mark P. Parillo, *The Japanese Merchant Marine in World War II* (Annapolis: Naval Institute Press, 1993), 192–93. For the actions with the PT boats See *Senshi sōsho*, 96:261, and PT Action Reports, 11–12 August 1943.

15. PT Operations.

16. *Senshi sōsho*, 40:65–67; *Senshi sōsho*, 96:288; 25th Air Flotilla Reports.

17. The Arundel battle is based on the following: 43rd Division, Operations Report; 172nd Infantry, Operations Report; 169th Infantry, Operations Report; 103rd Infantry, Operations Report; 25th Division, After Action Report; 27th Infantry, Combat Report; Employment of Tanks in Arundel Operation, Box 241, RG 127, NARA; Barker, *43rd Division Artillery*, 94–106; *Senshi sōsho*, 40:470–73, 478; Kumamoto hei dan, *Taiheiyō sensō hen*, 107–12; 13th Infantry, Situation Reports & 3rd Battalion Routine Meeting Reports, 14 August–11 September 1943, RJN, Item #814, NHHC.

18. Griswold, Diary, 21 September 1943. No criticism was implied; he thought it was simply too tired and too depleted.

19. COMAIRSOLS, Daily Intelligence Summary; 13th Infantry, 3rd Battalion Routine Meeting Reports.

20. 11th Marine Defense Battalion, "B" Battery, Box 243, RG 127, NARA.

21. The worst single day was 4 September, when the commander of VMTB-233, Major William J. O'Neill, made an emergency landing at Munda and his plane exploded near the operations tent, killing him and his crew and fourteen on the ground, wounding fourteen others, and destroying three aircraft and badly damaging three others. NGAF, SAR: VMTB-233, War Diary.

22. After he was hit, Larsen took the TBF up and told the others to bail out. Wood found his parachute badly burned "and sat in the pilotless plane while it performed a series of violent maneuvers, diving, pulling up in into a loop and falling out and diving again," until it leveled out and made a perfect landing. See VMTB-233, War Diary; Flickinger's report is in Strike Command, Summary of SBD Operations, September 1943, Shore Commands, Box 27, RG 127, NARA; Larsen's views on going in low are in BuAer, Interview

of Lieutenant Harold H. Larsen, Shore
Commands, Box 7, RG 127, NARA.

13. The Japanese Evacuation

1. Imai's statement is in Kumamoto
hei dan, *Taiheiyō sensō hen*, 115.

2. Japanese operations are based
on: *Senshi sōsho*, 96:288–304; *Senshi
sōsho*, 40:475–77, 479–502.

3. *Senshi sōsho*, 40:477; Waddell,
Report, 72; and VMF-215, War Diary.

4. The story is too long to repeat
here. See Waddell, Report, 73; CO-
MAIRSOLS, Daily Intelligence Summary, 2 October 1943.

5. Merrill had TG 39.1, *Montpelier*
and *Denver*; Captain Frank E. Beatty
had TF 39.2, his own *Columbia* and
Cleveland. Each group had four
destroyers.

6. COMAIRSOLS, Daily Intelligence Summary; COMSOPAC, War
Dairy; Gray Book.

7. Sasaki's loading chart and
instructions are in *Senshi sōsho*,
40:484–487.

8. The lack of intelligence from
the scouts is discussed at length in
COMAIRSOLS, Daily Intelligence
Summary, 3 October 1943.

9. Ten SB-24Ds under the command of Colonel Stuart P. Wright arrived at Carney Field 22 August, where
they were placed as a unit with the
394th Squadron, 5th Group. The SB-24
was the product of the low altitude
bombardment (LAB) project designed
for bombing by radar, the bombardier
peering into a special radar scope and
a computer translating the data to the
bomb release controls. See Rohfleisch,
Thirteenth Air Force, 200–206.

10. At 0210, a SB-24 spotted seven
destroyers off southwest Choiseul
headed up the Slot. 5th Bomb Group
(H), Consolidated Mission Reports. I
have not found any information on the
destroyers in the naval records.

11. 307th Bomb Group (H), Con-
solidated Mission Reports; 5th Bomb
Group (H), Consolidated Mission
Reports.

12. COMAIRSOLS, Daily
Intelligence Summary; ONI, *Combat
Narratives, Solomon Islands Campaign,
XI, Kolombangara and Vella Lavella, 6
August–2 October 1943* (Washington,
D.C., 1944), 42–44. A VMF-214 pilot
sent up as cover for Walker attacked a
PT boat and was shot down. This was
the last friendly fire incident with the
PT boats. See Bruce Gamble, *The Black
Sheep: The Definitive Account of Marine
Fighting Squadron 214 in World War II*
(Novata, Calif.: Presidio, 1998), 238–41.

13. ONI, *Combat Narratives, XI*,
44; Kumamoto hei dan, *Taiheiyō sensō
hen*, 113.

14. COMAIRSOLS, Mission Re-
ports; Destroyer Squadron 22, Action
Report, Operations against Japanese
Barges and Small Craft Nights of 1–2
and 2–3 October, 1943, 6 October 1943,
Box 605, RG 38, NARA; E. J. Jernigan,
Tin Can Man (Annapolis: Naval Insti-
tute Press, 1993), 144–45.

15. Destroyer Squadron 22, Action
Report, Barges. It would appear that
both destroyer divisions were to the
north of the Japanese destroyers close
in-shore against the mass of Kolombangara and made contact only as they
headed away.

16. *Senshi sōsho*, 40:500, 506.

17. The 20 September roster was compiled by Lieutenant Colonel Kamiya in *Senshi sōsho*, 40:507 and the losses in *Sensho sōsho*, 40:500.

18. TF 39, Action Report, Destroyer Squadron 22 Operations against Japanese Barges and Small Craft, Nights of 1–2 and 2–3 October 1943 [A Conclusive Summary of Japanese Tactics Employed in Subject Operations during their Evacuation of Kolombangara], Box 167, RG 38, NARA.

19. 35th Battalion, War Diary, WWII/1 Z157/1/21, NANZ.

20. 37th Battalion, War Diary, WAII/1 Z158/1/21, NANZ. Also captured was the engineer's diary, which is basically a ship's log and which is in RJN, Item #833, NHHC. Air drops are in *Senshi sōsho*, 96:305.

21. *Senshi sōsho*, 96:304–306; *Senshi sōsho*, 40:502–503.

22. *Senshi sōsho*, 96:306; Orange Intercepts, Eighth Fleet, Box 1090.

23. Commander Destroyer Squadron 4 (TG 31.2), Final Report of Action – *Selfridge*, *O'Bannon* and *Chevalier* with Enemy Forces off Sauka Point, Vella Lavella, Night of 6–7 October, 1943, Box 597, 26 October 1943, RG 38, NARA; Commander Destroyer Division 42, Actions by Surface Ships Off Sauka, Vella Lavella Night of 6–7 October 1943, 25 October 1943, Box 597, RG 38, NARA; *Senshi sōsho*, 96:306–308; Hara, *Japanese Destroyer Captain*, 202–12; Morison, *Breaking the Bismarcks Barrier*, 243–53; Dull, *Imperial Japanese Navy*, 283–86.

24. NGAF, SAR; VMF-213, War Diary; 18th Fighter Group, Combat Reports.

25. VP-23, Mission Report, 10 October 1943, Box 782, RG 38, NARA; PT Action Reports; Keresey, *PT 105*, 206–11.

26. Ijūin comes in for the most criticism (Morison, Dull, and Hara), Walker for not waiting for Larson (Dull), and Potter for being too cautious and not finishing off the Tsuruya Unit in the first place (Crawford and Gillespie).

14. The Bomber Offensive against Buin

1. Okumiya Masatake and Horikoshi Jiro with Martin Caidin, *Zero!* (New York: E. P. Dutton, 1956), 301–302.

2. 5th Bomb Group (H), Consolidated Mission Reports; *Senshi sōsho*, 96:242.

3. Robert C. Mikesh and Osamu Tagaya, *Moonlight Interceptor: Japan's "Irving" Night Fighter* (Washington, D.C.: Smithsonian Institution Press, 1985); a diagram of attack method is in *Senshi sōsho*, 96:155.

4. VB-101, Mission Report, 17 July 1943, Box 394, RG 38, NARA. 307th Bomb Group (H), Consolidated Mission Reports; No. 3 Bomber Squadron, War Diary; 5th Bomb Group (H), Consolidated Mission Reports. Conversations with the late Berton Burns.

5. *Senshi sōsho*, 96:319; 5th Bomb Group (H), Consolidated Mission Reports.

6. 5th Bomb Group (H), Consolidated Mission Reports; 307th Bomb Group (H), Consolidated Mission Reports; VMF-221, War Diary; VMF-214, War Diary. XIII Fighter Command, Mission Reports.

7. That is, with planes stepped low to high and resembling a downward pointing javelin when viewed in profile.

8. COMAIRSOLS pilots first reported sighting Ki-61s the first week of August, never in large numbers, and no doubt from the 68th Sentai. The one confirmation of Ki-61s at Buin in the sources I have comes from 13th Infantry, 3rd Battalion Routine Meeting Reports, 28 August, which states that three Type 3 fighters [Ki-61s] came over Kolombangara that morning. In addition, *Rikugun hikō sentaishi*, 152, says that the 68th chūtai were scattered, that the commanders were never able to unify the sentai, and that this was a persistent difficulty.

9. 307th Bomb Group (H), Consolidated Mission Reports; 5th Bomb Group (H), Consolidated Mission Reports; XIII Fighter Command, Mission Reports; VMF-221, War Dairy; and VMF-124, War Diary; Hata, *Japanese Naval Aces and Fighter Units*, 429. A much fuller account of the AAF fighter action can be found in William Wolf, *13th Fighter Command in World War II: Air Combat over Guadalcanal and the Solomons* (Atglen, Pa.: Schiffer, 2004), 193–213.

10. 5th Bomb Group (H), Consolidated Mission Reports; VMF-215, War Diary; No. 16 Squadron, War Diary; NGAF, SAR.

11. 5th Bomb Group (H), Consolidated Mission Reports; 307th Bomb Group (H), Consolidated Mission Reports; VMF-215, War Diary; No. 16 Squadron, War Diary, A 151/1, NANZ; VMF-214, War Diary.

12. 307th Bomb Group (H), Consolidated Mission Reports; 5th Bomb Group (H), Consolidated Mission Reports; XIII Fighter Command, Mission Reports; No. 16 Squadron, War Diary; VMF-123, War Diary; VMF-215, War Diary; VMF-124, War Diary. Walsh was awarded the Medal of Honor. See also, Hata, *Japanese Naval Aces and Fighter Units*, 279, 384. The number of Japanese pilots shot down but rescued is not known; after all, they were fighting over their own base. But for an incredible story of a pilot who landed his plane so badly wounded he never flew again, see Sakaida, *Aces*, 133–34.

13. The Japanese aircraft were parked on the airfields with little in the way of revetments. The Japanese say that the B-24s arriving first before dawn accounted for thirty planes and the B-25s with escorting P-38s arriving with the daylight accounted for seventy to eighty more. *Senshi sōsho*, 7:409. See also, Drea, *MacArthur's ULTRA*, 82–85.

14. *Senshi sōsho*, 96:369.

15. Dexter, *New Guinea Offensives*, 326–36.

16. The D4Y2 was developed by the navy at Yokosuka – hence the Y – as a replacement for the D3A and was built by Aichi. A few were flying reconnaissance in the Solomons, for on 30 August a F4U shot one down over Santa Isabel, and a recovery team in late September found the wreck and made the identification.

17. Much of the reorganization simply made official the changes made in August; for example, Sakamaki taking command of the 26th Air Flotilla at Buin and the disbandment of the 21st

Flotilla at Kavieng (both the 201st and the 253rd had originally belonged to the 21st). The 22nd Air Flotilla in the Marshalls – 252nd, 552nd, 755th, and 802nd – was left unchanged. The 938th and the 958th remained with 8th Fleet. See *Senshi sōsho*, 96:310–13.

18. Arnold had been pressing Twining for more results. Twining to Arnold, 7 October 1943; Arnold to Twining, 16 October 1943, H. H. Arnold Papers, Box 71, LC.

19. Briefly, when VMF-214 completed its second tour and the pilots were sent on R&R, they were replaced by pilots from the pool and Boyington took command. A few had combat experience, but most, while well trained, did not. (The reality bears no resemblance to the television series that aired 1976–78.) Gamble, *The Black Sheep*, 166–96.

20. The Lae operation began 4 September and ended the 14th. The D3A Unit of the 582nd participated in three raids – 4, 6, and 12 September – and lost one aircraft shot down and ten damaged. Five Zeros were lost. *Senshi sōsho*, 96:314; 25th Air Flotilla Reports.

21. In this case, oxygen problems. The introduction of a new aircraft was always attended by mechanical problems that had to be fixed.

22. COMAIRSOLS, Daily Intelligence Summaries; 5th Bomb Group (H), Consolidated Mission Reports; 307th Bomb Group (H), Consolidated Mission Reports; COMAIRSOLS, Mission Reports [VB-104].

23. 307th Bomb Group (H), Consolidated Mission Reports; 5th Bomb Group (H), Consolidated Mission

Reports; 18th Fighter Group, Combat Reports; VMF-213, War Diary; VMF-222, War Diary; VF-33, Mission Report, Box 449, RG 38, NARA. In regard to the Ki-61 claims here and later, Hata and Izawa, *Japanese Army Air Force*, list no 68th Sentai pilots killed in the Solomons after the 2 July raid on Rendova.

24. Okumiya, *Zero!* 292–293; COMAIRSOLS, Daily Intelligence Summaries; NGAF, SAR; Strike Command, Daily Intelligence Summary (September), Shore Commands, Box 24, RG 127, NARA; 307th Bomb Group (H), Consolidated Mission Reports; VMF-222, War Diary; 5th Bomb Group (H), Consolidated Mission Reports; 18th Fighter Group, Combat Reports; VMF-213, War Diary; VMSB-235, War Diary (includes VC-38 and VC-40); VMTB-233, War Diary; VF-33, Mission Report; VF-38, Mission Report, Box 450, RG-38, NARA. Japanese losses are from Hata, *Japanese Naval Aces and Fighter Units*, 429.

25. NGAF, SAR; 25th Air Flotilla Reports; *Senshi sōsho*, 96:303.

26. 42nd Bomb Group, (M), Consolidated Mission Reports; 18th Fighter Group, Combat Reports; VMF-222, War Diary; VF-33, Mission Report; VF-38, Mission Report.

27. 42nd Bomb Group (M), Consolidated Mission Report; NGAF, SAR; COMAIRSOLS, Mission Reports. The SBD reports for VC-38 and VC-40 (with VMSB-235) are in Box 415, RG 38, NARA; VMTB 233, War Diary, includes VC-38 and VC-40. Bruce Gamble, *Black Sheep One: The Life of Gregory "Pappy" Boyington* (Novato, Cal.: Presidio Press, 2000), 243–51. Gamble's bibliography

is a complete guide to the Boyington literature with the exception of John F. Wukovits, *Black Sheep: The Life of Pappy Boyington* (Annapolis: Naval Institute Press, 2011), which appeared later.

28. COMAIRSOLS, Daily Intelligence Summaries; NGAF, SAR; 25th Air Flotilla Reports; 18th Fighter Group, Combat Reports; 5th Bomb Group (H), Consolidated Mission Reports; 307th Bomb Group (H), Consolidated Mission Reports. Late in the day of 21 September, VMF-214 F4Us strafed Kahili and lost one aircraft to antiaircraft fire, but the pilot was safe at Vella Lavella. VMF-214, War Diary.

29. *Senshi sōsho*, 96:314; 25th Air Flotilla Reports; Hata, *Japanese Naval Aces and Fighter Units*, 429.

30. 18th Fighter Group, Combat Reports; No. 17 Squadron, Combat Reports, A 151/4, NANZ (also War Diary, A 152/1); VMF-213, War Diary; VMF-214, War Diary.

31. 5th Bomb Group (H), Consolidated Mission Reports; 307th Bomb Group (H), Consolidated Mission Reports; 339th and a combined VMF-213/VMF-214/VF-12 report is in COMAIRSOLS, Mission Reports.

32. 307th Bomb Group, Consolidated Mission Reports; RNZAF Fighter Wing, Air Operations, Solomons, A 118/22, NANZ; 18th Fighter Group, Combat Reports; VMF-213, War Diary; VMF-214, War Diary. The F4Us claimed seven shot down. Also, see Gamble, *Black Sheep One*, 255–58.

33. 307th Bomb Group (H), Consolidated Missions Reports; COMAIRSOLS, Missions Reports.

34. *Senshi sōsho*, 96:317. I could at least corroborate the G4M figure from 25th Air Flotilla Reports – the numbers check out exactly. My tabulation for COMAIRSOLS comes from SOPAC, Air Combat Intelligence.

35. Morton, *Strategy and Command*, 547–50; Drea, *In the Service of the Emperor*, 190–91; *Senshi sōsho*, 96:317–18, 322.

36. *Senshi sōsho*, 96:319–21. The 938th was the last air unit to leave, moving to Buka 1 November.

37. 5th Bomb Group (H), Consolidated Mission Reports; 307th Bomb Group (H), Periodic Activities Summary [October], 10 November 1943; 18th Fighter Group, Combat Reports; VMF-214, War Dairy; VMTB-232, War Diary.

38. *Senshi sōsho*, 96:321; Mason, *We Will Stand by You*, 127–28.

Epilogue

1. Command Air Northern Solomons (CANS) Operations Report, 25 October 1943–11 November 1943 in CANS, War Diary, Shore Commands, Box 8, RG 127, NARA; Operation Plan, No. T1-43, Task Organization, 33.1, Air Solomon Islands – COMAIRSOLS, Shore Commands, Box 7, RG 127, NARA.

2. *Senshi sōsho*, 96:371–73, 384–428; COMAIRSOLS, Daily Intelligence Summaries, 4 November–17 November 1943. For Halsey's two carrier strikes on Rabaul in which New Georgia–based fighters provided cover for the carriers in order that they could send off their full complements, see Commander TG 50.3, Attack on Enemy Ships at

Rabaul and Subsequent Enemy Aircraft Raid on Task Group 50.3, Action of, Box 176, RG 38, NARA. For the two heavy bomber missions staged through Munda, one to hit shipping north of Kavieng, the other in conjunction with Halsey's 11 November carrier strike, see 5th Bomb Group (H), Consolidated Mission Reports and 307th Bomb Group (H), Periodic Activities Summary [November].

3. Morison, *Breaking the Bismarcks Barrier*, 224.

4. Quoted in Miller, *Cartwheel*, 169.

5. SWPA, ATIS Bulletin # 366, in COMAIRSOLS, "Daily Digest," Daily Intelligence Summary, 11 October 1943.

6. Vice Admiral Samejima [Tomoshige], Observations, Morison, Office Files, Box 28.

7. Griswold, Lessons Learned from Joint Operations; Headquarters, New Georgia Air Command, Comments Based on the New Georgia Operation, in reference to COMINCH Doctrine (tentative) for Air Support, Shore Commands, Box 8, RG 127, NARA; Wilkinson's Report on the density needed for naval gunfire support in ONI, *Combat Narrative, X*, 54–55.

8. NGOF, Narrative Account of the Campaigns in the New Georgia Group, B. S. I., 214-0.3, RG 407, NARA; Rentz, *Marines in the Central Solomons*, 174.

9. *Senshi sōsho*, 40:507.

Bibliography

ARCHIVES

AFHRA: Air Force Historical Research Agency, Maxwell Air Force Base, Montgomery.

AWM: Australian War Memorial, Canberra.

MCNZA: Methodist Church of New Zealand Archives, Auckland.

MCU: Marine Corps University Research Center, Quantico.

NANZ: National Archives of New Zealand, Wellington.

NARA: National Archives and Records Administration, College Park.

NAVFAC: Naval Facilities Command, Archives, Port Hueneme.

NHHC: Naval Historical and Heritage Command, Navy Yard.

NIDS: National Institute of Defense Studies, Military Archives, Tokyo.

SINA: Solomon Islands National Archives, Honiara.

TNA: PRO: The National Archives, Public Record Office, London.

REFERENCES

Alden, John D. *U. S. Submarine Attacks during World War II*. Annapolis: Naval Institute Press, 1989.

Alexander, Joseph H. *Edson's Raiders: The 1st Marine Raider Battalion in World War II*. Annapolis: Naval Institute Press, 2001.

Altobello, Brian. *Into the Shadows Furious: The Brutal Battle for New Georgia*. Novato, Calif.: Presidio Press, 2000.

Barker, Harold B. *History of the 43rd Division Artillery, 1941–1945*. Providence, R.I.: John F. Green, 1960.

Batterton, Maj. Roy J., Jr. "You Fight by the Book." *Marine Corps Gazette* 33 (July 1949).

Bergerud, Eric. *Fire in the Sky: The Air War in the South Pacific*. Boulder, Colo.: Westview, 2000.

———. *Touched with Fire: The Land War in the South Pacific*. New York: Viking, 1996.

Bōeichō Bōei kenshūjō senshishitsu. *Senshi sōsho*. Vol. 7, *Tōbu Nyuginia hōmen rikugun kōkū sakusen*. Tokyo: Asagumo shinbunsha, 1967.

——. _Senshi sōsho._ Vol. 28, _Minami Taiheiyō rikugun sakusen (2): Gadarukanaru Buna sakusen._ Tokyo: Asagumo shinbunsha, 1969.

——. _Senshi sōsho._ Vol. 40, _Minami Taiheiyō sakusen (3): Munda Saramoa._ Tokyo: Asagumo shinbunsha, 1970.

——. _Senshi sōsho._ Vol. 83, _Nantō hōmen kaigun sakusen (2): Gadarukanaru tou tesshu made._ Tokyo: Asagumo shinbunsha, 1971.

——. _Senshi sōsho._ Vol. 96, _Nantō hōmen kaigun sakusen (3): Gadarukanaru tou tesshu go._ Tokyo: Asagumo shinbunsha, 1976.

Boyd, Carl, and Akihiko Yoshida. _The Japanese Submarine Force and World War II._ Annapolis: Naval Institute Press, 1995.

Britt, Sam S., Jr. _The Long Rangers: A Diary of the 307th Bombardment Group (H)._ Baton Rouge: Privately published, 1990.

Bulkley, Robert J., Jr. _At Close Quarters: PT Boats in the United States Navy._ Washington, D.C.: Naval History Division, 1962.

Calhoun, C. Raymond. _Tin Can Sailor: Life aboard the USS Sterett, 1939–1945._ Annapolis: Naval Institute Press, 1993.

Carey, Alan D. _We Flew Alone: United States Navy B-24 Squadrons in the Pacific, February 1943–September 1944._ Atglen, Pa.: Schiffer, 2000.

Carter, Worrall Reed. _Beans, Bullets, and Black Oil: The Story of Fleet Logistics Afloat in the Pacific during World War II._ Washington, D.C.: Department of the Navy, 1953.

Collins, J. Laughton. _Lightning Joe: An Autobiography._ Baton Rouge: Louisiana State University Press, 1979.

Condon-Rall, Mary Ellen, and Albert E. Cowdrey. _The Medical Department: Medical Services in the War against Japan._ Washington, D.C.: Center of Military History, 1998.

Corben, Elizabeth (Lisa). _My Father's Journey._ Alstonville, New South Wales: Privately published, 2001.

Cowdrey, Albert E. _Fighting for Life: American Military Medicine in World War II._ New York: Free Press, 1994.

Crawford, John, ed. _Kia Kaha: New Zealand in the Second World War._ Auckland: Oxford, 2000.

Crenshaw, Russell Sydnor, Jr. _South Pacific Destroyer: The Battle for the Solomons from Savo Island to Vella Gulf._ Annapolis: Naval Institute Press, 1998.

Davis, Donald A. _Lightning Strike: The Secret Mission to Kill Admiral Yamamoto and Avenge Pearl Harbor._ New York: St. Martin's, 2005.

DeBlanc, Jefferson. _The Guadalcanal Air War._ Gretna, La.: Pelican Press, 2008.

Dexter, David. _The New Guinea Offensives._ Canberra: Australian War Memorial, 1961.

Donovan, Robert J. _PT 109: John F. Kennedy in World War II._ New York: McGraw-Hill, 1961.

Drea, Edward J. _In the Service of the Emperor: Essays on the Imperial Japanese Army._ Lincoln: University of Nebraska Press, 1998.

——. _Japan's Imperial Army: Its Rise and Fall, 1853–1945._ Lawrence: University Press of Kansas, 2009.

——. *MacArthur's ULTRA: Codebreaking and the War against Japan, 1942–1945*. Lawrence: University Press of Kansas, 1992.

Dull, Paul S. *A Battle History of the Imperial Japanese Navy (1941–1945)*. Annapolis: Naval Institute Press, 1978.

Dyer, George Carroll. *The Amphibians Came to Conquer: The Story of Admiral Richmond Kelly Turner*. 2 vols. Washington, D.C.: Government Printing Office, 1969.

Eubank, William E. "Combat Engineers in the Solomon Islands." *Military Engineer* 36 (August 1944).

Evans, David C., and Mark R. Peattie. *Kaigun: Strategy, Tactics, and Technology in the Imperial Japanese Navy, 1887–1941*. Annapolis: Naval Institute Press, 1997.

Far East Command, Military History Section. *The Imperial Japanese Navy in World War II: A Graphic Presentation of the Japanese Naval Organization and List of Combatant and Non-Combatant Vessels Lost or Damaged in the War*. Japanese Monograph No. 116.

Feldt, Eric A. *The Coast Watchers*. New York: Nelson Doubleday, 1946, 1979.

Feuer, A. B., ed. *Coast Watching in the Solomon Islands: The Bougainville Reports, December 1941–July 1943*. Westport, Conn.: Praeger, 1992.

Foster, John M. *Hell in the Heavens: The True Combat Adventures of a Marine Fighter Pilot in World War Two*. Washington, D.C.: Zanger Publishing, 1961.

Francillon, Rene J. *Japanese Aircraft of the Pacific War*. Annapolis: Naval Institute Press, 1979.

Frank, Richard B. *Guadalcanal*. New York: Random House, 1990.

Frankel, Stanley A. *The 37th Infantry Division in World War II*. Washington, D.C.: Infantry Journal Press, 1948.

Friedman, Norman. *U. S. Amphibious Ships and Craft: An Illustrated Design History*. Annapolis: Naval Institute Press, 2002.

——. *U. S. Cruisers: An Illustrated Design History*. Annapolis: Naval Institute Press, 1984.

——. *U. S. Destroyers: An Illustrated Design History*. Annapolis: Naval Institute Press, 1982.

Gamble, Bruce. *The Black Sheep: The Definitive Account of Marine Fighting Squadron 214 in World War II*. Novato, Calif.: Presidio Press, 1998.

——. *Black Sheep One: The Life of Gregory "Pappy" Boyington*. Novato, Calif.: Presidio Press, 2000.

Gillespie, Oliver A. *The Pacific*. Wellington, New Zealand: War History Branch, 1952.

Glines, Carroll, V. *Attack on Yamamoto*. New York: Orion, 1990.

Griffith, Samuel B. "Action at Enogai: Operations of the First Raider Battalion in the New Georgia Campaign." *Marine Corps Gazette* 28 (March 1944).

Hackett, Bob, and Sander Kingsepp. *Sensuikan!* www.combinedfleet.com /sensuikan.htm.

Halsey, William F., and J. Bryan III. *Admiral Halsey's Story*. New York: McGraw-Hill, 1947.

Hara Takeshi and Yasuoka Akio. *Nihon rikukaigun jiten, konpakuto-ban – jō-kan/ge-kan* [Japan army/navy ency-

clopedia, abridged version, 2 vols.].
    Tokyo: Shinjinbutsu ōrai-sha, 2003.
Hara Tameichi, with Fred Saito and
    Roger Pineau. *Japanese Destroyer
    Captain*. Annapolis: Naval Institute
    Press, 1961, reprint 2011.
Hata Ikuhiko, and Yasuho Izawa. *Japa-
    nese Naval Aces and Fighter Units in
    World War II*. Translated by Don
    Cyril Gorham. Annapolis: Naval In-
    stitute Press, 1989.
Hata Ikuhiko, Yasuho Izawa, and
    Christopher Shores. *Japanese Army
    Air Force Fighter Units and Their Aces,
    1931–1945*. London: Grub Street,
    2002.
Howlett, R. A. *History of the Fiji Mili-
    tary Forces*. Suva, Fiji: Government
    Printer, 1948.
Jentschura, Hansgeorg, Dieter Jung,
    and Peter Mickel. *Warships of the
    Imperial Japanese Navy, 1869–1945*.
    Translated by Anthony Preston and
    J. D. Brown. Annapolis: Naval Insti-
    tute Press, 1970, 1977.
Jernigan, E. J. *Tin Can Man*. Annapolis:
    Naval Institute Press, 2010.
Jersey, Stanley Coleman. *Hell's Island:
    The Untold Story of Guadalcanal*. Col-
    lege Station: Texas A&M Press, 2008.
Joint Army-Navy Assessment Com-
    mittee. *Japanese Naval and Merchant
    Shipping Losses during World War II
    by All Causes*. Washington: Govern-
    ment Printing Office, 1947.
Kayama Homare. *Hosen nisshi*. N.p.:
    Privately published, 1987.
Keresey, Dick. *PT 105*. Annapolis: Naval
    Institute Press, 1996.
Kumamoto hei dan senshi hensan
    iinkai. *Kumamoto hei dan senshi:
    Taiheiyō sensō hen*. Kumamoto, Ja-

pan: Kumamoto nichi nichi shinbun-
    sha, 1965.
Kusaka Jinichi. *Rabauru sensen ijo
    nashi: warera kaku iki kaku tatakaeri*.
    Tokyo: Kowado, 1958.
Letourneau, Roger, and Dennis Letour-
    neau. *Operation Ke: The Cactus Air
    Force and the Japanese Withdrawal
    from Guadalcanal*. Annapolis: Naval
    Institute Press, 2012.
Lieberman, Joseph A. "Road Construc-
    tion on New Georgia." *Military Engi-
    neer* 36 (March 1944).
Lord, Walter. *Lonely Vigil: Coastwatch-
    ers of the Solomons*. New York: Vi-
    king, 1977.
Lucas, Jim. *Combat Correspondence*.
    New York: Reynal & Hitchcock,
    1944.
Lundstrum, John B. *The First Team and
    the Guadalcanal Campaign: Naval
    Fighter Combat from August to No-
    vember 1942*. Annapolis: Naval Insti-
    tute Press, 1994.
MacArthur, Douglas. *Reminiscences*.
    New York: McGraw-Hill, 1964.
Mason, Theodore C. *"We Will Stand
    by You": Serving in the Pawnee, 1942–
    1945*. Annapolis: Naval Institute
    Press, 1996.
McAuley, Les. *Battle of the Bismarck
    Sea*. South Australia: Burbank's,
    1999.
Mikesh, Robert C., and Osama Tagaya.
    *Moonlight Interceptor: Japan's "Irving"
    Night Fighter*. Washington, D.C.:
    Smithsonian Institution Press, 1985.
Miller, John, Jr. *Cartwheel: The Reduc-
    tion of Rabaul*. Washington, D.C.:
    Center of Military History, 1959.

Morison, Samuel Eliot. *Breaking the Bismarcks Barrier, 22 July 1942–1 May 1944*. Boston: Little, Brown, 1950.

Morriss, Mack. *South Pacific Diary, 1942–1943*. Edited by Ronnie Day. Lexington: University Press of Kentucky, 1996.

Morton, Louis. *Strategy and Command: The First Two Years*. War in the Pacific Series. Washington, D.C.: Center of Military History, 1962.

Nevitt, Allyn D. *Long Lancers*. www.combinedfleet.com/lancers.htm.

Office of Naval Intelligence. *Combat Narratives, Solomon Islands Campaign, IX, Bombardments of Munda and Vila-Stanmore, January–May 1943*. Washington, D.C., 1944.

———. *Combat Narratives, Solomon Islands Campaign, X, Operations in the New Georgia Area, 21 June–5 August 1942*. Washington, D.C., 1944.

———. *Combat Narratives, Solomon Islands Campaign, XI, Kolombangara and Vella Lavella, 6 August–7 October 1943*. Washington, D.C., 1944.

Okumiya Masatake. *Rabauru kaigun kōkūtai*. Tokyo: Asahi sonorama, 1976.

Okumiya Masatake and Jiro Horikoshi, with Martin Caidin, *Zero!* New York: E. P. Dutton, 1956.

Parillo, Mark P. *The Japanese Merchant Marine in World War II*. Annapolis: Naval Institute Press, 1993.

Prados, John. *Islands of Destiny: The Solomons Campaign and the Eclipse of the Rising Sun*. New York: New American Library, 2012.

Rems, Alan P. "Halsey Knows the Straight Story." *Naval History* 22, no. 4 (August 2008).

Rentz, John N. *Marines in the Central Solomons*. Washington, D.C.: USMC Historical Branch, 1952.

Rohfleisch, Kramer J. *Guadalcanal and the Origins of the Thirteenth Air Force*. USAAF Historical Study No.35. Air Force Historical Research Agency, 1945.

Ross, J. M. S. *Royal New Zealand Air Force*. Wellington, New Zealand: War History Branch, 1955.

Sakaida, Henry. *Aces of the Rising Sun*. Oxford: Osprey, 2002.

Sherrod, Robert. *History of Marine Corps Aviation in World War II*. Washington, D.C.: Combat Forces Press, 1952.

Sokyu banri: Rikugun hikō sentaishi. Tokyo: Rikugun hikō sentaishi kankō iinkai, 1976.

"Spring Offensives: New and More Powerful Allied Air Forces Helps Make Them Successful." *Life*, 12 April 1943.

Tagaya Osamu. *Mitsubishi Type 1 Rikko "Betty" Units of World War 2*. Oxford: Osprey, 2001.

Tamura Yozo. *Okinawa kenmin kaku tatakaeri*. Tokyo: Kodansha, 1997.

Tillman, Barrett. *U. S. Navy Fighter Squadrons in World War II*. North Branch, Minn.: Specialty Press, 1997.

Tully, Andrew P. "Neglected Disaster: Nisshin." *Mysteries/Untold Sagas of the Imperial Japanese Navy*. www.combinedfleet.com/atully10.htm.

Twining, Merrill B. *No Bended Knee: The Memoir of Gen. Merrill B. Twining, USMC (Ret)*. Edited by Neil Carey. Novato, Calif.: Presidio Press, 1996.

Ugaki Matome. *Fading Victory: The Diary of Admiral Matome Ugaki, 1941–1945.* Translated by Masatuka Chiyaya with Donald M. Goldstein and Katherine V. Dillon. Pittsburgh, Pa.: University of Pittsburgh Press, 1991.

Ulbrich, David J. "The Long-Lost Tentative Manual for Defense of Advanced Bases (1936)." *Journal of Military History* 71 (July 2007).

USN Bureau of Yards and Docks. *Building the Navy's Bases in World War II: History of the Bureau of Yards and Docks and the Civil Engineer Corps, 1940–1946.* 2 vols. Washington, D.C.: Government Printing Office, 1947.

Walker, Sam. *Up the Slot.* Oklahoma City: Walker Publishers, 1984.

Waters, S. D. *The Royal New Zealand Navy.* Wellington, New Zealand: War History Branch, 1956.

White, Geoffrey, David W. Gegeo, David Akin, and Karen Watson-Gegeo, eds. *The Big Death: Solomon Islanders Remember World War II.* Honiara & Suva: Solomon Islands College of Higher Education & University of the South Pacific, 1988.

Wolf, William. *13th Fighter Command in World War II: Air Combat over Guadalcanal and the Solomons.* Atglen, Pa.: Schiffer, 2004.

Wukovits, John F. *Black Sheep: The Life of Pappy Boyington.* Annapolis: Naval Institute Press, 2011.

Wyant, William K. *Sandy Patch: A Biography of Lt. Gen. Alexander M. Patch.* Westport, Conn.: Praeger, 1991.

Y'Blood, William T. *The Little Giants: U. S. Escort Carriers against Japan.* Annapolis: Naval Institute Press, 1987.

Zimmer, Joseph E. *The History of the 43rd Infantry Division, 1941–1945.* Nashville, Tenn.: Battery Press, 1982.

Zimmerman, Joseph C. "The Construction of Airfields during the New Georgia Campaign of 1943–1944: Lessons Learned by the United States Naval Construction Battalions." MA thesis, East Tennessee State University, 2008.

Index

TWENTIETH-CENTURY BATTLES

Edited by Spencer C. Tucker

RONNIE DAY (1939–2014) was Professor in the Department of History at East Tennessee State University. He was editor of *South Pacific Diary, 1942–1943.*

210 K